Ka Leung Wong, Ph. D. (2000), University of Edinburgh, is Assistant Professor of Biblical Studies at the University of Edinburgh, England.

THE IDEA OF RETRIBUTION IN THE BOOK OF EZEKIEL

SUPPLEMENTS

TO

VETUS TESTAMENTUM

VOLUME LXXXVII

THE IDEA OF RETRIBUTION
IN THE BOOK OF EZEKIEL

BY

KA LEUNG WONG

BRILL
LEIDEN · BOSTON · KÖLN
2001

This book is printed on acid-free paper.

Library of Congress Cataloging-in-Publication Data

Wong, Ka Leung
  The idea of retribution in the book of Ezekiel / by Ka Leung Wong.
      p.   cm. — (Supplements to Vetus Testamentum, ISSN 0083-5889 ;
    v. 87)
    Includes bibliographical references and indexes.
    ISBN 9004122567
    1. Bible. O.T. Ezekiel—Criticism, interpretation, etc. 2. Retribution–
  Biblical teaching. I. Title. II. Series.

  BS410 .V452 vol. 87   2001
  [BS1545.2]
  224'.406—dc21   2001035216
                                                                        CIP

Die Deutsche Bibliothek – CIP-Einheitsaufnahme

Wong, Ka Leung:
  The idea of retribution in the book of Ezekiel / by Ka Leung Wong. –
  Leiden ; Boston ; Köln : Brill, 2001
    (Supplements to Vetus testamentum ; Vol. 87)
    ISBN 90-04-12256-7

                              ISSN   0083-5889
                              ISBN   90 04 12256 7

PRINTED IN THE NETHERLANDS

CONTENTS

ACKNOWLEDGEMENTS

The present study is a slightly revised version of a doctoral dissertation submitted in 2000 to the University of Edinburgh. I was financially supported by the Overseas Research Students Award Scheme and the University of Edinburgh Postgraduate Research Studentship. The Studentship and the Gunning Foundation also allowed me to attend the Twelve World Congress of Jewish Studies held at Jerusalem in 1997.

I am grateful to my supervisor, Dr. David J. Reimer, who has graciously taken up the supervision after Dr. Iain W. Provan and Dr. A. Peter Hayman were called away to other duties. His warm encouragement, generosity in time, encyclopaedic knowledge, careful reading and ready accessibility have contributed much to the writing of the dissertation. I am thankful to Dr. Iain W. Provan, my first supervisor, who was most helpful in my search for a dissertation topic during my first year in Edinburgh. Even after he had left for Canada, he still showed interest in the work, kindly read the dissertation and offered comments. After Dr. Provan, Dr. A. Peter Hayman took up the supervision. His meticulous reading and knowledge of Hebrew saved me from a number of errors. I would like to thank Professor Johan Lust, who first introduced me to the world of Ezekiel when I was studying in Leuven. He also read part of the dissertation and raised some critical questions. Thanks are also due to the two examiners, Professor Graeme Auld and Professor John Barton, for their helpful comments and encouragement. I would also like to express my gratitude to Professor André Lemaire for accepting the dissertation for publication in the SVT series and for offering suggestions to improve the study.

I would like to thank Tyndale House, Cambridge, for allowing me to use their library. A number of friends were most helpful and showed their support in various ways. In particular, I would like to mention Dr. Rob Faesen sj and Dr. Bénédicte Lemmelijn, who helped procure additional books and articles, Richard Lew, who proofread the whole dissertation, improving its style and making it more readable, and Dr. Bobby Chum, who readily made available his computer expertise.

My deepest thanks go to my wife Wing Yee. She has been a source of unfailing love, constant support and immense encouragement, reminding me of the purpose of this undertaking and growing with me in this journey.

ABBREVIATIONS

AB	The Anchor Bible
ABD	*Anchor Bible Dictionary*
AES	*Archives européennes de sociologie*
AnBib	Analecta Biblica
ANET	*Ancient Near Eastern Texts Relating to the Old Testament*, 1969³
ANS	Abr-Nahrain Supplement Series
AOAT	Alter Orient und Altes Testament
ASTI	*Annual of the Swedish Theological Institute*
ASTS	ArtScroll Tanach Series
ATA	Alttestamentliche Abhandlungen
ATD	Das Alte Testament Deutsch
BA	*Biblical Archeologist*
BAT	Die Botschaft des Alten Testaments
BAZeP	Buchreihe der Anglia, Zeitschrift für englische Philologie
BBB	Bonner biblische Beiträge
BBC	Broadman Bible Commentary
BBET	Beiträge zur biblischen Exegese und Theologie
BCBC	Believers Church Bible Commentary
BDB	*The New Brown-Driver-Briggs-Gesenius Hebrew and English Lexicon*
BEATAJ	Beiträge zur Erforschung des Alten Testaments and des antiken Judentums
BETL	Bibliotheca Ephemeridum Theologicarum Lovaniensium
BibB	Biblische Beiträge
BibOr	Biblica et Orientalia
BIS	Biblical Interpretation Series
BKAT	Biblischer Kommentar: Altes Testament
BN	*Biblische Notizen*
BOT	De Boeken van het Oude Testament
BTSt	Biblisch-Theologische Studien
BWANT	Beiträge zur Wissenschaft vom Alten und Neuen Testament
BZ	*Biblische Zeitschrift*
BZAW	Beihefte zur Zeitschrift für die alttestamentliche Wissenschaft
CB	Century Bible
CBC	Cambridge Bible Commentary
CBET	Contributions to Biblical Exegesis and Theology
CBOT	Coniectanea Biblica, Old Testament Series
CBQ	*Catholic Biblical Quarterly*
CBSC	Cambridge Bible for Schools and Colleges
CC	Continental Commentaries
CCSOT	The Communicator's Commentary Series, Old Testament
CEB	Commentaire évangélique de La Bible
COT	Commentaar op het Oude Testament
COTC	Calvin's Old Testament Commentaries
CRB	Cahiers de la Revue Biblique
CR:BS	*Currents in Research: Biblical Studies*
CTJ	*Calvin Theological Journal*
Davidson	*Hebrew Syntax*, 3rd ed., by A. B. Davidson.
DBSup	*Supplément au Dictionnaire de la Bible*
DCH	*The Dictionary of Classical Hebrew*

DOTT	*Documents from the Old Testament Times*, ed. D. Winton Thomas
DSB	Daily Study Bible
EB	Echter Bibel
EBT	*Encyclopedia of Biblical Theology*, ed. Johannes B. Bauer
EdF	Erträge der Forschung
EHS	Europäische Hochschulschriften
EncyBib	*Encyclopaedia Biblica: A Dictionary of the Bible*
EpC	Epworth Commentaries
ERE	*Encyclopaedia of Religion and Ethics*
ETL	*Ephemerides Theologicae Lovanienses*
EvTh	*Evangelische Theologie*
ExpB	Expositor's Bible
FAT	Forschungen zum Alten Testament
Forum	*Foundations & Facets Forum*
FOTL	The Forms of the Old Testament Literature
FRLANT	Forschungen zur Religion und Literatur des Alten und Neuen Testaments
FzB	Forschung zur Bibel
GELS	*A Greek-English Lexicon of the Septuagint*, by J. Lust, E. Eynikel and K. Hauspie
Gibson	*Davidson's Introductory Hebrew Grammar: Syntax*, 4th ed., by John C. L. Gibson
GKC	*Gesenius' Hebrew Grammar*, 2nd English Edition
GS	Geistliche Schriftlesung
GTB	Van Gorcum's Theologische Bibliotheek
HALAT	*Hebräisches und aramäisches Lexikon zum Alten Testament*
HALOT	*The Hebrew and Aramaic Lexicon of the Old Testament*
HAR	*Hebrew Annual Review*
HBAT	Handbuch zum Alten Testament
HBK	Herders Bibelkommentar
HKAT	Handkommentar zum Alten Testament
HSAT	Die Heilige Schrift des Alten Testament
HSM	Harvard Semitic Monographs
HUCA	*Hebrew Union College Annual*
IB	Interpreter's Bible
IBCTP	Interpretation: A Bible Commentary for Teaching and Preaching
ICC	International Critical Commentary
IDB	*The Interpreter's Dictionary of the Bible*
ISBE	*The International Standard Bible Encyclopedia*
ITC	International Theological Commentary
J.-M.	*A Grammar of Biblical Hebrew*, 2 vols., by Paul Joüon and T. Muraoka
JANES	*Journal of the Ancient Near Eastern Society*
JAOS	*Journal of the American Oriental Society*
JBCOTC	The James Burton Coffman Series of Old Testament Commentaries
JBL	*Journal of Biblical Literature*
JBLMS	Journal of Biblical Literature Monograph Series
JETS	*Journal of the Evangelical Theological Society*
JJS	*Journal of Jewish Studies*
JNES	*Journal of Near Eastern Studies*
JNSL	*Journal of Northwest Semitic Languages*
JPOS	*Journal of the Palestine Oriental Society*
JPSTC	Jewish Publication Society Torah Commentary
JQR	*Jewish Quarterly Review*
JSOT	*Journal for the Study of the Old Testament*
JSNTSS	Journal for the Study of New Testament Supplement Series

JSOTSS	Journal for the Study of Old Testament Supplement Series
JSS	*Journal of Semitic Studies*
JTS	*Journal of Theological Studies*
KAT	Kommentar zum Alten Testament
KeHAT	Kurzgefaßtes exegetisches Handbuch zum Alten Testament
KHCAT	Kurzer Hand-Commentar zum Alten Testament
KKHS	Kurzgefaßter Kommentar zu den Heiligen Schriften
KVHS	Korte Verklaring der Heilige Schrift
LD	Lectio Divina
LSJ	*A Greek-English Lexicon*, by Henry G. Liddell, Robert Scott and Henry S. Jones
LTJ	*Lutheran Theological Journal*
LXX	Septuagint
MT	Masoretic Text
NAC	The New American Commentary
NCB	New Century Bible Commentary
NEB	Die Neue Echter Bibel
NICOT	New International Commentary on the Old Testament
NIDOTTE	*New International Dictionary of Old Testament Theology and Exegesis*
NIVAC	The NIV Application Commentary
NSOED	*New Shorter Oxford English Dictionary*
NTOA	Novum Testamentum et Orbis Antiquus
OBO	Orbis Biblicus et Orientalis
OBT	Overtures to Biblical Theology
OED	*Oxford English Dictionary*, Second Edition, 1989
OT	Old Testament
OTE	*Old Testament Essays*
OTG	Old Testament Guides
OTL	Old Testament Library
OTM	Old Testament Message
OTS	*Oudtestamentische Studiën*
PEGLMBS	*Proceedings, Eastern Great Lakes and Midwest Biblical Societies*
POT	De Prediking van het Oude Testament
PRE	*Pauly's Real-Encyclopädie der classischen Altertumswissenschaft*, 1932²
PRR	*The Presbyterian and Reformed Review*
QD	Quaestiones Disputatae
QS	Quaderni di Semitistica
RB	*Revue Biblique*
RGG	*Die Religion in Geschichte und Gegenwart: Handwörterbuch für Theologie und Religionswissenschaft*
RHPR	*Revue d'Histoire et de Philosophie Religieuse*
SANT	Studien zum Alten und Neuen Testament
SB	La Sainte Bible
SBB	Stuttgarter biblische Beiträge
SBFLA	*Studii biblici franciscani liber annuus*
SBLDS	Society of Biblical Literature Dissertation Series
SBLMS	Society of Biblical Literature Monograph Series
SBS	Stuttgarter Bibelstudien
SBT	Studies in Biblical Theology
SCS	Septuagint and Cognate Studies
SHCANE	Studies in the History and Culture of the Ancient Near East
SJLA	Studies in Judaism in Late Antiquity
SNSTMS	Society for New Testament Studies Monograph Series
SonB	Soncino Books of the Bible

SPOT   Studies on Personalities of the Old Testament
SSN   Studia Semitica Neerlandica
SVT   Supplement to Vetus Testamentum
TBC   Torch Bible Commentaries
TDNT   *Theological Dictionary of the New Testament*
TDOT   *Theological Dictionary of the Old Testament*
ThB   Theologische Bücherei
ThPh   *Theologie und Philosophie*
TLOT   *Theological Lexicon of the Old Testament*
TLZ   *Theologische Literaturzeitung*
TOTC   Tyndale Old Testament Commentary
TQ   *Theologische Quartalschrift*
TRE   *Theologische Realenzyklopädie*
TS   Theologische Studien
TT   Tekst en Toelichting
TWAT   *Theologisches Wörterbuch zum Alten Testament*
TWOT   *Theological Wordbook of the Old Testament*
TynBul   *Tyndale Bulletin*
TZ   *Theologische Zeitschrift*
UBL   Ugaritisch-Biblische Literatur
UCOP   University of Cambridge Oriental Publication
UF   *Ugaritische Forschungen*
USQR   *Union Seminary Quarterly Review*
UUÅ   Uppsala Universitets Årsskrift
VT   *Vetus Testamentum*
W.-O'C.   *An Introduction to Biblical Hebrew Syntax*, by Bruce K. Waltke and M. O'Connor
WBC   Word Biblical Commentary
WdF   Wege der Forschung
WestBC   Westminster Bible Companion
WestC   Westminster Commentaries
WMANT   Wissenschaftliche Monographien zum Alten und Neuen Testament
ZAW   *Zeitschrift für die alttestamentliche Wissenschaft*
ZLTK   *Zeitschrift für lutherische Theologie und Kirche*
ZPEB   *Zondervan Pictorial Encyclopedia of the Bible*
ZTK   *Zeitschrift für Theologie und Kirche*

CHAPTER ONE

INTRODUCTION

1. *General Introduction*

Events in the sixth century BCE formed a watershed in the history of Israel. In the first deportation by Nebuchadnezzar in 597 BCE, king Jehoiachin, the nobles and leaders of the people were taken away to Babylon. At that time the temple remained intact and the southern kingdom Judah was still allowed to be ruled by the puppet king Zedekiah. But his conspiracy with Egypt against Babylon in 589/588 BCE led to a dire consequence. About two years later in 587/586 BCE Nebuchadnezzar took Jerusalem. This time the temple was destroyed, more people were exiled. Zedekiah was captured in an attempt to flee and was later blinded. Judah as an independent state existed no more.

The two exiles brought about destruction and devastation. Many people were killed and a number of cities destroyed. The temple, which was the pride of the power of the people (Ez 24:21), and the cultic worship associated with it were brought to an end. The Davidic dynasty barely survived. Many were forced to leave the land which Yahweh had promised to give to their ancestor Abraham (cf. Ez 33:24). Both those in the exile and those remaining in Palestine had to face the challenges this event had brought upon them. They met the plight where the "old symbol systems"[1] were gone.

The Book of Ezekiel offers one of the many reactions to the two exiles. The book is attributed to Ezekiel, a priest who was deported to Babylon among many in 597 BCE. Although there has been much discussion on the locale of Ezekiel's ministry, most scholars today accept that his ministry was conducted in Babylon.[2] In the first six years of his ministry among the exiles, Ezekiel announced the end of Jerusalem, denouncing those prophets who declared "peace" for Jerusalem (Ez 13:1–16). He condemned the misconduct of the various

---

[1] Klein 1979:5.
[2] For a recent discussion, see McKeating (1993:30–61) and Renz (1999:27–38).

strata of the people: the king, the princes, the priests, the people of
the land and the ordinary people. He attempted, on the one hand,
to convict the people of their misbehaviour: it was because of what
they had committed that they should be responsible for what had
happened and what would happen.[3] And on the other hand, he
sought to convince them of the certainty of the coming disaster: God
would not relent until his anger had run its course (cf. Ez 24:14).

At that time, serious theological questions were undoubtedly raised
by the people. They wondered whether Yahweh was a God more
powerful than the Babylonian Marduk and whether or not he was
strong enough to keep them in the land (cf. Ez 36:20). They also
questioned whether what God had inflicted or would inflict upon
them was too heavy and whether he was just (cf. Ez 18:25). While
the former question is concerned with the omnipotence of God, the
latter concerns his justice in his retribution. The way that Ezekiel
addresses this latter question is the object of the present study.

Etymologically, the word "retribution" is composed of *re* + *tribuere*,
meaning literally "to pay back, to give back". It is this idea of paying back that underlines most modern definitions of "retribution" as,
for example, "deserved punishment for evil done, or conversely,
reward for good done".[4] According to this definition, retribution has
both a negative aspect, i.e., "deserved punishment for evil done",
and a positive aspect, i.e., "reward for good done". But contemporary usage rarely refers to the positive aspect.[5] In this book both
aspects are assumed for the word "retribution", although we will
focus only on the negative aspect. One important question concerning
retribution is "how is this achieved?", i.e., "how is punishment/reward
paid back?" This question contains two components. First, who will
execute retribution, the act of paying back the evil? Second, what
is the criterion or rule according to which what is paid back is deter-

---

[3] See Joyce (1989:33–77) for a discussion on the responsibility of Israel.

[4] Tullock 1994:757. Similarly, Towner (1976:742) defines retribution as "the
repayment of someone according to that person's just merits or deserts" and "[i]n
religious literature, the term usually refers to the rewards and punishments meted
out to persons by God . . ." (cf. Towner 1971:203). See also Gammie (1970:4) and
Zerafa (1973:465). Kuntz emphasises that retribution is different from mere consequence in that only the former "is tenacious in its claim that reward and punishment, in the form of just deserts, must be impartially dispensed by a conscious
agent" (1977:226n.19).

[5] Cf. *OED* 13:793.

mined? This second aspect is closely linked to the idea of just deserts. It is with these questions in mind that we turn to the discussion of retribution in the OT.

Since the Enlightenment the concept of retribution has been attributed to both the OT and God, and in the epoch of OT studies between Wellhausen and Gunkel the idea of retribution was seen as the fruit of the prophetic theology.[6] Moreover, these scholars seem to hold the view that retribution means the infliction of punishment on the offender for a deliberate violation of a norm.[7] As such, they understand the nature of retribution in juridical terms. That is to say, God (or sometimes a human) is the agent external both to the offender and the offence who actually pays back punishment to the offender according to the terms of the agreed norm broken by the offender. But there does not seem to be any intrinsic reason for restricting retribution to this juridical understanding. This becomes a point of contention for the discussion of retribution in OT. In the following we will present a brief overview of past scholarship on this question, thus setting the stage for the present study on the idea of retribution in Ezekiel.

2. *The Thesis of Koch*

Although many scholars understand retribution in the OT in a juridical manner, this is by no means a consensus. While some claim that a discussion of the relation between disobedience and punishment is still wanting,[8] some others hold that the relation is closer than a legal understanding would allow. Among holders of this latter view are Pedersen and Fahlgren.[9] Take Fahlgren as an example. He discovers that there are words which denote both an action and its consequence. For example, רשׁע means both being ethically depraved and its consequence, i.e., misfortune; חטאת denotes both sin and disaster; and עון both trespass and punishment.[10] The same applies to צדקה which means both righteousness and the fruit of righteousness,

---

[6] Janowski 1994:248–249. See, for example, Stade (1905:285), Gunkel (1931:1530).
[7] E.g. Eichrodt 1961:242–243.
[8] Koehler 1957:211.
[9] See Hubbard (1980:6–7) for a review of some other scholars.
[10] Fahlgren 1932:17, 24, 25, 31. Extracts of his book are published as Fahlgren 1972.

i.e., well-being.[11] The point for Fahlgren is that at some earlier time
in Israel's history people could not distinguish between cause and
effect and they viewed both as the same entity.[12] This state of mind
is termed the "synthetic view of life" ("synthetische Lebensauffassung").[13]
Only later does Yahweh gradually play a more important role. Thus,
according to Fahlgren, a deed and its consequence, and in particular an evil act and its disastrous consequence, are not to be distinguished. They are simply connected as a whole, and therefore the
consequence should not be seen (as in a juridical context) as the
result of intervention from outside the deed.

Inspired by and elaborating on Fahlgren's view, Koch's seminal
paper on the topic has set the agenda for subsequent discussion.[14]
In the paper Koch argues that there is "a built-in and inherent connection between an action and its consequences" and "there is an
apodictic alternative in force which very simply offers one either
blessing or destruction, without further delineation based on giving
special attention to how important an action is judged to be".[15] His
argument is based on a study of selected passages from Prov 25–29,
Hosea, Psalms and the Deuteronomistic History. He points out that
in some of these passages, Yahweh is not mentioned at all in the
connection between deed and consequence. Rather, what is depicted
in them is that an action will inevitably result in its consequence,
i.e., the consequence is part of the essence of the action. The deed-
consequence connection is like the connection between planting and
harvesting. The deed is like a seed and the consequence its fruit.[16]
The connection between deed and consequence is like the laws of
nature "which operate so that an action inevitably is followed by a
reaction".[17] By attributing a locative sense to the preposition ב in
expressions like ברשעתו (Prov 11:5), he asserts that a person is sur-
rounded or enveloped by one's own actions. Thus, the action "becomes
a powerful sphere of influence which was created by the person who
did something and is now caught by what he did".[18] Koch calls this

---

[11] Fahlgren 1932:88–89.
[12] Fahlgren 1932:51–52.
[13] Fahlgren 1932:50.
[14] Koch 1955 (ET 1983).
[15] Koch 1983:59–60.
[16] Koch 1983:61, 65, 72.
[17] Koch 1983:58.
[18] Koch 1983:72.

the "schicksalswirkende Tatsphäre". The action has "an in-this-world, material, self-activating quality about it".[19] He further notes that verbs like שלם (piel) and שוב (hiphil) do not mean "to reward" or "to requite", but rather "to make complete" and "to bring back" respectively.[20] The point is that passages with Yahweh as the subject of these verbs do not suggest that his role is that of a judge, but only like that of a midwife by *facilitating the completion of something which previous human action has already set in motion*".[21] It is the Septuagint which introduces the legal ideas by rendering these verbs with juridical terms.[22] There is, in fact, no Hebrew word meaning "punishment".[23] The use of passive verbal forms in describing the consequences further shows that there is no active intervention of Yahweh, but only an inherent connection between consequences and their originating actions.[24] Fahlgren's thesis that some Hebrew words denote both the action and its consequence points, according to Koch, to the same conclusion.

As a consequence of his argument, Koch concludes that there is no doctrine of retribution in the OT. His conclusion presupposes that retribution should be understood juridically. But if retribution is not restricted to this sense, then what Koch does amounts to proposing an alternative understanding of the concept of retribution instead of the often assumed juridical view. Koch's thesis of the mechanistic connection between deed and consequence is warmly received by von Rad,[25] McKane[26] and Wolff.[27]

---

[19] Koch 1983:65.

[20] Koch 1983:60, 63.

[21] Koch 1983:61 (his italics).

[22] Koch 1955:37–39.

[23] Koch 1983:77.

[24] Koch 1983:70.

[25] Von Rad 1962:266, 384–386, 436. Note, however, that the rendering of the German original "sein Blut (d.h. die Blutschuld) *komme* über . . ." as "let his blood (that is, his blood-guiltiness) *be* upon . . ." (p. 385, our italics) may blur a distinction which Koch and Reventlow want to make. For this, see Note 37 below. See also von Rad (1972:79, 128–129).

[26] E.g. McKane 1970:271. Commenting on Prov 1:19, he states that "the relationship between the actions of the fools and the bad end which overtakes them is inward and necessary, not superimposed as the consequence of a forensic verdict and penalty . . .".

[27] Wolff 1974:68.

3. Reactions and Further Discussion

A modification to Koch's thesis comes from Horst.[28] While scholars before him may have assumed the juridical nature of retribution, Horst argues for it. He holds that Yahweh's unchangeableness and exclusivity is the centre of all theological statements in the OT, and as such there is nothing autonomous and high-handed left in the world.[29] This character of Yahweh enforces the de-magicisation ("Entmagisierung") of the cultic rites, followed by their historicisation ("Historisierung"), thus relating them to Yahweh's special historical salvific actions.[30] The same de-magicisation and historicisation also play a role in the domain of secular law.[31] In doing so, the law has its origin and norm in the God who explains himself to Israel and in his salvific sovereign will.[32] That is to say, even if one asserts the origin of punishment in magical thought, at a later stage the religious language appropriates the language of private laws, thereby expressing the idea of punishment as, for example, a private revenge. Thus, it is God who sets in motion and brings to a fulfilment a legal case against a person who misbehaves.[33] The basic point of Horst is that although Koch is correct to detect a "primitive" notion of retribution in the Old Testament, he errs in rejecting any legal idea from Yahweh's act of connecting deed and consequence.[34]

A similar approach is taken up by Reventlow. In an article published in 1960, Reventlow traces the development of the use of the formula "sein Blut komme über sein Haupt". When it appears in a curse, it may take up the magical structure of a curse and hence come close to a mechanical outworking of a deed and its consequence.[35] Later, when the formula is uttered in the cult or a prayer, it is personalised in that God is supposed to be present and punish the guilty party.[36] A last step in overcoming the primitive understanding of the

---

[28] Horst 1956.
[29] Horst 1956:50, 51.
[30] Horst 1956:55–57.
[31] Horst 1956:58–66.
[32] Horst 1956:66–67.
[33] Horst 1956:74.
[34] See also Horst (1962).
[35] Reventlow 1960:314.
[36] Reventlow (1960:321–322) states: "Die Kundgabe des Rechts an Israel ist eine Wesensäusserung des göttlichen Herrn selbst, und auch die Fluchformel (welch primitiv-magische Vorgeschichte sie auch immer haben möge) ist da mithinein-

self-effecting deed-consequence connection is in the prophetic pro-
nouncement of the divine "I" as found especially in Ezekiel (e.g.
Ez 18:13).[37] Like Horst, Reventlow argues that there is a development in the idea of retribution from the mechanical to the juridical.

In two linguistic studies, J. Scharbert offers a critique of Koch's
thesis from another perspective.[38] In his study on the verb פקד, he
considers the various syntactical structures and different conjugations
involved when the verb is used transitively with person, things and
offence as objects and when it is used intransitively. He also pays
brief attention to its cognate substantives. He observes that when
God is the subject of the verb with a person as object it does not
always mean a self-originating and fateful consequence of an evil
act, but it also has to do with divine intervention.[39] Moreover, although
Koch noted correctly, "Das פקד im wohlwollenden Sinn hat aller-
dings nichts mit 'Lohn' zu tun . . .", Scharbert argues against Koch
that it "bezeichnet ein *gnädiges*, hilfsbereites und *heilsträchtiges Besorgtsein
Gottes* . . .".[40] These point out the presence of a personal God who
is certainly active in the world. In his second study, the verb שלם
is analysed in a similar fashion. This verb is of special importance
in the argument of Koch who renders its piel form as "to make
complete". But the verb is also capable of assuming the meaning of
"to give back, to pay, to remunerate, to substitute"[41] in contexts of
legal and economic life. It can even refer to the reactions of Yahweh
towards human behaviour in theological language. Although Koch
is right to hold that the verb in no way characterises Yahweh as a
judge, it speaks of God reacting to the morally relevant human
actions and operating with a "natural feeling of justice" ("natürliche

---

genommen. Es gibt keine Strafwirkung, hinter der nicht unmittelbar die Autorität
des göttlichen Herrn dahintersteht. Die magische Auffassung der Vorgeschichte ist
auf dieser Stufe längst überwunden."

[37] Reventlow 1960:324–325. In response to Reventlow, Koch (1962) modifies his
viewpoint. As the titles of this article and Reventlow's indicate, Koch holds that
"his blood *remains* on his head" instead of Reventlow's "his blood *comes* upon his
head". Thus, Koch maintains the close connection between deed and consequence.
However, he is ready to drop the notion of "mechanical" to describe the deed-consequence relationship and admit that God is a co-worker (still not a judge) in bringing the bloodguilt of a person back to him/her.

[38] Scharbert 1960, reprinted in Koch (1972:278–299); Scharbert 1961, reprinted
in Koch (1972:300–324).

[39] Scharbert 1960:283.

[40] Scharbert 1960:298 (his italics).

[41] Scharbert's "zurückgeben, (be)zahlen, begleichen, entgelten, ersetzen" (1961:309).

Gerechtigkeitsempfinden") demanding a corresponding "reward" for
every action.[42] The merit of Scharbert's studies lies in the detailed
treatment of the syntactic uses of the verbs in their various contexts.
This is in contrast to Koch who seems to limit the words to their
etymological meanings. But in the end, Scharbert holds that divine
retribution and the idea of *schicksalswirkende Tat* stand beside and supplement each other.[43]

Pax criticises Koch for not giving a precise definition of "retribution" and proposes the following: "die lohnende und strafende
Reaktion Gottes auf die guten und schlechten Taten der Menschen".[44]
Pax provides both a theological and a linguistic argument. Theologically, he points out that the Psalms show that God is intensively
involved in human affairs in relation to both salvation and calamity.[45]
This ambivalent character of Yahweh's action speaks against Koch's
one-sided emphasis on evil and calamity.[46] Moreover, the idea of
judgement as seen in its connection to the wrath of Yahweh on the
one hand, and in its relation to צדק which refers to community
faithfulness in the covenantal relationship between Israel and Yahweh
on the other hand, is not late but is anchored in the OT thought
from the beginning.[47] Linguistically, to argue on the basis of the
absence of the word "punishment" is basically an *argumentum e silen-
tio*. The lack of a word, for example, "parents", in Hebrew does not
mean that there is no such idea. This may also apply to the case
of the word "punishment".[48] From a literary-stylistic viewpoint, Pax
rejects Koch's idea that the use of impersonal terms in the *Unheilsphäre*
demonstrates the mechanical relationship between deed and consequence. Pax puts forward the rhetorical device Hysteron-Proteron,
i.e., the subjective side is placed before the objective side. For the
psalmist, the destruction of the enemy is so important to him (i.e.,
his subjective feeling) that it is placed before the temporally earlier
judgement of God (i.e., the objective fact) (e.g. Ps 9:16–17).[49] Related
to this is the idea of *Fait-Accompli-Darstellung* where an expected or

---

[42] Scharbert 1961:322–323.
[43] Scharbert 1961:324.
[44] Pax 1960/61:62 (his italics).
[45] Pax 1960/61:65–84.
[46] Pax 1960/61:68, 84.
[47] Pax 1960/61:82, 87.
[48] Pax 1960/61:103–104.
[49] Pax 1960/61:99.

possible event is pushed to the front as accomplished. In some of these cases the LXX renders a perfect in the MT as if it were an imperfect (e.g. Ps 109:17). That is to say, the LXX brings changes to the MT in order to maintain a logical flow.[50] Also classified under this category are those sayings using the pictures of seed and harvest, pit and net in which the evildoer is caught, the point of which is to express the irrefutability and truth of a state of affairs. They are concerned more with the subjective wishes of the speaker than the "gesetzmässigen inneren Entwicklung".[51]

Knierim enters the discussion through his study of different words for "sin". He holds a similar developmental view as Horst and Reventlow, i.e., the act-consequence connection moves from its original status as a neutral world principle, characterised correctly by Koch as a "schicksalswirkende Tatsphäre", to a personalised version in its later reception in the Yahwistic faith.[52] He also calls Koch's view "dynamistic" which "wird hier im Sinne einer aus sich bestehenden Bewegungsfreiheit der Macht . . . verwendet".[53] However, his distinctive contribution lies in his attempt to reconcile the opposition between the dynamistic and the legal views of retribution. He argues that the legal practice can be represented as a form of completing the dynamism. Legal practice and dynamism work in and with each other.[54] It is thus incorrect to say that the legal thinking overcomes or substitutes the dynamistic thinking, but only that the legal thinking undermines the autonomy of the dynamistic thinking through the Yahwistic faith. Both the legal and dynamistic thinking are taken as means or forms of expression of the rule of Yahweh. The fate-producing event has a dynamistic-autonomous quality and can be conceived as constituted by Yahweh at the same time.[55] As to the relationship between Yahweh and dynamism, Knierim asserts that the OT gives a different picture in different contexts depending on the extent to which Yahweh's sovereignty is underlined.[56]

Plöger in his discussion of Dt 28 devotes a section to "Vergeltung

---

[50] Pax 1960/61:100.
[51] Pax 1960/61:101.
[52] Knierim 1965:73–91, esp. 89–91.
[53] Knierim 1965:81n.164.
[54] Knierim 1965:80–81.
[55] Knierim 1965:83.
[56] Knierim 1965:83–89.

im Dt".[57] He argues that Koch's view is too limited to explain a number of passages in Deuteronomy.[58] Following Pax, he argues for the active intervention of Yahweh as shown in his anger and compassion. Yahweh indeed punishes and rewards. As such, Yahweh is more than simply a midwife.[59] Moreover, one should not fail to notice that Deuteronomy underlines the covenantal framework in the relationship between Yahweh and Israel. With it, the "Segen und Fluch werden zu einem Instrument göttlicher 'Vergeltung'". Blessings and curses stand in an inner correspondence with obedience and disobedience respectively. Consequently, "dokumentiert Dt 28 mit Segen und Fluch *das Prinzip* einer göttlichen Vergeltung".[60] The curse is not a magical power triggered by a human, but meted out by God who becomes the "strafenden Richter" when a people break the covenant.[61] Thus, apart from upholding the role of God in retribution, Plöger points out a *principle*, i.e., the covenantal blessings and curses determine how the consequence is related to the deed.

Criticising Plöger for failing to detect variations in the idea of retribution, Gammie seeks to delineate its different aspects in Deuteronomy. First, retribution appears as an impersonal and mechanical principle which states that an evil act is destined to bring guilt upon its actor. This is basically the same idea put forward by Koch. In this case, the other facet of retribution, namely, that a good act will effect a good outcome, is absent.[62] This facet appears in the second aspect of retribution, i.e., retribution is a principle according to which the faithful are assured that Yahweh will recompense them accordingly. Gammie emphasises that although passages indicating such an understanding seem to be theocentric, they are actually anthropocentric in that "God is only a reactor to man rather than the determiner of history".[63] Even God himself acts according to this principle. From this, there is a movement to a more theocentric notion of retribution. The third aspect of retribution is that retribution is a personal and theocentric conception to describe the relationship between God and the human. Here, God's initiative in

---

[57] Plöger 1967:196–213.
[58] Especially Plöger 1967:203–213.
[59] Plöger 1967:200–203.
[60] Plöger 1967:195 (our italics).
[61] Plöger 1967:216.
[62] Gammie 1970:6–7.
[63] Gammie 1970:7.

electing and imparting commandments to Israel is stressed. God can even restrain his anger so that human sins do not always get their due punishment.[64] The fourth aspect is the dissolution of the idea of retribution. Retribution is seen as inappropriate to describe the relationship between God and the human in face of other considerations. For example, God humbles Israel so as to test her (Dt 8:2); God lets Israel hunger in order to teach her that humans do not live by bread alone (Dt 8:3, 5); God dispossesses the nations because of their wickedness and also his promise to the patriarchs but not because of the righteousness of Israel (Dt 9:4–6). These stand as arguments correcting the fossilisation of the anthropocentric view above as a "dogma": "misfortune may be sent for reasons other than man's sin; prosperity is not necessarily a sign of man's virtue".[65] Again, Gammie proposes a developmental scheme. One may doubt if the four phases can be delineated as clearly as Gammie claims. One may also question whether Gammie has paid sufficient attention to the literary or rhetorical features of the text so that the objections raised against a dogmatised doctrine of retribution mentioned above may be taken as serving a different purpose.

Zerafa offers an almost point for point argument against Koch's position. First, like Pax he holds that the absence of a Hebrew word for "punishment" has no bearing on the argument.[66] Second, he points out that Koch stretches the etymological meaning of verbs like שלם too far in some cases (e.g. Dt 7:20; Gen 44:4).[67] Third, generally speaking there is no doubt that the OT speaks of God dispensing reward to the just and punishment to the wicked. In cases where retribution is referred to without mentioning God, either human agents are called upon or the agent of retribution is not mentioned at all. In the latter case, which happens mostly in the wisdom literature, the texts are not concerned with the mechanism of retribution, but they state the simple fact. This is just a literary way of presenting a fact.[68] Fourth, the attribution of good or bad is not by "some abstract standard, but only with respect to God". As a consequence, the result of all human activity depends on God.

---

[64] Gammie 1970:9–10.
[65] Gammie 1970:11.
[66] Zerafa 1973:478.
[67] Zerafa 1973:478–479.
[68] Zerafa 1973:480.

Legislation for the society necessarily expresses God's will of what
should be done to the righteous or the wicked. Zerafa finds it hard
to "believe that the Israelites ever admitted the so-called primitive
principle of an automatic return of good or evil".[69] Lastly, as the
lord of creation, God acts freely so that reward is a gift rather than
a strict human right and punishment is an expression of God's
response to an offence rather than an automatic return of evil done.[70]

In an article on natural law, Barton discusses the notion of poetic
justice which means "a divine judgment is declared in a way that
stresses its *appropriateness* to the sin which has called it down".[71] He
holds that by regarding those passages speaking of poetic justice as
exhibiting the Israelite synthetic view of life (as Koch does), one
reduces those assertions in the passages to tautology or vacuity. If
sin inevitably leads to suffering, then the "vivid images in which the
prophets show the congruence of sin and punishment become point-
less, utterly banal platitudes".[72] Barton's point is that texts bearing
the notion of poetic justice depict not the mechanism of retribution
for sin but the moral character of God who acts justly by repaying
the humans what they deserve. In asserting this, Barton claims that
the prophetic appeal to poetic justice makes sense only if the audience has some agreed notion of what is counted as just and what
is not, and this points to the idea of natural law. Thus Barton cau-
tions us to take into account the non-metaphysical use of language.

Miller challenges Koch's claim that there is no juridical character involved in the connection between offence and punishment.
Miller argues that even if we hold that a punishment grows from a
crime, their relation can still be understood in a judicial context as
witnessed by the Judicial Papyrus of Turin. Actually, Westermann's
analysis of the judgement speech points out the juridical-legal setting of this type of speech. Furthermore, by bringing out some correspondences between a particular crime and its punishment, the
principle of talion is reflected and hence the juridical character of
this type of speech is further accentuated.[73] Also important is Miller's
observation that the various passages he analysed show that there is

---

[69] Zerafa 1973:485.
[70] Zerafa 1973:494.
[71] Barton 1979:9 (his italics).
[72] Barton 1979:12.
[73] Miller 1982:134–136.

"a kind of synergism in which divine and human action are forged into a single whole or the divine intention of judgement is wrought out through human agency".[74] Thus, like Horst before him, Miller pays particular attention to the role of the human agent in the realisation of the *Tun-Ergehen-Zusammenhang* and its legal context.

Another important contribution of Miller is his observation on the rhetorical use of language. Re-examining some of the prophetic texts treated by Koch, Miller asserts that these texts deal more with a relation of correspondence between sin and punishment than consequence.[75] That is to say, these texts stress that punishment is like the sin committed. This emphasis on the correspondence between sin and punishment points not to the mechanism of cause and effect as held by Koch but to "a concept of *retributive justice*".[76] The idea of correspondence "sets at the center of Yahweh's judgment the affirmation of *appropriate justice*" and is used "to sharpen or heighten the relation between sin and judgment when the *Tun-Ergehen Zusammenhang* is not clearly evident and even when it is".[77] Miller identifies three possible sources for this correspondence. The first one is the general and universal patterns of speech and style. Secondly, depending on Lohfink, correspondences between sin and judgement by repetition of the same verbs can be traced back to treaties and covenants. The third source is a talionic style or way of thinking which can take many forms.[78] Miller's contribution to the study of retribution lies not only, as mentioned above, in restoring to its rightful place

---

[74] Miller 1982:138.

[75] For his earlier work on the correspondence of sin and judgement, see Miller (1978:27–36). See also Miller (1984).

[76] Miller 1982:134 (his italics).

[77] Miller 1982:136–137 (his italics). In this connection, we may mention Boogaart (1985). In the article, although Boogaart is somewhat reserved with respect to the argument of Miller against Koch, his treatment of Jdg 9, which seems to be an extended commentary on Koch's opinion that "the doer of mischief suffers in return the same evil he has inflicted on another" (48), remains very similar in tenor to Miller's. Not only does he detect a lot of correspondences between the evil deed of Abimelech and the men of Shechem and the fate they suffer because of it, he also mentions that it is "[a]*fter God's intervention*" that "the evil deed committed by Abimelech and the men of Shechem, i.e. fratricide, conspiracy, and killing upon a stone, return in the same form upon them" (52, our italics). On the scheme depicted on the same page, Boogaart clearly indicates when God delays in action, and when he responds to Jotham and sends "an evil spirit to return the violence and blood upon Abimelech and the Men of Shechem". It is thus surprising to find him arguing against Miller in favour of "the weight of the evidence marshaled by Koch" (54).

[78] Miller 1982:98–110.

the juridical character of those texts where the sin-judgement nexus
is mentioned but also in deepening our understanding of the use of
the language of correspondence. Miller and Barton's studies on the
use of the language of poetic justice caution us not to interpret hastily
the words too literally. One has to note not just the non-literal force
of the language but also the rhetorical effect. This constitutes another
criticism of Koch who reads, for example, metaphors involving natural and agricultural elements too literally and thus posits a narrow
notion of retribution.[79]

Taking up the idea of Knierim, Hubbard in his 1980 dissertation
discusses the dynamistic and legal language in the complaint psalms.
Two articles have been published on the basis of the dissertation,[80]
and his idea is further tested in Ruth.[81] The main objective of these
studies is to show how dynamistic and legal language can function
together. He basically develops Knierim's thesis mentioned above
that dynamistic and legal thought operate in and with each other
under the sovereign rule of Yahweh. There is, in fact, no opposition between them. In one of his articles, he proposes a termino-
logical correction of Koch's "Tatsphäre". He points out that the
act-consequence connection can be conceived not only as a sphere,
but also as a linear and even as a boomerang effect. He therefore
suggests the word "dynamic" as the comprehensive term for both
cases.[82] He also follows Knierim in using the term "Ganzheitsdenken".[83]
Since he calls Koch's idea "dynamic/dynamistic", it may be useful
to see how he employs the term. In his dissertation, he defines
"dynamism" as "the theory that acts beget consequences automati-
cally by virtue of an impersonal force which they are presumed to
release".[84] This is refined later as:

> The term "dynamism" . . . describes the theory that acts automatically
> release power which causes their corresponding consequences. Texts
> reflect the operation of dynamism in three ways: first, when they re-
> port someone's wish or prayer that another party receive an outcome
> commensurate with some prior or anticipated action; second, when

---

[79] For a similar comment, see Hoffman (1992:119).
[80] Hubbard 1982a, 1982b.
[81] Hubbard 1997.
[82] Hubbard 1982b.
[83] Hubbard 1982a:278; 1997:192; cf. Knierim 1965:99–100.
[84] Hubbard 1980:1n.1.

they report how a deed produced a subsequent result whose occurrence is traceable to the original deed; and third, when they use words
whose range of meanings encompasses both an act and its resulting
consequence.[85]

Hubbard holds that dynamism and law are interwoven and they
should both be put under the overarching ontological principle of
world order.[86] While the dynamic dimension underlines the "inevitability, equivalence, orderedness and even mysteriousness of the process",
the legal dimension "underscores the legality of the event".[87] Yahweh
is both a world judge and an overseer of the dynamic who "connects acts and consequences".[88]

Boström offers a renewed examination of Koch's interpretation of
the Proverbial material. Boström devotes a chapter to the triad God-
Retribution-Order. He sees retribution as the dispensation of reward
and punishment, and compares the ideas of retribution and order
found in both the God-sayings and other sayings in Proverbs. Some
of his conclusions relevant to understanding retribution are mentioned here. First, concerning the formulation of consequences, there
is little interest in Proverbs to specify the exact consequences of
actions. In particular, when the effects of bad behaviour are considered, there is a propensity to use impersonal or passive forms
which express an intentional ambiguity, leaving the cases open for
different interpretations.[89] But this "neither necessitates nor justifies
the introduction of an impersonal concept of order or of a strict
causal nexus between actions and consequences".[90]

Second, the God-sayings should not be considered as late. The
point is that "[t]o imagine a tradition in Israel or in the ancient
world that was devoid of a religious aspect is not historically credi-
ble".[91] Moreover, he approves the opinion of Gese that there is no
basic difference between the God-sayings and other sayings except
for the references to Yahweh in the former. This observation casts
doubt on a developmental theory of retribution.

---

[85] Hubbard 1997:193.
[86] Hubbard 1982a:273–274. Cf. Blenkinsopp's comment (1995:49) on Amos and
Jeremiah.
[87] Hubbard 1982a:276, 277. Cf. Hubbard 1980:287.
[88] Hubbard 1997:209.
[89] Boström 1990:112, 132, 135.
[90] Boström 1990:116.
[91] Boström 1990:135–136.

Third, a small number of proverbs evinces the active role of God in retribution while some others stress the sovereignty of God in relation to humans and the world. Boström thus summarises that the "God-sayings as a whole point towards a belief in the Lord as ruler and director of the world where his active role in the retributional process constitutes *one* facet".[92]

Fourth, regarding the notion of order, Boström argues that the term is appropriate if it denotes the world-view of the sages who believe that the world is marked by regularity, order and harmony. But when the term is used to designate a particular world-view in which order is seen as an impersonal principle governing all things in the world to such an extent that God's actions are rendered superfluous, then this use is misplaced. Any use of the word "order" to signify the world-view of the wisdom literature must be qualified by the idea that God is the ruler and sustainer of the world.[93]

Fifth, some sayings are characterised by anthropocentric thinking like those advocating that a person's own behaviour and attitudes are linked to certain consequences. Instead of regarding these as opposite to theocentricity, they should be seen as underscoring the responsibility of the human who can choose between right and wrong with their foreseeable consequences. However, one should note that various factors are involved in the retributive process, namely, a person's behaviour, his/her company and the community.[94]

Sixth, apropos of the relationship between acts and consequences, Boström suggests that in Proverbs consequences are not primarily related to actions but to the total life-style and attitude of the person. The term "character-consequence-relationship" is therefore more appropriate. However, since both the character and the consequence in the relationship are put in general terms, a precise picture of such a relationship cannot be determined. A re-examination of the use of שׁלם (piel) and שׁוב (hiphil) in texts on retribution shows that Koch's theory is unconvincing. Rather, God is active in the retributive process. He is more like a kinsman (גֹּאֵל) affected by a human's attitudes.[95]

Seventh, concerning the concept of God, as mentioned above, God is seen as actively participating in human affairs in association

---

[92] Boström 1990:136 (his italics).
[93] Boström 1990:136–137.
[94] Boström 1990:138.
[95] Boström 1990:138–139.

with human responsibility. He is portrayed not only as a judge and agent of the retribution process, but also as a kinsman of the people. The accent is put on the sovereignty of God who maintains justice, harmony and order. Although the anthropocentric viewpoint which underlines the responsibility of the people does exist, its tension with the theocentric viewpoint is resolved in some sayings by stressing the sovereignty of God who works out his plans independently of human activities. These two viewpoints are never seen as contradictory but as complementary.[96]

Boström's treatment of Proverbs is more comprehensive than that of Koch and therefore offers a more complete picture of the idea of retribution in Proverbs. Boström affirms not simply the role of God in retribution, but goes further in stressing the association between God and the human in retribution. Also noteworthy is his observation that many factors are involved in the retributive process so that any simplistic solution is doomed to be misleading.

In a study on different groups of people in the Proverbs, Delkurt holds that Proverbs is concerned with living in harmony with the will of God and it places community loyalty above personal success.[97] She affirms with Boström that the proverbs are formulated generally and have less to do with concrete actions.[98] While some proverbs may express established life patterns, some others simply point out what should be the case according to ethical standards.[99] As such, the proverbs underline which conduct would lead to which consequence rather than retrace which act could have triggered the existing consequence.[100] This speaks against Koch who interprets the proverbs as depicting the *Is* rather than the *Ought*. More directly, Delkurt argues that proverbial wisdom speaks against a rigid view of the deed-consequence connection. This is demonstrated by noting that some proverbs establish oppositions (e.g. 26:4–5), some speak of the abolition of consequences of evil acts (e.g. 28:13), and some which have a theological background point to the imponderability of life (e.g. 16:1).[101] Thus, the proverbs give much space to the work

---

[96] Boström 1990:139–140.
[97] Delkurt 1993:148–149.
[98] Delkurt 1993:144.
[99] Delkurt 1993:149.
[100] Delkurt 1993:147.
[101] Delkurt 1993:153–154.

of God. While the sages are conscious of their limits, they place their trust in Yahweh's personal intervention and uphold the will of Yahweh as a standard for their ethical action.[102]

Hausmann provides another study on Proverbs. Regarding the deed-consequence connection, she points out that the connection is not always clear, especially when there is a big time gap between the consequence and the deed. In this case, the connection can only be established by interpreting the past deed and the present consequence.[103] Moreover, this connection is expressed in various ways. The one who brings about this connection is sometimes not mentioned and sometimes is Yahweh. No pure immanent connection is to be expected.[104] At times, it is stressed that one should not seek retribution but wait on God to carry it out. Yahweh is the one who always intervenes on the side of the injured party.[105] Hausmann holds that there is no juridical sense in Proverbs, but one can still speak of retribution because there is an intervening agent, be it God or other humans.[106] Lastly, texts on the deed-consequence connection have an appellative function, i.e., they emphasise the responsibility of the actor and encourage one to live a righteous life.[107]

Responding to the question of "how does it happen that the deed returns to the actor?", Janowski first points out that the heart of the concept of retribution lies in the idea of reciprocity.[108] That is to say, instead of seeing the actor in him/herself, he/she is to be placed in the wider context of the society characterised by the principle of solidarity. All actions are connected with each other in the society. Involved in it is the idea of connective justice.[109] Drawing on the insight of Egyptian wisdom literature, Janowski holds that retribution belongs to the order of thinking-of-one-another ("Aneinander-Denken") and acting-for-one-another ("Füreinander-Handeln").[110] Justice is based on the principle of mutuality and is not a natural consequence of the good deed. It is rather a function of social

---

[102] Delkurt 1993:156.
[103] Hausmann 1995:235.
[104] Hausmann 1995:236–237.
[105] Hausmann 1995:238, 240.
[106] Hausmann 1995:243.
[107] Hausmann 1995:243–245.
[108] Janowski 1994:257. Cf. Towner 1971:203.
[109] Janowski 1994:259.
[110] Janowski 1994:260.

action.[111] Thus, proverbs like Prov 26:27 do not speak of a natural-law-like mechanism, but that the consequence will *certainly* appear. Some proverbs clearly point to someone other than the actor him/herself, and therefore reflect "die *Außenseite des Handelns*" (e.g. 28:18).[112] Some other proverbs with passive or impersonal formulation likewise refer to a second authority who is not named explicitly (e.g. 11:31). The point is that the deed returns to the actor not by itself, but through some other person. As such, retribution belongs to the category of social interaction.[113] In cases like Prov 25:21–22, where Yahweh is mentioned as the third party apart from the addressee and his enemies, Yahweh enters the scene and acts as a human would. His action follows the same principle of mutuality.[114] If retribution belongs to the category of social interaction, then it is a matter of *Ought* but not *Is*, and as such Koch's theory of *Tatsphäre* which attributes an ontic quality to actions, and therefore belongs to the domain of *Is*, is wrong.[115]

More recently, Kelly provides a fresh study on the idea of retribution and eschatology in Chronicles. Kelly does not give a clear definition of the term "retribution" in his book, but in a footnote he points out that the term is used "neutrally to signify both divine reward and punishment".[116] With respect to the theme of retribution Kelly seeks to re-examine the prevalent view that retribution in Chronicles is mechanical, individual and immediate by considering both the theological vocabulary and the narrative structure of the book. The question is therefore not whether God is the retributor, but how he dispenses retribution. Of special relevance to the present discussion is Kelly's contention that the Chronicler's thought can be traced partly to his reflection on the Sinaitic covenant, in that reward and punishment are closely related to the blessings and

---

[111] Janowski 1994:261. We may mention Keller's study (1977), in which he argues one-sidedly that retribution is based *only* on the principle of mutuality.

[112] Janowski 1994:262 (his italics).

[113] Janowski 1994:264–266.

[114] Janowski 1994:268–269.

[115] Janowski 1994:271. Cf. von Rad's "ontological definition of good and evil" (1972:128).

[116] Kelly 1996:29n.1. On the same page, he suggests that there is a strong link between "obedience and blessing, and disobedience and punishment, within the lifetimes of individuals and generations" in 2 Chr 10–36. Such a link can also be seen as an understanding of the meaning of the term "retribution".

curses of that covenant.[117] The importance of the notion of covenant is affirmed in the narrative structure of the Chronicles. Kelly shows that the topic of reward and punishment in Chronicles is seen less generally as a general theory of divine action in history than specifically as part of the covenantal relationship between Yahweh and his people. The founding principle employed seems to be the blessings and curses of the Sinaitic covenant which is seen as underlying the Davidic covenant, carrying with it the temple-oriented promise of forgiveness and restoration.[118] Moreover, when the Chronicler differs from the judgements of Kings (e.g. over Solomon, Rehoboam, Abijah and Manasseh), he does not furnish a better picture of these kings but underscores the covenantal goodness of Yahweh.[119] The Chronicler is not concerned with the question of the origin of evil, nor the justification of divine action, nor the question of innocent suffering (cf. 1 Chr 21:17; 2 Chr 25:13). It is not stated or even implied that every calamity (such as invasion and illness) is the consequence of sin, but when punishment is meted out, it is shown to be deserved and appropriate for the sin. The basic point of using the theme of blessing and punishment is to serve the fundamental concern of "*Yahweh's mercy and restorative will toward his sinful people*".[120] There is no strict balance between blessing, "which comes *consistently* whenever Israel 'seeks Yahweh', and judgment, which can be mitigated or remitted entirely".[121] Relevant for us is that the involvement of covenant in retribution implies a juridical overtone. This not only indicates that Yahweh intervenes as a judge, but also that he metes out blessings or curses according to the terms of the covenant. As such, it points to a principle which dictates how retribution is dispensed.[122]

---

[117] Kelly 1996:61–62.

[118] Kelly 1996:106. In this connection, we may mention Johnstone's studies on Chronicles (1986, 1996). He argues that Israel's sin consists in מעל and that this is a central concept in Chronicles. The Chronicler borrows it from Lev 5:14–26 and also Lev 26. The punishment for this sin includes the forfeiture of land, an idea going back to Lev 26. Although Johnstone does not explicitly refer to the covenantal framework of Lev 26, his discussion seems to presuppose it.

[119] Kelly 1996:107.

[120] Kelly 1996:108 (his italics).

[121] Kelly 1996:108 (his italics).

[122] Charette (1992:21–62) surveys the OT, with special emphasis on Deuteronomy and Jeremiah, and concludes that the Sinaitic covenant plays an important role in the OT schema of recompense. With his interest in the land in mind, he underlines that obedience to the laws and commandments of the covenant will lead to

The dynamistic view of retribution is again raised recently and supported by Tucker. He defines the "dynamistic" point of view as that which "sees actions—whether good or bad—as entailing or setting into motion their consequences".[123] He repeats some previous arguments such as the absence of a Hebrew word for "punishment", or that the words עון and חטאה can denote both the evil act and its consequence,[124] or that some consequences are formulated passively.[125] He further holds that impurity is seen as virtually "automatic" and that defilement is not punishment imposed from without.[126] Since the Israelites should be aware of the principle of cause and effect, they could apply this principle to sin and its effects. Even in cases in which Yahweh is said to intervene, there is no juridical perspective for the sanction is the same as the violation (e.g. Hos 4:9).[127] Although he affirms the presence of dynamistic thought, he holds that it is not necessarily a more primitive but a "less self-consciously reflective point of view".[128]

4. *Summary and Comments*

It is time to take stock. Koch's article is chosen as the point of departure for our discussion of retribution in the OT. His position is refined or refuted on different fronts. His preference for the dynamistic over the juridical view of retribution is challenged. While some reject the dynamistic view as either the residue of a historical development or simply wrong because of the active intervention of God or his action through human agency (e.g. Pax, Miller, Boström),[129] some seek to harmonise it with the juridical view (e.g. Knierim, Hubbard). But the latter's move is problematic because these two views do not seem to be reconcilable. For Koch, the dynamistic view underlines the force immanent in an act which produces its consequence.

---

continuing existence in the land, while disobedience will lead to devastation of and ejection from the land.

[123] Tucker 1997:374–375.
[124] Tucker 1997:379, 385.
[125] Tucker 1997:383.
[126] Tucker 1997:380.
[127] Tucker 1997:386.
[128] Tucker 1997:388.
[129] See also Rankin (1936:32), van Oyen (1967:68), Towner (1971:204–205) and Burger (1989:85).

But the juridical view presupposes the intervention of an agent external to the act and its actor. It seems impossible to hold simultane-
ously that the consequence of a deed is both produced by an
impersonal force of the act and by the intervention of an external
agent. These two views can only be reconciled by changing the
meaning of either or both of them. Consider, for example, Hubbard's
definition of dynamism mentioned above. It is doubtful whether the
three ways he listed in which a passage reflects dynamistic thinking
can really do so. Firstly, how can a report of an outcome commensurate with some anticipated action be an indication that the
action "releases power which causes their corresponding consequences"?[130] A punishment inflicted by a judge can easily be commensurate with the misdeed. Secondly, when a result is traceable to
the original deed, it can well be a punishment traceable to the original offence. Thirdly, words expressing both an act and its consequence say nothing about the metaphysical connection between an
act and its consequence. At this particular point, Fahlgren's and
therefore Koch's reliance on words possessing this property is ill-
founded. More than thirty years ago Barr already confuted the thesis that a linguistic structure reflects or corresponds to the thought
structure. One example he mentioned may be used to illustrate this
point.[131] It is absurd to say that English speakers cannot distinguish
between knowing facts and knowing people because there is only
one word "know", whereas German or French speakers can do so
because the former has "wissen" and "kennen", and the latter "savoir"
and "connaître". It is equally absurd to claim that since there are
Hebrew words meaning both an act and its consequence, the Hebrews
are not aware of the difference between them and see them as one
synthetic whole. Thus, texts having any of these three properties
listed by Hubbard can in no way reflect what he wants them to
reflect. Similarly, Tucker's definition of "dynamism" is equally problematic. There is certainly a difference between saying that actions
entail or set in motion their consequence and that actions produce
their consequence by virtue of the forces immanent in them in a
natural law-like manner. Again, the first can imply a juridical intervention but the latter cannot. Thus, Koch's idea of "dynamism" is

---

[130] Hubbard 1997:193.
[131] Barr 1961:36.

modified by his successors so that it can be incorporated within a legal framework. Moreover, as just mentioned, there is an intrinsic difficulty with Koch's view because it presupposes a correspondence between linguistic and thought structures. Related to this is Koch's claim that the fact that there is no Hebrew word in the OT for "punishment" supports the thesis that actions have built-in consequences. This, of course, is equally absurd, as Pax and others have pointed out. The lack of a word in a language system does not imply that this language user has no such idea. Would Koch say that the Israelites have no sense of history since there is no Hebrew word for "history" in the OT? As a matter of fact, there is no Hebrew word for "schicksalswirkende Tatsphäre", otherwise Koch would not have had to argue for the concept it represents. However, it is also unsatisfactory for Pax to explain this absence on the basis of the fact that Hebrew lacks abstract nouns.[132] Barr provides a still further relevant criticism against Koch. Barr warns the danger of taking the etymological meaning of a word as its most important meaning and trying to read this meaning into its various contexts.[133] Koch committed precisely that mistake as has been readily noted by scholars (e.g. Scharbert, Zerafa).[134]

Furthermore, Koch's argument is also untenable from a stylistic point of view. He argues that passive or impersonal formulations in some descriptions of the disastrous consequence show that there is an inherent connection between deed and consequence. Other scholars are quick to point out that stylistic features may play a role (e.g. Pax, Zerafa, Boström). Sometimes the passive formulations suggest a second party or even a third party who brings about the consequence (e.g. Hausmann, Janowski). In some of these cases, Yahweh is seen as that intervening party. Hausmann rightly notes that in Proverbs, retribution belongs to Yahweh. That last observation also shows that Koch sometimes pays attention to sayings isolated from their broader contexts.

More important is the way that Koch sees how language functions. For him, language seems to work in only one way, namely, description of reality. The seed-harvest saying is taken literally as

---

[132] See Barr (1961:27–30) for a refutation.
[133] Barr 1961:107–160.
[134] We may note that Peels (1995:305) finds fault with Koch for omitting to study the word נקם which, Peels avers, often suggests a strong juridical context.

depicting the mechanism of deed and consequence. The preposition
ⴗ is interpreted in a locative sense (although not limited to that) to
give the idea of a *Tatsphäre*. Equally problematic is Hubbard's idea
of a "linear" or "boomerang" motion of the action. Texts which
speak of the deed-consequence connection have nothing to do with
depicting the dynamism (between deed and consequence). They are
not dealing with the *Is* of the world. Rather, these texts are expressions of the *Ought*. In cases where there is a temporal separation
between a deed and its consequence,[135] the connection between them
is not self-evident. Thus, their connection can only be made by interpreting the past deed and present consequence through the specta-
cle of the deed-consequence connection (e.g. Hausmann). Hence, the
deed-consequence connection is not the result of a generalisation
from daily experiences, but a trust and confirmation of the moral
world order even in view of conflicting experiences.[136] It points to
the idea of distributive and/or connective justice (e.g. Delkurt,
Janowski). It also has what Krüger calls an "appellative function"[137]
which underlines "in besonderer Weise die Verantwortung des
Menschen für sein eigenes Ergehen".[138] It aims at motivating people to be responsible, appealing to them to act according to this
world order and to lead a life in good conduct.[139] This rhetorical
function of language is simply not taken into consideration by Koch.

   In a discussion of retribution it is important to consider not only
who or what brings about the deed-consequence connection, but also
in what sense the consequence (or punishment) inflicted is deserved
or just. This point has not been brought up in most cases. While a
juridical view of retribution includes such a consideration, a dynamistic
view omits it. The use of the (Sinaitic) covenant as a basis for retribution (e.g. Plöger, Kelly)[140] can be seen as a form of the juridical view. Since the blessings and curses to be meted out as the
retributive consequence are the agreed terms of the covenant, they

---

[135] Noted by Krüger (1989:90) and Janowski (1994:262). Koch is not clear on
this point. Although he uses the seed-harvest metaphor which implies a temporal
distance between a deed and its consequence, he also claims that an action has "*an
immediate effect*" on the actor (1983:61, his italics).

[136] Miller 1982:134; Krüger 1989:90. Cf. Barton 1979:12.

[137] Krüger 1989:91n.145.

[138] Hausmann 1995:245n.90.

[139] Krüger 1989:91; Boström 1990:101.

[140] Also Peels (1995:304).

are also the just deserts. Apart from this, the idea of just deserts is also found in texts depicting poetic justice or correspondences between deed and consequence. In these texts the consequence is shown to be appropriate to the deed through correspondences between them. Instead of taking these texts as depicting the dynamistic view as Koch claims, they are, as Barton writes, more concerned with the moral character of God who acts consistently in rendering human persons "*what they deserve*".[141] These texts show what sort of consequence is a just desert for what sort of deed. That is to say, the consequence bears resemblance to the deed. But whether these texts imply a juridical view remains to be seen.

The view that the deed-consequence connection is mechanistic or dynamistic is not tenable. But what needs to be explored more is firstly the claim of some scholars that retribution is not always juridical in nature (e.g. Scharbert, Hausmann). Is there a non-juridical understanding of retribution? Tucker mentions the idea of impurity. But his idea needs further clarification since there are different types of impurity and not all can be qualified morally and hence be the subject of retribution, which is basically a moral issue. If Ezekiel presents one of the most important responses to the question of retribution when confronted with the exile, he can certainly shed some light on this issue. The second question which needs to be addressed is what makes a consequence a just desert. A juridical understanding of retribution presents one solution to this question. The agreed norm within a juridical context serves as the criterion by which a punishment is meted out. In following the norm, the punishment is just. But are there any other ways of talking about just deserts apart from juridical ones? Again Ezekiel may have something to offer since he is also concerned with the justice of Yahweh in dispensing retribution. "Was his punishment too heavy?" and "Was his way of dealing not just?" are some of the challenging questions to which Ezekiel must face and respond.

5. *Ezekiel and Retribution*

The idea of retribution in Ezekiel with respect to the two aforementioned aspects has not been dealt with previously. More often

---

[141] Barton 1979:12 (his italics).

Ezekiel is referred to in relation to the issue of corporate and individual responsibility.[142] While our study will have some implications for this issue, it is not the purpose of this book to deal with it. Specific studies on other aspects of retribution in Ezekiel are few and they basically stress the unsystematic character of Ezekiel. In an article on Jer 5:1–6, Carroll tries to show that Jeremiah's attack on the people is actually rhetoric used to justify God's punishment of Jerusalem. Then Carroll considers some other texts which deal with similar problems as the Jeremian passage. He notes that in face of the coming calamity Ezekiel presents three different positions with respect to the fate of the righteous and the wicked: (1) some of the wicked will be spared, though exiled; (2) the righteous in the city will be spared and the wicked destroyed; (3) both the righteous and the wicked will be killed.[143] These divergent views demonstrate that Ezekiel is not systematic with respect to the idea of retribution.

A more detailed study is carried out by Fishbane, who deals with sin and judgement in Ez 4–24. In these chapters the sins of the Israelites are proclaimed by Ezekiel in order to confirm the utter wickedness of the people and God's justified punishment so that no false hope should be cultivated among the people. However, the perspectives shown in Ez 14, 18, 20 and 21 are contradictory. The message of Ez 14 is that there is no vicarious salvation. Ez 18 affirms that view and also that each person can change his/her fate by returning to God. However, Ez 20 presents a totally negative picture of Israel's history whose message is, in Fishbane's words, *"diametrically opposed to the teaching of chapter 18"*.[144] Ez 21 goes a step further by announcing the annihilation of both the righteous and the wicked. These chapters thus present different ideas of retribution in Ezekiel. Although words like יַעַן, עַל כֵּן and לָכֵן create a link

---

[142] For a pioneering work on the issue, see Robinson (1911, 1936, 1937). His idea is adapted by, for example, Johnson (1949, 1961). Some discussions can be found in Gruenthaner (1942), Daube (1947:154–189), Mendenhall (1960), Hempel (1964:32–67), Porter (1965), Rogerson (1970, 1977, 1978). For a recent discussion see Krašovec (1994, 1999) and Kaminsky (1995). For a discussion of the issue with respect to Ezekiel, see, for example, Herzog (1923:61–70), Rankin (1936:83–86), May (1961), Lindars (1965), Schenker (1981), Maag (1982:70–72, 131–137), Lust (1987), Joyce (1989), Matties (1990), Kaminsky (1995:155–178) and Krašovec (1999:463–483).
[143] Carroll 1984:30.
[144] Fishbane 1984:143 (his italics).

between the sins and the divine punishments, the relationship between them is not uniform. The point is that "the rhetorical strategy appears more designed to demonstrate *the reality of divine providence* and *the logic of sin-judgment* than any strict principle of legal retribution or equivalent".[145]

Uffenheimer examines the relationship between Ezekiel's deterministic view of history and his conception of ethics.[146] The former is depicted in Ez 16, 20 and 23, and touched upon in Ez 11, 33 and 34. In these chapters, Israel's history is portrayed as a history of total depravity in an utterly pessimistic tone so that no hope whatsoever is possible for Israel. Thus, the divine punishment of Israel is completely justified and divine justice should not be questioned at all. This collides with the ethics of Ezekiel (found, for instance, in Ez 18) which pinpoints the freedom of the individual to repent so that even the past of the individual would not weigh him/her down if he/she returns to God. Uffenheimer claims that "it is impossible to bridge the tensions between these two poles by any kind of harmonizing exegesis . . .".[147] This tension is set up because Ezekiel wants to prepare the exiles for the worst by announcing the devastating judgement on Jerusalem and at the same time to keep alive the hope for future redemption for the exiles by calling each individual to be responsible for his/her actions.

The unsystematic character of Ezekiel is likewise pointed out by Joyce, Kaminsky and Greenberg.[148] But the opposite opinion is also voiced. Duguid examines the fate of the various groups of leadership of Israel, i.e., kings and princes, priests and Levites, prophets and lay leadership. By considering Ezekiel's critique of these groups and proclamation of their future, Duguid attempts to prove that there is

> *a coherent and connected attitude* taken toward these leadership groups throughout the book: those singled out for the most reproach in Ezekiel's critique of the past are marginalized in his plan for the future, while those who escape blame are assigned positions of honour. Both upward mobility and downward mobility are evident. . . .[149]

---

[145] Fishbane 1984:149 (his italics).
[146] Uffenheimer 1992.
[147] Uffenheimer 1992:221.
[148] Joyce 1989:82; Kaminsky 1995:177; Greenberg 1997:469.
[149] Duguid 1994:1 (our italics).

By "their future", Duguid considers not only the punishment inflicted upon the groups as announced by Ezekiel, but also their place in the eschatological future temple displayed in Ez 40–48. Thus, it seems that Ezekiel is more systematic in the treatment of at least a distinct category of people in Israel.

It is not easy to reconcile the various contradictory viewpoints within Ezekiel. It may not even be possible to do that, since Ezekiel may have held different viewpoints at different times, or he may have wanted to stress one aspect over another on a particular issue. Thus, this has to be taken into account in our discussion of the idea of retribution in Ezekiel.

6. *A Note on the Approach Taken*

A few words remain to be said on the approach adopted in this study. A history of the studies of the authorship and unity of the Book of Ezekiel can be found in many introductions to the OT and need not be repeated here.[150] While these studies mostly employ various diachronic approaches, the Book of Ezekiel has increasingly been treated from a synchronic perspective.[151] Recently, Joyce has produced a survey of diachronic and synchronic perspectives on the Book of Ezekiel.[152] As those diachronic studies have shown, the Book of Ezekiel has undoubtedly undergone many redactional changes. But it is questionable whether these different layers of redaction can be attributed to the work of an "Ezekielian school" over a long period of time as proposed by Zimmerli,[153] or whether they can be determined so precisely as claimed by some scholars (e.g. Garscha, Ohnesorge). The variety of results of these studies certainly serves as a caveat to those who are embarking on the diachronic task. On the other hand, synchronic studies often point out literary features which indicate the interconnectedness of different parts of a peri-

---

[150] See, in addition, Lang (1981:1–31), Lust (1986:1–3), Joyce (1989:21–31), Duguid (1994:3–8). To Duguid's discussion we may add the work of Ohnesorge (1991).

[151] E.g. Parunak 1978, 1980; Boadt 1980, 1986; Greenberg 1983a, 1984, 1997; Newsome 1984; Tromp 1986; Matties 1990; Galambush 1992; Stevenson 1996; Nay 1999; Renz 1999.

[152] Joyce 1995. To his list we may add the rhetorical studies of Good (1970), Durlesser (1987, 1988) and, more recently, Renz (1999). In comparison, Darr's survey (1994) pays little attention to synchronic studies on Ezekiel.

[153] See Clements's criticism (1982, 1986) on Zimmerli.

cope or even of the Book. These studies reinforce the homogeneity of the Book of Ezekiel, thus increasing the difficulty of making "any straightforward division between primary and secondary material".[154] Thus, there is a tendency to attribute the bulk of the Book of Ezekiel to the prophet Ezekiel himself. On the basis of these observations and as a reading strategy, the approach we adopt is basically synchronic. The object of study will be the book in its present form instead of the history of formation of the book. This does not mean that the MT will be accepted without reservation. But any change brought to the MT will only be made when there is enough support from both external grounds (i.e., textual traditions) and internal grounds (i.e., literary features and internal coherence). For the sake of simplicity, we will use the word "Ezekiel" to denote both the author of the Book of Ezekiel and the book itself.

7. *Conclusion*

In this chapter we have briefly reviewed studies on the concept of retribution, paying particular attention to the question of who or what brings about retribution and in what sense the consequence is a just desert. Koch's seminal idea of the dynamistic nature of retribution is rejected after considering the role of God within the OT, the linguistic studies of some key words such as שׁלם (piel), the stylistic features of the biblical texts, the functions of language, and the relationship between linguistic structure and thought structure. Although a juridical view of retribution is affirmed in some of the studies, it is questionable if it is the only possible view. The search for other viewpoints continues.

In the studies reviewed, not much has been said with respect to what makes a consequence a just desert. The juridical view of retribution helps to justify the consequence since it is meted out according to *agreed norms*. Similarly, covenantal blessings and curses can be seen as just deserts within a covenantal relationship. By appealing to the general feeling of justice that the consequence should be like the deed, texts displaying poetic justice point out that the consequence is appropriate to the deed by showing that the consequence resembles the deed.

---

[154] Joyce 1995:118.

In the rest of this book, we will examine in detail Ezekiel's idea of retribution. There is no doubt that for Ezekiel Yahweh is the one who is responsible for retribution, although in some cases he employs human agents to carry it out. Of greater importance is how Ezekiel argues that Yahweh's retribution is just. We will demonstrate that for Ezekiel the relationship between deed and consequence is determined by three principles, i.e., the covenant (Chapters Two and Three), the disposal of impurity (Chapters Four and Five), and poetic justice (Chapter Six). Thus, the consequence for a deed is not meted out by Yahweh arbitrarily, but according to some principles, and hence it is appropriate and just.

CHAPTER TWO

COVENANT AND RETRIBUTION (I)

1. *Introduction*

In the first chapter, we mentioned that some studies have attributed some importance to the notion of covenant in relation to retribution. A simple counting reveals that in the prophetic books, the word "covenant" (ברית)[1] occurs 12 times in Isaiah, 24 times in Jeremiah, 18 times in Ezekiel,[2] and 15 times in the Twelve (5x in Hosea, 1x in Amos, 1x in Obadiah, 2x in Zechariah and 6x in Malachi). Thus, relatively speaking, these figures show *prima facie* that the notion of covenant is of some importance in Ezekiel. However, this importance is evaluated differently by scholars. Zimmerli remarks that in Ezekiel there is no well-defined covenant theology.[3] This is followed, for example, by Baltzer, Begg and Joyce.[4] But Reventlow, Mayo and Gray hold otherwise.[5] The difference is, of course, partly dependent on how much of the material on covenant is considered authentic. Since the MT is taken as our point of departure, it is not our concern here to enter into this debate. In the present and next chapters we will examine the relationship between covenant and retribution. In this chapter we will examine three passages in which retribution is shown to be related to the terms of the covenant between two parties (Ez 16, 17, 20). Associated with the covenant are the curses and blessings which are delivered to those who violate or keep the covenant respectively. Resemblances between covenants in the OT and ancient Near Eastern treaties and resemblances between the

---

[1] We adopt the traditional translation of ברית as "covenant". Barr (1977:36) says that in "talking about the biblical covenant, . . . the word is for most users something of an empty word" and its meaning is to be derived from the biblical usage. But Nicholson (1986:105–106) argues that "covenant" is suitable for rendering ברית in some contexts.

[2] 16:8, 59, 60 (2x), 61, 62; 17:13, 14, 15, 16, 18, 19; 20:37; 30:5; 34:25; 37:26 (2x); 44:7.

[3] Zimmerli 1979:46.

[4] Baltzer 1986:172; Begg 1986:81; Joyce 1989:119.

[5] Reventlow 1962:157–159; Mayo 1973; Gray 1979:159.

kinds of doom foretold by the prophets and the threats contained
in ancient Near Eastern treaty-curses have been noted by scholars.[6]
Thus, this idea is also important in the relationship between covenant
and retribution. This will be examined in the next chapter.

2. ברית *as a Marriage Covenant: Ez 16*

2.1. *Introductory Remarks*

Ez 16 is a literary unit demarcated in content from its neighbour-
ing chapters 15 and 17. It is divided in three units: vv.2–43bα,
43bβ–58 and vv.59–63, each ending with the concluding formula
"says the Lord Yahweh".

In terms of form, the first unit is an oracle of judgement. An
expanded accusation is found in vv.2–34. This is followed by an
announcement of judgement, first introduced by the transitional word
לכן in v.35. This is followed by a summary of accusations introduced by יען in v.36. Then a proper announcement is again introduced by לכן in v.37. This unit depicts a foundling abandoned by
her parents. She is rescued by a man who later marries her. But
the bride commits adultery, inciting the anger of and punishment
from her husband.

This unit can be further subdivided. Greenberg proposes to demar-
cate the subunits as vv.3–8, 9–14, 15–19, 20–22, 23–29, 30–34, and
35–43 on the basis of the use of the concluding formula.[7] Krašovec
detects an antithetic structure and divides the text in four parts:[8]
The initial plight of the abandoned girl (vv.3–5) is reversed by
Yahweh's loving care (vv.6–14). His love (vv.6–14) is contrasted with
the unthankful behaviour of the bride (vv.15–34). And her behaviour (vv.15–34) is countered by Yahweh's punishment (vv.35–43).

The second major unit is delimited by the combination of "lewdness" (זמה) (found first in v.27) and "abominations" (תועבות) (found
in vv.2, 22 in the first unit) in v.43bβ and v.58.[9] It extends the
metaphor started in v.3 by providing two siblings to the woman

---

[6] Tsevat 1959; Mendenhall 1962; Fensham 1962, 1963; Hillers 1964; Baltzer
1971b; McCarthy 1981.
[7] Greenberg 1983a:292–294.
[8] Krašovec 1983:96–98.
[9] Parunak 1978:268.

Jerusalem. The sisters of Jerusalem are introduced in vv.43bβ–46. A comparison between their conduct and that of Jerusalem is found in v.47 and vv.51b–52, thus forming an inclusion. In between, Jerusalem is compared only to Sodom in vv.48–50 and only to Samaria in v.51a.[10] In v.53, the restoration of the fortunes of the three sisters is announced, indicating a new theme. This continues until v.58, where the concluding formula rounds off the unit. Thus, this unit can be subdivided into vv.43bβ–46, 47–52, and 53–58.

The third major unit begins with the emphatic כִּי plus the messenger formula in v.59. This unit builds upon the idea of the covenant in v.8. It is concerned with Yahweh's establishment of a covenant with Jerusalem and her accompanying shame. This unit has many echoes in the previous two units (e.g. "days of youth": vv.22, 43, 60). The ability "to remember", which is found lacking in Jerusalem in v.22 and v.43, is found first with Yahweh (v.60), and only then with Jerusalem (vv.61, 63). A connection with the second unit is forged by a transformation of Jerusalem's sisters into her daughters. Note that the "shame" motif runs through all three major units, especially the second and third: כְּלִמָּה in vv.52 (2x), 54, 63, כְּלַם in vv.27, 54, 61, and בּוֹשׁ in vv.52 and 63. The recognition formula in v.62b gives the impression that this unit is a two-part proof saying which, according to Hals, forms the basic structure of this unit where there is twice the pattern of intervention of Yahweh (vv.59aγb–60 and vv. 61b–62a) followed by a result (v.61a and v.62b), and a conclusion in v.63.[11] On the other hand, Jüngling proposes a chiastic reading: עשׂה forms the outer ring (vv.59 and 63b), כלם-הקים ברית- זכר forms the inner ring (vv.60–61aα and 62–63a), with the centre at v.61aβb.[12]

From the point of view of content, we suggest the following for the whole chapter:[13]

A	vv.2–43bα	Prophecy against Jerusalem
	v.2	Ezekiel called to accuse
	vv.3–5	Jerusalem's origin and initial plight
	vv.6–7	Yahweh's first passing by: adoption

---

[10] Hals 1989:108.
[11] Hals 1989:105. But compare the bipartite structure of Renaud (1986:336).
[12] Jüngling 1993:142–143.
[13] The chiastic structure proposed by Swanepoel (1993:93) for the chapter is not convincing.

		vv.8–14	Yahweh's second passing by: marriage and endowment
		v.15	Announcement of Jerusalem's idolatry to the passer-by
		vv.16–22	Jerusalem's idolatry: cultic
		vv.23–34	Jerusalem's idolatry: political
		vv.35–43bα	Announcement of punishment
	B	vv.43bβ–58	Jerusalem and her Sisters
		v.43bβ	Introductory accusatory question
		vv.44–46	Jerusalem's sisters
		vv.47–52	Jerusalem is worse than her sisters
		vv.53–58	The restoration of the three sisters
	C	vv.59–63	Yahweh's future re-establishment with Jerusalem

2.2. *Ez 16:8*

2.2.1. *A Preliminary Note: Two Basic Approaches*

There are two basic approaches to the section comprising vv.3–43bα. The first is to regard it as an allegory in the sense that it is "a narrative in which each element represents something or someone else in the real world, so that a point for point correspondence can be drawn between the allegory and its referent".[14] Thus, historical events corresponding to what is said in the biography are sought. A typical example of this approach is the Targum.[15] Some modern commentators also call the text an allegory but recognise at the same time the presence of non-allegorical elements. Thus, they provide historical correspondences only as they deem appropriate.[16] Even then, their attempts are not always convincing.[17] More recently, schol-

---

[14] Galambush 1992:10. See also the definition of allegory in Soulen (1981:15) and Maier (1994:86).

[15] For the Aramaic text, see Sperber (1962). Levey (1987) provides an English translation. Bloch (1955) goes furthest in this direction.

[16] E.g. Davidson 1916:109; Cooke 1936:159; Fisch 1950:83; Fohrer 1955:84; Zimmerli 1979:334–335; Cody 1984:76–77; Brownlee 1986:220; Block 1997:471.

[17] Since this has no direct bearing on our concern, we will refer to it only briefly. While Davidson (1916:110–111), Greenberg (1983a:301), Brownlee (1986:223–224) and Krüger (1989:184) find some historical references in the details given in 16:3–7, Allen (1994:237) says explicitly that no historical counterpart should be expected. Evidently, the connection between the word "field" (v.5) and the working place of the Israelites as slaves in Egypt is too loose to be convincing. Nor would one find the correspondence between the rejection of the baby and the emigration of the family of Jacob persuasive. Given that it is difficult to determine the historical counterparts for 16:3–7, can we have more certitude in the case of 16:8? The opinion that the oath and covenant in 16:8 refers to the oath and covenant in 20:5–6 deserves some attention. But we must first reject Greenberg's suggestion (1983a:278)

ars have begun to treat the story as a metaphor or an extended
metaphor. Their concern is not only with the reality presented in
the story, but also with the various effects the choice of such a
metaphor has on the reader and the relation between the symbol
and the symbolised.[18] For our purpose, the priority is to understand
the meaning of the extended metaphor.

2.2.2. *Analysis*

Chapter 16 opens with the word reception formula אֵלַי וַיְהִי דְבַר־יְהוָה
לֵאמֹר, which almost as a rule marks the beginning of a new speech
unit.[19] The prophet, who is addressed as בֶּן־אָדָם,[20] is commanded to
make known (הוֹדַע) to Jerusalem her abominations. Such an act can
also be found in 20:4 and 22:2 (cf. הַגִּיד in 23:36) where it is associated with judgement. It therefore has a legal and forensic tone.[21]
After this commission and the messenger formula, the biography[22]
of Jerusalem as a girl[23] begins.

---

that the oath in 16:8 is a fusion of the oath to the patriarchs and the mutual obligation connected with the Exodus since in 20:5–6 there is no mention of an oath
to the patriarchs. Rather, the scene begins in Egypt. Moreover, the patriarchs do
not seem to play any important role in Ezekiel. Another point worth noting is that
although the "swearing" language is found in most modern translations of Ez 20
(which points to a connection with the "to swear" in 16:8) and elsewhere in Ezekiel,
the actual Hebrew wording is יָדִי (אֶת־)נָשָׂא/וָאֶשָּׂא נָשָׂאתִי/ (20:5, 6, 15, 23, 28, 42; 36:7;
44:12; 47:14). Some scholars (e.g. Lust 1967:517–524, 1994:160–164; Bettenzoli
1979:201) doubt if one could equate "to swear" (נִשְׁבַּע) with this expression which
always has God as subject. The point is that if this equation is not valid, then the
identification of 16:8 with 20:5–6 and therefore with the Sinaitic covenant is problematic. In addition to that, Jüngling (1993:137) warns us not to identify Jerusalem
too readily with Israel. If so, it would be even more problematic to identify the
covenant in 16:8 as the Sinaitic covenant.

[18] E.g. Hals 1989:109; Galambush (1992:4–11) discusses the moral dimensions
and the participation of the readers; Maier (1994:87) speaks of the "sprachschöpfer-
ische Funktion" of the metaphor. See also Stienstra (1993:17–40). Fuhs (1984:80)
and Pohlmann (1996:223) refuse to call it an allegory ("Allegorie") and use the term
"Bildrede" instead. Jüngling (1993:138) says explicitly that "[d]ie Bildrede ist keine
Allegorie; so widersetzen sich die Einzelzüge der Icherzählung einer direkten Über-
setzung auf Vorgänge der Stadtgeschichte".

[19] For a discussion of the formula, see Zimmerli (1979:25–26, 144–145) and
Hossfeld (1977:26–27).

[20] This designation of the prophet is peculiar to Ezekiel with a total occurrence
of 93 times and in 24 cases it is accentuated by a preceding וְאַתָּה.

[21] Zimmerli 1979:335; Greenberg 1983a:273. For a basic discussion on the form
of the judgement oracles, see Westermann (1967:169–189). See also de Roche (1983).
For the רִיב oracles in Ezekiel see Block (1997:459–462).

[22] Greenberg 1983a:299.

[23] For a discussion of the ancient Near Eastern background depicting a city as

The story of Jerusalem begins with her origin. She is from the
land of the Canaanite, thus stressing her alien origin more than her
geographical location. This pagan origin is reinforced by noting that
her father is an Amorite and her mother a Hittite. The Amorites
and the Hittites are Israel's enemies whose practices are not to be
followed (cf. Ex 23:24). This presentation of the origin of Jerusalem
is hardly neutral. The phrase "on the day when you were born"
provides a frame to vv.4–5 which describe the plight of the new-
born child. Four negative phrases indicate that she was denied the
normally expected treatment for a new-born necessary for life: her
navel cord was not cut, she was not washed, not rubbed with salt
and not swaddled in bands. These omissions are interpreted in v.5
as a lack of compassion for the child.[24] What is more, the child was
cast on the field[25] to die because her life was disgusting. The omissions and the casting out of the new-born not only show a physical
rejection but also have a legal meaning. Malul argues that the cutting of the navel cord, washing, rubbing with salt and clothing the
new-born are legal acts of legitimation. That is, by doing these the
parents recognise the child as their lawful child and decide to keep
it.[26] By omitting these, therefore, the parents relinquish their rights
to the child. Malul further points out that the word "field" (שׂדה)
represents a domain outside another domain, a sense comparable to
the idea of the wilderness (מדבר). With the verb "to cast out" (השׁליך)
the phrase "cast on/to the field" means "to get rid of something
and to remove it from one's legal domain to the outside domain".[27]
The legal meaning of all these is that the baby girl was given up
by her parents who cut off all legal links with her. Continuing this
line of thought, Block, citing Lev 26:40 for support, argues that since
נעל together with מאס in association with the covenant means "to
repudiate a covenantal obligation", the expression נעל נפשׁך here

----

a woman in general and the portrayal of Jerusalem as a woman in the OT in particular, see Fitzgerald (1972, 1975) and Steck (1989).

[24] The phrase "no eye looked compassionately on you" is used elsewhere in
Ezekiel to describe Yahweh's action towards Israel (5:11; 7:4, 9; 8:18; 9:5, 10). The
positive "my eyes looked compassionately" is used only in 20:17.

[25] Cogan (1968) argues that the phrase השׁליך על פני השׂדה is a technical expression for exposure.

[26] Malul 1990:109.

[27] Malul 1990:100–103.

should be interpreted as "a legal renunciation of parental obligations by Jerusalem's parents".[28]

At this point, Yahweh passes by for the first time (v.6) to come to the rescue. While there was no compassionate look on the child (v.5), Yahweh *saw* it wallowing in its birth blood. The word בדמיך, which occurs three times in v.6, requires some explanation. The plural form of "blood" is used in cases of blood shed violently. Hence some ask if the use of the plural here may allude to the bloodguilt of Jerusalem mentioned elsewhere in Ezekiel.[29] The plural form, however, may also refer to the menstrual discharge (e.g. Lev 12:4–5). In the present context, the blood refers to the amniotic fluid and blood that the baby girl's mother discharged at her birth. According to Malul, the taking of a child in its blood and amniotic fluid underlines the fact that the child taken is abandoned and thus the one who takes it has full rights to it. Moreover, he argues that the command בדמיך חיי can be seen as a formal declaration of adoption.[30] Lastly, in the context of adoption, the expression רבבה ... נתתיך means the raising up of the adopted child by the adopter.[31] Here the image of Jerusalem as a girl is changed to that of Jerusalem as the "sprout of the field".[32] But this image soon gives way to the former one. She matures with the formation of her breasts and the growth of her pubic hair. Thus, on the level of the images used here, the passer-by adopts and brings up the baby girl.[33] But less clear is the last phrase of v.7 which does not seem to fit in well with the adoption interpretation. It seems that the girl was left on

---

[28] Block 1997:476. See also Malul (1990:117n.32).

[29] Carley 1974:96; Zimmerli 1979:323. For the connection between the plural form and shed blood, see Koch (1962:406) and Kedar-Kopstein 1978:236.

[30] Malul 1990:106–112.

[31] Malul 1990:113.

[32] Maier (1994:91) suggests that this image is based upon the idea of a creator God who creates by his word and lets the field flourish by his blessing.

[33] Malul's opinion is followed by most scholars (e.g. Galambush 1992; Allen 1994; Block 1997). Pohlmann (1996) remains an exception. In failing to see the adoption language here, he (1996:225) states that the passer-by seems to stand at a distance from the girl in v.6 whereas later in vv.8–12 his contact with the grown up girl is much more direct. In almost all commentaries published before Malul's article, the relationship between that of the passer-by and the child was not characterised as one of adoption. Davidson (1916:111) is a notable exception. Thus, Malul (1990:99) is almost right to say that "no scholar has seen the ties between the passer-by and the foundling as those of adoption".

her own (in the field) and remains naked.[34] However, this helpless situation of the girl prepares for what follows in v.8 and finds a complete resolution later in v.10.[35]

In v.8 we find the second passing-by of Yahweh.[36] The timing is perfect since the baby girl who has grown up is now at a time of love. She has arrived at sexual maturity. V.8 seems to speak of a marriage event between the passer-by and the woman. For a clear look at it, we present the text as follows:

ואעבר עליך	8a	And I passed by you
ואראך	8b	and saw you,
והנה עתך עת דדים	8c	and behold, your time was a time of love.
ואפרש כנפי עליך	8d	And I spread my skirt over you
ואכסה ערותך	8e	and I covered your nakedness.
ואשבע לך	8f	And I swore to you
ואבוא בברית אתך	8g	and I entered into a covenant with you,
נאם אדני יהוה	8h	says the Lord Yahweh,
ותהיי לי	8i	and you became mine.

As in the case of v.6, after the initial passing by, beholding of the girl, and description of her, the passer-by's action is mentioned. The spreading of the skirt or the edge of a garment over the woman (v.8d) results in or aims at covering her nakedness (v.8e). A similar expression is found in Ru 3:9 (ופרשת כנפך על־אמתך).[37] Kruger notes firstly that in some ancient Near Eastern texts the hem of the wife's garment was cut in divorce procedures to bring about the dissolution of the marriage. Secondly, the uncovering of a wife's nakedness is a punishment of the woman for committing adultery (cf. Is 47:2–3; Hos 2:12; Nah 3:5),[38] which at the same time means the end of the marriage. Thus, the opposite of the action here, i.e., the spreading of the hem,[39] is the symbolic act of a marriage proposal, or, it is an

---

[34] Despite Malul (1990:112), who does not recognise that v.7 forms a link between the image of the girl as an adopted daughter and that of the girl as a bride.

[35] Cf. Pohlmann 1996:226.

[36] Aalders (1955:257) seems to hold that there is only one passing-by.

[37] In Ru 3:9, the MT reads a plural (כְּנָפֶךָ) but the LXX and Syriac have the singular, which is to be preferred. Generally speaking, the plural form refers to wings whereas the singular form refers to a mantle. For reading the singular form in Ru 3:9, see Campbell (1975:123), Hubbard (1988:207n.9), Sasson (1989:81), and Viberg (1992:143).

[38] Also Greenberg (1983a:287).

[39] Viberg (1992:136–137) argues that כנף here does not mean the hem but the whole mantle. But see Dommershausen (1995:231).

act of "establishing a new relationship" and "extending his [= the man's] authority over her [= his wife]".[40] Some other scholars also regard the expression in Ru 3:9 as a proposal for marriage.[41] In our case here, the spreading of the skirt over the woman not only covers her nakedness in a physical sense (as a partial resolution of the nakedness in v.7) but also has a symbolic meaning of engaging her in marriage.[42] An additional reason for supporting the claim that a marriage is involved here is that in the marriage laws of the ancient Near East, the husband is obliged to provide his wife with food, clothes and oil.[43] And this is found precisely in what follows: oil in v.9, clothes in v.10 and food in v.13a. The act of spreading the garment is sometimes taken as euphemism for sexual intercourse.[44] But whether this is true or not,[45] marriage is intended.

After the marriage proposal, the passer-by swore (שבע) to the woman (v.8f) and entered into a covenant with her (v.8g).[46] This culminates in the last sentence "and you became mine" (v.8i), which resembles a declaration formula in marriage: "he is her husband and she his wife". These phrases again pinpoint the marriage context, especially v.8i. But the meaning of v.8fg and their relation to the marriage context in v.8de is more controversial than it appears in the first place. The central questions are whether an oath is taken in a marriage and whether marriage can be characterised as a covenant. Some scholars refer to Mal 2:14 and Prov 2:17 as support for the idea.[47] But this is doubted by others.[48] Hugenberger has discussed in some detail the basic objections raised by Milgrom and

---

[40] Kruger 1984:80–82; quotation from p. 84.
[41] Phillips 1980:39; Davies 1981:144; Nielsen 1985:206–207.
[42] This act could mean a promise of protection (Wevers 1969:96) or an act of acquiring (Greenberg 1983a:277). But these can be seen as part of the marriage proposal.
[43] Paul 1970:56–61; Jackson 1975:152; Kruger 1984:81.
[44] Brownlee 1986:225; Viberg 1992:138–139, 144; Pope 1995:393.
[45] Hugenberger (1994:304) argues that this is false. However, his arguments are open to question. For instance, the claim that it is anomalous to have sexual union before betrothal is contradicted by Ex 22:15–16. His discussion relating to the phrase נלה ערות is also problematic.
[46] Note that שבע occurs elsewhere not infrequently with "covenant". See Jüngling (1993:132n.52).
[47] Davidson 1916:112; Cooke 1936:163; Zimmerli 1979:340; Allen 1994:238 (only Prov 2:17); Block 1997:483.
[48] Kraetzschmar 1900:147; Herrmann 1924:99; Milgrom 1976a:133–134; Kalluveettil (1982:79) regards the use of ברית in Mal 2:14; Ez 16:8 and Prov 2:17 as "figurative"; Greenberg 1983a:278; Pohlmann 1996:226.

Greenberg: (1) no marriage laws or contracts in the ancient Near East stipulate an oath; (2) nowhere is marriage called a covenant; (3) nowhere is the husband expected to take an oath in marriage; (4) the use of the word "covenant" here is only metaphorical, referring to the relationship between God and Israel.[49] These objections, however, are not without their difficulties. Objection (1) is simply wrong. Among the Babylonian marriage contracts collected by Roth, some contain an oath which is taken against any person who would violate the terms of the agreement.[50] Moreover, the special character of the law should be noted. It is well-known that ancient Near Eastern laws in general and biblical laws in particular are not complete codes but have many gaps and they "regulate only matters as to which the law is dubious or in need of reform or both".[51] Greengus in his study of Babylonian marriage contracts argues that marriage contracts were not always written, but when they were written the purpose "was not to record marriage, but to record important transactions which could affect the status and rights of husbands and wives".[52] Similarly, Kalluveettil comments that "[s]ince the main concern of marriage contracts were [sic] economic, the marriage ratifying rites as such were not described in them".[53] Thus, the omission of an oath connected with marriage in laws and contracts is hardly surprising even if such an oath was common or compulsory.

The second objection is connected with the interpretation of Mal 2:14 and Prov 2:17. We pointed out above that some scholars think that these two texts refer to marriage as a covenant. In particular, Hugenberger argues convincingly that the word "covenant" in Mal 2:14 refers to marriage.[54] If his argument is accepted, there is at least one instance in the MT where a marriage is regarded as a covenant.[55] If that is the case, then "covenant" in Ez 16:8, given the marriage context, could very well refer to marriage.

---

[49] Milgrom 1976a:134; Greenberg 1983a:278.

[50] Roth 1989:19. For a discussion of these contracts, see Hugenberger (1994:187–189). Fohrer (1955:87n.1) also refers to the marriage contracts of the Jewish community in Elephantine and in the Nuzu texts for the claim that oath is taken in marriage.

[51] Daube 1961:257. Cf. Fishbane 1985:91; Greengus 1992:243.

[52] Greengus 1969:512.

[53] Kalluveettil 1982:110.

[54] Hugenberger 1994:27–46. He also discusses Prov 2:17 (1994:296–302).

[55] Kalluveettil (1982:79–83) provides some other biblical and non-biblical examples where marriage is designated as a "covenant".

Objection (3) is equally problematic. First of all, it seems that there is no intrinsic reason why the husband (instead of the wife) cannot take an oath in marriage. One may argue analogically that since in a vassal treaty it is the lower status vassal who should take an oath of allegiance to the suzerain, so it is the woman who should be expected to take an oath instead of the husband. But this analogy fails because it is not always the case that only the vassals take an oath. Kalluveettil states that "[o]ath-taking by the overlord is not unknown in the ANE treaties". He lists a number of extra-biblical examples as well as biblical examples for support.[56] In addition, Hugenberger cites some Elephantine marriage contracts in which the husband is found to say the oath. He also cites some biblical cases as evidence.[57] The point is that there is evidence that the husband can take an oath in a marriage. Lastly, one should note the whole tenor of the passage. That is to say, in vv.3–14, and especially vv.6–14, the initiative of the passer-by is constantly underlined whereas the girl is depicted as passive. She is passive with respect to her birth and the omission of caring acts to a new-born. She remains alive; she grows up; she is adorned with all sorts of beautiful clothes. All these do not result from her own effort, but are brought about by the actions of the passer-by. If this is the case, then to portray the passer-by as the one who takes the oath is but just one facet of the emphasis of the passage.

The last objection is basically the result of the first three objections. If it is true that an oath is not taken in a marriage, and that marriage is not characterised as a covenant, and that it is strange to have the husband taking a marriage oath, then indeed one can only seek an explanation of the text outside the image of the metaphor itself, i.e., in the historical dimension. But such a reference to the historical realm for an explanation of the image of the metaphor is unnecessary since the various parts of the extended metaphor which portray a marriage cohere well.

Having dealt with the various objections, we now examine in more detail the expression ואבוא בברית אתך, which is seldom discussed. The phrase בוא בברית is found only three more times in the MT: 1 Sam 20:8; 2 Chr 15:12; Jer 34:10. In 1 Sam 20:8, it is said that

---

[56] Kalluveettil 1982:87–88, and n.329. Quotation from p. 87.
[57] Hugenberger 1994:225–228 (for the contracts) and 230–238 (for biblical cases).

Jonathan brought (הבאת) David into the covenant of Yahweh (בברית
יהוה) with him (עמך). Different from Ez 16:8, the hiphil form of בוא
is used. This resembles Ez 20:37: והבאתי אתכם במסרת הברית. Similar
to Ez 16:8, the other party with whom the covenant is made is indicated by a preposition with a suffix. This making of the covenant
between Jonathan and David recalls the one they made earlier in
1 Sam 18:1–4. There the verb כרת, most commonly used in connection with making a covenant, is employed. Here, the term ברית יהוה
is used for the covenant between Yahweh and humans.[58] It is probably because David and Jonathan swore in the name of Yahweh
that their covenant was elevated to the status of Yahweh's covenant.
In the context of 2 Chr 15:12, after King Asa heard the words of
Azariah son of Oded, he repented. He then gathered in Jerusalem
some tribes of Israel (v.9) who are said to have entered into a covenant
to seek Yahweh (ויבאו בברית לדרוש את יהוה) (v.12). This covenant
was not made between Yahweh and the people but was a binding
agreement between the king and the people to serve Yahweh.[59]
Jer 34:8–22 reports a covenant made between King Zedekiah and
all the people in Jerusalem to release all the male and female slaves.
At first the people did that but then they revoked the decision
(vv.10–11). This incurred God's accusation that they failed to obey
the command that they should release their slaves every seventh year
(vv.12–16). This is followed by an announcement of punishment
(vv.17–22). Various constructions with the word "covenant" can be
found:

1. כרת ברית: between Zedekiah and the people (v.8), between God
   and the fathers (v.13), between the people (v.15). Note that the
   accusative marker את is not used.
2. בוא בברית: the officials and the people are the subject (v.10).
3. העברים את בריתי: the people transgressed the covenant of Yahweh
   (v.18).
4. לא הקימו את דברי הברית: the people did not keep the terms of
   the covenant (v.18).

Noteworthy is the description of the ceremony of cutting a calf into
two parts and passing through them. This shows a wordplay not

---

[58] Kalluveettil 1982:12.
[59] Williamson 1982:271; Japhet 1989:112–115, 1993:726; Kelly 1996:55–56.

only of the verb "to cut" (כרת) but also "to pass, transgress" (עבר). Those who passed through (עבר) the parts are those who took part in the covenant. If they later transgressed (עבר) the covenant, they would be punished. Jüngling lists two relevant points of this passage to Ez 16:8. First, the expression "to enter into a covenant" is used with a special connection with Jerusalem, i.e., it is done in Jerusalem. Second, the wordplay of עבר is also found in Ez 16:8 (and also vv.6, 15, 25) and it is therefore possible that the twofold "I passed by you" in Ez 16:6, 8 hints already at the "I entered in a covenant with you".[60] However, it is not clear that 1 Sam 20:8 points to a Jerusalem context. The wordplay of עבר in the Jeremian passage is interesting but the description has a parallel only in Gen 15. Moreover, it is only in Dt 29:11 that the expression עבר בברית means the making of a covenant. Elsewhere, עבר in connection with covenant always means the transgression of a covenant. Thus, the connection between עבר and the making of a covenant is less clear than Jüngling thinks.

We may offer two other observations. First, the expression בוא בברית is used for covenants between people. This is the case for 1 Sam 20:8 and 2 Chr 15:12. The case of Jer 34:10 needs some explanation. In v.8, Zedekiah made a covenant with the people and in v.10 this group of people are qualified as those who had entered in the covenant (אשר followed by באו בברית). This indicates that the expression "to enter into a covenant" denotes a covenant between humans.[61] Note further that in Jer 34:15, the people is not said to have made a covenant with God, but before him, invoking his name. It is perhaps because of this invoking of God's name that the covenant is later called בריתי in Jer 34:18, referring to God's covenant. A comparison can be made with Ez 17 where the covenant (and oath) made between Nebuchadnezzar and Zedekiah (17:13–18) is also called Yahweh's covenant (and oath) (17:19).[62] In the case of Ez 16:8, on the level of the metaphor, the above observation also applies because it involves a covenant between the passerby and the girl. The expression "to enter into a covenant" indicates basically an inter-personal relation.

---

[60] Jüngling 1993:134.

[61] This is also accepted by Duhm (1901:280), Weiser (1955:320), Rudolph (1958:205), Thompson (1980:611) and Carroll (1986:649). Cf. Kalluveettil 1982:7.

[62] Hillers 1964:52; Kalluveettil 1982:12n.25. This answers the objection raised by Baltzer (1971b:55) that the "my covenant" in Jer 34:18 implies that the covenant is not civil but one between Yahweh and the people.

Second, both 2 Chr 15:12 and Jer 34:10 seem to depict the case that it is a king who initiates the covenant and then his officials join in. That is to say, those with a lower status join in the terms set out by one with a higher status. 1 Sam 20:8 follows this pattern. Jonathan, who is the son of king Saul, causes David, a fugitive, to enter into a covenant to the advantage of the latter. In the case of Ez 16:8, perhaps the making of a marriage proposal imposes already upon the passer-by an obligation which he subsequently enters into. On this understanding, the passer-by joins in the terms which he sets for himself.[63]

Now consider v.8i: ותהי לי ("and you became mine"). Elsewhere in the MT when a marriage relationship between a man and a woman is mentioned, the combination לאשׁה + ל + היה is used.[64] What is absent in Ez 16:8 is the word אשׁ׳ and the love-motif which is sometimes found in a marriage context (e.g. Gen 24:67). Actually, the word אהב, which occurs seven times in Ezekiel (16:33, 36, 37 (2x); 23:5, 9, 22), is found six times in the form of the piel masculine participle and denotes a woman's extra-marital sex partners. But the absence of אהב in describing the relationship between the passer-by and the woman does not imply that there is no caring relationship between them, as claimed by some.[65] In v.8c the form דדים means "love" in general and "physical sexual relationship" in particular.[66] In the Song of Songs, the word and its singular form denote a love relationship which pays no attention to the identity of or any particulars about the lovers themselves.[67] Whether they are married or not is not mentioned, nor is it a matter of importance. What is important is that they enjoy each other and they belong to each other. This is expressed in Song 2:16 (דודי לי ואני לו) (cf. 6:3). This formula emphasises not only mutual possession[68] but also "the feeling of deepest and most intimate connectedness".[69] Occasionally,

---

[63] Cf. Jüngling 1993:131. The analogous expression ובאים באלה ובשבועה in Neh 10:30 seems to exhibit the same above-mentioned two characteristics.

[64] Gen 20:12; 24:67; Dt 21:13; 1 Sam 25:42; 2 Sam 11:27; 1 Kg 4:11; 2 Kg 8:18; Ruth 4:13.

[65] E.g. Joyce 1989:100.

[66] Sanmartin-Ascaso 1978:151. Cf. Pope 1977:299; Brownlee 1986:224; Maier 1994:91; Block 1997:482. The word occurs once more in Ezekiel (23:17), where it denotes the sexual relationship between Oholibah and the Babylonians.

[67] Sanmartin-Ascaso 1978:156.

[68] Murphy 1990:141, 173 (on 6:3).

[69] Keel 1994:114.

instead of the expression of mutual belonging, a one-way expression is found (e.g. 7:11 "אֲנִי דוֹדִי").[70] Thus, Song 2:16 provides a parallel for the connection between Ez 16:8c and 8i.[70] Note also that the word יָפֶה, commonly rendered as "beautiful",[71] may have the sense of "desirable" in Ez 16:13.[72] Thus, the whole context uses the language of (erotic) love to describe the relationship between the passer-by and the girl.[73] Lastly, the passer-by supplies food, cloth and oil to the woman whom he marries.[74] This expresses his responsible and caring action.[75] With the gift of clothes, the nakedness of the woman in v.7 finds a complete resolution. The narrative reaches a climax in v.14: her beauty is said to be perfect, she became a queen and was renowned among the nations. But a quick reminder follows. All these she got from the passer-by; her beauty was but the reflection of his splendour.

2.2.3. *Summary*

Some conclusions can be drawn regarding the use of the word בְרִית in 16:8. First, it does not seem necessary to resort to historical details in order to understand the extended metaphor. Moreover, the extended metaphor is not an allegory and no one-to-one correspondences between the components of the metaphor and historical events exist. Thus, reference to the Sinai covenant and perhaps 20:5–6 for an explanation of "covenant" in 16:8 is unnecessary. Second, the action of spreading the hem over the girl and covering her nakedness imply a marriage proposal (and perhaps coition). The oath taken and the entering into a covenant indicate a marriage relationship between the passer-by and the woman. Third, the phrase "to enter into a covenant" is used for an interpersonal covenant. It also means entering into obligations set up by a higher authority. In Ez 16:8, it implies the passer-by's entering into a binding obligation towards the woman set up by himself. However, this does not mean that the

---

[70] Jüngling 1993:131.

[71] BDB 421.

[72] Keel 1994:164.

[73] Thus, Jüngling (1993:131) rightly objected to Malul's characterisation of the relation here as that of a political treaty (1990:113).

[74] This gift is sometimes taken as a dowry. E.g. Greenberg 1983a:279; Westbrook 1991:145–146.

[75] Cf. Klee 1998:103, who further argues that the man's love is shown by his readiness to cleanse blood, a source of impurity, from the girl.

woman has no obligation to the man, for within the marriage relationship, the woman is equally obliged to him. Fourth, although the
word אהב ("to love") is not used in describing the relationship between
the passer-by and the woman, there are other clues which indicate
the presence of the man's caring action within the relationship. The
use of the word "lovers" to designate those with whom the woman
commits sexual offences is meant to be sarcastic.

2.3. *Ez 16:59–63*

2.3.1. *Analysis*

This last section of Ez 16 opens in v.59 with a summarising statement concerning the conduct of the woman: she despised the oath
(בזה אלה),[76] explicated as breaking a covenant (הפר ברית[77]),[78] that is,
to invalidate the covenant.[79] That an oath is used to ratify a covenant
and that a covenant is also called an oath are well accepted.[80] But
which covenant did Jerusalem break? The word "oath" (אלה) which
first occurs in Ezekiel here together with "covenant" recalls 16:8,
where the passer-by is said to have sworn to the girl and entered
into a covenant with her.[81] Although in v.8 the girl is not said to
have sworn and partaken in the covenant, it is undoubtedly so. Thus,
it is the marriage covenant which Jerusalem broke.[82] This is confirmed
by the various actions that Jerusalem performed which violate the
marriage. Her whoring acts (זנה) are notable.[83] But Yahweh remembers his covenant (i.e., the marriage covenant)[84] with Jerusalem in

---

[76] The phrase בזה אלה is found only in Ez 16:59; 17:16, 18, 19, and in these
cases, the parallel expression הפר ברית is found.

[77] The LXX reads τὴν διαθήκην μου. Allen (1994:232) explains it as assimilation to v.60 and suggests that the parallelism supports the MT.

[78] According to Weinfeld (1977:261), הפר ברית is priestly language whereas עבר
ברית is Deuteronom(ist)ic. See also Thiel (1970).

[79] Ruppert (1989:777) states that הפר ברית means "eine Verpflichtung einseitig
(auf)lösen" or "einen Vertrag brechen/für ungültig (nicht mehr bindend) erklären".
See also Kutsch (1997:1031–1032).

[80] Mendenhall 1954:28; Tucker 1965:488–490; Barr 1977:32; Scharbert 1977:264;
Weinfeld 1977:256; Nicholson 1986:103; Hugenberger 1994:182–184.

[81] The combination of ברית and אלה is uncommon outside Ezekiel. Cf. Gen 26:28;
Dt 29:11, 13, 20; Hos 10:4.

[82] Kraetzschmar 1900:155; Fisch 1950:98–99; Wevers 1969:103; Brownlee 1986:251;
Vawter and Hoppe 1991:96; Allen 1994:246.

[83] The verb זנה occurs 22 times in Ezekiel, 12 times in Ez 16, and 7 times in
Ez 23. The noun תזנות occurs 20 times in Ezekiel (and only in it), 9 times in Ez 16
and 11 times in Ez 23. The words זנונים and זנות are also found in Ez 23.

[84] Block 1997:516; Jüngling 1993:146, against some who refer to the covenant

the days of her youth. The expression "the days of your youth", which occurs first in vv.22 and 43, supports this understanding. The phrase זכר ברית with God as the subject is rarely found in the prophetic books.[85] According to Schottroff, it is used when either the covenant or the covenant partner (with God) is in danger, and it is used in opposition to the breaking of the covenant.[86] In Jer 14:21 and Lev 26:44–45, זכר ברית is used in contrast to הפר ברית. Both actions have God as the subject. The same opposition occurs here in Ez 16:60, although the subject of הפר ברית is the woman. The verb זכר denotes more than simply a thought process of the past. The point is that it involves not only a thought process, but also an action;[87] and it concerns not merely the past, but the present and the future as well.[88] Here the result of Yahweh's remembering the marriage covenant is that he הקים ברית עולם for Jerusalem.[89] But does that mean Yahweh is setting up a new covenant or maintaining an old one? One cannot decide on the basis of the uses of הקים ברית or ברית עולם, since both expressions can refer to a previous or a new covenant.[90] Ez 16:60 contrasts the covenant between the passer-by and the woman in her youth with the everlasting covenant. This is a contrast between young and everlasting. Thus a continuity is in view. In Jer 14:21 and Lev 26:44–45, the contrast of "to break a covenant" is not to make a new one, but "to remember the covenant". This remembrance clearly points to a continuity with the old covenant. It is therefore more likely that maintaining of the old covenant is spoken of here. Moreover, it is not uncommon

---

as one Yahweh made either with the Israelites after the Exodus (e.g. Keil 1876a:230–231; Fisch 1950:99; Greenberg 1983a:303) or with the patriarchs (e.g. Grant and Bloore 1931:94).

[85] With God as subject, the expression also occurs in Gen 9:15, 16; Ex 2:24; 6:5; Lev 26:42, 45; Ps 105:8; 106:45; 111:5; Jer 14:21, and with a human subject in Am 1:9 and 1 Chr 16:15. *Contra* Block (1997:516n.301). Neh 13:29 is a misquote in Jüngling (1993:143n.71).

[86] Schottroff 1964:216–217.

[87] Groß 1960:229, 230. Cf. Schottroff 1997:383. See also Eising (1980:69–72) for biblical examples.

[88] Eising 1980:67.

[89] Woudstra (1971:29) says, "'Remembering' in the Old Testament is more than a mere calling to mind" but "is tantamount to making the covenant operative again".

[90] For הקים ברית: previous covenant in Ex 6:4; Dt 8:18; new covenant in Gen 6:18; 9:9. For ברית עולם: previous covenant in 1 Chr 16:17; Is 24:5; new covenant in Is 55:3; Jer 32:40. Ezekiel is unique in having ברית עולם as the direct object of הקים.

to qualify a covenant mentioned previously as an everlasting covenant later (e.g. Gen 9:9, 15–16; 17:7, 9). Thus, it is probable that the everlasting covenant here refers to the covenant remembered by Yahweh.

As a consequence of this, Yahweh will give Jerusalem's elder and younger sisters to her as daughters. The announcement of this gift is followed by the much discussed nominal clause ולא מבריתך (v.61bβ). The point of contention is to identify the reference of "covenant" and the meaning of the clause.

First, the covenant here could refer to either (1) an old covenant,[91] or (2) the confirmed or new covenant.[92] Second, it is clear that the suffix refers to Jerusalem, but the covenant can be one between (3) Jerusalem and the daughters or between (4) Jerusalem and God. Options (1) and (2) can combine with (3) or (4) and each can also combine with different meanings of מן. Regarding options (1) and (2), note that in the context of vv.59–63, Yahweh's faithfulness to his covenant is highlighted so much so that he maintained the covenant broken by Jerusalem as an everlasting covenant. And if the consequence of re-establishing the covenant is the gift of the sisters as daughters, then it is not possible that the clause ולא מבריתך would function as a negation or restriction of this consequence of the covenant just re-established.[93] That is to say, the clause must refer to an old covenant which is negated here. Thus, we opt for (1), the choice of most scholars. To determine what that old covenant is we need first to deal with options (3) and (4). Those who accept option (3) usually take the preposition מן concessively, thus interpreting the phrase as meaning that there is an incorporation of the sisters as daughters into Jerusalem *even though* their previous covenant did not designate that.[94] One difficulty with this interpretation is that a Jerusalem covenant with the sisters has never been mentioned before

---

[91] This is held by most scholars. E.g. Keil 1876a:232; Davidson 1916:127; Redpath 1907:80; Fisch 1950:99; Taylor 1969:142; Wevers 1969:103; Greenberg 1983a:292; Dijkstra 1986:156; Maarsingh 1988:31; Vawter and Hoppe 1991:97; Allen 1994:246.

[92] Brownlee (1986:251) also takes the מן privatively (see W.-O'C. §11.2.11e) and interprets the clause as "not outside your covenant", meaning that the daughters share the same covenantal blessing and obligation as Jerusalem. As one possible interpretation, Zimmerli (1979:353) suggests the opposite, i.e., the sisters will not be made members of the same covenant.

[93] Cf. Kutsch 1973:98.

[94] Cooke 1936:181; Wevers 1969:103; Maarsingh 1988:31; Block 1997:518.

in Ez 16, not even in vv.44–58 where Jerusalem has been compared with her sisters Sodom and Samaria. Its appearance here is unexpected. Another difficulty is that this view seems to underscore the status of Sodom and Samaria (e.g. Block; cf. Brownlee). However, this is not the emphasis of vv.59–63, whose focus is on the restoration of Jerusalem by unexpectedly promoting her above her sisters. Concerning option (4), note first that no one seems to hold that the suffix is a subjective genitive with God as object.[95] Taken as an objective genitive, the subject God is occasionally stated explicitly in translations.[96] Some interpret the phrase as "not because of your conduct in the covenant".[97] But it is difficult to see why "your covenant" means "your conduct in the covenant" or "fulfilment of your obligation in the covenant"—both of these find no precedent in the MT.[98] A second group of scholars interprets the "not of your covenant" as meaning "but of divine grace".[99] Such a contrast between covenant as binding and God's grace as something free from obligation, thus reflecting the contrast between law and grace, poses a false dichotomy which is simply not found in Ezekiel. There seems to be no distinction between covenant and grace for Ezekiel. The most probable interpretation is simply to take the "covenant" as referring to the only one covenant mentioned in the passage, the marriage covenant first mentioned in 16:8 and then in vv.59, 60a.[100] This covenant is described in v.59 as one broken by Jerusalem and in v.60a as one made in the days of her youth. Here in v.61 it is simply בריתך at least for the reason that the word בריתי is inappropriate since it can refer to either the old or the confirmed everlasting covenant. The meaning of the clause is starkly made by Dijkstra in his translation: "ook al zijn ze niet uit mijn huwelijk met jou geboren".[101] The message is that Yahweh remembers his marriage covenant and remains

---

[95] Cooke (1936:181) mentions this possibility, and Woudstra (1971:42) argues against it.

[96] E.g. NRSV; NIV; Auvray 1957:66; Dijkstra 1986:156; Allen 1994:226.

[97] Hitzig 1847:115; Kraetzschmar 1900:155; Herrmann 1924:97; Bertholet 1936:60; Fohrer 1955:91; Kraeling 1966:448–449; Greenberg 1983a:292; Krüger 1989:330n.220; Vawter and Hoppe 1991:97; Jüngling 1993:147.

[98] Cf. Keil 1876a:232; Eichrodt 1970:201; Renz 1999:169n.103.

[99] Heinisch 1923:86; Cooke 1936:181; Kutsch 1973:98; Greenberg 1983a:292; Fishbane 1984:138; Maarsingh 1988:31; Vawter and Hoppe 1991:97; Allen 1994:246.

[100] Stienstra (993:153) speaks of a return to the marriage metaphor in vv.59–63.

[101] Dijkstra 1986:156: "even though they were not born from my marriage with you" (my translation).

faithful to it by confirming it. As a consequence, he will give her
sisters to her as daughters, thus resuming her motherly position which
she once assumed but forfeited by sacrificing her children (v.20). In
re-establishing this marriage, she is given daughters who are not from
the former marriage (i.e., ולא מבריתך). So Jüngling says, "Wenn jetzt
die Störung der Liebe durch das Gedenken an den Bund beseitigt
und die Frau als Mutter eingesetzt wird, kommt genau das zur Vollen-
dung, was mit dem Eid und dem Bund in Ez 16,8 begonnen hatte".[102]

The confirmation of the covenant will arouse in Jerusalem a knowledge of God (v.62). The recognition formula is expanded in v.63
with a purpose clause introduced by למען. She will remember and
be ashamed (בוש), and she will not have an open mouth because of
her shame (כלמה) when God forgives all she did. In 36:31–32 we
find again the idea that remembering one's evil past would lead to
a feeling of shame (בוש and כלמה). And because of the guilt, she is
ashamed and will boast no more (as she once did in v.56).[103]

2.3.2. *Summary*

Ez 16:59–63 can be interpreted as a continuation of the extended
metaphor in vv.1–43. It speaks of the old marriage covenant which
was broken by Jerusalem. But Yahweh will remember it and confirm
it as an everlasting covenant. As a consequence of this, Yahweh will
give Jerusalem's sisters to her as daughters, thus resuming Jerusalem's
motherhood which she lost through sacrificing her sons and daughters. This can be seen as an act of forgiveness. The other effects of
this covenant on Jerusalem are her (1) remembering of her past
deeds; (2) arriving at a knowledge of God; and (3) feeling so ashamed
that there will no longer be any boasting.

2.4. *Covenant and Retribution*

In this section, we will show in what ways Jerusalem has violated
the marriage covenant and how the punishment inflicted on her is
appropriate for that.

Jerusalem's misconduct is announced in v.15 as whoring (זנה). The
verb זנה primarily refers to having "a sexual relationship outside of

---

[102] Jüngling 1993:147. Cf. Stienstra 1993:154.
[103] Kraetzschmar 1900:155; Eichrodt 1970:217; Zimmerli 1979:353; Greenberg
1983a:294; Brownlee 1986:252; Allen 1994:246.

a formal union",[104] including therefore both pre-marital and extra-marital sexual relationships. It also has the meaning of "to practise prostitution".[105] It is perhaps because of the latter usage that the verb has predominantly woman as its subject. When an illicit sexual act is committed with a woman, either a restitution must be made (e.g. Dt 22:28–29) or the two partners involved are penalised by death (e.g. Dt 22:22–27).[106] The practice of prostitution is not outlawed and it is rarely mentioned that the prostitute should be punished.[107]

Vv.16–19 portray Jerusalem's whoring acts with her husband's gifts. First, Jerusalem takes some garments and makes for herself colourful high places (במה), and then on the garments[108] she plays the whore. The word במה can denote not only a high place, but also a raised pedestal for (cultic) prostitutes.[109] Second, she melts the gold and silver jewellery and turns it into male images. These images can refer either to phallic forms[110] or to whole human figures,[111] but the latter is more likely in view of the treatment in vv.18–19. The woman then plays the whore with these images. It is not clear whether this should be taken literally or as referring to cultic prostitution. Third, she clothes the images and sets before them oil and incense. Fourth, she places before the images the choice flour, oil and honey which her husband gave her. She probably mixes and burns them to produce a fragrant smell (cf. Lev 2:1–2). All these acts are not without parallels in the ancient Near East, but such a description is unique in the Bible.[112] In vv.16–19, all that which the husband gave to the woman is abused by her. That this misuse implies a violation of the marriage and therefore may incur a punishment is not foreign in the ancient Near East. There are some laws in the Code

---

[104] Erlandsson 1980:100. But the word is not used for incest, homosexual relation or bestiality.

[105] Hall 1996:1123.

[106] Dempsey (1998:71) wrongly claims that Dt 22:20–24 is concerned with *harlotry*.

[107] E.g. Lev 21:9. See also Bird (1989:77) and Frymer-Kensky (1989:92).

[108] The masculine suffix of עליהם refers not to the high places (which is feminine) but the garments. Cf. Zimmerli 1979:326; Block 1997:486; against Brownlee 1986:227; Galambush 1992:69.

[109] Eissfeldt 1936:287; Block 1997:488. A recent discussion on במה can be found in Gleis (1997).

[110] E.g. Ehrlich 1912:55; Herrmann 1924:93; Fohrer 1955:89.

[111] E.g. Redpath 1907:72; Maarsingh 1988:19; Allen 1994:239.

[112] Greenberg 1983a:280.

of Hammurabi pertaining to this point. The phrase "wasting her house", which appears in §§141 and 143 of the Code and means "filling her own pocket at her husband's expense and so impoverishing him",[113] may serve as a parallel. This offence in conjunction with others may result in divorce or capital punishment. More recently, Brewer argues that the terms of the marriage covenant as expressed in Ex 21:10–11 are expected to be reciprocated. Thus, the woman's actions described here clearly shows that she has broken the marriage covenant.[114]

In vv.20–21, she is said to sacrifice the children whom she bore to her husband as food to the images. Her action is described by three phrases: זבח, שחט and נתן בהעביר. The first verb means basically "to slaughter (an animal)" by a butcher or as part of a religious ritual.[115] The word שחט means "(die Kehle) durchschneiden", used mostly for ritual killing for a cultic celebration.[116] The third phrase is similar to וּמִזַּרְעֲךָ לֹא־תִתֵּן לְהַעֲבִיר לַמֹּלֶךְ (Lev 18:21). It could be a conflation of two idioms:[117] נתן מזרעו למלך ("give his offspring to Molech")[118] and לְהַעֲבִיר אֶת־בְּנֵיהֶם וְאֶת־בְּנוֹתֵיהֶם לַמֹּלֶךְ ("to offer up their sons and daughters to Molech").[119] It is possible that the sacrifice to Molech consists of slaughtering and then burning.[120] Elsewhere in the Bible, when these three phrases are associated with the sacrifice of children, the imagery of "playing the whore" or "adultery" can also be found. For example, those who sacrifice (זבח) their children (Ps 106:37) are said to "prostitute themselves in their doings" (וַיִּזְנוּ בְּמַעַלְלֵיהֶם) (Ps 106:39). In Is 57:5, the one who slaughters (שחט) her children is said to be an offspring of an adulterer (זֶרַע מְנָאֵף). It is similar for Ez 23:39. Lastly, those who offer their children to Molech in Lev 20:2–4 are described as "prostituting after Molech" (לִזְנוֹת אַחֲרֵי לַמֹּלֶךְ).[121] The same can be said of Ez 23:37. Thus, Ezekiel shares the same convention by using the sexual imagery to describe this Molech cultic act.[122] In v.22, these acts are further characterised

---

[113] Driver and Miles 1952:300.
[114] Brewer 1996:7–8, 9.
[115] Bergmann, Ringgren and Lang 1980:11.
[116] Clements 1993:1214, 1215.
[117] Block 1997:490.
[118] Lev 20:2, 3, 4.
[119] Jer 32:35. Cf. 2 Kg 23:10.
[120] Cooke 1936:169; Heider 1985:366n.722, 374; Day 1989:17; Allen 1994:239.
[121] Cf. Lev 18:21, which is placed within a context of sexual relations.
[122] Cf. Day 1989:23.

as "abominations",[123] which denotes mostly cultic offences in Ezekiel and is also the case here.[124]

Vv.23–29 then gives an account of the whoring acts (the root זנה occurs six times) of the woman with different groups of people. For herself she builds a brothel (גב)[125] and makes a booth (רמה)[126] in every square and at every street crossing. Her promiscuous behaviour is described coarsely as "parting her legs to every passer by" (v.25). She first receives the Egyptians, which provokes her husband to anger. In his fury, he stretches his hand against her (נטה יד על). This expression appears seven more times in Ezekiel. In these seven cases, the object of this action can be a country (Israel in 6:14 or other nations in 14:13; 25:7, 13, 16; 35:3), or an individual (14:9). The result of this action is total destruction, be it of the land or the people. In comparison, the result in 16:27 seems less harsh. First, there is a reduction (not a total withdrawal) of the ration (חק). In the present context, "ration" may refer to a prescribed portion of food.[127] If it is the obligation of the husband to provide food to his wife, the

---

[123] The word is not rendered in the LXX. It is deleted by Herrmann (1924:93), Fohrer (1955:87), Zimmerli (1979:326). Allen (1990:228), followed by Block (1997:487), suggests that its omission is probably due to its graphical similarity to the following Hebrew word.

[124] Humbert 1960:227–231; Hossfeld 1977:112; Zimmerli 1979:190; Ohnesorge 1991:39; Gerstenberger 1997:1431. Note that the substantive תועבה occurs 43 times and the verb תעב twice in Ezekiel.

[125] Basically, there are two interpretative options for גב: (1) BDB (146) suggests the meaning "mound, for illicit worship" for Ez 16:24, 31, 39. This is followed by DCH (2:297), Davidson (1916:117), Fisch (1950:90), Aalders (1955:264), Wevers (1969:99) and Eisemann (1988:259). Cf. HALOT 170. (2) It refers to a secular structure connected with prostitution. The LXX renders it as οἴκημα πορνικὸν (v.24) and τὸ πορνεῖον (vv.31, 39). This is accepted by Herrmann (1924:93), Eichrodt (1970:200), Greenberg (1983a:281), Brownlee (1986:217), Dijkstra (1986:140), Allen (1994:229) and Hugenberger (1994:307). We opt for the second option since it suits the context better.

[126] The word רמה is sometimes identified as the במה in v.16 (e.g. Zimmerli 1979:342). In this line of thinking, HALOT (1240) states its meaning as "high places ... [for] cultic prostitution". See also Davidson (1916:117) and Eisemann (1988:259). However, the LXX understands it differently. It is rendered as ἔκθεμα (v.24), τὰ πορνεῖα (v.25), and βάσις (vv.31, 39), which, according to LSJ and GELS, mean "public notice (to brothel)", "brothel" and "steps, pedestal" respectively. Admittedly the LXX is guessing, but the context requires a meaning related to brothel. It is accepted by Herrmann (1924:93–94), Cooke (1936:170), Allen (1994:224, 229), Greenberg (1983a:281–282) and Hugenberger (1994:307).

[127] For this meaning of חק, see Gen 47:22; Prov 30:8; 31:15; Job 23:12. For this interpretation, see Greenhill (1645–67:374), Keil (1876a:209), Fisch (1950:91), Aalders (1955:265), BDB 349. Cf. Hos 2:11 for another biblical example.

reduction of this commodity indicates a warning, a first step taken to treat the woman not as his wife. Second, he will deliver her to the will (נתן בנפשׁ)[128] of her enemies, the Philistine women who compete "with Jerusalem for these international paramours".[129] But even they are ashamed of her lewd ways.[130] The expression נתן בנפשׁ occurs elsewhere only in Ps 27:12; 41:3. In these two places, the expression is preceded by the negative אל ("not") and used as an imperative. The psalmist asks God not to abandon him to the will of his adversaries. There the expression is contrasted with the protection of God. This could also be the meaning here. Thus, the husband not only reduces the food, but withdraws his protection.[131] This punishment, however, has no effect on her. She continues her harlotry with the Assyrians and the Chaldeans. Three times she is said to "increase her whoring" (vv.25, 26, 29) and three times she is described as "not satisfied" (vv.28a, 28b, 29). Her whoring acts reach a climax in vv.30–34.

In vv.30–34, the woman is called a "whore" (זונה) for the first time (v.30).[132] But she is no ordinary whore who would receive payment from her clients. Instead, she gives gifts to her lovers to bribe them to have sex (בוא אל) with her. That she is an unnatural whore is stressed by the twofold use of "contrariness" (הפך) in v.34. She is not just a whore, she is also an adulterous wife (האשׁה המנאפת v.32) since she takes strangers while she is still under the authority of[133] her husband.

---

[128] נפשׁ is translated as "will, desire" in Greenberg (1983a:283), Allen (1994:225), BDB (660). It is also rendered as "greed" in the expression נתן בנפשׁ. E.g. Kraus 1960:221, 311; Weiser 1962:250; Eichrodt 1970:197; Zimmerli 1979:327; Craigie 1983b:29; Brownlee 1986:217.

[129] Block 1997:496.

[130] On the construction of מדרכך זמה, see GKC §131r; Gibson §41. The context here speaks for the meaning "lewdness" for זמה (Steingrimsson 1980:90; Allen 1994:229; Block 1997:492; BDB 273) instead of "depravity" (e.g. Greenberg 1983a:283).

[131] Cf. *DCH* 3:299.

[132] Greenberg (1983a:284) puts forward the interpretation that the word שׁלטת (v.30), which is illuminated by the Elephantine Papyri, means "a woman authorised to dispose at will of property given to her by her husband". This is endorsed by Block (1997:497). But this interpretation seems unlikely in the context. It also contradicts vv.16–19. The meaning "domineering, imperious" given by BDB (1020), accepted by Cooke (1936:172), Fisch (1950:92), Brownlee (1986:217) and Allen (1994:229), is more likely.

[133] For this meaning of תחת, see Herrmann (1924:94), Aalders (1955:268), Greenberg (1983a:284). Cf. Ez 23:5. The preposition תחת can also mean "instead of", held by Fisch (1950:92), Eichrodt (1970:20), Dijkstra (1986:140), Allen (1994:225), Block (1997:493).

The woman's offences are summarised in v.36 in reverse order: whoring with the lovers;[134] involvement with abominable idols; bloodguilt in child sacrifice. These are offences against the husband in one way or another. In reaction to this, the husband announces his punishment. The first one involves the gathering of her lovers—all those she loved and hated—from around to turn against her. Before, she bribed them to come from around (מסביב) to make love with her, now they come from around (מסביב) against her.

Secondly, the husband will expose her nakedness. It is generally agreed that the exposure of the body is a symbolic act of punishment of adulterers and this is probably done before witnesses (the lovers here). It is also associated with divorce.[135] Physically, it also reverses the provision of clothing by a husband for his wife.

Thirdly, the husband passes[136] on her the sentences applied to adulteresses (נאפות) and those who shed blood[137] (v.38a). He will make her a bloody object[138] of wrath and jealousy,[139] meaning a death sentence[140] (v.38b). And according to the priestly law, this is the appropriate penalty.[141] In this connection, one may question why the lovers are not also punished according to the law.[142] The answer lies in the dual role of the woman—she is a wife and prostitute at the same time. From the point of view of her husband, she commits adultery with other men. But from the lovers' point of view, she is a prostitute

---

[134] It is possible to read v.36a with v.36bα (e.g. Pohlmann 1996:218), but most scholars follow the Masoretic accentuation. E.g. Zimmerli 1979:330; Greenberg 1983a:272; Allen 1994:230.

[135] Kruger 1984:82; Westbrook 1990:559. Block (1997:502n.231) provides a list of ANE parallels. See also Hos 2:4–5; Nah 3:5; Jer 13:22, 26.

[136] Bovati (1994:206n.92) remarks that שפט here means "to hand down sentence". See also Cooke (1936:174), Aalders (1955:270), Brownlee (1986:218). Fisch (1950:93) and Zimmerli (1979:330) render it as "to judge", and Eisemann (1988:265) as "to punish".

[137] Bovati (1994:210) holds that משפטי נאפות ושפכת דם is an expression specifying the kind of sentence. See also Brownlee (1986:218), Allen (1994:225), Block (1997:499). Cf. Krüger 1989:175, 193.

[138] For this understanding of the text, see Keil (1876a:215), Ehrlich (1912:58), Aalders (1955:270–271), Greenberg (1983a:286), Block (1997:499). There is no need to emend the text to ונתתי בך, as claimed by Toy (1899:24), Bertholet (1936:57), Cooke (1936:176), Auvray (1957:64), Zimmerli (1979:330) and Pohlmann (1996:218).

[139] For wrath and jealousy as the reaction of the husband to an adulteress, see Prov 6:34. For the reference of קנאה to "marital jealousy", see Sauer (1997:1146).

[140] Allen 1994:225; Block 1997:502.

[141] For adultery, Lev 20:10; Dt 22:22; for murder, Lev 24:17. Cf. Fishbane's "measured retribution" (1984:138).

[142] McKeating 1979:62.

and there seems to be no law against a client of a prostitute.[143]

The punishment inflicted on the woman takes place in several steps. The buildings associated with her whoring are destroyed (vv.39aα, 41aα). Although no law decrees such an action, it seems appropriate to do so.[144] Her marital gifts—the clothes and other beautiful objects—are taken away so that she returns to her former state, bared and naked (cf. v.7). By that, she is divorced. Furthermore, a group of people is summoned up to stone her to death according to the law (Dt 22:23–24; cf. Dt 22:21).[145] As if that were not enough, her body is cut by swords (v.40). This deserves some attention. The Hebrew בתק, a hapax legomenon, is often rendered as "to cut to pieces".[146] It may then recall the Levite's cutting his concubine into pieces in Jdg 19:19. However, the Hebrew used there is נתח, which means "to cut into pieces".[147] According to Greenfield, the root btq, well-known in Semitic languages, means "to cut, sever limbs".[148] The emphasis is then on mutilation. In this sense, the action done to the woman has a parallel not with Jdg 19:19, but with Ez 23:25. Paul argues that according to Mid-Assyrian Law, a man can mutilate his wife's nose if he catches her with another man *in flagrante delicto*.[149] This punishment is found in Ez 23:25. Of significance is that there the husband allows the woman to be punished according to the laws of her lovers (23:24) and the Assyrians are listed among her lovers (23:5, 7, 9, 12, 13). If the mutilation of the nose or ears as a punishment of an adulteress is known to Ezekiel, as 23:25 testifies, the possible parallel passage in Ez 16:40 with the use of the verb בתק could very well mean the same. By allowing all this to happen to her, the husband stops her from being a whore who gives payments.

---

[143] The Assyrian and Sumerian laws decree the freedom of the man who is ignorant of the marital status of the woman he slept with. See Westbrook (1990:550). Compare the case of Judah in Gen 38. Failing to notice that, Dempsey (1998:72) comments that the "metaphorical language of the text admits of a strong bias against women".

[144] Smend (1880:100), followed by Hugenberger (1994:308), suggests a comparison with Dt 13:16–17; Ez 23:25, 47. Keil (1876a:218) holds that this represents an intensification of the usual punishment.

[145] McKeating (1979:61–62) suggests that in Ez 16 stripping and public humiliation is an alternative punishment for adultery, but not an additional punishment.

[146] E.g. NRSV; Zimmerli 1979:330; Allen 1994:225; Pohlmann 1996:218.

[147] E.g. BDB 677.

[148] Greenfield 1958:220. Cf. Cooke 1936:175; Paul 1990:344n.48.

[149] Paul 1990:345; also noted by Westbrook (1990:558). It is followed by Block (1997:751). See also the discussion in Lafont (1999:82–85).

One main idea governing retribution in this chapter is the marriage covenant. Between the establishment of the covenant (v.8) and the formal announcement of the breaking of the covenant (v.59) lies a description of how the covenant is broken along with its corresponding punishments. By entering into the marriage covenant, there are mutual obligations to keep. The man does that by providing at least food, cloth and oil. However, the woman breaks the covenant by (1) misusing the property of the husband to make idols and playing the whore with them; (2) sacrificing her children born to her husband, thus committing murder; and (3) being a harlot and receiving different people. Hence, the husband passes on her sentences applied to adultery (and bloodguilt). She is punished according to the terms of the covenant. She is stripped naked, divorced, stoned to death, mutilated, and her brothels are torn down and burned.

2.5. *Summary*

Ez 16 presents an extended metaphor on the relationship between Yahweh and Jerusalem. By entering into a marriage covenant, both Yahweh and Jerusalem have obligations to fulfil. However, Jerusalem shows infidelity to the covenant by committing adultery and sacrificing her children. In reaction to this, punishments appropriate to (mainly) adultery are inflicted on her: her brothels are destroyed, she is stripped naked and divorced, and she is stoned and mutilated. That the different possible punishments for an adulteress are conglomerated here is uncommon, but that serves to heighten the hideous crime the woman has committed. The various punishments are inflicted because each of them is seen as appropriate to the misconduct within the marriage covenant. The marriage covenant also functions in the restoration of the relationship in that Jerusalem is granted her motherhood, which she forfeited when she sacrificed her children, by giving her daughters who are not born from the marriage. In this understanding, the marriage covenant forms the focus of the whole chapter.

3. ברית *as a Vassal Treaty: Ez 17:11–21*

3.1. *Introductory Remarks*

The word reception formula in v.1 marks the beginning of Ez 17. In v.2 the prophet is addressed, commanded to propound a riddle

(חידה), and speak a parable (משל) which begins in v.3 and extends
to v.10. In v.11 the word reception formula marks the start of an
interpretation of the parable which ends in v.21 with a variation of
the recognition formula. Then the messenger formula opens an oracle of salvation in v.22 which concludes in v.24. Instead of this tripartite division, Parunak proposes a chiasm: vv.1–10//vv.22–24 where
both are parables, and v.11–18//vv.19–21 where each is an interpretation of its adjacent parable.[150] Even then, the basic subdivision
of the chapter remains vv.1–10, 11–21, 22–24.

The first unit, vv.2–10, consists of two parts whose beginnings are
indicated by the messenger formula in v.3 and v.9. A narrative of
past events is found in vv.3–8 whereas vv.9–10 consider the future
consequence, presented in the form of questions. This form shows
resemblances to a bipartite oracle of judgement[151] but it lacks the
usual connective לכן joining the accusation and judgement.

Within the second unit (vv.11–21), a break is indicated by the
word לכן followed by the messenger formula in v.19. While vv.12–18
interpret the parable in terms of Zedekiah's infidelity to Nebuchadnezzar and his subsequent fate, vv.19–21 speak of Zedekiah's infidelity
to Yahweh. Building upon Parunak's study, Greenberg calls the first
(vv.12–18) and second (vv.19–21) subunits interpretations on the
earthly plane and divine plane respectively.[152] Within the first subunit, vv.12b–15a represent the accusation and vv.16–18 the punishment. The question raised in v.15b is answered in v.18.[153] Whereas
the first oath formula (v.16) introduces punishment in the human
sphere, the second one (v.19) does that in the divine sphere. Block
follows Greenberg's scheme but puts the units in the form of a step-
like progression.[154]

The third section, vv.22–24, is an oracle of salvation, employing
the vocabulary used in the previous sections. It has the form of a
two-part proof saying. After the messenger formula in v.22aα, the
positive message in vv.22aβ–23 culminates in the extended recognition formula in v.24aα. Then the section closes with an elaborated
formula for divine speech.

---

[150] Parunak 1978:270.
[151] Allen 1994:254.
[152] Greenberg 1983a:320.
[153] Parunak (1978:273) argues that vv.15–18 form a chiasm.
[154] Block 1997:526.

The structure of the chapter is as follows:

A vv.2–10   A parable of two eagles, a cedar and a vine
   vv.2–3aα   Introduction
   vv.3aβ–6   The first eagle and the deeds of the cedar turned
                    vine
   vv.7–8   The second eagle and the vine
   vv.9–10   The fate of the vine
B vv.11–21   An interpretation of the parable
   v.11   Introduction
   vv.12–18   Nebuchadnezzar and Zedekiah
   vv.19–21   Yahweh and Zedekiah
C vv.22–24   Yahweh's restoration of the cedar

3.2. *Analysis*

The general thrust of vv.11–21 is clear. Nebuchadnezzar, the king of Babylon, came to Jerusalem and took its king, i.e., Jehoiachin, and his officials to Babylon.[155] Then Nebuchadnezzar set up Zedekiah, Jehoiachin's uncle, as the puppet king of Judah. But Zedekiah rebelled by sending envoys to Egypt asking for help. As a result of his action, Zedekiah was punished. The emphasis of the interpretation (as well as the parable) is on the fate of Zedekiah as shown by the length of the text devoted to it. This last phase of the political history of Judah can also be found in 2 Kg 24:8–25:21 and Jer 37:1–39:10.

In the present passage, "covenant" functions as a catchword (vv.13, 14, 15, 16, 18, 19). In four cases the word is used with "oath" (אלה) (vv.13, 16, 18, 19). "Covenant" is once the object of כרת (v.13), once of שמר (v.14), and four times of הפר (vv.15, 16, 18, 19) where it is three times used in parallel to בזה אלה (vv.16, 18, 19). The last phrase indicates the concern of this passage. In v.13 we find ויכרת אתו ברית followed by ויבא אתו באלה. While the first expression is the most common one for the making of a covenant, the second expression is much less frequent, found only in Neh 10:30 (ובאים באלה ובשבועה)[156]

---

[155] Hossfeld (1977:78), Lang (1978:55–56) and Allen (1994:250), following Kutsch, argue that the verb לקח in v.13bβ means to take the leaders into a covenant. But this seems unlikely. See Jüngling (1993:121n.18). Besides, לקח has often been used to mean deportation as in v.12. A chiastic use of the word in vv.12b–13, noted by Greenberg (1983a:314) and Maarsingh (1988:39), argues against Hossfeld.

[156] In 1 Kg 8:31 (//2 Chr 6:22), the expression ובא אלה is found. While Dillard (1987:46) takes it as a syntactic equivalent of ובא באלה, Gray (1977:216) and Japhet (1993:584) regard its syntax as impossible and suggest the alternatives ובא ואלה (with

where different groups of people following the lead of others showed their determination to observe the laws of God brought by Ezra by entering into an oath. The use of the qal form of בוא in Neh 10:30 recalls a similar phrase בוא בברית mentioned above in 2 Chr 15:12 and Jer 34:10 where a similar situation is to be found, namely, a person of a superior status initiates some terms of an agreement and then people of a lower status join in. The use of the hiphil of בוא in this case resembles the case in 1 Sam 20:8, for in both cases it depicts a relationship between only two persons of unequal status. The purpose of Nebuchadnezzar's action is that "the kingdom be low, not to exalt itself".[157]

The phrase שמר ברית in v.14 is used sixteen times in the MT to denote the keeping of the covenant,[158] but only in Ezekiel is a human treaty in view. What is of some interest is whether the suffix of לעמדה[159] represents the covenant[159] or the kingdom.[160] In favour of the former is the observation that since a suffix usually refers to what is just mentioned, the suffix in this case must refer to the covenant.[161] Moreover, "covenant" is the object of the hiphil form of עמד in Ps 105:10 (//1 Chr 16:17).[162] In favour of the latter, one can argue that it makes the sentence less tautologous. That is, "by keeping the covenant, the kingdom may continue" is more informative than "by keeping the covenant, the covenant may stand". Secondly, the whole tenor of v.14 seems to be on the kingdom: to be low, not to exalt itself, and that by keeping the covenant the kingdom may continue.

LXX and Syriac) or ובא באלה. Note that *DCH* (1:272) lists as one possibility that אלה is the subject of ובא.

[157] The subject of התנשא can be either the king or the kingdom. The first option is held by Lang (1978:56), Greenberg (1983a:308) and Block (1997:534), while the second by BDB (672), Zimmerli (1979:357), Dijkstra (1986:161), Breuer (1993:139) and Allen (1994:250). The choice seems to depend on whether one reads לבלתי התנשא in connection with the making of the covenant in v.13, or with the preceding phrase להיות ממלכה שפלה, respectively. In view of the immediate context and a comparison with 29:15, the second option is preferred.

[158] With a human subject: Gen 17:9, 10; Ex 19:5; 31:16; 1 Kg 11:11; Ps 78:10; 103:18; 132:12; Ez 17:14. With God as subject: Dt 7:9, 12; 1 Kg 8:23; 2 Chr 6:14; Neh 1:5; 9:32; Dan 9:4.

[159] Kraetzschmar (1900:159) (citing Is 54:10 and Ps 89:29 for support, but in neither case does the word עמד appear); Cooke 1936:193; Auvray 1957:69; Hossfeld 1977:67; Lang 1978:50; Zimmerli 1979:357; Allen 1994:250; Block 1997:534.

[160] Keil 1876a:242; Heinisch 1923:88; Aalders 1955:287; Wevers 1969:106; Brownlee 1986:258; Pohlmann 1996:236.

[161] Hossfeld 1977:67.

[162] Allen 1994:252.

Thus, once the covenant was violated, the kingdom, not just Zedekiah (vv.16, 20), suffered (vv.17, 21). Lastly, some key words in vv.13–14 are found in 2 Kg 23:3 where Josiah made a covenant (כרת ברית) before Yahweh to keep (שׁמר) his commandments, and all the people stood in the covenant (ויעמד בברית).[163] Based on this, the Ezekiel text could mean "by keeping the covenant, the kingdom stands (in the covenant)".

The last expression to be discussed is נתן יד in v.18.[164] This action is generally taken as belonging to the rite of covenant making.[165] Viberg adds that the action probably took place at the same time as the oath since both the action and the oath are used to ratify the vassal-suzerain treaty between the two parties.[166]

Undoubtedly, ברית refers here to a vassal treaty between Zedekiah and Nebuchadnezzar. The phrase ממלכה שׁפלה meaning vassal kingdom (also in 29:15) supports this.[167] As noted above, a covenant is usually accompanied by an oath invoking the gods as witness and guarantor,[168] although in this case some question if Nebuchadnezzar himself also took the oath.[169] That Yahweh was invoked as a witness is supported both by 17:19 where the oath and covenant are said to be Yahweh's[170] and by 2 Chr 36:13 where Nebuchadnezzar is said to have made Zedekiah swear by God (השׁביעו באלהים). But Greenberg questions this interpretation. He argues that (1) there is no evidence that the practice of invoking gods as witnesses in a vassal treaty was followed in neo-Babylonian times; (2) 2 Chr 36:13 is not an independent source but is dependent on Ezekiel; and (3) the covenant in 17:19 is actually referring to that between Israel and Yahweh.[171] Laato criticises Greenberg with respect to argument (1). In addition to the neo-Assyrian treaty between Esarhaddon and Baal of Tyro where the gods of both the suzerain and the vassal are called as witnesses—the only treaty Greenberg reckons as exemplifying

---

[163] The parallel text in 2 Chr 34:32 uses the hiphil of עמד.

[164] Also in 2 Kg 10:15; 1 Chr 29:24; 2 Chr 30:8; Ezr 10:19; Jer 50:15; Lam 5:6.

[165] E.g. Hossfeld 1977:83; Kalluveettil 1982:14.

[166] Viberg 1992:38. Cf. Block 1997:535n.76.

[167] Tsevat 1959:201; Lang 1978:56n.19.

[168] Aalders 1955:286; Tsevat 1959:201–204; Thiel 1970:216; Hossfeld 1977:83–84; Lang 1978:57; Maarsingh 1988:39; Allen 1994:256.

[169] Scharbert 1977:264; Maarsingh 1988:40.

[170] Brichto 1963:38.

[171] Greenberg 1983a:320–322.

such a practice—Laato lists five more.[172] Laato admits that this does not constitute proof that such was practised in Babylonian times, but it adds to the likelihood.[173] As to the dependence of 2 Chr 36:13 on Ez 17:13, Greenberg gives no proof for his claim.[174] Greenberg's weakest argument is to make a distinction between the covenant in v.18 and v.19. In referring 17:19 to 16:59 Greenberg "confuses two distinct passages and the relation between them".[175] He also misses the link between v.18 and v.19 forged strongly by the word לכן. Lastly, notice that elsewhere in the Bible a covenant among humans is sometimes referred to later as "my covenant", denoting God's covenant (e.g. 1 Sam 18:1–4 and 20:8; Jer 34:8–10 and 34:18). This phenomenon is best explained by the supposition that each of these covenants was accompanied by an oath taken in the name of the god involved. The point is that by taking an oath in Yahweh's name, Yahweh becomes the guarantor of the treaty. Within the vassal treaty, there are obligations for both the suzerain and the vassal. For the vassal, this includes the giving up of independence in political matters and the paying of tribute to the suzerain (cf. 2 Kg 17:3–4).[176]

In 17:11–21, "covenant" is used (five times) to denote a vassal treaty between Nebuchadnezzar and Zedekiah, with obligations for the latter. The emphasis on this covenant is not found elsewhere. With this treaty, the kingdom of Judah was supposed to remain humble so that it may survive. But Zedekiah rebels against the treaty, resulting in disaster. At the same time, this violation is to be seen as breaking Yahweh's covenant in that a ratifying oath was taken in Yahweh's name. That "covenant" is used together four times with "oath" points to the importance of honouring one's oath in God's name. In this passage, we may have a unique combination of עמד (qal) with ברית.

3.3. Covenant and Retribution

In this section we will consider the idea of retribution involved in Ez 17.

---

[172] Laato 1992:160–161.
[173] Cf. Dillard 1987:300; Allen 1994:259.
[174] Nor do Japhet (1993:1070) and Allen (1994:259).
[175] Allen 1994:259.
[176] Lang 1978:56–57.

As mentioned above, it is the duty of the vassal to give up independence in external politics and to pay a tribute. In Ez 17, Zedekiah attempts to violate the vassal treaty by sending envoys to Egypt to secure military assistance. It is not impossible that Zedekiah withheld the tribute as well.[177] The fate of Zedekiah in connection with his breaking the vassal treaty is envisaged several times in Ez 17. The rhetorical question in v.15 hints already at the death of Zedekiah. The word מלט (niphal) is used primarily of those escaping from enemies, usually in connection with wars.[178] It denotes not the process of fleeing, but the successful end result of the flight.[179] That Zedekiah was not able to escape is made explicit in v.16. The announcement of the death penalty in v.16 has the form of a legal verdict[180] pronounced in the absence of the guilty party.[181] Here God plays the role of a judge, mediating between Zedekiah and Nebuchadnezzar and delivering the verdict. Basically the same language is found in v.18 with the additional information of the ceremony of "giving the hand", which seems to function in the same way as the oath.[182] Not only is Zedekiah himself punished, so is the kingdom. Many lives will be cut off (v.17),[183] choice soldiers[184] will fall by the sword (v.21) and the people will be scattered.

So far the violation of the treaty and its corresponding punishment are on the human level with Yahweh as the judge. However,

---

[177] Lang 1978:57.

[178] Ruprecht 1997:987.

[179] Hasel 1989:596.

[180] Several features of a sentence suggested by Bovati (1994:355, 357n.34) can be found here. First, it takes the form of a declaration. Second, there is an indication of the motivation. Third, the sentence is accompanied by an oath which guarantees the irrevocable nature of the sentence. See also Lang (1978:59).

[181] Liedke 1971:129n.4.

[182] Hugenberger 1994:213.

[183] Note that there is a wordplay on the cutting of a covenant (כרת ברית) and the cutting of many lives (להכרית נפשׁות רבות).

[184] The word מברחו is textually problematic. It is emended to מבחרו, suggesting that there is a metathesis, because: (1) מברח is a hapax in the OT; (2) מבחר is supported by the Targum, Syriac, LXX[86] (οἱ ἐκλεκτοί) and some other Hebrew manuscripts; (3) the word מבחר occurs four more times in Ezekiel (23:7; 24:4–5; 31:16); (4) מבחר seems to function better in its context: the soldiers are mentioned in v.21aα whereas the fugitives or the survivors in v.21aβ (Zimmerli 1979:358; Allen 1994:253; Block 1997:535); and (5) a comparison with a similar description in 12:14 favours the reading מבחר (Block 1997:535). Barthélemy (1992:121–123) gives only a grade C to the MT reading. Few scholars keep the MT reading (e.g. Keil 1876a:243–244; Greenberg 1983a:309, 316).

the parallel between the breaking of a treaty and despising an oath, which appears three times (vv.16, 18, 19), points to the divine domain because the oath was taken in the name of the God who guarantees the treaty. The turn in v.19, where the oath and covenant are said to be Yahweh's, is therefore not surprising. Yahweh's action is described as "to spread a net" so that Zedekiah "will be captured in a trap". The syntagm פרש רשת occurs nine times[185] and תפש במצודה twice in the OT.[186] In Ezekiel the first expression is used mostly with the divine punishment of rulers.[187] In the two occurrences of the second expression, the role of Yahweh is explicit. Further on, Yahweh will bring him to Babylon and charge him for treason (מעל), which refers to the violation of an oath.[188]

Apart from Ez 17, the fate of Zedekiah is also mentioned in Ez 12. In the explanation of the symbolic action there, Ezekiel refers to the fate of "the prince" (הנשיא) in Jerusalem, who is generally recognised to be Zedekiah.[189] Three descriptions of him are found in 12:12. First, he will lift up his baggage and flee from Jerusalem in darkness (i.e., after sunset) (cf. Jer 39:4; 2 Kg 25:4). Second, the invaders[190] will breach the wall and bring him out. Third, he will cover his face because he will not see the land. The sentence in 12:12bβ is difficult.[191] Of relevance to us is whether or not "he will not see the land" refers to Zedekiah's blindness.[192] This interpretation seems unlikely. Rather, in the context of the exile the phrase means that Zedekiah will never see the *land of Palestine* again (cf. Jer 22:12).[193] Three phrases in 17:20 are also found in 12:13: (1) "spread my net over him" (12:13aα); (2)

---

[185] Ps 140:6; Prov 29:5; Lam 1:13; Ez 12:13; 17:20; 19:8; 32:3; Hos 5:1; 7:12.

[186] Ez 12:13; 17:20.

[187] Bodi 1991:164–170.

[188] This usage finds a precedent in Lev 26. The violation of the covenant (הפר ברית) in v.15 is regarded as treason committed against God (במעלם אשר מעלו־בי) in v.40. See Milgrom (1976a:19–20). Against Ringgren (1997:462), who regards the act of מעל in 17:20 as being of a general nature.

[189] Cooke 1936:132; Zimmerli 1979:274; Allen 1994:181; Block 1997:373.

[190] Some take the subject of יחתרו as either citizens (Zimmerli 1979:274; Brownlee 1986:170) or the king's attendants (Keil 1876a:160). However, it is more likely that the subject is the Babylonians (Uehlinger 1987:138; Allen 1994:181; Block 1997:375; cf. Garscha 1974:110–111).

[191] See the discussion in Allen (1994:173) and Block (1997:363–364).

[192] Redpath 1907:54; Davidson 1916:84, 86; Cody 1984:62; Stuart 1989:110; Blenkinsopp 1990:66; Cooper 1994:150.

[193] Aalders 1955:209; Greenberg 1983a:211; Allen 1994:180; Block 1997:375–376. Cf. Lofthouse 1907:119; Davidson 1916:84.

"he will be caught in my snare" (12:13aβ); and (3) "I will bring him to Babylon" (12:13bα). The phrase "he will not see it" (12:13bβ), whether regarded as original or a later addition, is often taken to refer to the blinding of Zedekiah (mentioned in 2 Kg 25:7).[194] This seems reasonable because the suffix of ואותה refers to its nearest antecedent which is the land of the Chaldeans, and the word שם in 12:13bβ also has the same referent. That is to say, the punishment that Zedekiah will die in Babylon and at the same time not able to see the land there must mean that he will be blind at that time.[195]

The idea of retribution in Ez 17 is expressed in two ways. First, it is couched in legal terms. Yahweh as the guarantor of the vassal treaty serves as a judge who delivers a verdict on the party who violates the treaty. Zedekiah, who transgresses the conditions laid down in the treaty, will not be able to escape from the consequence. Yahweh mediates between Zedekiah and Nebuchadnezzar, judges according to the terms and therefore sentences Zedekiah in his absence to his deserved death penalty. The one who executes this death penalty is not mentioned explicitly but v.17 hints that the Babylonians are responsible. Thus, although the deity is the judge, the execution of the verdict remains on the human level. Though not found in Ez 17, the fate of Zedekiah mentioned in Ez 12 contains elements pertaining to curses in treaties. Greenberg refers to a treaty between Ashurnirari V of Assyria and Mati'ilu of Arpad in the eighth century BCE in which if Mati'ilu breaks the treaty, he, his family and his people will be removed from his country, not return to it, and not behold it again.[196] This resembles the fate of Zedekiah depicted in Ez 12. Moreover, if the blindness of Zedekiah is alluded to in Ez 12, then we have one more item on the list of curses in the treaty. Deist refers to I Sefire A 35–40 wherein one curse for the breach of treaty is the blinding of the offender.[197] These extra-biblical sources provide a parallel to the biblical materials, indicating the curses imposed upon the one who breaches a treaty.

Secondly, Zedekiah sins against God by despising the oath which he swore in Yahweh's name. This is taken as treason against Yahweh,

---

[194] Keil 1876a:160; Aalders 1955:209; Wevers 1969:82; Lang 1978:21; Zimmerli 1979:274; Greenberg 1983a:215; Stuart 1989:110; Allen 1994:182.

[195] See Block (1997:377–378) for a different opinion.

[196] Greenberg 1983a:211; also in *ANET* (532) and Parpola and Watanabe (1988:8).

[197] Deist 1971:72. Cf. *ANET* 660. See also *ANET* (538, 540), Parpola and Watanabe (1988:45, 57).

whose punishment of Zedekiah is couched in the stereotypical language of "spreading of net and snare", which in Ezekiel refers to the divine punishment on rulers. Lastly, the idea of being trapped in a snare also resembles some curses in ANE treaties, listed by Hillers.[198]

3.4. *Summary*

In Ez 17:11–21 the word ברית refers to a vassal treaty between Zedekiah and Nebuchadnezzar which is made with an accompanying oath taken in Yahweh's name who then serves as the protector and guarantor of the treaty. Retribution was then considered on both the level of the treaty and of the oath. Violation of the vassal treaty will result in the death penalty, permanent removal from one's own homeland, and being blinded. Violation of the oath implies treason against Yahweh and will result in divine punishment whose nature is unclear.

4. ברית *as a Future Covenant: Ez 20:37*

4.1. *Introductory Remarks*

Thematically Ez 20 stands out from its surrounding chapters 19 and 21. It is a literary unit comprising two subunits: vv.1–31, 32–44. The chapter begins with a date, followed by a delegation of elders to consult Yahweh. The word reception formula in v.2 introduces a command from Yahweh who refused to be consulted (v.3). Then a history of Israel is recounted: Israel in Egypt (vv.5–9), the first generation in the wilderness (vv.10–17), the second generation in the wilderness (vv.18–26), and Israel in the land (vv.27–29). The oracle then moves back to the present in vv.30–31. It is concluded in v.31 where Yahweh's refusal to be consulted is restated, forming an inclusion with v.3.[199]

The second subunit of this chapter is a disputation speech.[200] According to Graffy, this speech consists of the following parts: (i)

---

[198] Hillers 1964:69–70.
[199] Against those who make a division after v.32. E.g. Heinisch 1923:102; Aalders 1955:326; Fohrer 1955:107; Stuart 1989:184.
[200] Zimmerli 1979:413–414; Graffy 1984:65; Allen 1990:7.

an introduction (v.32a), (ii) a quotation (v.32b), (iii) a programmatic refutation (v.33), and (iv) a refutation (in three parts: vv.34–38, 39–42, 43–44).[201] This can be subjected to some refinement. Agreeing with Baltzer, Allen suggests that a medial break is found only after v.38.[202] While the section is split into vv.33–38, 39–44 on the basis of form and contrast in content by Baltzer, and on the basis of the different locales (wilderness of the peoples in vv.32–38 and the land of Israel in vv.39–44) by Krüger,[203] Allen structures it in four parts: vv.32–33, 34–38, 39–42, and 43–44 with the first part as an introduction and the last part as a conclusion.[204]

4.2. *Analysis*

The lack of a formal introduction in v.32 seems to suggest that this subunit (vv.32–44) is related to what precedes.[205] The quotation in v.32 can be regarded either as a defiant claim of the people to be like the nations[206] or as a resigned expression of the people for being exiled among the nations.[207] The difference is whether the exiles actively will to be like the nations or are unwillingly absorbed by their surroundings. The second option is more likely.

First, the serving of wood and stone is a curse for disobedience (e.g. Dt 4:28; 28:36, 64) and that is what the people will (or are afraid to) suffer here.[208] The combination "wood and stone" (עץ ואבן) occurs in basically two contexts: as materials for vessels or houses[209] and as gods of the nations (or idols).[210] The less frequently found combination "stone and wood" is attested mostly in the first context[211] and once as the object of Judah's adulterous action.[212]

---

[201] Graffy 1984:65.
[202] Baltzer 1971a:2; Allen 1990:8.
[203] Baltzer 1971a:2; Krüger 1989:201.
[204] Allen 1990:8.
[205] Sedlmeier (1990:311) notes the continued use of participles from vv.30–31 to v.32.
[206] E.g. Keil 1876a:279; Skinner 1895:182; Davidson 1916:159; Fisch 1950:128; Eichrodt 1970:277.
[207] E.g. Andrew 1985:102; Dijkstra 1986:205; Klein 1988:79; Krüger 1989:226; Clements 1996:91.
[208] Graffy 1984:66. Carley (1975:49) also points out that the exilic situation induces pessimism.
[209] E.g. Ex 7:19; 1 Kg 5:32; 18:38; 2 Kg 12:13; 22:6; Zech 5:4; 1 Chr 22:14; 29:2.
[210] E.g. Dt 4:28; 28:36, 64; 29:16; 2 Kg 19:18; Is 37:19; Ez 20:32. Cf. Jer 2:27.
[211] E.g. Lev 14:45; Ez 26:12; 1 Chr 22:15 and 2 Chr 2:13.
[212] Jer 3:9.

Wood and stone are explicitly referred to as gods (אלהים) among the peoples (עמים) or in the nations (גוים) in Dt 4:28; 28:36 (גוי); 28:64; 29:16; 2 Kg 19:18; Is 37:19. In the parallel passages 2 Kg 19:18 and Is 37:19, "wood and stone" are immediately qualified as no gods but the work of human hands. The first three Deuteronomic passages speak of a curse on the Israelites when they fail to obey Yahweh: they will serve (עבד) wood and stone in the foreign nation(s). These texts seem to depict an exilic situation. This is absent in other texts. In Dt 29:16 and Jer 3:9, Israel's connection with wood and stone is more of a voluntary action—she wants to do it. And because of this action the people will be punished. The case of Ez 20 is more similar to the three Deuteronomic texts than to the latter two passages in pinpointing the exilic situation. First, 20:1 is a frame which indicates a conversation between Ezekiel and the elders in the exile. Secondly, the phrase "clans of the countries" (משפחות הארצות) in 20:32 has a parallel only in Zech 14:17 (משפחות הארץ), in which the phrase is parallel to "nations" (גוים) in Zech 14:16.[213] Thirdly, Yahweh's reply in 20:34 points again to an exilic situation. Thus, by comparing the usage of "wood and stone" (or "stone and wood") elsewhere, it is more likely that in Ez 20:32, the worship of wood and stone does not express a voluntary action on the part of the worshippers but the result of a curse. If that is the case, then in the background of the text already lies a covenantal idea.

Secondly, Graffy holds that in other disputation speeches in Ezekiel, those quotations attributed to the exiles express despair and dejection (12:27; 33:10; 37:11) whereas those attributed to the Jerusalemites show arrogance and pride (11:3, 15; 12:22; 18:2; 33:24).[214] This is generally correct although one may question if 12:27 belongs to a dispute with the exiles or if 37:11–14 should be seen as a dispute with the people in Judah.[215]

Thirdly, the overall positive response seems more likely to be a reply to a despondent expression.[216] Even though in vv.33–38 the niphal of שפט with God as the subject is used three times, there is

---

[213] The parallel use of משפחה and גוי is attested elsewhere in the MT. See Zobel (1986:89).

[214] Graffy 1984:66–67. Cf. Aalders 1955:325–326; Zimmerli 1979:414.

[215] Pohlmann 1992:117.

[216] Herrmann 1924:125; Beuken 1972:49–50; Graffy 1984:67; Allen 1990:13.

a distinction between two groups of people. The message is not totally negative.

From v.33 on, the future of Israel is in view.[217] In v.33a, the oath formula, strengthened by the messenger formula, introduces Yahweh's reaction to the saying in v.32. Vv.33b–34 are framed by the three-fold expression "with a strong hand and with an outstretched arm and with outpoured wrath".[218] That the first two expressions are connected with the Exodus event is pointed out frequently.[219] The third expression is unique to Ezekiel and it echoes the phrase שפך המה which, with one exception, is found only in him.[220] It always has Yahweh as the subject, and mostly refers to the wrath of Yahweh poured out on Israel, but also on a country (which acts treacherously against Yahweh) in general (14:19) or on Egypt in particular (30:15). Some scholars regard the third expression as modifying negatively the first two expressions which are positive for Israel,[221] presuming that the third expression refers to the judgement of Israel. This presumption is probably based on the use of the phrase שפך המה in 20:8, 13, 22.[222] Whether this is true we can only determine after examining אמלוך עליכם in v.33, which is the only place in Ezekiel where Yahweh is said to act as a king.[223] Apart from Ez 20:33, Yahweh is the subject of the verb 12 times in the MT.[224] In some cases Yahweh is depicted as king over the nations, or Yahweh as

---

[217] Sedlmeier 1990:341.

[218] Cf. Greenberg 1983a:371. This speaks against those who find a separation between vv.33 and 34. See, for example, Bettenzoli (1979:198) and Graffy (1984:65), who sees v.33 as a programmatic refutation to be expanded in what follows.

[219] Keil 1876a:279; Carley 1975:14; Zimmerli 1979:415; Andrew 1985:103; Hoffmeier 1986:384–386; Block 1997:650. Both expressions are found in the context of the Exodus in Dt 4:34; 5:15; 7:19; 11:2; 26:8; Jer 32:21; Ps 136:12 (otherwise also in 1 Kg 8:42//2 Chr 6:32). "Strong hand" is found alone in Ex 3:19; 6:1; 13:9; 32:11; Nu 20:20; Dt 3:24; 6:21; 7:8; 9:26; 34:12; Neh 1:10; Dan 9:15. "Outstretched arm" appears alone in Ex 6:6; Dt 9:9; 2 Kg 17:36; Jer 32:17. Note that in some cases these expressions are also used of humans.

[220] The exception is Jer 10:25 (//Ps 79:6).

[221] Greenberg 1983a:372; Allen 1990:14; Ohnesorge 1991:157; Koenen 1994:48; Block 1997:650.

[222] Zimmerli 1979:415.

[223] The verb is used once more in Ezekiel in 17:16 as a hiphil. In Ez 34, Yahweh is designated as a shepherd (רעה), which, according to Soggin (1997b:1248), "clearly represents a variant of the title *melek* 'king'".

[224] Ex 15:18; 1 Sam 8:7; Ps 47:9; 93:1; 96:10; 97:1; 99:1; 146:10; Is 24:23; 52:7; Mi 4:7; 1 Chr 16:31. For a list of passages where Yahweh is given the title מֶלֶךְ, see Soggin (1997a:677).

king rules over the chaotic forces. No case seems to indicate that
the kingship of Yahweh is threatening to Israel.[225] Even some who
suggest a menacing tone here admit that such usage is singular.[226]
Why should the kingship of Yahweh be intimidating to Israel? Rather,
the reign of Yahweh is a positive note, associated with the first
Exodus in Ex 15:18 (cf. Nu 23:21–22). In addition, Lust argues that
the kingship of Yahweh is also linked with the "gathering and return"
theme,[227] which is found at first in the Exodus from Diaspora in
20:34a (note the words "peoples" and "countries"). Framing this idea
is the combination of the three phrases "with a strong hand", "with
an outstretched arm" and "with outpoured wrath". The last phrase
is not directed to Israel, but to the nations (cf. Ez 14:19; 30:15).[228]
Thus, we should read vv.33–34 as an entirely positive answer to the
resigned quotation in v.32. With power Yahweh will be king over
Israel by performing for the Israelites a second Exodus from the
nations.

Like the first generation in the wilderness which was brought out
by Yahweh not to the promised land but to the wilderness (v.10),
so will the Israelites here. Thus, "the desert of the people" to which
the people will be brought (v.35a) designates less a geographical location and more a "typological counterpart" to the desert of Egypt.[229]
There (שם) God will enter into judgement with them. The niphal of
שפט occurs three times in vv.35–36. Apart from a few cases where
it denotes the passive,[230] the niphal form means generally "to enter
into a controversy with someone",[231] often in a juridical context.[232]
Yahweh will confront the people "face to face". The phrase פנים אל

---

[225] One doubts if Vawter and Hoppe (1991:103) are correct in claiming that
"king" in prophetic literature is a title of doom. Cf. Is 43:15; Zeph 3:15.

[226] Cooke 1936:221; Krüger 1989:266–267.

[227] Lust 1981b:139.

[228] Herrmann 1924:125; Dijkstra 1986:206.

[229] Keil 1876a:280; Baltzer 1971a:7n.33; Zimmerli 1979:416; Krüger 1989:268;
Allen 1990:14; Ohnesorge 1991:159 (cf. Sedlmeier 1990:356); against Cooke 1936:221;
Fohrer 1955:116; Greenberg 1983a:372.

[230] The niphal of שפט occurs 17 times in MT: 1 Sam 12:7; Is 43:26; 59:4; 66:16;
Jer 2:35; 25:31; Ez 17:20; 20:35; 20:36 (2x); 38:22; Jl 4:2; Ps 9:20; 37:33; 109:7;
Prov 29:9; 2 Chr 22:8. It is used as passive only in Psalms.

[231] Bovati 1994:49; Niehr 1995:419. Cf. BDB 1048.

[232] Niehr 1995:419; Schultz 1996:219. Ohnesorge (1991:197) takes it as "einen
Rechtsstreit führen". Against Hossfeld (1977:455), who suggests the meaning "ein
vernichtendes Gericht halten".

פָּנִים, which occurs four more times in the MT,[233] is not used here to refer to an actual past encounter of the people with God (such as on Sinai).[234] Rather, it means that the encounter is "persönlich und unmittelbar",[235] thus emphasising the individual aspect (in contrast to the collective whole of Israel referred to in previous verses).[236] This individual aspect is accentuated by the use of the shepherd metaphor in v.37. This entering into judgement with the Israelites is compared to a similar event which happened before. In the context of Ez 20, this must refer to God's entering into judgement with the first and second generations in the wilderness (vv.10–17, 18–26) who disobeyed the statutes and ordinances given by God.

V.37 resumes the series of w-qatal phrases (from v.34 on). Vv.37–38 seem to make more explicit what is said in vv.35–36.[237] The expression עבר תחת השבט occurs only once more in Lev 27:32 (where the qal of עבר is used). There the picture is that as the sheep pass under the rod, a shepherd counts his sheep and every tenth is taken as a tithe. The image used here underlines again each individual. Although in Leviticus the expression does signify some sort of selection, it has nothing to do with quality (cf. Lev 27:33). If quantity but not quality is also the concern here (cf. Jer 33:13),[238] this seems to indicate that all[239] and every[240] Israelite who is brought to the wilderness is under consideration. After this inspection, *all* the Israelites are brought into the rule[241] of the covenant[242] (v.37b). Following Fisch, who holds

---

[233] Gen 32:31 (God and Jacob); Ex 33:11 (God and Moses); Dt 34:10 (God and Moses); Jdg 6:22 (Gideon and an angel of God). The expression פָּנִים בְּפָנִים, referring to the Sinaitic encounter between God and the Israelites, occurs only in Dt 5:4.

[234] Sedlmeier 1990:358; against Zimmerli (1979:416) and Baltzer (1971a:7n.32).

[235] Fohrer 1955:116.

[236] Ohnesorge 1991:197.

[237] Sedlmeier 1990:362.

[238] Krüger 1989:269; Sedlmeier 1990:367; Ohnesorge 1991:197. Against Greenhill 1945–67:513; Keil 1876a:281; Herrmann 1924:137; Fisch 1950:129; Eichrodt 1970:280; Greenberg 1983a:372; Block 1997:652.

[239] Krüger 1989:269.

[240] Sedlmeier 1990:364.

[241] The word מָסֹרֶת has caused much discussion. The proposals are: (1) The LXX renders it as (ἐν) ἀριθμῷ, reflecting מִסְפָּר "number". E.g. Smend 1880:134; Toy 1899:136; Bertholet 1936:72; Schumpp 1942:105; Auvray 1957:80; Wevers 1969:120; Eichrodt 1970:262; Mosis 1978:244; Zimmerli 1979:403; Hals 1989:131; Ohnesorge 1991:90n.39; *HALOT* 2:608; cf. *BHS* apparatus. (2) Theodotion (ἐν παραδόσει) and the Targum take it as "tradition", probably deriving it from מסר "to deliver, offer". (3) Aquila (ἐν δεσμοῖς), Symmachus (διὰ κλοιοῦ) and Vulgate (*in vinculis*) interpret it as "bond, fetter", thus reading it as מַאֲסֹרֶת, from אסר. E.g. Kraetzschmar 1900:174;

that only those who pass the selection process will be "reconsecrated under the covenant", Greenberg argues that only those who pass will be made to accept the obligation of the covenant.[243] But this is not likely since the same pronominal suffix "you" is retained from v.32. Only in v.38 do we find a partition (מכם).[244] Thus, all Israelites are to be put under the rule of the covenant. But that does not mean that all of them can keep it. Those who cannot are the rebels (הַמֹּרְדִים) and transgressors (הַפּוֹשְׁעִים) against God[245] and they will be purged out (ברר) from among the Israelites. In this understanding, the selection process does not begin in v.37a, but in v.37b.[246] The "rule of the covenant" can be likened to the "statutes and ordinances" which Yahweh gave to the first and second generations in the wilderness who could choose to observe them or not. Just as these "statutes and ordinances" include both promise and punishment, so does "the rule of the covenant".[247] Thus, there is no need to restrict its meaning to "covenantal curses".[248] If Bovati is right in

Cooke 1936:225; Aalders 1955:327; Maarsingh 1988:88; BDB 64. Similarly, Ehrlich (1912:77) takes it as מֹסֶרֶת, also from אסר, meaning "Halfter, Leitseil". See also J.-M. §16a n.2. Greenberg (1983a:372–373, 1983b) argues for the meaning "obligation, duty" with the rendering "bond", a metaphoric equivalent. His opinion is followed by Allen (1990:4), Krüger (1989:268) (who further points out that MT has the *lectio difficilior*), Sedlmeier (1990:54–56) and Block (1997:648). (4) Syriac has "chastisement", and thus takes the word as מוּסַר, from יסר "to discipline, chasten, admonish" (cf. Prov 13:24; 22:15; 23:13 for the parallel between שׁבט and מוּסַר). This understanding is taken up by Cornill (1886:296–297), Bertholet (1897:109), and Heinisch (1923:103). Driver (1935:297) suggests מֻסֶרֶת, also from יסר. (5) Hitzig (1847:138), followed by Herrmann (1924:121), reads מֶסְרַת, the construct state of מַשְׂרֵת which is a hapax found in 2 Sam 13:9, meaning "pan, crucible". (6) Gertner (1960:271) argues that the word should be read as מִסְרָה, derived from שׂרר (שׁרד) "to rule, command", much as does Koenen (1994:46). To conclude, while options (1), (2) and (5) are less likely, the other options do not differ too much, especially (3) and (6). We may take the meaning to be "bond, rule".

[242] Following the LXX, some commentators (see proposal (1) in previous note) delete הברית as dittography of the following word וברותי. But this can also be a haplography on the part of the LXX. Hitzig (1847:138), in view of וברותי in v.38, repoints the word as חַבְּרִית, meaning "purification". Thus the phrase במסרת הברית means "in the crucible of purifying". Greenberg (1983a:373), followed by Allen (1990:4) and Koenen (1994:45), holds that "the high incidence of repetition and alliteration in vss. 33–40 speaks for the originality of the sequence *hbryt wbrty*".

[243] Fisch 1950:129; Greenberg 1983b:42. Cf. Allen 1990:14.

[244] Sedlmeier 1990:364, 365–366; Koenen 1994:46.

[245] For a discussion of these expressions, see Ohnesorge (1991:160).

[246] Cf. Dijkstra 1986:127: "De Here zal de Israëlieten onder het juk van het verbond brengen door hen opnieuw tot de keuze to dwingen: God of afgoden".

[247] Keil 1876a:282; Aalders 1955:327; Koenen 1994:46. Cf. Greenberg 1983b:42.

[248] Kraetzschmar 1900:174; Noordtzij 1957:225.

saying that in a two-party controversy both parties must refer to
some norms which "regulate the rights and duties of each",[249] then
the rule of the covenant can serve precisely that purpose. In this
connection, a further parallel between the rule of the covenant and
the statutes mentioned in Ez 20:11–12, 18–20 can be found. Thus,
Krüger suggests rightly that those statutes can be understood as
"Bundes(erneuerungs)angebot" in as far as it aims at a relationship
between God and the people in which "das Handeln beider Instanzen
durch *explizite Normen* reziprok typisiert ist".[250]

The phrase אֶרֶץ מְגוּרִים ("the land of sojourning", v.38aβ) occurs
five more times in the MT.[251] It denotes the land of Canaan promised
to the patriarchs but not yet possessed. In Gen 36:7 it has a more
restricted meaning as a part of Canaan. Ezekiel changes its reference
but retains its sense. It still means the land where the Israelites are
residing as aliens, but the reference is now the land of exile.[252] The
rebels will, together with other Israelites, be taken out from the land
of exile, but their punishment, like that of their fathers in the wilderness of Egypt, is that they will not enter the land of Israel (cf. 20:15).

The quotation in v.32 represents a pessimistic resignation of the
exiles. This triggers a positive reply from Yahweh who promises to
carry out for them a second Exodus. But this Exodus is qualified by
a selection so that the rebels will be purged out and excluded from
the land of Israel. The selection is done by putting all Israelites under
the rule of the covenant, which can be compared to the statutes and
ordinances given to the fathers in the Egyptian wilderness. This rule
is served as the standard by which the people are assessed if they
are rebellious or not. In this understanding, the covenant is one
between Yahweh and the Israelites which consists of norms for appropriate conduct for both sides.

4.3. *Covenant and Retribution*

In the above discussion, we argue that the phrase מָסֹרֶת בְּרִית ("rule
of the covenant") can be likened to the "statutes and ordinances"
(חֻקּוֹת וּמִשְׁפָּטִים) given by Yahweh to the first and second generations

---

[249] Bovati 1994:30.
[250] Krüger 1989:222 (our italics).
[251] Gen 17:8; 28:4; 36:7; 37:1; Ex 6:4.
[252] Keil 1876a:282–283; Zimmerli 1979:416; Ohnesorge 1991:161.

in the wilderness. These statutes and ordinances can be seen as the terms of the covenant between Yahweh and Israel, the observance of which will lead to life and the violation of which will lead to punishment. The rule of the covenant has a similar function. The covenantal overtone in the present pericope (20:32–38) is shown not only by the occurrence of the word ברית, but also by המרדים and הפושעים.

In political contexts, מרד means to rebel against a superior power with the aim of gaining independence and is mostly used to refer to Judah/Israel's unsuccessful attempt to break away from a superior power.[253] It denotes therefore a vassal's violation of a treaty relationship with the suzerain.[254] It is not to be equated with "to fall away, to become apostate" which denotes completed events.[255] The verb is found in Ezekiel at 17:15, referring to Zedekiah's action against Babylon. In theological contexts, the word refers to rebellion against Yahweh which is always illegitimate. It means the attempt to break a covenantal relationship with Yahweh. In Ezekiel, the verb occurs four times (2:3 (2x); 17:15; 20:38). In 2:3 the participle המורים is used in apposition to "sons of Israel", followed by a relative clause employing the same verb again. The participle denotes not a single action, but a continued activity,[256] thus indicating the rebellious character of the Israelites. This observation also applies to 20:38.

The verb פשע, when used in a context of international relations, refers to a breach of allegiance through the violation of a treaty or covenant (e.g. 1 Kg 12:19; 2 Kg 1:1; 8:20, 22; Ez 21:29).[257] As such, it signifies a completed action (in contrast to מרד)[258] and a wilful violation from a norm or standard.[259] It is a thoroughly negative concept.[260] The above understanding also applies to the theological domain. With Israel as the subject, it denotes a break, a completed separation from Yahweh the suzerain of Israel and therefore a breach of the covenant with Yahweh (e.g. 1 Kg 8:50; Is 1:2; Hos 8:1).[261] In Ezekiel, the verb פשע occurs three times[262] and the noun פֶּשַׁע ten

---

[253] Schweinhorst 1998:2.
[254] Knierim 1997a:685; Schweinhorst 1998:2.
[255] Knierim 1997a:685.
[256] GKC §116a.
[257] Cover 1992:32.
[258] Knierim 1997b:1034.
[259] Youngblood 1978:202; Cover 1992:32; Knierim 1997b:1034.
[260] Seebass 1989:797.
[261] Carpenter and Grisanti 1996:708; Knierim 1997b:1036.
[262] 2:3; 18:31; 20:38.

times.[263] In all these cases, the verb has Israel as the subject and the noun refers to the actions of Israel. With the exception of 21:29, which refers to Israel's transgression against Babylon, all the rest indicate either explicitly or implicitly from the context that the object of Israel's transgression is Yahweh. In both 14:11 and 37:23 "all their transgressions" (בכל פשעיהם) is placed in contrast to the covenantal formula. Thus, in these two passages, פשעים is connected with the breaking of a covenant.[264]

In the theological domain, both מרד and פשע have to do with the violation of a covenantal relationship with Yahweh. While the former represents a futile attempt to do so, the second denotes a successful and wilful deviation from known standards. The combination of מרד and פשע occurs only in Ez 2:3 and 20:38 within the OT. In the first text, both verbs are used to characterise the general conduct of the Israelites. In the second, they denote those who refuse or fail to follow the rule of the covenant, those who attempt to break away from God and those who have violated the norms. Thus, in this case, the terms of the covenant in the sense of statutes and ordinances are used as criteria to determine the fate of the Israelites.

4.4. *Summary*

Ez 20:32–38 (39–44) is a disputation speech in which Yahweh responds with a positive message to the resigned expression of the Israelites. Instead of suffering the covenantal curse to serve wood and stone among the nations, Yahweh will carry out a second Exodus and lead the Israelites to the wilderness of the peoples where they will enter into a controversy. Within the controversy both Yahweh and the Israelites must refer to some norms to regulate their rights and duties. These norms are precisely the so-called "rule of the covenant" by which each and all of the Israelites are judged. The rebels and transgressors are those who fail to respond positively to the rule and thus break away from Yahweh their suzerain. This passage shows clearly that how the people fare is determined by these norms, the rule of the covenant. More precisely, those who pass will enter the land and those who fail will not. In the past Yahweh's election (בחר) of Israel (20:5) is linked to the land as the main, if

---

[263] 14:11; 18:22, 28, 30, 31; 21:29; 33:10, 12; 37:23; 39:24.
[264] Cf. Sedlmeier 1990:392.

not the sole, concern (20:6) and whether they can enter the land
depends on their reaction to the statutes and ordinances. It is the
same in the future. Again each of them will be put under the rule
of the covenant and only those who pass will be allowed to enter
the land.

5. *Conclusion*

It is the objective of this chapter to show that there is a relationship between covenant and retribution in its negative sense in Ezekiel.
We attempted to demonstrate that covenant is a principle governing the transition from sin to punishment, from deed to consequence.
Three passages from Ezekiel are examined as test cases.

In Ez 16 the word ברית is used six times in an extended metaphor
depicting a marriage covenant which symbolises a covenant between
Yahweh and Jerusalem. According to Adler, the use of the marriage
covenant as a metaphor for the covenantal relationship between
Yahweh and Israel underscores four aspects: the obligation of exclu-
sive fidelity, election, the legal and artificial nature of the bond, and
the emotional and intimate nature of the relationship.[265] Of special
relevance to us is the legal aspect of the marriage covenant. Each
partner of the covenant has obligations to fulfil. While the husband
offers food, clothes and protection to his wife, she violates the marriage covenant by abusing the property of the husband, sacrificing
his children and committing adultery with others. The punishments
inflicted on her are appropriate to these crimes according to the
legal stipulations for the marriage covenant. While it is uncommon
to have all these different punishments imposed on her, it is used
to underscore the severity of the crime. In this case, the misdeeds
of Jerusalem and their consequences are related through the marriage covenant.

The word ברית is also used six times to denote a vassal treaty between Zedekiah and Nebuchadnezzar in Ez 17. To ratify the treaty,
an oath is taken in the name of the gods, who then serve as the
witnesses and guarantors of the treaty. The idea of despising the
oath by breaking the treaty comes to the fore in this passage. In a
vassal treaty the vassal is supposed to give up his international auton-

---

[265] Adler 1990:43–93.

omy and pay a tribute. Zedekiah fails to do the former and probably the latter. Regarding the breaking of the treaty, Zedekiah is
punished according to the terms of the treaty. In this case, ancient
Near Eastern parallels are helpful in pointing out the punishments
as the death penalty, permanent removal from one's homeland and
blinding. Regarding the breaking of the oath, this is equivalent to a
violation of covenant with Yahweh and treason against him. The
corresponding punishment is couched in stereotyped language. In
both the human and divine domains, what Zedekiah did and then
suffered as a consequence are connected through the covenant. He
who breaks a covenant will suffer according to the terms of covenant.

Ez 20:32–38 (39–44) speaks of a future second Exodus of the
Israel from among the nations through a mighty act of Yahweh. In
the future as in the past, whether one obeys the covenantal terms
becomes the criterion for determining whether one is allowed to
enter the (promised) land (20:37). The rule of the covenant becomes
the norm against which the conduct and consequence of each is
measured.

These three cases demonstrate that although ברית admits of different
references, it is related to retribution in the sense that the consequence of one's misdeed is determined by the terms of the covenant.
The punishment is meted out according to the terms of the covenant. The punishment is thus justified and just. It is justified because
it is the consequence of a violation of the agreed norms. It is just
because it is dispensed according to the terms of the agreement. The
juridical view of retribution is affirmed in these cases. Moreover, the
role of Yahweh is stressed. He is the one who pronounces the punishment as a judge according to these norms. While he may not
always be involved directly in executing the punishment, he uses
human agents to carry out the punishment. Even in the case of the
secular vassal treaty between Zedekiah and Nebuchadnezzar, that
Zedekiah will die in Babylon is paralleled by Yahweh's bringing him
there and judging him for his treason against Yahweh himself. What
happens in the human domain reflects what happens in the divine
domain. Yahweh's direct and active involvement in retribution is not
to be doubted.

CHAPTER THREE

COVENANT AND RETRIBUTION (II)

1. *Introduction*

In Chapter Two we have considered the relationship between covenant and retribution (Ez 16, 17, 20) in the sense that the move from misdeed to its consequence is mediated by the terms of the covenant. This chapter explores this relationship further by noting the similarities between the covenant in the OT and ancient Near Eastern treaties. The studies of Mendenhall, Baltzer, Weinfeld, McCarthy and others have shown many similarities between them.[1] Integral to the treaty is the list of curses and blessings which serves as enforcement for the treaty. Those who keep the treaty will be rewarded with blessings and those who break it with curses. Regarding the prophetic materials, Mendenhall holds that there is a general resemblance between the disasters announced in the judgements and the threats in treaty curses.[2] In greater detail Hillers examines the parallels found in the prophetic books to the treaty curses. He concludes that the prophets often used traditional curses in their judgement oracles, and this use was deliberate because of the association of the curses with the covenant.[3] This idea of curses and blessings within the framework of a covenant plays an important role in explaining the kind of language Ezekiel uses in some of his oracles of judgement and restoration.[4] It is the objective of this chapter to show that covenant plays a role in the idea of retribution in that what has happened (or will happen) to Israel are covenantal curses which are realised (or will soon be realised). By violating its covenant with Yahweh, Israel will suffer the curses which are part and parcel of the covenant. Thus, the punishment is not random but meted out according to the terms of the covenant.

---

[1] Mendenhall 1954, 1955; Baltzer 1971b; Weinfeld 1972:116–129; McCarthy 1981. See also Nicholson (1986:56–82) for a summary and critique.
[2] Mendenhall 1962:720.
[3] Hillers 1964:88. See also Fensham (1962, 1963).
[4] Cf. Raitt 1977:23.

2. *Ezekiel and Lev 26*

Lev 26:3–46 forms the epilogue to Lev 17–26, the so-called Holiness Code (H).[5] It is composed of three sections—blessings (vv.3–13), curses (vv.14–39), possibility for restoration (vv.40–45)—and a post-script (v.46).[6] Lists of blessings and curses following a collection of laws can be found elsewhere in the OT (e.g. Dt 28) and in the ancient Near East in general (e.g. Code of Hammurabi).[7] Such a list is often found at the end of a treaty. In his study on Hittite treaties, Korošec shows that a list of curses and blessings forms an integral part of a typical treaty.[8] Hillers shows further that treaties of a later time also contain curses and blessings.[9] The purpose of the list is to motivate treaty partners to keep to the terms of the treaty by invoking the gods to act as witnesses to punish those who breach the treaty and to reward those who keep it.[10] Usually, curses are elaborated upon more than blessings.[11] In the case of Lev 26, the relationship between Yahweh and the Israelites is summarised by the word בְּרִית ("covenant") which appears six times within the chapter (vv.9, 15, 25, 42, 44, 45). In v.15, the violation of the statutes, ordinances and commandments is equivalent to the breaking the covenant. Thus, those statutes and ordinances "are expressly oriented toward the 'covenant'",[12] and they can be seen as the terms of the covenant which the Israelites are admonished to keep. The blessings and curses in Lev 26 then provide motivation for keeping the covenant. They serve precisely the same function as those of ancient Near Eastern treaties.

Similarities in diction and themes between Ezekiel and Leviticus (in particular Lev 26) have been noted by many scholars. The relationship between H and Ezekiel is variously explained: H is dependent

---

[5] The name "Heiligkeitsgesetz" was first coined in 1877 by Klostermann (1877).

[6] Hartley 1992:457; Budd 1996:360. Cf. Elliger 1966:363.

[7] Driver and Miles 1955:95–107. For other examples, see Levine (1987a:32n.2).

[8] Korošec 1931.

[9] Hillers 1964:7–11. Cf. Levine 1989:283n.1 to Excursus 11.

[10] Barton (1998:84) regards the curses and blessings as future motivations for good conduct.

[11] Hillers 1964:6, 33; Wenham 1979:328n.4; Levine 1987a:10. Although, with reference to Lev 26, Reventlow (1961:149) holds that the lists of blessings and curses originally had the same length.

[12] Gerstenberger 1996:409.

on Ezekiel,[13] Ezekiel is dependent on H,[14] both of them have the same source,[15] or there is some mutual influence in their growth.[16] Some arrive at these explanations through positing a compositional history for H and/or Ezekiel which admits of no consensus. While it is possible that both H and Ezekiel have the same source, we tend to agree with scholars who hold that Ezekiel is dependent on H on the basis of their close lexical links, having the same sequence of blessings/curses, some theological considerations, and the general claim that Ezekiel is a frequent quoter.[17] Some of these will be considered below. In this section we will give a list of lexical similarities between Ezekiel and Lev 26. This provides the basic data for a close look at select passages from Ezekiel which show a connection with Lev 26. Our concern is to show that by appropriating the curse language from Lev 26 within the covenantal framework, Ezekiel actually argues that Israel has suffered or will suffer the covenantal curses (expressed in Lev 26). Thus, by violating the covenant Israel will meet its fate as decreed in the covenantal curses.

A list of similarities between Lev 26 and Ezekiel is given below in Table One. The first column gives the chapter and verse of Ezekiel which has the same or similar expression in Lev 26 which is given in column two. Some variations in phraseology are given in parenthesis. Expressions unique to Leviticus and Ezekiel are marked with an asterisk.

Table 1

Ez Chapter	Verse	Lev 26 Verse		Expression
4	10(מאכל במשקול)	26a	*	לחם משקל
	16	26a		שמר מטה־לחם
	16	26a	*	לחם משקל
	17	39a,b	*	מקק בעון

[13] E.g. Bertholet 1901:94; Herrmann 1924:XIX; Levine 1989:275–284; Grünwaldt 1999:348–365.

[14] E.g. Paton 1896; Haag 1943:136; Reventlow 1962:157–159; Allen 1994:92–96; Milgrom 1997; Levitt Kohn (1999:502–509).

[15] E.g. Fohrer 1952:144–148.

[16] E.g. Kilian 1963:182–186; Zimmerli 1979:46–52; Sun 1992:256.

[17] For the last point, see especially Burrows (1925).

Table 1 (cont.)

Ez Chapter	Verse	Lev 26 Verse		Expression
5	2(זרה לרוח)	33a		זרה בגוים
	2	33a	*	הריק חֶרֶב אחרי
	6	3a		בחקות הלך
	6	43b	*	מאס במשפט
	7	3a		בחקות הלך
	8	45b		לעיני הגוים
	10	29a		אכל בנים
	10(זרה לכל־רוח)	33a		זרה בגוים
	12(זרה לכל־רוח)	33a		זרה בגוים
	12	33a	*	הריק חֶרֶב אחרי
	14	31a,33b(היה)		נתן חָרְבָּה
	15(+תוכחת)	28a		(+יסר) (Yhwh's) בחמה
	16	21b		יסף על
	16	26a		שמר מטה־לחם
	17(שלח)	cf.6b(not)		חרב עבר בארץ
	17	22a	*	שלח חיה
	17(famine & beast)	22a		שכל (beast)
	17	25a	*	הביא חרב על
	17(עבר)	25b		שלח דבר
6	3	25a	*	הביא חרב על
	3(אבד)	30a		השמיד במות
	4(נשבר)	30a		הכרית חמנים
	4	cf.30a	*	נתן פגרים . . . גלולים
	4(שמם מזבחים)	cf.31a		שמם מקדשים
	5	30a	*	נתן פגרים . . . גלולים
	5(אשם,חרב מזבחים)	cf.31a		שמם מקדשים
	6(שמם)	30a		השמיד במות
	6(נדע)	30a		הכרית חמנים
	6(עיר חֶרֵב)	31a,33b(היה)		נתן חָרְבָּה
	8(זרה בארצות)	33a		זרה בגוים
	13	cf.30a	*	נתן פגרים . . . גלולים
	13	31b		בריח ניחח
	14(נתן)	33b		היה ארץ שממה
7	21	25b		נתן ביד
	24(שבת גאון עז)	19a	*	שבר גאון עז
8	18	28a		(+יסר) (Yhwh's) בחמה
11	8	25a	*	הביא חרב על
	9	25b		נתן ביד
	12(בחקים הלך)	3a		בחקות הלך

Table 1 (cont.)

Ez Chapter	Verse	Lev 26 Verse		Expression
	16(פוץ בארצות)	33a		זרה בגוים
	17(פוץ בארצות)	33a		זרה בגוים
	20	3a		בחקות הלך
	20	12		covenant formula
12	14(זרה לכל־רוח)	33a		זרה בגוים
	14	33a	*	הריק חֶרֶב אחרי
	15(זרה בארצות)	33a		זרה בגוים
	15(פוץ בגוים)	33a		זרה בגוים
	18(eat with terror/fear)	5b(cf.26b)		אכל לחם לשֹבע
	19(eat with terror/fear)	5b(cf.26b)		אכל לחם לשֹבע
	20(עיר חָרֵבָה)	31a,33b(היה)		נתן חָרְבָּה
	20	33b		היה ארץ שממה
13	10	43b	*	יען ובִיעַן
	13(2x)	28a		בחמה (Yhwh's) (+יסר)
14	8	17a	*	נתן פנים ב
	11	12		covenant formula
	13(famine)	22a	*	הכרית בהמה
	13	26a		שמר מטה־לחם
	13(no ב)	40a		מָעַל מַעַל ב
	15(העביר)	6b		השבתי חיה רעה
	15	cf.6b(not)		חרב עבר בארץ
	15(beast)	22a		שֹכל (beast)
	15	33b		היה ארץ שממה
	16	33b		היה ארץ שממה
	17	6b(not)	*	חרב עבר בארץ
	17(sword)	22a	*	הכרית בהמה
	17	25a	*	הביא חרב על
	19(pestilence)	22a	*	הכרית בהמה
	19	25b		שלח דבר
	21(שלח)	6b		השבתי חיה רעה
	21	22a	*	שלח חיה
	21(4 evils)	22a	*	הכרית בהמה
	21	25b		שלח דבר
15	7	17a	*	נתן פנים ב
	8(נתן)	33b		היה ארץ שממה
	8(no ב)	40a		מָעַל מַעַל ב
16	19	31b		ריח ניחח
	39	25b		נתן ביד
	59	15b,44a		הפר ברית

Table 1 (cont.)

Ez Chapter	Verse	Lev 26 Verse		Expression
	60	9b		הקים ברית
	60	42a,45		זכר ברית
	62	9b		הקים ברית
17	15	15b,44a		הפר ברית
	16	15b,44a		הפר ברית
	18	15b,44a		הפר ברית
	19	15b,44a		הפר ברית
	20	40a		מָעַל מַעַל ב
18	9	3a		בחקות הלך
	17	3a		בחקות הלך
	24(no ב)	40a		מָעַל מַעַל ב
19	6	12a		התהלך בתוך
	7(עִיר הָרֵב)	31a,33b(היה)		נתן חָרְבָּה
20	1	3a		בחקות הלך
	3	3a		בחקות הלך
	9	45b		לעיני הגוים
	11	46a		נתן משפטים
	13(no ב)	43b		מאס במשפט
	14	45b		לעיני הגוים
	16	3a		בחקות הלך
	16	43b	*	מאס במשפט
	18(בחקים הלך)	3a		בחקות הלך
	19	3a		בחקות הלך
	21	3a		בחקות הלך
	22	45b		לעיני הגוים
	23(זרה בארצות)	33a		זרה בנוים
	23(פוץ בנוים)	33a		זרה בנוים
	24	15a	*	בחקות מאס
	25	46a		נתן משפטים
	27	40a		מָעַל מַעַל ב
	28	31b		בריח ניחח
	33	28a		בחמה (+יסר) (Yhwh's)
	34	28a		בחמה (+יסר) (Yhwh's)
	34(פוץ בארצות)	33a		זרה בנוים
	41	31b		בריח ניחח
	41(פוץ בארצות)	33a		זרה בנוים
	41	45b		לעיני הגוים
21	36	25b		נתן ביד

Table 1 (cont.)

Ez Chapter	Verse	Lev 26 Verse		Expression
22	15(זרה בארצות)	33a		זרה בגוים
	15(פוץ בגוים)	33a		זרה בגוים
	16	45b		לעיני הגוים
	20	28a		(+יסר) (Yhwh's) בחמה
23	9	25b		נתן ביד
	28	25b		נתן ביד
24	21(חלל)	19a	*	שבר גאון עז
	23	39a,b	*	מקק בעון
25	4	11a	*	נתן משכן ב
	13(Edom)	22a	*	הכרית בהמה
	13	31a,33b(היה)		נתן חָרְבָּה
26	19(עיר חָרֵב)	31a,33b(היה)		נתן חָרְבָּה
28	7(no אחרי)	33a		הריק חֶרֶב אחרי
	14	12a		התהלך בתוך
	23	25b		שלח דבר
	25(פוץ ב)עמים)	33a		זרה בגוים
	25	45b		לעיני הגוים
	26	5b		ישב לבטח (באָרץ)
29	8(sword and Egypt)	22a	*	הכרית בהמה
	8	25a	*	הביא חרב על
	9	33b		היה ארץ שממה
	10	31a,33b(היה)		נתן חָרְבָּה
	10(נתן)	33b		היה ארץ שממה
	12(עיר חָרֵב)	31a,33b(היה)		נתן חָרְבָּה
	12(זרה בארצות)	33a		זרה בגוים
	12(פוץ בגוים)	33a		זרה בגוים
	12(נתן)	33b		היה ארץ שממה
	13(פוץ ב)עמים)	33a		זרה בגוים
	15	17b		רדה ב
30	6(ירד)	19a	*	שבר גאון עז
	7(עיר חָרֵב)	31a,33b(היה)		נתן חָרְבָּה
	11(no אחרי)	33a		הריק חֶרֶב אחרי
	12(חָרְבָה)	31a,33b(היה)		נתן חָרְבָּה
	12	32a	*	שמם ארץ (hiphil)
	14	32a	*	שמם ארץ (hiphil)
	18(first two words)	13b		שבר מוטה על
	18(שבת)	19a	*	שבר גאון עז

Table 1 (cont.)

Ez Chapter	Verse	Lev 26 Verse		Expression
	(זרה בארצות)23	33a		זרה בגוים
	(פוץ בגוים)23	33a		זרה בגוים
	25	25b		נתן ביד
	(זרה בארצות)26	33a		זרה בגוים
	(פוץ בגוים)26	33a		זרה בגוים
31	11	25b		נתן ביד
32	(אבד)13	22a		כרת בהמה
	(נתן)15	33b		היה ארץ שממה
33	2	25a	*	הביא חרב על
	10(only מקק)	39a,b		מקק בעון
	15	3a		בחקות הלך
	(שבת)28	19a	*	שבר גאון עז
	(נתן)28	33b		היה ארץ שממה
	(נתן)29	33b		היה ארץ שממה
34	(את)4	17b		רדה ב
	24	cf.12		covenant formula
	25	5b		ישב לבטח (בארץ)
	25	6b	*	השבתי חיה רעה
	25a	6b+9a		שלום + ברית
	(הורדתי)26	4a		נתן גש(מי)ם בעתם
	27	4b,20		נתן הארץ יבול
	27	4b,20	*	נתן עץ השדה פרי
	(היה)27	5b		ישב לבטח (בארץ)
	27	13a		to be servant
	27	13b		שבר מוטה על
	28	5b		ישב לבטח (בארץ)
	28	6a		אין מחריד
	30	cf.12		covenant formula
35	(שים)4	31a,33b(היה)		נתן חָרְבָּה
	(נתן)7	33b		היה ארץ שממה
36	3	43b	*	יען וביען
	6	28a		(יסר+) (Yhwh's) בחמה
	9–11	9a	*	ופניתי אליכם...והרביתי
	12(mountain)	22a		שכל (beast)
	13(mountain)	22a		שכל (beast)
	13	38b		devour people
	14(mountain)	22a		שכל (beast)
	14	38b		devour people

Table 1 (cont.)

Ez Chapter	Verse	Lev 26 Verse	Expression
	19(זרה בָּאֲרָצוֹת)	33a	זרה בנוים
	19(פוץ בנוים)	33a	זרה בנוים
	27(בחקים הלך)	3a	בחקות הלך
	28	12	covenant formula
	34	33b	היה ארץ שממה
	35(עָרִים חֲרֵבוֹת)	31a,33b(היה)	נתן חָרְבָּה
	36	36a,39a	שאר
	38(עָרִים חֲרֵבוֹת)	31a,33b(היה)	נתן חָרְבָּה
37	23	12	covenant formula
	26	6b+9a	שלום + ברית
	26(only והרביתי)	9a	ובניתי אליכם...והרביתי
	27(היה + על)	11a	נתן משכן ב
	27	12	covenant formula
38	8	5b	ישב לבטח (בארץ)
	11	5b	ישב לבטח (בארץ)
	14	5b	ישב לבטח (בארץ)
	23	45b	לעיני הגוים
39	6	5b	ישב לבטח (בארץ)
	23	25b	נתן ביד
	23(no מַעַל)	40a	מָעַל מַעַל ב
	26	5b	ישב לבטח (בארץ)
	26	6a	אין מחריד
	26	40a	מָעַל מַעַל ב
	27	45b	לעיני הגוים
44	7	15b,44a	הפר ברית

From Table One, the first cluster of curses can be found in Ez 4–6. Although some references to Lev 26 can be found within Ez 7–13, they are either general expressions depicting the disobedience of the people (e.g. לא בחקים הלך) or merely isolated expressions. A second cluster of curses is found in Ez 14:12–23. Some similarities to Lev 26 are detected in Ez 16, but in general they have less to do with the curses themselves and more with the word "covenant" (e.g. Ez 16:59–63). The same can be said of Ez 17. A third cluster is in Ez 20 which concentrates on the theme of disobedience, acting before the nations and scattering among the nations. The rest of the oracles of judgement against Israel (Ez 21–24) contains only isolated references. Within the oracles against the nations (Ez 25–32), lists of curses are found mostly in Ez 28–30, i.e., in the oracles against Tyre and Egypt. In the oracles of restoration (Ez 33–48), Ez 34:23–31 has a number of references to the blessings in Lev 26. More are found in Ez 36; 37:23–28; 39:21–29.[18] In the following, we will deal with select passages in Ezekiel which contain a cluster of references to Lev 26. We will look at their similarities more closely and the changes made by Ezekiel. Our thesis is that Ezekiel employs the curses and blessings from Lev 26 to convey the message that the curses have come or will certainly come upon the Israelites because of their violation of the covenant, and that in the future restoration, God's blessings will come to them in a covenantal relationship. In this understanding, the first part of Ezekiel (chapters 1–24) is related to the third part (Ez 33–48) at least partly by the use of the curses and blessings theme.[19]

3. Ez 4–6

3.1. Introductory Remarks

Ez 4–5 is a literary unit composed of a series of symbolic actions against Jerusalem, although opinions differ as to whether Ez 3:22–27 or Ez 3:16–27 should be considered as its introduction.[20] Basically it consists of four symbolic actions (4:1–3, 4–8, 9–17; 5:1–4) which begin with the same structural marker, i.e., ואתה followed by an imperative to act (4:1, 4, 9; 5:1).[21] The first interpretation 5:5–6 develops into an oracle of judgement in 5:7–10. This is followed by a three-part proof saying in 5:11–13 composed of accusation, sentence and recognition formula. Two further modified judgement oracles are in 5:14–15 and 16–17 which contain only announcements of punishment without giving any reason.[22] While Ez 4–5 is confined

---

[18] This observation nuances Boadt's claim that "most extensive parallels" between Lev 26 and Ezekiel are found in "Ezekiel 4–7 and 34–37" (1992:719).

[19] See Rendtorff (1993) for other connections.

[20] For the former opinion, see Zimmerli (1979:154), Greenberg (1983a:117). For the latter, see Allen (1994:55).

[21] Against Boadt (1986:188) who claims only three.

[22] Hals (1989:31) explains this by pointing out that the emphasis of Ez 4–5 is on the fact of punishment rather than the reason for it, and some reasons for punishment have been given in 5:5–13.

to Jerusalem, Ez 6 is concerned with the mountains of Israel. This is further extended to the four corners of the land in Ez 7.[23] Ez 6 is a literary unit consisting of two oracles, vv.2–10, 11–14. The beginnings of these two oracles are marked by the messenger formula (vv.3, 11) and a divine command to perform some actions (vv.2, 11). Both of these are extended bipartite proof sayings, i.e., an announcement of judgement with a closing recognition formula extended further with statements of judgement.[24]

3.2. *Ez 4*

In Ez 4, the similarities to Lev 26 appear in vv.16–17, the interpretation of a symbolic action concerning a limited supply of food. If it is linked to the symbolic action in 4:1–3, then it depicts the siege and exile diets. While some scholars regard the section on exile (vv.12–15, especially v.13) as secondary,[25] Block holds that the dichotomy between siege and exile is artificial and suggests the following chiastic structure:[26] A: Siege diet (4:9–11); B: Exilic diet (4:12); B': Interpretation of the exilic diet (4:13); A': Interpretation of the siege diet (4:16–17). The section 4:12–15 on unclean food will be dealt with in a later chapter. Here we will concentrate on vv.9–11, 16–17.

The symbolic action consists of the making of bread from different grains and vegetables (v.9), and the rationing of food and water (vv.10–11). The interpretation of this act, given in vv.16–17, is that food and water will be scarce. More importantly, the scarcity is the result of Yahweh's action for he *will*[27] break the staff of bread in Jerusalem so that food and water will be scarce. The use of the word משקל in connection with the rationing of food is found within the Bible only in Lev 26:26 and Ez 4:10. And the phrase שבר מטה־לחם is found only in Lev 26:26; Ez 4:16: 5:16; 14:13; Ps 105:16.[28] Ez 4:16 closely resembles Lev 26:26, but restricts the breaking of staff of bread to Jerusalem, and adds דאגה (fearfulness) and שממון

---

[23] Boadt 1986:188.
[24] Hals 1989:37–38.
[25] Herrmann 1924:31; Wevers 1969:56; Zimmerli 1979:149–150, 170.
[26] Block 1997:169.
[27] On the use of הנה plus a participle to refer to an event which is imminent or sure to happen, see GKC §116p. Cf. J.-M. §121e.
[28] In Ps 105:16 the phrase refers to the famine at the time of Jacob.

(dismay). The relationship of v.16 to v.17 is not immediately clear due to the use of למען. The usual sense of "in order that"[29] is strange after v.16 which already states the scarcity of food and water and also the people's state of mind. Greenberg's opinion that it should mean "so [= with the result] that" is forced.[30] It is better to read v.17 as the completion of what Yahweh begun in v.16.[31] That is to say, ונמקו בעונם also belongs to Yahweh's purpose apart from his reducing the food supply and that each one be appalled.

The phrase מקק בעונם (niphal) occurs only in Ez 4:17; 24:23 and Lev 26:39. In Leviticus it describes the fate of the exiles in the land of their enemies while in Ez 4:17 it refers to the fate of those who are in a famine situation in Jerusalem. The verb מקק refers to festering of wounds (Ps 38:6) or the decomposition of flesh (Zech 14:12). It therefore denotes the "slow but steady erosion of people's lives".[32] The preposition ב in בעונם is rendered as "in",[33] "because of",[34] or "(caused) by".[35] While the first translation is more literal, the second and the third give a better link between מקק and עונם, i.e., that the Jerusalemites will waste away is due to their עון. This meaning of ב in בעון is also attested elsewhere in Ezekiel (e.g. 18:17, 18, 19, 20; 39:23). The word עון has different meanings: iniquity, guilt, or punishment.[36] Here almost unanimously the translation is "iniquity/guilt/ *Schuld*".[37] Whether one adopts the meaning of "because of" or "(caused) by" for ב, its combination with עון as iniquity or guilt points to a punishment from Yahweh. Thus, vv.16–17 not only mention the coming intervention of Yahweh, but also regard it as his punishing action.

---

[29] BDB 775.

[30] Greenberg 1983a:108.

[31] Zimmerli 1979:150; Allen 1994:51n.17a; Block 1997:189. Another possibility is to read v.17 as the start of a new sentence and take למען as "because". See Keil (1876a:78), Auvray (1957:33), Einheitsübersetzung. Cf. NRSV.

[32] Hartley 1992:468.

[33] Keil 1876a:78; Zimmerli 1979:150; Greenberg 1983a:99; Pohlmann 1996:79.

[34] Herrmann 1924:29; van den Born 1954:44; Auvray 1957:44; Fuhs 1984:36; Brownlee 1986:74; Hartley 1992:453; Block (1997:139), who more specifically takes it as ב *pretti* (i.e., ב of price paid or exchanged).

[35] Allen 1994:48. Cf. Aalders 1955:105 ("veroorzaken").

[36] BDB 730–731; *HALOT* 800.

[37] A notable exception is NRSV which reads "punishment". In addition, note that while RSV/NRSV and Fohrer (1955:29) consistently render עון in 4:4–8 as "punishment" (cf. Brownlee 1986:59), most scholars have the translation "iniquity/ guilt/*Schuld*".

The presence of phrases unique to Ez 4:16–17 and Lev 26 points
to an intertextual relationship. The restriction of the curses to Jerusalem
and the explanation of "break the staff of bread" in Ez 5:16; 14:13
as famine demonstrate that Ezekiel is dependent on Lev 26.[38] Granted
that, the punishment of Yahweh as described in Ez 4:16–17 is linked
to the series of covenantal curses in Lev 26. That is to say, "the
siege is to be Yahweh's punishment of Israel for breaking their
covenant with him by failing to honor its terms".[39] The threat in
Lev 26 will soon become reality. And it is an even more harsh reality. The wasting away will not happen in the exile as in Lev 26,
but even earlier in the siege of Jerusalem.

3.3. *Ez 5*

In Ez 5:1–4 Ezekiel is told to shave some hair and divide it into
three parts as a symbolic action. He has to burn the first one-third,
strike the second third with a sword, take some from last third and
scatter the rest. This is followed by a series of judgement oracles in
vv.5–17.

The passage 5:5–17 has been examined in some detail by Krüger.
He discerns four epochs in the text: (1) Yahweh's original action on
Jerusalem; (2) Israel's guilty action; (3) the judgement action of
Yahweh; and (4) the aftermath of the completion of Yahweh's action.
Yahweh's original action consists in placing Jerusalem in the midst
of the nations (v.5). Then v.6 refers to Jerusalem's breaking of statutes
and ordinances. The connection between vv.5 and 6, according to
Krüger, can be seen by considering Is 2:2–4 and Mi 4:1–4 which
show a link between the spatial position of Jerusalem and its legal
dimension. Decisive for his argument is that Jerusalem appears sometimes as a singular feminine entity and sometimes as plural masculine. The former refers to Jerusalem as a local unit and the latter a
social unit.[40] This "mythical" unity of the local and social dimensions

---

[38] Cf. Reventlow 1962:24–25; Milgrom 1997:60–61; against Levine (1989:281).

[39] Allen 1994:70. Cf. Block 1997:189.

[40] Whether this claim of Krüger is true needs further support. At least in 5:6a
Jerusalem as "she" and therefore a local unit is said to rebel against Yahweh's ordinances and statutes. This rebellious action should more appropriately be said of
Jerusalem as "they" as in 5:6b. Also, the use of both the singular and plural forms
in 5:12 does not seem to warrant a strict differentiation in the denotation of these
forms. Equally problematic is Krüger's interpretation of 5:5 that Jerusalem is at the
geometric centre of the world with nations surrounding it. Talmon (1978:438) holds

belongs to Zion theology. The purpose of the judgement oracles in 5:5–17 is to break up this unity. Even if the mythical unity can be broken by the misconduct of the people, "erfordert der Übergang von der Analyse zur Prognose, vom Schuldaufweis zur Gerichtsankündigung, weitere Regeln, wenn das angekündigte Eingreifen Jahwes nicht nur als *möglich*, sondern . . . als *notwendig* oder mindestens *wahrscheinlich* erscheinen soll".[41] Further consideration leads Krüger to conclude that the human action and divine intervention is correlated in a covenant relation so that Jerusalem's violation of the statutes and ordinances brings about the covenantal curses.[42] The covenant context serves as the backbone for this oracle.

The combination of מֹשְׁפָּטִים ("ordinances") and חֻקּוֹת ("statutes") in v.6a is found mostly in the Priestly source whereas מֹשְׁפָּטִים with חֻקִּים appears more often in Deuteronomy.[43] The rejection of these is expressed by the phrases וּבְמִשְׁפָּטַי מָאָסוּ and חֻקּוֹתַי לֹא־הָלְכוּ בָהֶם in v.6b. The first phrase appears only in Lev 26:43 and Ez 5:6; 20:16 (without בְ in 20:13). The second phrase is found more often. While Krüger regards the plural (masculine) verbal form as deliberately chosen to represent the activity of the Jerusalemites,[44] some take this as one of the many cases in which Ezekiel quotes from Leviticus.[45] In addition, we may point out that the absence of Lev 26:43bβ in Ez 5:6 is an example of the trend that primitive idioms are increasingly dropping out of usage. The point is that "the background underlying *Lev.* xxvi is definitely earlier here than that of Ez".[46] Thus, v.6b, which resembles Lev 26:15 and is the reversal of Lev 26:3, refers to the violation of covenant stipulations.[47] The premise for the dispensing of curses is satisfied.

---

that expressions like בְּתוֹךְ, בְּקֶרֶב and בְ "simply indicate the position of an object within a certain perimeter . . . without necessarily referring to a geometrical or cosmic center".

[41] Krüger 1989:86 (his emphasis).

[42] Krüger 1989:112–113.

[43] Weinfeld 1972:337. Cf. Matties 1990:178.

[44] Krüger 1989:78.

[45] Reventlow 1962:7–9; Greenberg 1983a:111; Rooker 1990:62; Allen 1994:73.

[46] Hurvitz 1982:104–107; quotation from p. 107.

[47] In this connection, we may cite Gerstenberger's opinion on covenant and law (1965:146): "Aber 'Nichthalten der Gebote' meint sofort und radikal: Bruch, Auflösung des Bundesverhältnisses. Der Bund manifestiert sich in den Geboten. Die Gebote, im Kontext des Bundes verstanden, sind Ausdruck der personalen Beziehung, des personalen Treueverhältnisses". Similarly, Hillers (1969:130) also remarks that מֹשְׁפָּט is a "common term for the legal norms demanded by the covenant". Hence, the violation of מֹשְׁפָּט means the breaking of a covenant. See also Block (1997:199).

In Ez 5:7, the second person plural is found instead of the third person plural in v.6. The shift is probably occasioned by a move from presenting the accused with a summary of the charges in vv.5–6 to speaking directly to the accused in what follows. That is, a move from the past conduct to the present judgement.[48] The violation of the statutes and ordinances is again put forward in the accusation (note the use of יען).

The punishment is announced in v.8 by the use of the formula הנני עליך, followed by גם אני. Humbert calls the first formula the "challenge formula" ("Herausforderungsformel") which might have its origin in a challenge-to-a-duel.[49] It almost always has a threatening sense and refers to a threat in the near but not distant future.[50] The second expression is typical of an announcement of punishment expressing correspondence especially in retribution.[51] The phrase "in the sight of the nations" occurs otherwise in Ezekiel in basically two contexts.[52] First, Yahweh's name is not to be profaned before the nations.[53] Second, Yahweh gathers Israel from the nations/Egypt and displays his holiness before the nations/Egypt.[54] In the case of Lev 26:45, it is used in the second context. Here in v.8, the punishing of Israel before the nations is more connected with the first context. While in 20:9, 14, 22 Yahweh does not want his name to be profaned before the nations by leaving Israel unpunished, here he asserts that he will execute punishment on Jerusalem before the nations. Thus, it is only here that the nations will witness God's punishment of Jerusalem.[55]

The concrete punishments are found especially in vv.10, 12, 14–15 and 16–17.[56] The cannibalism mentioned in v.10 often appears in ancient Near Eastern treaty curses.[57] It can also be found elsewhere in the Bible in situations of cities under siege (e.g. Dt 28:53–57; 2 Kg 6:28–29; Jer 19:9; Lam 2:20; 4:10). It also aligns with the

---

[48] Reventlow 1962:9; Krüger 1989:69; Block 1997:197, 200.
[49] Humbert 1933:107.
[50] Humbert 1933:104.
[51] BDB 169.
[52] See further Reventlow (1959) and Joyce (1989:95–97) on the expression.
[53] 20:9, 14, 22; 22:16.
[54] 20:9, 41; 28:25; 36:23; 38:23; 39:27.
[55] Cf. 5:14, 15.
[56] Krüger 1989:96.
[57] Hillers 1964:62–63.

curse found in Lev 26:29a. Ezekiel, however, expands this to a two-sided cannibalism, i.e., parents eating children and children eating parents,[58] in order to illustrate the extraordinary action of Yahweh (v.9). The phrase וזריתי . . . לכל־רוח (v.10b) reappears with little change in v.12 (אזרה לכל־רוח). This echoes the curse אתכם אזרה בגוים in Lev 26:33a while the use of רוח in Ezekiel "was dictated by the symbolism of the context".[59]

V.12 refers back to and interprets the symbolic action in 5:1–4, and at the same time, it makes clear that the symbolic action represents the punishing action of Yahweh by the use of the first personal singular forms.[60] In v.12 the phrase אזרה לכל־רוח is followed by the phrase וחרב אריק אחריהם which is unique to Ezekiel and Leviticus. Moreover, this sequence is found only again in Ez 5:2; 12:14 (cf. Jer 9:15) and Lev 26:33. It is interesting to note that while the subject of the scattering is Ezekiel (in the symbolic action) in 5:2, it is Yahweh in 5:10, 12 and 12:14; and the subject of unsheathing the sword is Yahweh alone in 5:2, 12; 12:14. Thus, in the case of 5:2, there is an intrusion of Yahweh's own action into a command to Ezekiel to perform a sign action. This intrusion has been taken as a gloss or later addition.[61] But it can also be seen as a quotation from Lev 26:33 with minimal changes (from second person plural suffix to third person plural),[62] especially when the same sequence of "scatter-unsheathe the sword" is observed. Lastly, the combination of דבר and חרב here is also found in Lev 26:25 as punishment of those who breach the covenant.[63]

In v.14 ואתנך לחרבה finds a parallel in Lev 26:31 (ונתתי את־עריכם חרבה) or Lev 26:33 (ועריכם יהיו חרבה). The expression נתן (ל)חרבה is found, with an exception, only in Ezekiel and Leviticus.[64] All these expressions refer to the desolation of a city/cities although the word

---

[58] Milgrom 1997:61. This may also be due to Ezekiel's casuistic style (cf. 3:16–21; 18).

[59] Allen 1994:95.

[60] Pohlmann 1996:100.

[61] Herrmann 1924:29; Cooke 1936:58; Fohrer 1955:33; Wevers 1969:57; Zimmerli 1979:151.

[62] Greenberg 1983a:109; Rooker 1990:61–62; Allen 1994:71.

[63] Peels (1995:106) argues that the phrase נקם ברית, which means "the vengeance for/because of the covenant", indicates that vengeance is the fitting response to the breaking of a covenant. Budd (1996:370) suggests that the phrase "has the sense of taking action against a breach of faith and loyalty".

[64] The exception is Jer 25:18.

חרבה can also be applied to countries (e.g. Ez 25:13; 29:20). Here, not only the siege but also the destruction of the city is envisaged. The word משמה in v.15 may reflect שממה in Lev 26:33 by sharing the same root שמם.[65]

A number of parallels occur in vv.16–17. The combination יסף and על, with the former an independent verb, means "add something to something" or "to increase in size or number".[66] It occurs quite often in the Bible but only in Ez 5:16bα and Lev 26:21 (cf. Dt 32:23; Jer 45:3) is Yahweh its subject while referring to the multiplication of disasters. Both texts also have the same עליכם. While the combination is used more generally to refer to God's sevenfold punishment in Leviticus, it is used specifically to refer to famine in Ezekiel.[67] The second person plural masculine form in v.16bα differs from the third person plural masculine form in v.16aα (בהם). Some therefore propose to emend בהם to בכם.[68] However, v.16aα is probably dependent on Dt 32:23–24.[69] These texts have similar contexts and the words רע, הצי and רעב are found in both texts. Interestingly, the persons to whom God's arrows are directed are "they", expressed by בם in Dt 32:23 and also "they", expressed by בהם in Ez 5:16. This supports the view that Ezekiel is dependent on the Deuteronomic text but not the reverse. The "breaking the staff of bread" recalls the curse in Lev 26:26. It is closer (than Ez 4:16) to Lev 26:26 by the use of לכם (which is absent in Ez 4:16).

In v.17 the sending of animals (שלח חיה) which bereave (שכל)[70] echoes Lev 26:22 except that the piel instead of the hiphil of שלח is used in Ezekiel.[71] The phrase הביא חרב על is unique to Lev 26:25 and Ezekiel. In Lev 26:25 the threat of the sword leads the people to withdraw to the cities, but then a pestilence comes to them, and enemies are allowed to take the city. In 5:12, Ezekiel works from Jerusalem to its immediate vicinity and then further outwards. There

[65] Cf. Krüger 1989:97.
[66] André 1990:121, 123.
[67] The LXX has a minus of v.16aβbα. The plus in MT is generally taken as a gloss explaining v.16aα. E.g. Hitzig 1847:39; Zimmerli 1979:153; Allen 1994:54.
[68] Bertholet 1936:20; Zimmerli 1979:153; cf. *BHS* apparatus.
[69] Greenberg 1983a:116; Allen 1994:77; Block 1997:213.
[70] The LXX has τιμωρήσομαί σε ("I will take vengeance on you") for ושכל. This happens also in 14:15. Most scholars retain the MT and even Cornill (1886:207) regards the LXX as a free translation.
[71] See Hillers (1964:54–56) and Wächter (1967:140–145) for the theme in extra-biblical treaties.

is famine and pestilence within the city, the sword in its vicinity and then they are scattered to the nations. It looks as if the famine and pestilence would force the people to escape from the city, but then they will be struck by the sword and scattered. In 5:17 a summary is given of all four punishments: wild animals, famine, pestilence[72] and the sword, all of which can be found in Lev 26:22 (wild animals), 25–26 (famine, pestilence and sword). This occurs also in Ez 14:21. Elsewhere only the trio of famine, pestilence and sword[73] or the wild animals is found. Thus, it seems more likely that Ezekiel is using the Leviticus text by putting these punishments together.

The similarities in both ideas and diction between Ez 5 and Lev 26:21, 22, 25, 26, 29, 31, 33, 43, 45 point to a close relationship between them. From the above observations, it is more likely that Ezekiel is dependent on Leviticus.[74] The rejection of God's statutes in 5:6 shows that the premise for God's curses is satisfied (Lev 26:15) and so God is justified in meting out the curses. Allen is then right to say that "[t]here is a deliberate historicizing of the phases of deterrent curses in terms of an imminent catastrophe".[75] For Ezekiel, God's punishing actions directed to the people for their breach of the covenant are actualised curses known to the Israelites. Thus, "the judgement that will befall Jerusalem is neither arbitrary nor unfair"[76] but is retribution in the strict sense of the word.

3.4. *Ez 6*

In Ez 6:2 שׂים פנים אל may be an allusion to נתן פנים ב (Lev 26:17) which is unique to Leviticus and Ezekiel. Reventlow argues that the two phrases are interchangeable. First, the verb נתן in the formula appearing in Lev 20:3, 6 is replaced by שׂים in Lev 20:5 without any apparent change in meaning. A similar phenomenon can be found in Ez 15:7a (נתן) and 15:7b (שׂים). Second, the נתן formula occurs in Ez 14:8.[77] This seems reasonable except that in both Lev 20:5 and

---

[72] Cooke (1936:62), followed by Allen (1994:77), takes דבר ודם as a hendiadys, meaning "a fatal plague".

[73] E.g. Jer 14:12; 21:7, 9; 24:10; Ez 5:12; 6:11, 12; 7:15. Cf. 2 Sam 24:13.

[74] Similarly, Greenberg (1983a:127) says that "[a]ll indications are of Ezekiel's dependence upon Lev 26".

[75] Allen 1994:78.

[76] Duguid 1999:100.

[77] Reventlow 1962:27–28.

Ez 15:7b, the preposition ב is used instead of אל (על). In addition, we note that both phrases seem to be used in a hostile sense.[78]

The addressee of the oracle is the mountains of Israel (הרי ישראל). This phrase appears 16 times in Ezekiel and only in him.[79] Its reference admits of two possibilities. First, it denotes only the highlands and mountainous area of Israel.[80] Second, it refers to the whole land of Israel.[81] The latter option is more likely because the four-fold addressee given in v.3bα (mountains, hills, ravines and valleys) shows that not just the highlands are intended (cf. 36:4). That the same combination in 36:6 is used in parallel to אדמת ישראל further supports this interpretation. As to its connotation, two aspects can be discerned. First, it emphasises the difference between the Babylonian plains and the more mountainous area of Israel.[82] Second, it connotes the places where "Israel has defiled itself with false worship".[83] A polemic against sacrifices (זבח) on the mountains can be found first in Hos 4:13, and later in Dt 12:2 and Is 65:7.[84] Accompanying these sacrifices is the eating of the meat of the sacrificial animal.[85] This seems to be the reference of the phrase אכל על ההרים,[86] found only in Ez 18:6, 11, 15 and 22:9.[87] That in these Ezekielian texts the action of eating on the mountains is given a negative evaluation shows that Ezekiel is following the tradition of condemning such an illegitimate practice. Ez 6:13 supports this understanding. According

---

[78] Levine 1989:185; Hartley 1992:464. The phrase שים פנים occurs nine times in Ezekiel (6:2; 13:17; 21:2, 7; 25:2; 28:21; 29:2; 35:2; 38:2; cf. 15:7) and always in an oracle of judgement. See also Cooke (1936:68), Cooper (1994:107n.55), Block (1997:34–35), against Aalders (1955:124).

[79] 6:2, 3; 19:9; 33:28; 34:13, 14; 35:12; 36:1(2x), 4, 8; 37:22; 38:8; 39:2, 4, 17. The variation הר(י) מרום ישראל is found only in Ez 17:23; 20:40; 34:14. The singular "mountain of Israel" occurs in Jos 11:16, 21.

[80] Herrmann 1924:43; Taylor 1969:88; Greenberg 1983a:130; Allen 1994:86.

[81] Keil 1876a:94; Wevers 1969:60; Talmon 1978:433; Zimmerli (1979:185) regards it as a synonym for אדמת ישראל; Alexander 1986:775; Hals 1989:39; Vawter and Hoppe 1991:51; Block 1997:221.

[82] Greenberg 1983a:130; Allen 1994:86; Block 1997:221. Note that Israel was known as the people of the mountains (cf. 1 Kg 20:23, 28). See Becker (1971:27).

[83] Boadt (1986:190), citing 6:13; 18:6, 11; 22:9; 32:5–6 as support. But he omits 18:15. And 32:5–6 has nothing to do with Israel. See also Hals (1989:39) and Blenkinsopp (1990:41).

[84] Holladay 1961.

[85] Wolff 1974:86.

[86] Zimmerli 1979:380; Matties 1990:164; Allen (1994:274), citing 1 Sam 9:12–13 as support.

[87] Cf. LXX of Lev 19:26.

to Weinfeld, Ez 6:13 combines the traditions of Hosea (4:13) and Deuteronomy (12:2).[88] If so, then "mountains of Israel" is chosen by Ezekiel in this case probably because of its connotation of false worship. This explains why some curses which have to do with false worship in Lev 26 are used by Ezekiel here.

The phrase אני מביא עליכם חרב in v.3a (like 5:17) is undoubtedly connected to Lev 26:25 as noted above. The use of הנני אני is emphatic,[89] indicating the role of God. The action of God is spelled out further. In v.3b God will destroy[90] the high places (ואבדתי במותיכם) which echoes Lev 26:30aα[1] (והשמדתי את־במתיכם). Ezekiel may have replaced שמד with אבד which he uses more often.[91] In Ez 6:4aα, ונשמו מזבחותיכם lacks a counterpart in Lev 26. The inclusion of the altars here may have to do with its natural association with the cultic high places (במות) on the one hand[92] and with the chapels (המנים)[93] on the other hand.[94] The plural form of מזבח occurs 54 times in the OT. With a few exceptions it is used in the context of idol worship.[95] Outside Ezekiel, when it is qualified by a plural suffix, it appears only in the context of idol worship.[96] The same holds also for Ezekiel (6:4, 5, 6, 13).

The parallel goes further in v.4aβb and Lev 26:30aα[2]β:

ונתתי את־פגריכם על־פגרי גלוליכם	ונתתי את־המניכם	והכרתי את־חמניכם Lev 26:30aα[2]β
והפלתי חלליכם לפני גלוליכם		ונשברו המניכם Ez 6:4aβb

---

[88] Weinfeld 1972:366.

[89] It occurs only in Ez 6:3; 34:11, 20 in the OT. For its emphatic function, see GKC §135e, Muraoka (1985:62, 139).

[90] The LXX has καὶ ἐξολεθρευθήσεται, implying וְאָבְדוּ. This is probably an assimilation to the plural form in v.4. See Allen (1994:82). Cf. Zimmerli 1979:179. Against Cornill (1886:208), Herrmann (1924:41).

[91] אבד occurs 14 times in Ezekiel but שמד only four times.

[92] Zimmerli 1979:186.

[93] The word המנים occurs only eight times in the OT (Lev 26:30; Is 17:8; 27:9; Ez 6:4, 6; 2 Chr 14:4; 34:4, 7). It has been thought to designate a cultic object connected with the altar, and often taken to be incense altars which are placed as ornament on the great altar of burnt offering. E.g. Aalders 1955:125; Taylor 1969:90; Wevers 1969:60; Eichrodt 1970:94; Zimmerli 1979:186; Greenberg 1983a:132; Nielsen 1986:45; Levine 1989:188; Hartley 1992:467; Allen 1994:87. But more recent discussion points to the meaning "chapel". See Fritz (1981), Drijvers (1988), Xella (1991:204–225) and Block (1997:225).

[94] Is 17:8; 27:9; 2 Chr 34:4, 7.

[95] Possible exceptions are Nu 3:31; 23:1, 4, 14, 29; 1 Kg 19:10,14. Cf. Dohman 1997:224.

[96] Ex 34:13; Dt 7:5; 12:3; Jdg 2:2; Jer 17:1, 2; Hos 10:2, 8; 12:12; 2 Chr 34:5.

Both texts mention the destruction[97] of the chapels (חמנים) and the laying of dead bodies before the idols (גלולים).[98] In the case of Ezekiel, there is a change in the addressee in v.4b, from the mountains to the Israelites.[99] The sins of the mountains are actually the sins of the inhabitants. Instead of פגריכם in Lev 26:30, Ezekiel employs חלליכם. The word חלל occurs 35 times in Ezekiel (of which 25 occurrences are plural) and refer to those slain in battle, murdered or executed, and wounded.[100] It is often connected with the sword, meaning slain by the sword.[101] Thus, the use of this word is occasioned by the context, i.e., God's bringing of his sword.[102] That the slain (חלל) should fall (נפל) is common both within and without Ezekiel.[103] Here the hiphil of נפל is used to stress the role of God in bringing down the slain before their idols.[104] Thus, although the niphal forms are used in v.4a, the first person verbal forms in vv.3b and 4b clearly demonstrate that the agent of all these destructions is God.

V.5a provides a closer parallel to Lev 26:30 than v.4b.[105] It serves as an explanation for v.4b, making explicit that the second person suffixes in v.4b refer not to the mountains but to the Israelites.[106] The word פגריכם of Lev 26:30 is replaced by פגרי בני ישראל, and consequently there is a change from the second person suffix of גלוליכם to the third person suffix in Ez 6:5a. Moreover, the use of

---

[97] The word ונשברו in Ez 6:4aβb is not attested in LXX. But Kraetzschmar (1900:65) holds that it is needed for the parallelism and Zimmerli (1979:179) explains its absence as a case of simplification of the Hebrew text.

[98] גלולים occurs 48 times in the OT of which 39 times appear in Ezekiel. Bodi (1993) provides a detailed discussion of the word.

[99] Smend 1880:37; Zimmerli 1979:186; Allen 1994:87–88.

[100] Eissfeldt 1950. Cf. Dommershausen 1980:418–420; Block 1997:227.

[101] E.g. 21:19; 28:23; 30:4, 11, 24.

[102] Cf. Zimmerli 1979:187.

[103] E.g. Dt 21:1; Jdg 9:40; 1 Sam 17:52; Jer 51:4, 47; Ez 6:7; 28:23; 30:4; 35:8.

[104] Cf. Ez 32:12.

[105] That v.5a is not attested in the LXX and the anomalous third person suffix is used cause many scholars to regard v.5a as a gloss depending on Lev 26:30. E.g. Heinisch 1923:49; Herrmann 1924:41; Cooke 1936:69; Simian 1974:117–118; Zimmerli 1979:179; Greenberg 1983a:132; Brownlee 1986:95; Allen 1994:82. Fohrer (1955:37) differs from them in taking it as a gloss from Jer 8:1–2. However, its absence in the LXX can be seen as a result of homoioteleuton (Aalders 1955:125; Block 1997:220). The third person suffix can be a reference to בני ישראל (Becker 1976:136).

[106] Aalders 1955:125; Greenberg 1983a:132; Brownlee 1986:97; Allen 1994:82. Cf. Smend 1880:37.

corpses in v.5a provides a better parallel to the bones in v.5b,[107] which, however, has no parallel in Lev 26. To scatter their bones before the idols serves two purposes. The first is to deny burial, and this would "mar the future of the dead".[108] Although not mentioned in Lev 26, non-burial is taken as a curse.[109] The second is to pollute the cultic places.[110] A similar instance can be found in 2 Kg 23:14 (cf. vv.16, 20). Thus, the people can find no favour before their idols which are powerless to relieve them of their disaster.[111]

While the punishment in vv.3–5 is centred on the high places, idolaters and idols, it is extended to their locations in v.6. The expression "in all your settlements" (בכל מושבותיכם) is a priestly expression[112] not found in Lev 26. While Lev 26:31 has "cities" and "sanctuaries" (מקדשים) in parallel, Ez 6:6 has "cities" and "high places" in parallel. The noun חרבה is used of cities in Lev 26:31 (also 26:33) and its cognate verb תחרבנה is used also of cities in Ez 6:6. While the sanctuaries in Lev 26:31 are the object of שמם (hiphil), the high places in Ez 6:6 are the subject of תישמנה, derived from the rare form ישם,[113] also meaning "to be desolate".[114] Ezekiel's use of במות instead of מקדשים is not haphazard. Among the 30 occurrences of מקדש in Ezekiel, only twice is it plural (21:7; 28:18).[115] While the plural in 21:7 is a plural of extension,[116] that in 28:18 refers to Tyre's sanctuaries. In the other 28 occurrences, the singular form refers to either the Jerusalem temple or the future temple.[117] Thus, Ezekiel's replacement of מקדשים in Lev 26:31 with במות in Ez 6:6 is based on a theological consideration. Introduced by

---

[107] Becker 1976:136.

[108] Toy 1899:107. Cf. Kraetzschmar 1900:66.

[109] See Hillers (1964:68–69) and Fensham (1987:59–60) for examples in ANE treaties and OT.

[110] Kraetzschmar 1900:66. Cf. Wevers 1969:60.

[111] Greenhill 1645–67:155–156.

[112] E.g. Lev 3:17; 7:26; 23:3, 14, 17, 21, 31. See also Reventlow (1962:30n.144), Greenberg (1983a:132), Allen (1994:88).

[113] Cooke 1936:74. There is no need to repoint it as if from שמם (cf. BHS apparatus) since the root ישם is also attested in Ez 12:19; 19:7.

[114] BDB 445.

[115] Thrice if we include 7:24 where the rare מקדשיהם is often repointed as מקדשיהם.

[116] Greenberg (1997:419), citing W.-O'C. §7.4.1c and König's grammar (§260f) as support.

[117] The exception is 11:16 where Yahweh himself becomes a sanctuary to the exiles.

למען, which has a consequential meaning,[118] v.6b further mentions
the destruction of altars, idols and chapels. It should be noted that
the destruction of the idols, which is mentioned here for the first
time, has no counterpart in Lev 26. Following Lev 26, Ezekiel demonstrates in vv.4–5 the impotence of the idols to protect their worshippers. But Ezekiel goes a step further by stating explicitly the
destruction of the idols themselves. The slain are again mentioned
in v.7a. It provides an inclusion to v.6aα, "so that the loss of human
life is widened from shrines to cities".[119] Like 5:17, where the four
agents of God's punishment are put together, 6:6b–7a summarises
together the total destruction of everything and everyone involved
in the illegitimate worship.

Vv.1–7 which constitute the first part of the oracle of this chapter indicate that cultic deviation is the reason for God's punishment.
No explicit terminology on the idea of cultic purity or impurity is
found. Instead, idolatry is seen as the violation of the covenant
between Yahweh and the Israelites. Curses related to idol worship
in Lev 26 are employed and expanded here to show that the breaking of the covenant in terms of illegitimate worship will be repaid
with curses mentioned before (i.e., the destruction of the high places,
altars, idols, chapels, places of worship and the idolaters). It is interesting to note, as pointed out by Allen, that within this oracle, the
links between Ez 6 and Lev 26 "move consecutively through the
catalogue of curses" in Lev 26.[120]

Another series of curses is found in 6:13–14 which forms the conclusion of the second oracle. This second oracle begins in v.11 with
Yahweh commanding Ezekiel to perform three actions concerning
the house of Israel—strike with a hand, stamp his foot, and say
"Aha". This is followed by the triad sword, famine and pestilence
which is first found in Ez 5:12 as punishment applied to Jerusalem
but now extended to the house of Israel. V.13aβ recapitulates vv.4–5
and seems to combine the ideas of the presence of the slain before
the idols and the scattering around the altars. Here the altars are
said to be found everywhere, expressed by means of two pairs of
parallel lines: on every high hill and on all mountain tops, under

---

[118] Greenberg 1983a:133; Allen 1994:81.
[119] Allen 1994:88.
[120] Allen 1994:94.

every green tree and under every leafy oak.[121] These are the places where the people offer pleasing odour (ריח ניחח) to all their idols. The expression ריח ניחח, found often in P to describe God savouring the sacrifices, has in Ezekiel almost exclusively a negative connotation, related to pagan worship (6:13; 16:19; 20:28). Only in 20:41 is it used positively where it appears metaphorically in the context of a future restoration, referring to the people as a pleasing odour. Hurvitz regards this as a tendency to avoid describing God in anthropomorphic terms, thus implying that the Ezekielian text is later than the Levitical one.[122] This can also be seen as an intensification of the curses in Lev 26 from Yahweh's conditional rejection of the "pleasing odour" (Lev 26:31) to unconditional rejection since it is associated with idolatry and is therefore rejected *per se*. In v.14 the devastation of the land harks back to Lev 26:32a, 33b. The combination of the cognate terms שממה and משמה has a superlative sense,[123] meaning total devastation. The comprehensiveness of destruction is further expressed by "in all the settlements", and "from the wilderness to Riblah",[124] i.e., from south to north. Thus, no place can escape God's destruction.

In 6:11–14, the references to Lev 26 also follow the sequence in the chapter (26:30a, 31b, 32a, 33b). An intensification of the sense of the curses in Lev 26 is found not only in the change in meaning of the phrase ריח ניחח, but also in the sixfold use of כל, qualifying the locations of idolatry (four times in v.13 and once in v.14) and the idols. Despite such an intensification, the text shows clearly

---

[121] The second and fourth phrases are absent in the LXX. Some therefore regard these as a later insertion (e.g. Wevers 1969:61; Zimmerli 1979:181). But Cornill (1886:210–211) retains them. Greenberg (1983a:136), followed by Allen (1994:83, 90), regards these as an innovative adaptation from familiar phrases. Block (1997:236) holds that the LXX simplifies the MT.

[122] Hurvitz 1982:53–58. But see Blenkinsopp (1996:513) for a different opinion.

[123] GKC §133 l, followed by Kraetzschmar (1900:70), Greenberg (1983a:137) and Block (1997:236).

[124] There are two textual problems concerning ממדבר דבלתה. First, scholars agree almost unanimously that there is a ד/ר error associated with דבלתה. Second, there are basically two exegetical options regarding the meaning of the phrase. The first one is to keep the Masoretic accentuation and take the phrase a comparative, i.e., "more than the wilderness of Riblah". E.g. Ehrlich 1912:22. The second one is to vocalise the first word as an absolute, i.e., מִמִּדְבָּר, and render it as "from (the) wilderness to Riblah". Both have problems. The first option needs to account for the ה-directive, whereas the second lacks a definite article. But this lack of a definite article can be a case of poetic style and Smend (1880:40) finds similar cases in prose. This option is taken up by most scholars.

that God maintains his covenant in the sense that the breaking of
the covenant will evoke God's reprisal according to the curses of the
covenant.[125] God's retribution is not arbitrary, but keeps to the terms
of the covenant.

3.5. *Summary*

In this section we have examined the similarities between Ez 4–6
and Lev 26 (mainly the section on curses). We found that the curses
in Lev 26 are selected to suit the particular contexts Ezekiel is considering: a limited food supply in the context of the siege of Jerusalem,
being chased by the sword, the scattering and destruction of cities
in the context of war, and the destruction of idolaters, altars and
high places in the context of idol worship. Some modifications and
expansions have been made in view of these contexts. In some cases,
Ezekiel even follows the same order of curses as in Lev 26. But the
different uses of the curse language all point to one idea, namely,
Yahweh will repay the people with covenantal curses for their violation of the covenant (in terms of idolatry and disobedience to
statutes and ordinances). In this understanding, Yahweh's retribution
is juridical because it is meted out according to agreed norms, and
it is just because it is dispensed according to these norms.

4. *Ez 14:12–23*

4.1. *Introductory Remarks*

The first part of Ez 14 is often taken as belonging to the larger unit
12:21–14:11.[126] The rest of Ez 14, i.e., 14:12–23, is demarcated from
what precedes by the word reception formula in v.12 and a difference
in content. While 12:21–14:11 comprises a series of oracles on true
and false prophecy, no such concern can be found in 14:12–23. In
its present context, 14:12–23 exhibits many links with 15:1–8: the
phrase מַעַל מָעַל (14:13; 15:8); the desolation of the land (14:15–16;
15:8); the expression אַף כִּי (14:21; 15:5); and the concern for the

---

[125] Allen 1994:91; Block 1997:239.
[126] This has been noted by Ewald (1880:73), followed by Smend (1880:67), Cooke
(1936:135), Talmon and Fishbane (1975/76:136), Dijkstra (1986:119), Allen (1994:193),
Block (1997:384).

tate of Jerusalem (14:21–23; 15:6–8).[127] These links suggest that 14:12–23 and 15:1–8 may have been composed as a literary unit.

The recognition formula in v.23 shows that 14:12–23 is a proof saying, addressed to Ezekiel's companion exiles. The first half of the unit vv.12–20 is put in a test-case format consisting of four cases, each concerning an agent of punishment. The second half vv.21–23 is introduced by the messenger formula, followed by an announcement of punishment of Jerusalem. This unit concludes with a modified recognition formula.

4.2. *Analysis*

After the word reception formula (v.12), the oracle begins in v.13aα with "if a land sins against me by acting treacherously" (אֶרֶץ כִּי תֶחֱטָא־לִי לִמְעָל־מַעַל). According to Zimmerli, the use of כִּי after the subject indicates the use of sacral-legal language which can be found in the casuistic form of the priestly regulations.[128] The structure of what follows until v.20 needs some comments. The rest of v.13, i.e., וְנָטִיתִי . . . וּבְהֵמָה, can be taken either as a sub-condition of the protasis in v.13aα[129] or as the apodosis of it.[130] The first option is preferred. Firstly, it is grammatically possible to understand the וֹ prefixing the various verbs after אֶרֶץ כִּי as indicating a sub-condition.[131] A similar case is found in Ez 33:2–4 where after the initial כִּי אֶרֶץ, the sequence of verbs prefixed by וֹ forms a sub-condition to the protasis with the apodosis being found without any prefixed וֹ in v.4b. Secondly, taking v.13 in this way, there will be no difficulty in incorporating v.14a as part of the protasis (beginning in v.13aα) with the apodosis given in v.14b.[132] Lastly, note first that the אוֹ in vv.17 and 19 has the meaning "or if",[133] which indicates a second supposition[134]

[127] Mosis 1978:263n.155; Fuhs 1984:79; Brownlee 1986:214; Allen 1994:214; Block 1997:438.

[128] Zimmerli 1954:7; 1979:302; cf. Reventlow 1962:39.

[129] Kraetzschmar 1900:140; Herrmann 1924:87; Noordtzij 1957:154; Greenberg 1983a:256; Allen 1994:211; Block 1997:439.

[130] Brownlee 1986:205; Pohlmann 1996:195. Dijkstra (1986:133) offers a variation: "Stel nu dat een land . . . en ik straf het . . ., zodat ik daar mens en dier uitroei . . .". Cf. LXX.

[131] J.-M. §167e.

[132] Cf. Cooke (1936:156), who claims that the protasis . . . כִּי אֶרֶץ is resumed in v.14. Also Aalders (1955:246).

[133] *DCH* 1:148.

[134] J.-M. §167q, although not all examples given are correct.

or introduces subordinate clauses especially in legal material.[135] The
לו in v.15 is more problematic. Its general use for unreal conditions[136] does not seem to fit the context. Either it is emended to או[137]
or its usage is extended to ordinary cases.[138] In either case, vv.15–16
can still be taken as a sub-condition to the main protasis in v.13aα.[139]
Thus, to regard . . . ונטיתי as a sub-condition gives a better parallel
to the grammatical structure of the other three cases found in vv.15–16,
17–18, 19–20 where the divine action is again taken as a sub-condition and the deliverance of the three men (Noah, Daniel, Job) as
the corresponding apodosis.[140]

The point of the above consideration is that it is *not* the concern
of the text to depict the four cases of divine action as possible consequences for the treacherous action against God. The argument
concerns whether anyone in the land will be saved because of the
presence of the three righteous men under different divine actions.
The relationship between the treacherous action of the land and the
various divine reactions is not argued but assumed.

The four divine reactions find their parallels mainly in the curses
of Lev 26. The first case, to break the staff of bread and send famine
and cut off human and animals, echoes Lev 26:22, 26. The second
case, to send wild animals to bereave the land and make it desolate, parallels Lev 26:22, 33. The third case, to bring a sword, parallels Lev 26:25a. It is followed by a saying of God (חרב תעבר בארץ)
which is the negation of a promise in Lev 26:6 (וחרב לא־תעבר בארצכם).
The absence of a pronominal suffix for ארץ in Ez 14:17 fits its context better. Moreover, this direct speech of God in Ezekiel seems to
be a deliberate negation of the Levitical promise.[141] The last case,
to send pestilence, corresponds to Lev 26:25. The order of this combination, i.e., famine, wild beasts, sword and pestilence, differs from
that in Lev 26, i.e., wild beasts, sword, pestilence and famine. Although
Lev 26 has the idea of famine (v.26), the word רעב is not used.
Ezekiel supplies the word and places it in the first position, and then

---

[135] W.-O'C. §39.2.6b.
[136] GKC §159l, x, y; W.-O'C. §38.2e; J.-M. §167f.
[137] Cornill 1886:254; Cooke 1936:156; Zimmerli 1979:310; Allen 1994:212.
[138] Greenberg 1983a:258; Block 1997:439.
[139] Against Aalders (1955:247), who takes v.15 as the start of a second case
whereas v.13 starts the first case with כי.
[140] Cf. Joyce 1989:71.
[141] Cf. Milgrom 1997:59.

adds the הכרית formula to the combination (vv.13, 17, 19, 21).[142] Another change made by Ezekiel is found in the initial protasis which has a parallel in Lev 26:40 (במעלם אשר מעלו־בי). Thus, Ezekiel takes over the curses and blessings from Lev 26 and reworks them in the form of a casuistic case. The connection between acting treacherously and the consequential divine reaction is simply assumed. And then in v.21 the quaternary is explicitly said to be four deadly judgements (ארבעת שפטי הרעים), applied to Jerusalem. In connection with the word מעל, we may add the observation that Lev 26:40–41 seems to imply a causal link between the act of מעל (as an example of עון) and the exile, and this link is made explicitly in Ez 39:23.

Although the casuistic form may give the impression that a general case is discussed and then applied to Jerusalem in v.21, it is not really so. Firstly, Jerusalem is not a country (ארץ) in the strict sense of the word. Secondly, in the rest of Ezekiel the term מעל is used only of Israel/Israelites (15:8; 17:20; 18:24; 20:27; 39:23; 39:26).[143] The term basically refers to a violation of Yahweh's rights, especially in sancta trespass and oath violation.[144] In particular, in Lev 26:40 it refers to the violation of the covenant between Yahweh and Israel. The taking over of this Levitical passage and making it the basic protasis here points out that the prophet has Israel in mind.[145] Thirdly, the use of diction and ideas from Lev 26 again stresses the covenantal relationship between Israel and Yahweh. Fourthly, the use of אף כי, meaning "all the more/less",[146] in v.21 does not emphasise that it is Jerusalem which will suffer more than the hypothetical nation mentioned previously, but that Jerusalem will suffer more when all four punishments are applied to it instead of any one of these four. The concern of the oracle remains Israel/Jerusalem throughout. Lastly, Joyce notes that Old Testament prophets in general are concerned less with abstract theory and more with concrete situations. The legal case format is used here as a "teaching technique". The point of the oracle is to tell the Israelites that the sins

---

[142] According to Milgrom (1997:59), the absence of the הכרית formula in connection with the wild animals, in contrast to its presence in Lev 26:22, is more logical and therefore shows a reworking of the Levitical material by Ezekiel.

[143] Bertholet 1897:75; Aalders 1955:245; Allen 1994:217.

[144] Milgrom 1976a:16–21.

[145] Cf. Duguid 1999:193.

[146] GKC §154a rem.1(c). Cf. Fishbane 1985:420n.9.

of Israel are so great that punishment is imminent and thorough.[147] Thus, this oracle conveys the idea that Jerusalem, because of treachery against Yahweh, will be punished by actualising the covenantal curses. The punishment will not be averted by the presence of some righteous persons.

4.3. *Summary*

In Ez 14:12–23 the four possible divine punishments are put as sub-conditions for the basic protasis "if a land sins against me by acting treacherously". The basic protasis and the four punishments employ diction and ideas from Lev 26, especially the curses, although not confined to them. The quotation of a divine saying in v.17, which is the negation of a promise in Lev 26, demonstrates that Ezekiel is also aware of the promises in Lev 26. The framework of Lev 26 in which curses are consequential to treacherous actions against God is taken over by Ezekiel and applied to Jerusalem. The fate of Jerusalem will be dictated by this rule. The presence of any righteous person, even if it has any, will not be able to avert its fate (cf. 1 Sam 2:25). The oracle is based on the presupposition that a breach of the covenant will inevitably bring upon Israel the covenantal curses.

5. *Ez 34:23–31*

5.1. *Introductory Remarks*

Ez 34 is a literary unit independent from Ez 33 and 35. The first major subunit runs from v.2 to v.16. The accusation of the shepherds in vv.2–6 (as a woe oracle) is followed by an announcement of punishment, introduced by לכן in vv.7, 9. This is followed by an oracle of salvation, introduced by the explanatory כי and the messenger formula in v.11, where God will be the shepherd of his flock (vv.11–15). V.16 is a transitional verse, moving from vv.11–15 to v.17. Thus, vv.2–16 is both an oracle of judgement and an oracle of salvation. Willmes calls this type of oracle "differenzierende Prophezeiungen".[148] The second subunit extends from v.17 to v.24. The

---

[147] Joyce 1989:74.
[148] Willmes 1984:259–268; 1986.

dominant theme is the judgement between sheep and sheep (vv.17, 20, 22). There is a minor break between v.22 and v.23, but the absence of a concluding formula in v.22 and an introductory formula in v.23 suggests reading vv.23–24 with what precedes.[149] The last subunit, vv.25–31, which maintains some of the shepherd language,[150] is a proof saying. It contains a series of (covenantal) promises similar to those of Lev 26:4–13. Allen detects a double scheme within this unit: wild animals (vv.25aβ, 28aβ), fertility (vv.26b–27aαβ, 29abα) and the nations (vv.28aα, 29bβ).[151] This oracle ends properly at v.30 with a combination of three formulae: recognition formula, covenant formula and the divine saying formula. V.31 is an amplification which seeks to draw together the themes in vv.25–30 and the shepherd language in vv.2–24.[152]

5.2. *Analysis*

In this section, we will not dwell on the relationship between Ez 34 and Jer 23:1–8; 30:8–11 which has already been dealt with by others.[153] The unit vv.25–31 is filled with covenantal themes. The phrase כרת ברית implies the making of a new covenant instead of the confirming of an old covenant. Yahweh will make a covenant of peace with[154] the flock/people.[155] The expression "covenant of peace", because of its paucity within the OT,[156] is probably not a fixed term.[157] This covenant "inaugurates a relation of שלום"[158] between

---

[149] Hossfeld 1977:253; Zimmerli 1983:212–213; Dijkstra 1989:113; Krüger 1989: 453–455; Greenberg 1997:706. Against Allen (1990:159) and Westermann (1991:169). Maarsingh (1991:36) seems to be the only one who breaks after v.23.

[150] Levin 1985:221; Allen 1990:163; Greenberg 1997:707. Against Zimmerli 1983:220; Hals 1989:249.

[151] Allen 1990:160–161.

[152] Herrmann 1965:269–270; Allen 1990:159.

[153] Miller 1955:106; Levin 1985:218–219; Vieweyer 1993:98–104.

[154] The use of ל following כרת to indicate the party of the covenant is common in MT. Greenberg (1997:702) remarks that "[a]s a rule the subject of *krt byrt l-* is a superior who obligates himself (grants terms) to another". See also Weinfeld (1977:259). Against Kraetzschmar (1900:244) who incorrectly interprets להם as "for them" but not "with them".

[155] The LXX reads τῷ Δαυιδ for the Hebrew להם. It may have been influenced by 2 Sam 7 (cf. Cornill 1886:404) or Ps 89:4, 29 (cf. Jahn 1905:240). See also Greenberg (1997:702).

[156] Only in Ez 34:25; 37:26. Similar expressions are in Nu 25:12 and Is 54:10. See also Mal 2:5.

[157] Stendebach 1995:36; against von Rad 1977:403.

[158] Baltzer 1971a:161; von Rad 1977:403.

Yahweh and the people and hence the word "peace" indicates "the reality of which a covenant in any case consists".[159] It is, nevertheless, concretised in some consequences for Israel.[160] First, the evil animal (חיה רעה), used as an instrument of God's punishment in Ez 5:17; 14:15, 21,[161] is removed from the land (probably of Israel). The wilderness (מדבר) and the forest (יער), normally for animals but not human habitation,[162] become a place where the sheep/people can dwell securely (לבטח)[163] and sleep. The same idea recurs in v.28 although there "the animal of the land" (חית הארץ)[164] is mentioned. This may correspond to the danger noted in vv.5, 8 where "the animal of the field" (חית השדה) is mentioned.[165] Second, the fruitfulness of the land is granted (vv.26–27a). This idea, which reappears in the negative statement "they shall no more be carried off by famine in the land" in v.29bα, corresponds to the good pasture in vv.14, 18.[166] The third element of the covenant is freedom from the dangers posed by the nations: being the plunder (בז) (v.28aα, which corresponds to vv.7, 22) and bearing the reproach (נשא כלמה) (v.29bβ) of the nations. Being slaves (v.27bβ) can also be put under this category. These three aspects are related to the main theme of being safe and secure (לבטח in vv.25, 27, 28 and אין מחריד in v.28). Lastly, in vv.30–31 the covenant idea is found through the use of the covenant formula.

In this text, the covenant of peace[167] denotes for the sheep/people a future Yahweh-given state of security and freedom from the

---

[159] Zimmerli 1983:220. Cf. Taylor 1969:224. Commenting on a similar expression in Is 54:10, Schoors (1973:136) holds that the genitive שלום is "a *genitivus appositionis* or *epexegeticus*, defining the true content of the covenant".

[160] Baltzer 1971a:161.

[161] The phrase occurs otherwise in Gen 37:20, 33; Lev 26:6.

[162] For the wilderness, see Talmon (1997:101); for the forest, see Ps 50:10; 104:20; Is 56:9; Jer 5:6; 12:8; Hos 2:12; Am 3:4.

[163] Note that in the Exodus tradition in Ps 78, Yahweh led out his people like a flock (צאן), guided them in the wilderness, and led them securely (לבטח) so that they did not fear (vv.52–53). Thus, the *shepherd* language is not out of place in this Ezekielian passage.

[164] The expression occurs in Gen 1:24, 25, 30; 9:2, 10; Ez 29:5; 32:4; 34:28; Ps 79:2; Job 5:22. This may be a priestly term.

[165] This is a more common expression and occurs 31 times in the MT.

[166] Allen 1990:163.

[167] Batto (1987) provides a study on the mythological background of the covenant of peace, though one may question if his conclusion can be applied to Ez 34. By referring to the basic meaning of שלם, Gerleman (1973) regards ברית שלום as alluding to events in the past that need compensation. Apart from Barr's criticism (1961:107–160) on the undue use of etymological meaning, see also the criticism of Renner (1985) and Jarick (1986).

dangers posed by wild animals, famine and the nations, while recognising a covenantal bond between them and Yahweh.[168]

5.3. *Ez 34:23–31 and Lev 26*

In this section we will concentrate on the similarities and differences between this unit and Lev 26. A glance at Table One above indicates that Ez 34:23–31 relates closely to Lev 26:4–6, 9, 12–13. The making of a covenant of peace in Ez 34:25 has no direct parallel to Lev 26, but it seems to combine Lev 26:6 (שלום) and 9 (ברית). In doing so, the ונתתי in Lev 26:6 is changed to וכרתי in Ez 34:25.[169] However, while peace is a consequence of keeping the covenant in Lev 26, it is the content of the covenant in Ez 34.

The phrase והשבתי חיה רעה מן־הארץ (Lev 26:6) is found exactly in Ez 34:25a. Note that the expression חיה רעה occurs only in Gen 37:20, 33 outside these two verses. The image of sheep requires the change from dwelling securely "in their land" (בארצכם) in Lev 26:5b to dwelling in both the desert and forest in Ez 34:25b and also "on their earth" (על־אדמתם) in Ez 34:27a. The sending of the rain followed by its consequences (i.e., trees bear fruit and earth yields produce) is found in both Ez 34:26b–27a and Lev 26:4. A negation of such fruitfulness appears as a curse in Lev 26:20b. The idea of the breaking of the bar of the yoke and being enslaved (עבד ב) no more is found in both Ez 34:27b and Lev 26:13. While in Leviticus the idea is related to the past Exodus event and hence the use of the *wayyiqtol* forms וָאֶשְׁבֹּר and וָאוֹלֵךְ after the *qatal* הוֹצֵאתִי, Ezekiel changes it to refer to a future event.[170] The phrase וְאֵין מַחֲרִיד appears in Ez 34:28 and Lev 26:6a. In both passages, the covenantal formula serves as a climactic conclusion to the salvific actions of God.[171]

Animals, an agent of punishment elsewhere in Ezekiel, are here banished by God. Another agent, the sword, in the sense of war and being attacked by the nations, will not happen anymore. This corresponds in meaning to Lev 26:6b. The third agent, famine, will

---

[168] Cf. Ohnesorge 1991:414.

[169] Milgrom 1997:58.

[170] Against Grünwaldt (1999:351), who holds that the past tense in Leviticus means that the *exile* was over for the author, and hence the Levitical passage is later and based on Ezekiel.

[171] The dependence of Ezekiel on Leviticus has been argued by Reventlow (1962:44–50), Baltzer (1971a:158), Hossfeld (1977:273–276) and Milgrom (1997:57–59).

not appear because of the fruitfulness of the land. Interestingly, there is no mention of the fourth agent, pestilence, which often appears in Ezekiel. But this absence finds a parallel in the blessing section in Lev 26 which again has no reference to pestilence which only appears in the list of curses (26:25).

Some differences between Ez 34:23–31 and Lev 26 can be found. Lev 26:5abα has no echo in Ez 34 probably because it does not fit the sheep metaphor. Although the overthrow of enemies is mentioned in Lev 26:7–8, it is not found in Ez 34. This is not surprising in view of the exilic situation of the prophet[172] and the sheep metaphor. The blessing of "be fruitful and multiply" in Lev 26:9a is not reflected in Ez 34, but it is echoed in Ez 36:9–11 and partly in Ez 37:26. Of course, there is no need for Ezekiel to employ all the blessings in Lev 26, as he does not do so for the curses. The omission of any blessing from Lev 26 is less significant than the use of a number of them. This consideration serves to buttress the argument that Ezekiel is drawing from the blessing-curse theme which is part and parcel of the covenantal framework in Lev 26.

The most significant difference between Ezekiel and Leviticus is that the blessings found in Ez 34 are not contingent upon the obedience of the people as in Lev 26. This is probably a modification introduced by Ezekiel. The blessings as the content of the covenant of peace are promised by God unilaterally without regard to the people's conduct. It is an unconditional action of God.[173] This is related to the idea of "radical theocentricity" in Ezekiel.[174] One example is Yahweh's gift of a new heart and a new spirit to the people in Ez 11:19, the result of which, indicated by למען and stated in 11:20, is that the people will walk in God's statutes and keep his ordinances and do them (cf. 36:26–27).[175] This is precisely the same condition which the Israelites have to fulfil in order to obtain the blessings of God in Lev 26, with only the slight difference in the use of משפטים in Ez 11:20 and מצות in Lev 26:3.[176] In this case, it is God himself

---

[172] Greenberg (1997:707, 760) suggests that the restored Israel is under divine protection (e.g. Ez 38–39) and hence promises like "victory in war" found in Leviticus need not be mentioned.

[173] Cf. Baltzer 1971a:161.

[174] See Joyce (1989:89–124).

[175] More recently, Mein (1996:174–207) explains this human passivity in terms of the social location of the exiles.

[176] While the word משפטים appears in Lev 26:15, מצות never occurs in Ezekiel.

who enables the people to fulfil the condition for the blessings. And in the case of Ez 34, the condition is not even mentioned.

5.4. *Summary*

A consideration of Ez 34:23–31 shows that Ezekiel not only utilises the curse section of Lev 26, but also its blessing section. Not only that, Ezekiel also places the blessings within a covenantal frame-work—the blessings are the content of the covenant of peace. It consists mainly in security from dangers posed by wild animals, famine and the nations. This buttresses the argument that Ezekiel has the covenantal framework in mind, being seen in both his oracles of judgement and salvation. His main departure from Lev 26 is that the blessings are not dependent on the conduct of people but only on the grace of God.

6. *Ez 37:24–28*

6.1. *Introductory Remarks*

Ez 37 is composed of two oracles. The first oracle (vv.1–14) is concerned with the dry bones in the valley and the second (vv.15–28) with the reunification of Israel and Judah.[177] After the word reception formula in v.15, the prophet is commanded to perform a symbolic action (vv.16–17). A hypothetical question from the audience and a command to answer with the messenger formula lead to a first explanation of the symbolic action (vv.18–19). This explanation, which is put in metaphorical language, is further clarified.[178] The clarification extends to at least v.22.[179] V.22 flows into v.23 with a series of "no longer" (vv.22bα, 22bβ, 23a).[180] The unit is concluded with the covenant formula. The expression "my servant David" forms an inclusion for vv.24–25. While the idea of "one shepherd" in v.24a links vv.24–25 to what precedes, v.24b is often taken with what

---

Matties (1990:177) suggests that the absence of מצות in Ezekiel may have to do with his deliberate avoidance to identify with that (Deuteronomic) tradition.

[177] Barth (1977) argues for the thematic unity of the chapter.

[178] Allen 1990:191; Greenberg 1997:758.

[179] Bertholet 1936:129; Fohrer 1955:210.

[180] Hals 1989:272–273. Cf. Greenberg 1997:758.

follows.[181] But it is also possible to read it with v.24a because the pattern of external (v.22) and internal conditions (v.23) of Israel is repeated in v.24a and 24b respectively,[182] and v.24 hints that one good shepherd (v.24a) will lead the people to obey God's laws (v.24b).[183] Vv.26–27 is again a unit demarcated by an inclusion of theme of covenant: the making of a covenant in v.26aα and the covenant formula in v.27aβb. To regard vv.25–28 as a section because it deals with the external condition of the restored Israel[184] may not be justified, although it is dominated by the fivefold use of עולם. The whole oracle concludes with the recognition formula, thus showing that it is a proof saying.[185] We can divide this unit as v.15, vv.16–17, vv.18–19, vv.20–28 (vv.20–23, 24–25, 26–27, 28).

6.2. *Analysis*

After the symbolic action of joining together the two sticks bearing the names "Judah" and "Joseph" into one stick (vv.16–17) and its metaphorical explanation (vv.18–19), a more concrete explanation is given. The Israelites will be gathered from the nations and brought to their own land. There they will be made one nation and have one king over them. The idea of oneness dominates v.22. The sequence of gathering the people and then appointing one leader here finds a parallel in 34:11–24.[186] After that, the idea of cleansing appears in v.23, which occurs already in more detail in 36:25–27. Yahweh will save them and cleanse them, and they will be his people and he their God.

V.24 reverts back to v.22, but now the future one king is called "David". This designation of a future king finds a precedent in Hos 3:5 and Jer 30:9. But as in 34:23–24, this Davidide is qualified as both a servant and a shepherd. This qualification is perhaps added to downplay the political tone associated with the kingship,[187] although one must not overlook that in v.24 the future ruler will be a king over them (עליהם). Similarly in 34:23, the future shepherd, also

---

[181] Zimmerli 1983:272; Allen 1990:192. Cf. Ohnesorge 1991:347.

[182] Krüger 1989:439. Cf. Klein 1988:152.

[183] Schumpp 1942:191; Greenberg 1997:757.

[184] Krüger 1989:439. Cf. Herrmann 1965:286–287.

[185] Zimmerli 1983:272; Hals 1989:273; against Allen 1990:191.

[186] Greenberg 1997:755–756.

[187] Allen 1990:194; Ohnesorge 1991:386.

called David, will be set over the people (עליהם). But it is added immediately in 34:24 that this David will be a prince among the people (בתוכם). In both Ez 34 and 37, this relationship of David with the people "involves authority as well as service".[188] V.24b can be seen as the consequence of v.24a, which goes back to the "deuteronomistic conception of the Davidic dynasty as model and monitor of the covenant law"[189] (cf. 2 Kg 23:3). The king guarantees the obedience of the people which shows that the condition for blessing is fulfilled (cf. Lev 26:3).[190] This may lead to v.25a where obedience to Yahweh's statutes and ordinances[191] will enable the people to dwell on the land. Such a sequence is also found in 36:27–28. This dwelling is further qualified as an everlasting one (עד־עולם) in v.25bα. Jenni suggests that עד־עולם, in contrast to לעולם, "almost always indicates successive temporal continuation in the future".[192] This understanding fits the context well. V.25bβ forms an inclusion with v.24a, but with two differences. First, David is no longer called a king, but a prince (נשׂיא).[193] Second, he is said to be a prince forever (לעולם). This idea of the eternity of the Davidic dynasty goes back to 2 Sam 7.

Yahweh is the subject of a series of verbal clauses in vv.26–27. This unit opens with the making of a covenant of peace in v.26aα and concludes appropriately with the covenant formula in v.27aβb.[194] What lies between gives the content of the covenant.[195] The covenant of peace, found in Ez 34:25, reappears here and is further called an eternal covenant. It contains statements that Yahweh will establish the people,[196] multiply them (v.26bβ), and put his sanctuary (מקדש)

---

[188] Duguid 1994:49. *Contra* Hals 1989:254.

[189] Allen 1990:194. See also Bunn (1971:344), Maarsingh (1991:93), Greenberg (1997:757).

[190] Garscha 1974:227.

[191] The combination of הלך משפט and שמר חקה is unique in the Bible.

[192] Jenni 1997:855.

[193] On the titles נשׂיא and מלך in Ezekiel, see Zimmerli (1983:277–279) and Duguid (1994:11–33).

[194] Fuhs 1988:213.

[195] Toy 1899:173; Alexander 1986:927; Fuhs 1988:213.

[196] The word ונתתים is not attested in the LXX and Syriac. The LXX has a further minus of והרביתי אותם. Some suggestions have been made: (1) The whole phrase is deleted as secondary by Cornill (1886:420–421), Heinisch (1923:1923:180), Fohrer (1955:211). Some others delete only the word ונתתים. E.g. Bertholet 1897:187; Schumpp 1942:186; Einheitsübersetzung. (2) Kraetzschmar (1900:254) proposes to read ונתתים as ונטעתים on the basis of Am 9:15 and Jer 24:6, and keeps the rest. Note that the verb נטע occurs only twice in Ezekiel (28:26; 36:36). (3) Bertholet

in their midst forever (v.26bγ). This last idea is put slightly differently in v.27aα as "my dwelling place (מִשְׁכָּנִי) shall be over them". This gift of Yahweh's sanctuary among the people (בְּתוֹכָם) implies his presence among them,[197] and this presence is forever. The word מִשְׁכָּן is frequently used by P to refer to the dwelling-sanctuary in the wilderness period.[198] But here it seems to refer to the temple which is situated higher than its surroundings, and hence "above them" (עֲלֵיהֶם).[199] Here the juxtaposition of מִקְדָּשׁ and מִשְׁכָּן[200] and also that of מִשְׁכָּן and עַל are unique in the Bible.

The recognition formula in v.28 concludes the proof saying. The subject of "to know" is the nations who will know that it is Yahweh who sanctifies Israel.[201] The verb קָדַשׁ carries with it the meaning of

---

(1936:128) emends the text to וְהִנַּחְתִּים without giving any reason. (4) Herrmann (1924:234) suggests that אוֹתָם וּנְתַתִּים is a doublet of אוֹתָם וְנָתַתִּי. His opinion is endorsed by Cooke (1936:406) and Zimmerli (1983:270–271). (5) Perles (1911/12:121) suggests that (i) וְהִרְבֵּיתִי אוֹתָם was first added to the text after יִהְיֶה אוֹתָם on the basis of Jer 30:19; Ez 36:10, 11, (ii) a second scribe then made a correction by writing on the margin ס֗ וְנָתַתִּי, meaning the reader should jump over וְהִרְבֵּיתִי אוֹתָם to וְנָתַתִּי אֶת מִקְדָּשִׁי, (iii) this gloss was then contracted to one word and entered into the text. (6) Parunak (1978:437) explains the minus in Greek as a result of homoioteleuton in אוֹתָם with the preceding and homoioarcton in וְנָתַתִּי with what follows. (7) Allen (1990:191) opines that an original text אוֹתָם וְהִרְבֵּיתִי אוֹתָם וְנָתַתִּי lost וְהִרְבֵּיתִי אוֹתָם by parablepsis, a text attested by the LXX. A correction וְהִרְבֵּיתִי אוֹתָם וְנָתַתִּי was then made in the margin, which later entered into the text. Then the first וְנָתַתִּי was adapted by adding the pronominal suffix. (8) The Targum interprets וְנָתַתִּים as "and I will bless them", probably inspired by 34:26. This is followed by Ehrlich (1912:136), RSV and NRSV. (9) Barthélemy (1992:300–301) argues on the basis of 17:22 and 34:26 that "l'emploi du verbe נתן au sens de 'établir en une position et un lieu bien choisis' était caractéristique du livre d'Ézéchiel". Cf. Vulgate ("fundabo eos"). See also Fisch (1950:252), Aalders (1957:208), Auvray (1957:142). In the absence of clear evidence supporting any emendation or the different textual history suggested above, we adopt Barthélemy's proposal.

[197] Bettenzoli (1979:147) interprets מִקְדָּשׁ as the sacral laws whose obedience makes possible Yahweh's presence among his people. This is at odds with the use of the word elsewhere in Ezekiel and is not deducible from the context here.

[198] Kellermann 1986:68; Hulst 1997:1329.

[199] Bertholet 1897:186; Cooke 1936:403; Wevers 1969:198; Eichrodt 1970:511–512 (but the German original "über ihnen ragen" is mistranslated as "shall be with them"); Allen 1990:191; Maarsingh 1991:95. Against (1) the translation of עַל as "bei/bij" by Herrmann (1924:234), van den Born (1954:222), Fohrer (1955:211) and Zimmerli (1983:277); (2) the interpretation of מִשְׁכָּן by Hitzig (1847:287) as Yahweh's heavenly dwelling, by Bettenzoli (1979:147) as the basic structure of the people's life, and by Davidson (1916:296), Aalders (1957:208) and Greenberg (1997:757–758) as Yahweh's protective presence.

[200] Cf. Ex 25:8.

[201] For this idea, see also Ex 31:13; Lev 20:8; 21:8, 15, 23; 22:9, 16, 32; Ez 20:12; 37:28.

selection.[202] In this case, it is clearly the presence of Yahweh's sanctuary which sanctifies the Israelites. This presence is no longer seen as part of God's promise but already as a result of this promise, hence the change from נתן מקדש to היה מקדש.[203]

While the covenant of peace in Ez 34:25 is concerned with security from dangers posed by wild animals, famine and the nations, in Ez 37:26 it is concerned with the establishment and multiplication of the people, and more importantly, with Yahweh's presence as exhibited in the presence of the physical sanctuary among/over the people. The possession of the sanctuary is, therefore, better seen as the content of the covenant than as the guarantee for the covenant of peace.[204] Also, to treat vv.25–26 as a sequence of four promises, all characterised by "forever" with the last one being the most significant,[205] is dubious. The covenant of peace is granted after the people, following the lead of the future king, obey the ordinances. While the blessings in Ez 34:25 are given unconditionally, here the conditions are explicitly stated to be fulfilled.

6.3. *Ez 37:24–28 and Lev 26*

In this unit, parallels to Lev 26 are limited to a few, but important, instances. In the last section, we have briefly mentioned the omission of some blessings from Lev 26 in Ez 34:23–31. Some of these, however, appear in Ez 37:24–28. The first one is God's multiplying the people, found in a longer form in Lev 26:9aβ (והפריתי אתכם והרביתי אתכם) and a shorter one in Ez 37:26bα (והרביתי אותם). Another important one is the presence of Yahweh among the people:

ונתתי משכני בתוככם	Lev 26:11a
ונתתי את־מקדשי בתוכם	Ez 37:26bβ
והיה משכני עליהם	Ez 37:27aα
(בהיות מקדשי בתוכם	Ez 37:28b)

Actually, Ez 37:26bβ–27 is almost a duplicate of Lev 26:11–12 in which God's presence is followed by the covenant formula but for the absence of two consecutive phrases in Lev 26:11b–12aα. This absence is readily explained by Hurvitz as the tendency to drop

---

[202] Taylor 1969:241; Wevers 1969:198; Bunn 1971:344; Zimmerli 1983:277.
[203] Ohnesorge 1991:399–400.
[204] Bertholet 1936:129; Bunn 1971:344.
[205] Zimmerli 1983:276–277; Klein 1988:152–153.

primitive idioms and anthropomorphism regarding God.[206] Relevant for us is the conclusion that the Ezekielian text is later than the Levitical text. Thus, apart from the ideas that food is overstocked (Lev 26:5a, 10) and enemies are overthrown (Lev 26:7–8), basically all the blessings of Lev 26 are paralleled in Ez 34 and 37. But the first idea as an extension of the blessing that the earth will be fruitful (Lev 26:4) is already taken up in Ez 34:27. The second idea does not seem to suit the exilic context well. Thus, it seems that Ez 37:26–27 deliberately fills the gaps left by Ez 34.[207]

Two more observations can be made. First, the filling in of the gaps does not only happen in Ez 37, but already in Ez 36. In Lev 26:9aα we find ופניתי אליכם which appears exactly in Ez 36:9. The consequence of this favourable action of God, stated in Lev 26:9aβ, is found in Ez 36:10–11 in which we find the same idea and use of the same verbs (והרביתי vv.10, 11; ורבו v.11; ופרו v.11). In addition, there is a reversal of the curse of desolation of cities in Ez 36:10. Second, as in Ez 34 the blessings are the result of God's actions alone. We mentioned above that the sequence of obeying the statutes and ordinances, followed by the dwelling on the land, is found also in Ez 36:26–28. There the foundation of the obedience is God's gift of a new heart and spirit. Here this gift is not mentioned; it is rather seen as the consequence of the rule of the future Davidide who will be installed by God. The point is again that while curses will be dispensed when the people break the covenant, blessings will be given without regard to the conduct of the people, or, to be more precise, the people will be enabled by God so that they can meet the condition for the blessings.

6.4. Summary

Most of the blessings in Lev 26 but not in Ez 34:23–31 are found in Ez 37:24–28. Thus, Ez 37:24–28 supplements Ez 34:23–31 regarding the list of blessings. Like Ez 34:23–31, Ez 37:24–28 also places these blessings within the covenant of peace. In this case, they have to do mainly with the multiplication of people and the presence of Yahweh among his people. Following the lead of the future leader

---

[206] Hurvitz 1982:102–107.
[207] See Baltzer's synopsis of texts from Lev 26, Ez 34 and 37 (1971a:156–157). Cf. Allen 1990:194.

David, the people will obey Yahweh's statutes and ordinances. Thus, this fulfils the condition for God's blessings which actually follows in the text. In this case, that they can fulfil this condition is seen as the result of God's initiative.

7. *Conclusion*

In this chapter we have demonstrated that covenant plays a role in Ezekiel's idea of retribution through analysing his use of the language of curses and blessings. While it is true that in these instances in Ezekiel, the judgement or salvation are never literally claimed as curses or blessings respectively,[208] they are undoubtedly so. In Lev 26 the covenant forms the framework for the blessings and curses—the keeping of the covenant in terms of doing God's statutes and ordinances will be rewarded with blessings, and the failure to do so will be repaid with curses. By employing diction and ideas from Lev 26, Ezekiel presupposes and invokes the covenantal framework. His use of the curse language from Lev 26 is sometimes rather general, but more often it is appropriate to the situation he is presenting. For the former case we may consider Ez 14:12–23. For the latter case one may note the curse of "breaking the bread of staff", cannibalism, the sword, and pestilence which all suit well the situation of the siege of Jerusalem; the curse of scattering describes well the aftermath of the conquest of Jerusalem; the curse of breaking the high places and chapels, and the placing of carcasses around the idols are appropriately directed against idolatry. These curses are presented as imminent punishment to the people. Although in many cases the offences are not detailed, there is no doubt that they are taken as actions against the covenant, the statutes and ordinances of God.

Ezekiel uses not only the curses, but also the language of blessing. In Ez 34 and 37 the blessings are explicitly associated with the covenant of peace, and together they have almost exhausted the list of blessings in Lev 26. This use of the language of blessing reinforces the argument that Ezekiel employs the curse/blessing scheme of Lev 26. But we have noted an important difference between Ezekiel and Leviticus. In Ezekiel the blessings are no longer contingent upon the obedience of the people as in Lev 26, but only

---

[208] Cf. Raitt 1977:26.

upon God's initiative. He not only grants the blessings unilaterally; in some cases it is even said explicitly that he will make the people fulfil the condition for the blessings by giving them one new ruler or a new heart/spirit.

There are two ways by which Ezekiel employs the covenant language to depict the relationship between sin and punishment. The first one is to state plainly that the covenant is violated. In the last chapter we have shown that the offences committed by Israel broke the agreements made within the covenant. Punishment is then meted out accordingly, i.e., according to the terms of the covenant. The second way is to use the curses/blessing language conceived within a covenantal framework in Lev 26. In this case, the precise offence committed is not always given. Sometimes it is said simply that God's statutes and ordinances are not observed, and in some cases a generic description such as idolatry is given. The punishment is then meted out according to the curses, with some modification and expansion. Despite these two different uses, the juridical idea (in the sense of an involvement of an external agent, i.e., God, and agreed norms) and the idea of justice (in the sense that punishments are meted out according to agreed norms) are present.

Some conclusions concerning the idea of retribution and the role of God can be drawn. First, the active role of God in meting out punishment is underscored, either by the use of first person verbs or the use of some emphatic expressions such as הנני אני. There is no case in which punishment is seen as an automatic consequence of the sin committed. God is an executor of punishment. Second, not only does God play an active role, he is passionately involved. Some texts mention his wrath and jealousy. A sin is an act directed against him and angers him. This shows that the breaking of a covenant is also a breaking of a relationship. Third, although in some cases the punishment announced is rather general (e.g. Ez 17:20), in some other cases the punishments are dispensed according to the crime. The judgement is therefore not random but just and justified. Fourth, the certainty of the punishment is underlined by the use of curse language. A violation of the covenant in terms of not keeping the statutes and ordinances *will* result in curses realised as foretold (in Lev 26). Apart from being certain, the punishments are also imminent—they will soon arrive. Fifth, even when the violation of statutes and ordinances is sometimes said to set in motion the curses, the process is never a mechanical one independent of God. The text stresses clearly that the curses are delivered by God. It is God who sends the sword, the wild animals, the famine and the pestilence. It is God who scatters the bones of idolaters and destroys the high places. And even when God is not said to act directly, he uses human agents to execute punishments on his behalf.

CHAPTER FOUR

IMPURITY AND RETRIBUTION (I)

1. *Introduction*

That Ezekiel is influenced by the priestly tradition is rightly claimed by many scholars.[1] In particular, the priestly concern for holiness and purity[2] features prominently in Ezekiel. One scholar claims that the "Kern und Stern des ezechielischen Gottesgedankens ist . . . Jahwes Heiligkeit".[3] Another is willing to go as far as to say that "Ezekiel evolved his doctrine of holiness with the consciousness, and in the manner, of a theologian" who "thinks . . . in a logical, consistent, coherent and systematic fashion".[4] While not all scholars would agree with that, it is certainly true that Ezekiel employs the vocabulary of holiness and purity more than any other canonical prophet.[5] For example, Ezekiel distinguishes himself in consistently designating the sins of the people as profanation and impurity.[6] Ezekiel also stresses the holiness of God which is connected especially with his name.[7] Although the language of holiness and purity is dominant in Ezekiel, not many studies have been devoted to examine this aspect of the Ezekielian theology. The earlier study by Baudissin is more concerned with what and who can be called holy in the OT in gen-

---

[1] E.g. Zimmerli 1965:523–524; Carley 1975:62–65.

[2] The usage of "pure/impure" to render טהר/טמא is not consistent. While BDB uses predominantly "clean/unclean", *DCH* uses mostly "pure/impure". The *HALAT* has "rein/unrein" which is translated in *HALOT* by a mixture of "clean/unclean" and "pure/impure". Jenson (1992:43n.5) claims that "the word 'purity' in English has a positive content lacking in the Priestly טהור". But in the following, no distinction is made between these two sets of terminology.

[3] Brögelmann 1935:32. Similarly, Ackroyd (1968:104) says that Ezekiel has a "profound sense of the holiness of God".

[4] Gammie 1989:45.

[5] The statistics provided by *TLOT* under, for example, the word קדש show clearly that it occurs in Ezekiel more than any other prophet (Müller 1997:1106–1107). Similarly for חלל, טהר and טמא. Cf. Muilenburg (1962:622), who says that "Ezekiel's awareness of the divine holiness is more awesome, more sublime and majestic, more cosmic and 'tremendous' than that of his prophetic predecessors".

[6] McKeating 1993:86; Mills 1998:83. Cf. Muilenburg 1962:622.

[7] Nine times in Ezekiel out of a total of 21 in the OT.

eral, and less in the individual books.[8] Ringgren's brief study devotes less than two pages to Ezekiel.[9] Theological dictionaries do not necessarily discuss holiness in Ezekiel.[10] There are some specific studies on the idea of holiness in Ezekiel, namely, those of Bettenzoli, Haik, Gammie and Miao,[11] but these studies pay less attention to the idea of purity/impurity in Ezekiel. There is, therefore, a need to examine this idea more thoroughly and, in view of our concern, its relationship to retribution.

Since the idea of purity/impurity cannot be considered in isolation from its related concepts, we will start with a discussion of the general idea of the holiness word group, paying particular attention to purity/impurity. Then we will probe into Ezekiel's idea of purity/impurity. This forms the basis for the next chapter in which we will deal with the relationship between impurity and retribution in Ezekiel.

2. Holiness and Purity: An Introduction

2.1. The Holiness Word Group

Since one cannot discuss the concept of holiness or purity in isolation from its related concepts,[12] we will in this section briefly examine the holiness word group as found in the OT. The terms of the word group of holiness can be found in Lev 10:10:

ולהבדיל בין הקדש ובין החל   to distinguish between the holy and the common

ובין הטמא ובין הטהור   and between the impure and the pure

While each of the two opposed pairs, holy/profane and impure/pure, appears elsewhere individually, the two pairs are found together only again in Ez 22:26 and 44:23. The relations between these two pairs are subjected to various interpretations. The interpretation that

---

[8] Baudissin 1878.

[9] Ringgren 1948:28–29.

[10] E.g. Procksch (1964:92–94) spends two-thirds of his discussion of holiness in the prophetic theology on Isaiah (and Deutero-Isaiah) but ignores Ezekiel.

[11] Bettenzoli 1979; Haik 1980; Gammie 1989:45–59, 173–194; Miao 1998. See also Wells (2000:160–184).

[12] This is one of Gammie's critiques of Otto's idea of the holy (1989:7–8).

Lev 10:10 exhibits a strict parallelism[13] might be thought to support the older equation of the holy and the impure. This interpretation and equation are untenable. The equation of holiness and impurity, which goes back to William Robertson Smith, is based upon an understanding of taboo no longer held by contemporary anthropologists.[14] Moreover, Lev 10:10 does not seem to offer a strict parallelism. Rather, the terms holy and pure may be aligned, and so may profane and impure, but they are not identical.[15] Barr depicts the relations between the four terms as follows:[16]

The vertical lines represent absolute oppositions and the cross lines indicate compatibility. In this scheme, holiness is opposed to impurity but akin to purity. But one may question if holiness and impurity always stand in such absolute opposition.[17] More will be said below.

Wenham provides a more dynamic picture of the holiness word group:

The above diagrams can be combined as:[18]

---

[13] Cf. Podella 1997:478.

[14] Smith 1894:153–154. Cf. Söderblom 1913:736. For a detailed discussion, see Amorim (1985:13–44), Budd (1989:275–282). Recently, Maccoby (1999:208) also suggests this connection in some particular cases.

[15] Hartley 1992:141; Jenson 1992:44. *Contra* Neusner (1973:18), who equates holiness with purity.

[16] Barr 1972:15.

[17] Even if holiness is opposed to impurity, it is wrong to claim that "קָדוֹשׁ is the antonym of טָמֵא" (Milgrom 1989:105). Strictly speaking, the antonym of "holy" should be "common/profane". Cf. Wright 1992:246.

[18] Wenham 1997:35. This diagram shows a modification of his opinion in his commentary on Leviticus (1979:19) after accepting Jenson's research. The main difference is the insertion of "common" in the middle of the diagram.

According to Wenham, anything is either holy or common. And common things are either clean or unclean. Clean things can be sanctified to become holy, but unclean things cannot. Clean things can be polluted to become unclean. Holy things may be profaned to become common, or polluted to become unclean. But this scheme is only true generally. For example, it does not seem possible for an unclean animal to become clean in any way, and the move from holy to clean via profanation has no justification. The problem, as we will explain below, is that there are different types of cleanness and holiness, and not all of these types can be fit into the above diagrams.

A more recent attempt to characterise the holiness word group is to express it as a "Holiness Spectrum". Jenson proposes the following continuum:[19]

| קדש קדשים — קדש — טהור — טמא — טמא |
| very holy — holy — clean — unclean — very unclean |

In the diagram, terms far away are opposites and adjacent terms are more closely related, although there is a larger distinction between clean and unclean than the diagram implies. Jenson admits that one disadvantage of this scheme is the omission of חל ("profane"), but its rarity justifies that. In this scheme, different types of impurity can be represented by different points on the continuum according to some criteria of gradations. This scheme is then applied to four dimensions of the priestly texts: spatial, personal, ritual and temporal. This scheme is not without its difficulties. First, the use of the same word טמא to represent both "unclean" and "very unclean" is confusing. Second, in the personal dimension, the categories of high priest, regular priests, Levites and lay Israelites, are not phenomenologically continuous with the categories of major and minor impurities.[20] Third, the scheme cannot be applied to the temporal dimension because there is no clean/unclean time.[21] The schemes of both

---

[19] Jenson 1992:44.
[20] Jenson 1992:37.
[21] Wright 1994:162.

Wenham and Jenson are only true generally and the combination of the two opposite pairs holy/profane and purity/impurity is problematic. It would be better to keep them apart, and at the same time to allow for both gradations within each pair and interactions between the two pairs.

While holiness has more to do with the divine and its relation to the world, impurity/purity has more to do with the earthly realm of human existence.[22] Moreover, the distinction between holiness on the one hand and purity on the other can be seen in the distinction between desecration and defilement.[23] While desecration denotes losing holiness, defilement means acquiring uncleanness. Their differences can be seen in the agents of the action, the objects affected by the action and the causes of the action.[24] An example is that the Sabbath is never the subject or object of טמא, but only the object of חלל. The point is that the two pairs holy/profane and clean/unclean are neither totally overlapping nor totally separated.

2.2. *Basic Ideas of Holiness*

In the OT, holiness is basically an attribute of Yahweh. It is not just one attribute among many, but the essential nature of Yahweh.[25] Persons or objects which are said to be holy derive their holiness in relation to Yahweh. The holiness of persons or objects is therefore less an attribute and more a relationship.[26] In the priestly theology, Jenson shows that there is a gradation of holiness. That is to say, the proximity of persons or objects to God determines their degree of holiness. For example, from a spatial point of view, the tabernacle and the camp define different zones possessing different degrees of holiness: the Holy of Holies, the outer chambers of the tabernacle and the altar, the court, and the camp. Corresponding to this spatial dimension is the personal dimension: high priest, priests, Levites, Israelites.[27] Apart from spaces and persons, different rituals and festivals also have different degrees of holiness.

---

[22] Jenson 1992:47. Cf. Amorim 1985:345.
[23] Against those who regard them as synonyms. E.g. Block 1997:308n.45.
[24] Amorim 1985:338–345.
[25] Hartley 1992:lvi.
[26] Baudissin 1878:45; Brögelmann 1935:24; Ringgren 1948:13; Joosten 1996:124; cf. Milgrom 1963:292.
[27] Jenson 1992:89–148.

There are various concepts relating to holiness. The first one is separation.[28] Israel is a holy people because she is separated by God from other nations (e.g. Lev 20:26). But the concern is not just separation *from* something, but also separation *to* Yahweh.[29] Secondly, holiness has a dreadful and fearful dimension. The holy God is to be feared.[30] Thirdly, holiness is contagious by touch under certain conditions.[31] Cases of sancta contagion can be found in Ex 29:37; 30:26–29; Lev 6:11, 20.[32] Fourthly, holiness has a sense of wholeness.[33] For example, physical perfection is required of priests and sacrifices (Lev 21–22) although this requirement does not apply to the laity. Fifth, holiness seems to have an ethical dimension. This point is controversial. Some scholars detect a material aspect of holiness which lacks any ethical connotation. In this understanding, holiness is a mysterious power which operates "in what could be termed an amoral universe".[34] While this may be true in some cases, the ethical demand in connection with holiness is prominent in many other passages, especially in the priestly texts (e.g. Lev 19:2; 20:7–8).[35]

While Yahweh is always holy, persons and objects may lose their holiness.[36] Amorim usefully distinguishes two types of profanation or desecration.[37] Positive desecration should probably be called desanctification[38] which means a voluntary and necessary process by which a person or object moves from a holy realm to a common realm. For example, a Nazirite needs to offer a sacrifice and shave his head at the end of the time of consecration (Nu 6:13–20). Negative desecration is an act which treats persons or objects considered holy as profane. An example is that a person profanes God's name by swearing by it falsely (Lev 19:12).

---

[28] Baudissin 1878:19–22. This idea can be traced back to medieval Jewish commentators. See Wilson (1994:85).

[29] Snaith 1944:30; von Rad 1962:205; Milgrom 1989:105.

[30] Ringgren 1948:10.

[31] Ringgren 1948:14; Amorim 1985:155–157; Joosten 1996:124. Against Wood 1975:177; Levine 1987b:246–247; Hartley 1992:97.

[32] Although Hag 2:10–12 is often taken as a counter-example, a more detailed examination shows that it does not deny the contagious character of holiness, but only limits the extent of the contagion. For a thorough discussion, see Milgrom (1991:443–456).

[33] Douglas 1966:51–53; Wenham 1979:203; Amorim 1985:161; Hartley 1992:lx.

[34] Kaminsky 1995:63, 88.

[35] Amorim 1985:159–161; Houston 1993:222.

[36] Hänel 1931:41; Ringgren 1948:9.

[37] Amorim 1985:164.

[38] Milgrom 1991:732.

2.3. *Basic Ideas of Purity*

We mentioned above that purity/impurity has to do with the human realm. The consideration below is based on the priestly texts. In doing so, we are not unaware of some of the complications involved. First, the dating of the priestly texts is still far from a consensus.[39] A comparison between them and Ezekiel should bear this in mind when the question of dependence is involved. Second, even within the priestly texts, different strata and therefore development have been detected and discussed. Most notable is the relationship between the P texts and H texts.[40]

There are different categories of impurity or uncleanness which should be distinguished. First, animals are classified as clean and unclean (Lev 11–12). An unclean animal can never become clean and that is why some scholars call this type "permanent uncleanness".[41] Permanent uncleanness is not contagious. Unclean animals do not pass on their uncleanness unless they are dead.[42] Unclean animals cannot be eaten or sacrificed.

The second type of impurity has different nomenclatures: levitical,[43] religious,[44] cultic,[45] ritual,[46] ceremonial,[47] physical,[48] permitted,[49] or tolerated impurity.[50] We shall call it ritual impurity. Ritual impurity has different sources: a human corpse or an animal carcass, leprosy,[51] and regular and irregular sex related emissions from the human body. We may also include here impurity contracted unintentionally.[52]

---

[39] See, for instance, the recent study of Blenkinsopp (1996).

[40] For a recent discussion, see the Introduction in Milgrom (1991), esp. 13–49, Knohl (1995), Wright (1999).

[41] Wenham 1979:20–21.

[42] This point is contested. Some claim that unclean animals render unclean everyone in contact with them. E.g. Douglas 1966:55; André and Ringgren 1986:332–333; Hartley 1979:719 (who later changes his position in his Leviticus commentary). But other scholars argue that only the carcasses of unclean (and also clean) animals can defile. E.g. Feldman 1977:50; Wenham 1979:21; Amorim 1985:271; Milgrom 1991:669; Hartley 1992:158.

[43] Büchler 1928:214.

[44] Büchler 1928:269.

[45] Noth 1966:56; Bauer 1970:118.

[46] Toombs 1962:644; Frymer-Kensky 1983:404; Hartley 1992:141.

[47] Gray 1903:81.

[48] Averbeck 1996a:478.

[49] Wright 1988:180.

[50] Wright 1991:151.

[51] For a recent discussion on the disease, see Wright and Jones (1992).

[52] Wright (1991:159) classifies this impurity as our third type of impurity.

Ritual impurity is mostly contagious[53] and impermanent. Ritual impurities can be classified according to their degree of severity.[54] We may consider two examples. First, semen pollutes the man who emits it, the woman with whom he has sexual intercourse, and any object in contact with it. They all remain unclean until the evening and require washing (Lev 15:16–18). Second, a corpse pollutes a man who touches it or is in the same tent with it (Nu 19). He will become unclean for seven days. Water of purgation is needed to sprinkle on him on the third and seventh days. Washing the clothes and bathing are also required. Moreover, anyone or anything in touch with a corpse-contaminated person will be unclean for one day. Bathing or destruction (in the case of earthenware) is also needed. These two examples illustrate the different contagious power of the sources and the difference in severity of the impurity.

The first two types of impurity have nothing to do with morality.[55] Whether an animal is clean or unclean certainly has no relation to human morality. Most of the ritual impurities are inevitable or even necessary in daily life. A woman cannot help but menstruate. Dead bodies have to be taken care of. Sexual intercourse is necessary (at that time) for procreation to fulfil the command to be fruitful and multiply. Even though leprosy has been used as a punishment in the cases of Miriam (Nu 12:10–15), Gehazi (2 Kg 5:27) and Uzziah (2 Chr 26:19–21), there seems to be no necessary connection between leprosy and the transgressions of lepers.[56] The point is that "it is not sinful to be ritually impure, and ritual impurity does not result from sin".[57] However, that does not mean that ritual impurity is something that can be taken lightly. Leprosy results in isolation from the community. All bearers of impurity are restricted from the sanctuary and sacred materials within their habitation[58] (cf. Lev 15:31). When an unclean layperson eats the peace offerings (Lev 7:19–21)

---

[53] For a study on the degree of communicability of different ritual impurities, see Wright (1987:179–228).

[54] Some criteria for gradations are: (1) duration of impurity; (2) method of purification; (3) power of contagion; (4) degree of isolation. See Amorim (1985:287n.2), Wright (1991:155n.3), Douglas (1993:154).

[55] Against Gray (1903:81) who includes ritual impurity in the idea of sin.

[56] Frymer-Kensky 1983:403–404; Douglas 1996:97; Klawans 1997:2–3. But see Milgrom (1991:820–823).

[57] Klawans 1997:3. See also Hartley (1992:141), Douglas (1996:96).

[58] Frymer-Kensky 1983:403; Wright 1991:156. Cf. Bauer 1970:119.

or an unclean priest consumes a sacred portion (Lev 22:3–9), they
will be cut off from the people. Any person who is contaminated by
a corpse and yet performs no purification would defile the sanctuary and incur the same penalty (Nu 19:13). Subsequent to Korah's
rebellion, one duty of the priests and Levites is to guard the holy
things and the Tent from encroachers[59] (Nu 18:1–5; cf. 2 Chr 23:19).
Thus, there is a need to minimise impurity lest any contact between
impurity and the sacred brings about grave consequences.

The third type of impurity is also called by different names: spir-
itual,[60] moral,[61] figurative or metaphorical,[62] prohibited impurity,[63] or
danger-beliefs.[64] We shall call it moral impurity. It includes impurities arising from (1) sexual sins such as adultery, incest, bestiality,
and homosexuality (Lev 18:6–23); (2) idolatry such as the Molech
cult (Lev 20.2–5), (3) illicit divination (Lev 19:26, 31); (4) intention-
ally eating sacrifices while unclean (Lev 7:19–21; 22:3–7); and (5)
bloodshed (Nu 35:33–34).[65] By committing any of these acts, people
can defile themselves with moral impurity (Lev 18:24). They can
also defile the land of Israel (Lev 18:25, 27) and even the sanctuary (Lev 20:3).

The relationship between moral impurity and ritual impurity deserves some attention.[66] Moral impurity is often said to be used in
a "figurative" or "metaphorical" way.[67] To say so means for some
scholars that there is no real defilement taking place. But as Klawans
points out, there is no reason to deny a literal reading of these passages (e.g. Lev 18) and to hold that sin can defile.[68]

Some differences between ritual impurity and moral impurity can
be discerned.[69] First, moral impurity is not contagious by touching.

[59] Milgrom 1970:19–33.
[60] Büchler 1928:214. Cf. Amorim 1985:309.
[61] Toombs 1962:641; Meyer and Hauck 1965:416; Milgrom 1991:37; Klawans
1997:3. Cf. Amorim 1985:309.
[62] Neusner 1973:14; Levine 1989:134; Milgrom 1991:37; Wright 1991:163; Averbeck
1996b:365.
[63] Wright 1991:151.
[64] Frymer-Kensky 1983:404.
[65] For more details, see Büchler (1928:212–237).
[66] Milgrom (1991:37) attributes texts on ritual impurity to the Priestly Torah (P)
and those on moral impurity to the Holiness School (H).
[67] See above. Cf. Büchler 1928:235; Maccoby 1999:200.
[68] Klawans 1997:5–6.
[69] The claim by Toombs (1962:647) or Zink (1967:360) that the OT makes no
distinction between ritual and moral impurity is a moot point.

One does not contract any impurity by touching a murderer. Second, while there are purification rites for a person's ritual impurity, there are no such rites for moral impurity.[70] Rather, the person may be subjected to the כרת punishment.[71] Third, ritual impurity does not defile the land, but moral defilement of the land may lead to exile (Lev 18:28).[72] Fourth, a morally impure person is not necessarily ritually impure.[73] A case in point is idolatry. Thus, one can come up with the surprising conclusion that "an idolater would be granted access to the sanctuary while one simply defiled by touching a dead rat is not".[74] Fifth, ritual and moral impurity differ in their relation to controllability. According to Eilberg-Schwartz, the reason why menstrual blood and non-seminal discharge are defiling but urine is not is that the former is uncontrollable but not the latter. Similarly, tears, saliva and mucus are controllable and thus not (ritually) defiling.[75] That may also explain why excrement is not listed as ritually impure.[76] On the contrary, moral impurity is caused precisely by actions which are controllable such as incest and adultery.

One implication of the distinction of the three types of impurity is that the *general* claim that "the antipathy between holiness and impurity was absolute"[77] needs to be nuanced. A priest is consecrated and therefore holy (Lev 8–9). But he can be married and have sexual intercourse with his wife. By doing so, he becomes ritually unclean. But this uncleanness does not seem to compromise his state of being holy.[78] It only bars him from approaching the sanctuary. Another example concerns the sanctuary which can be defiled by the ritual uncleanness of the people (Lev 15:31) or sacrifice to Molech (Lev 20:3). But again this does not seem to compromise its holiness.[79] Wright holds that some purgation offerings are holy and impure at the same time.[80] Lastly, Amorim suggests that the uncleanness of the people of Israel is not necessarily incompatible with their

---

[70] Büchler 1928:216; Wright 1991:162; Klawans 1997:3.
[71] For a discussion of the כרת punishment, see Chapter Five Section 2.2.3.
[72] Cf. Amorim 1985:327.
[73] Büchler 1928:235.
[74] Wright 1991:164n.1. But see Ps 24:3–4.
[75] Eilberg-Schwartz 1990:187.
[76] Eilberg-Schwartz 1990:189.
[77] Jenson 1992:53.
[78] Averbeck 1996a:481–482.
[79] Amorim 1985:230; Jenson 1992:49.
[80] Wright 1992:246–247.

holiness.[81] The point is that there are different types of impurities and they have different effects on different things/persons. It is just not true to simply say that "what is holy is always clean".[82] Rather, the antipathy between impurity and holiness is found where the sanctuary is concerned. That is to say, any ritually impure person/thing is barred from the sanctuary and sacred materials.

Concerning purity, we can be brief. Corresponding to the three types of impurity are the three types of purity. First, animals can be pure/clean. Second, persons or objects can be ritually pure. This is their neutral state. Third, persons can be morally pure. None of these types of purity is contagious.

2.4. *Approaches to Purity and Impurity*

In this section, we will briefly discuss the various approaches adopted by scholars in their studies on the idea of purity and impurity[83] which is our main concern. The discussion is not meant to be exhaustive. It aims at giving a general picture of the current studies. That some scholars are cited under one approach does not necessarily imply that these scholars use only that particular approach in their studies. Rather, most scholars adopt a variety of approaches in their research.

2.4.1. *Descriptive Approach*
Those who seek to describe rather than explain the biblical or extra-biblical materials on purity/impurity are said to adopt a descriptive approach. This approach seeks to answer the questions of what comes under the rubric of pure/impure. The description can be limited to the biblical texts or can be extended to texts in other historical periods such as the Qumran scrolls, Mishnah and Talmud. Description of biblical materials appears both as entries to dictionaries and encyclopaedias,[84] and in monographs.[85] They may list the different kinds of ritual impurities, their sources, their effects, and the rites for their purification. But the description can go beyond the biblical corpus

---

[81] Amorim 1985:325.

[82] Hartley 1992:141. Thus, it is equally wrong to say that "[t]he unclean and the holy are two states which must never come in contact with each other" (Wenham 1979:19–20) or "the sacred may never be impure" (Milgrom 1991:732).

[83] Neyrey (1988) has a different classification.

[84] E.g. Toombs 1962; Bauer 1970; Hartley 1979; André and Ringgren 1986.

[85] E.g. Baudissin 1878; Ringgren 1948; Amorim 1985; Gammie 1989.

and include texts from other periods. This includes Neusner who gives a survey of materials from the Hebrew Bible, literature of the second temple period and the Talmud, Newton who examines the idea of purity in Qumran and Paul, and Harrington who deals with the impurity systems of Qumran and the rabbis.[86]

2.4.2. *Explanatory Approach*

Instead of asking the question of what comes under the rubric of the purity language, some scholars raise questions like "What is the basis of classification of pure and impure animals?", "Why are there purity laws?", or "Why is there purity language at all?". These scholars seek to *explain* the phenomenon of the purity language and therefore we shall call their approaches explanatory. These approaches may take different forms.[87] The first one may be called reductionistic. It seeks to explain what is impure by reducing it to something else. It includes a hygienic theory which reduces impurity to disease-causing power,[88] a cultic theory which reduces what is impure to objects of pagan cult,[89] and a demonic theory which reduces impurity to demonic forces.[90]

The second way to explain the purity language is to uncover the worldview of the people and how they use the language to order their world. This is based on the theory that the way a culture classifies objects/persons into pure/impure reflects the worldview of this culture. This task is undertaken by many cultural anthropologists whose results are adopted and modified by biblical scholars. Among them, two groups can be distinguished. The first one can be called idealist or structuralist and the second materialist.[91] While the first group uses more abstract notions to denote the worldview, the second group employs more materialistic notions. Scholars in the first group use the notions of order vs. anomaly and wholeness vs. defects,[92] or herbivores vs. carnivores, extended to wholeness vs. blemish,[93] or

---

[86] Neusner 1973; Newton 1985; Harrington 1993.

[87] Houston (1993:68–123) gives a survey and criticism of various approaches to the biblical laws of clean and unclean animals.

[88] Döller 1917:231–235; Clements 1970:43; Harrison 1980:121–126.

[89] Meyer and Hauck 1965:417; Noth 1966:56–59.

[90] Döller 1917:242–247; Elliger 1966:197; Snaith 1969:69; Levine 1974:77–78.

[91] This distinction is made by Hunn (1979:112), adopted by Jenson (1992:81).

[92] E.g. Douglas 1966.

[93] Soler 1979.

nature vs. culture,[94] or controllable vs. uncontrollable.[95] Scholars in the second group employ the notion of death/life.[96]

The third way to explain the purity language is to consider its function within the society in which it is used. The function can be social or theological. It can be used to support the moral order of the society,[97] to inculcate a reverence for life,[98] to help to differentiate and define different religious groups,[99] to serve as a mechanism for social survival and maintenance for the exilic community as a minority group,[100] or in particular in Ezekiel to characterise the exilic community as the true remnant.[101] Theologically, the purity language serves to distinguish Israel as a nation separated from other nations.[102]

3. *Purity and Impurity in Ezekiel*

In the last section we have briefly indicated the importance of the purity/holiness language in the Book of Ezekiel. As a basis of our study on Ezekiel, we have also discussed the holiness word group, and the various basic concepts associated with holiness and purity. Lastly, a brief overview of different approaches to holiness/purity has been given.

In this section we are going to investigate what has been put under the rubric of the purity language in Ezekiel. Our approach here will be *descriptive*. Following the distinctions made, both ritual and moral impurity will be examined. Since the latter aspect is our main concern, the former aspect will be dealt with only briefly. Our discussion is mostly restricted to Ez 1–39 although Ez 40–48 certainly contains material pertaining especially to the issue of ritual impurity. A complete investigation of the idea of purity/impurity and holiness in Ezekiel would therefore require a thorough study of

---

[94] Carroll 1978.
[95] Eilberg-Schwartz 1990:186–189.
[96] Dillmann 1897:521; Paschen 1970:63, 64; Feldman 1977:34–35, 35–45; Füglister 1977:157–160; Wenham 1983; Amorim 1985:285; Kiuchi 1987:63–65; Milgrom 1989:108; Eilberg-Schwartz 1990:182–185; Maccoby 1999:207. Cf. von Rad 1962:277.
[97] Douglas 1966:129–139; Wright 1991:170.
[98] Milgrom 1990a.
[99] Neusner 1973:108.
[100] Smith 1989:11, 139–151. Cf. Herzog 1923:109–113.
[101] Siedlecki 1991.
[102] Gispen 1948:196; André and Ringgren 1986:331; Wright 1991:167, especially the dietary laws.

Ez 40–48 after the fashion of Jenson's *Graded Holiness*[103] which is beyond the scope of the present study.

3.1. *Ritual Impurity*

Ritual impurity does not seem to be featured much in Ez 1–39. It is restricted to a few cases: the idea of impure food, the defiling power of corpses, and the impurity of menstruants. Our discussion here will be brief since ritual impurity does not play an important role in Ezekiel's idea of retribution.

3.1.1. *Food*

The concern for food impurity is found in Ez 4:12–15, which is part of 4:9–17—a symbolic action concerning food supply. While some scholars hold that Ez 4:9–17 deals with the siege food, with the possible exception of the secondary v.13 which introduces an exilic setting,[104] others treat 4:12–15, whether secondary or not, as a whole relating to exilic food.[105] We accept the latter option basically because v.12 cannot be seen as a continuation of vv.9–11 for the following reasons: (1) the reversion to food in v.12 after mentioning food and drink in vv.10–11 is odd; (2) v.12 mentions a barley cake which is different from the siege food mentioned in v.9; (3) the feminine suffixes to the two verbs plus the feminine pronoun (in v.12) agree with the feminine עגת שערים but not the masculine לחם (v.9) or מאכל (v.10).[106]

In v.12 Yahweh asks Ezekiel to eat a barley cake which is to be baked by using human excrement. An explanation of this action is given in v.13 from the mouth of Yahweh: "Thus the sons of Israel shall eat their bread, unclean, among the nations to which I will banish them." The questions concerning this verse are what is unclean

---

[103] Some discussion can be found in Haran (1979), Tuell (1992) and Kasher (1998).

[104] Cooke 1936:55; Eichrodt 1970:78 (who also rearranges the text); Brownlee 1986:77; Allen 1994:70–71; also Aalders (1955:102) and Cooper (1994:97), without positing the secondary character of v.13.

[105] Herrmann 1924:31; Wevers 1969:53–54; Carley 1974:34; Garscha 1974:90; Zimmerli 1979:170–172; Greenberg 1983a:119; Fuhs 1984:35; Pohlmann 1996:81; Block 1997:169.

[106] Both וענת שערים and והיא can be seen as *casus pendens* (Greenberg 1983a:107; Block 1997:181). To regard the verbal suffixes as neutral is forced (Keil 1876a:81; Aalders 1955:102). Translations like "you shall eat it as a barley cake" are also mistaken (e.g. NRSV; Keil 1876a:78; Fisch 1950:22; Coffman 1991:55; cf. Toy 1899:6).

and what causes the uncleanness. We will return to this. In v.14,
the prophet raises the objection that his throat[107] has not been
defiled.[108] Some examples are then given: (1) an animal died of itself
(נבלה); (2) an animal torn by wild animals (טרפה); and (3) carrion
flesh (בשׂר פגול). The first two types are regarded as unclean and forbidden to eat (Lev 7:24; 22:8; cf. Ez 44:31). On the basis of Lev 7:18
and 19:7, the third one refers probably to sacrificial meat in the
peace offering which becomes an abomination if not eaten until the
third day.[109] The examples cited are all concerned with ritual impurity. In response to his complaint, Yahweh allows Ezekiel to use
cow's dung instead of human dung.

That the word "unclean" qualifies "their food" in v.13 is not questioned.[110] Various reasons are given to explain the uncleanness. First,
the cake is unclean because it is made of a mixture of grains, which
is forbidden according to Lev 19:19 or Dt 22:9–11.[111] But this not
only presupposes that the barley cake in v.12 is the same as the
bread in v.9, which we have argued against, but also misinterprets
Lev 19:19 or Dt 22:9–11 which says nothing about bread made
from a mixture of grains.[112]

Second, the uncleanness is caused by the way of cooking, i.e., by
using human dung as fuel, citing Dt 23:13–15 as support.[113] This
view assumes that human dung is impure and its impurity is contagious. But Dt 23:13–15 does not say that human dung is impure,
only that it is something indecent (ערות דבר).[114] And the precaution
is taken when the Israelites are at war (Dt 23:9).[115] We noted above
that excrement is not said to be impure in the priestly texts prob-

---

[107] This rendition of נפשׁ as "throat" provides a better parallel to "mouth" later.
See Greenberg 1983a:107; Allen 1994:51; Block 1997:186.

[108] The use of לא instead of אין before the participle gives a more forceful negation. See Davidson §100 Rem.3; J.-M. §160c.

[109] Zimmerli 1979:171; Greenberg 1983a:107; Wright 1987:140–143; Allen 1994:70;
Block 1997:186. Kraetzschmar (1900:1900:53), followed by Cooke (1936:56), suggests that the word is used here in a wider sense referring to ritually unclean food.

[110] Cf. NIV "defiled food". However, the grammatical relationship between לחמם
and טמא is not always noted. It is explained by various grammarians. E.g. Davidson
§32 Rem.2; Gibson §42 Rem.2; W.-O'C. §14.3.3c. See also Kraetzschmar (1900:53).

[111] Aalders 1955:103; Eichrodt 1970:86; Fuhs 1984:35; Brownlee 1986:77.

[112] Alexander 1986:770.

[113] Davidson 1916:36; Cooke 1936:55; Fisch 1950:23; Becker 1971:25; Greenberg
1983a:107; Brownlee 1986:77; Allen 1994:69; Cooper 1994:97; Biggs 1996:17.

[114] Houston 1993:18; Tigay 1996:214.

[115] Mayes (1979:318) calls it a law of the holy war.

ably because it is controllable.[116] Although God's concession made in 4:15 seems to imply that the issue has to do with the human dung, there is no clear evidence from the Pentateuch that human excrement is unclean.[117] Also, we should note that strictly speaking Ezekiel's reply in v.14, which is concerned with unclean meat, has nothing to do with the vegetarian bread. Thus, it may be more appropriate to say that the use of human dung addresses the sensibilities of the priest Ezekiel.[118] That is to say, human dung is repulsive and loathsome but not ritually impure. If that is the case, then the use of cow dung would remove the repulsion, and is equally ritually allowable.[119]

Third, since the cake is prepared in a foreign land which is considered unclean, it is unclean. Josh 22:19; Am 7:17 and Hos 9:3 are cited as support.[120] Undoubtedly these verses state that foreign lands are unclean. What is not clear is why and whether this would render food prepared there unclean. The impurity of foreign lands can be caused by the foreigners' idolatrous actions (e.g. Lev 18:24–27; Ezr 9:11)[121] or the fact that the lands are ruled by foreign gods (e.g. 1 Sam 26:19) or that no Yahwistic cult is possible.[122] In the first case, it is not clear why food would be affected unless it is part of the idolatrous worship. In the second case, food normally eaten after sacrifice has been made would no longer be prepared in such a way in foreign lands. No matter which is the case, Ezekiel's reply in v.14 does imply that it is *possible* to eat ritually pure food even in exile since at the time of this sign action Ezekiel is already in Babylon.[123]

In conclusion, it is not clear what exactly causes the uncleanness of the food. It is possible that Ezekiel extends some of the purity laws so that the use of human dung as fuel renders the food unclean. It is also possible that the use of human dung, although ritually

---

[116] Eilberg-Schwartz 1990:187.

[117] Milgrom 1991:767.

[118] Cody 1984:37; Vawter and Hoppe 1991:44. Against Craigie (1983a:34) who holds that human dung is ritually but not naturally repugnant.

[119] Against those who claim that cow dung is ritually impure. E.g. Kraetzschmar 1900:53; Aalders 1955:104; Greenberg 1983a:108; Calvin 1994:122; Block 1997:187.

[120] Lofthouse 1907:79; Cooke 1936:56; Zimmerli 1979:171; Greenberg 1983a:107; Alexander 1986:770; Allen 1994:71; Block 1997:186; Friebel 1999:248.

[121] Greenberg 1983a:107; Amorim 1985:320–321.

[122] Rudolph 1971:259; Jeremias 1983:116. Cf. Davies 1992:216.

[123] One may consider the case of Daniel and his friends in Dan 1 where they can remain ritually pure regarding food even in the Babylonian royal palace.

allowed, indicates an extreme condition which is repugnant and far
from desirable as in the case of the exile. There may be cases where
the Israelites would not know whether the food they consume is
clean or not. Without the cult the people may have no way to cleanse
their ritual impurity. In any case this is a concern of ritual rather
than moral impurity.

3.1.2. *Corpses*

A corpse is the only source of impurity that defiles persons and
objects for seven days where the defiled are able to pollute further
(Nu 19:14–16). Thus, in order to confine the impurity, corpses are
removed from human habitation.[124] Similar restrictions and exclu-
sions of other communicable impurities can also be found.[125] In
Ezekiel, the defilement of corpses is found indirectly in Ez 39:11–16.
After Gog and his armies are defeated by Yahweh, their bodies have
yet to be buried. For seven months a group of searchers locate and
signpost any human bone, and then a group of buriers collect and
bury it in a designated place. The purpose of this action is not to
honour the dead,[126] but, as said thrice in the passage, to cleanse
(טהר) the land (vv.12, 14, 16). Although the word טמא does not
appear, the context implies that the corpses defile the land. However,
nowhere else in the OT is the land said to be polluted by corpses.
Dt 21:23 may be an exception but its exact meaning is by no means
certain.[127] The cleansing here in Ezekiel seems to be the concern of
ritual impurity.[128] Hence, this case should not be confused with the
sort of land pollution in 36:18 where moral impurity is concerned.[129]

---

[124] Although the priestly texts rarely talk about moving a corpse outside the camp
(Lev 10:4–5; Nu 5:2–4), Wright (1987:115–128) argues that the non-priestly texts
reflect an ideal of moving corpses outside human habitation, citing archaeological
evidence for support.

[125] Wright 1987:224–228.

[126] Hitzig 1847:297.

[127] Fisch 1950:261; Aalders 1957:235; Cooper 1994:343. References are also made
to Josh 8:29; 10:26–27, but what exactly defiles the land is not clear. Driver
(1902:248–249) suggests that the person must have committed a heinous offence if
his body was hanged, and thus the offence pollutes the land. Tigay (1996:198) holds
that the land is polluted if the body is spread by birds, etc. Craigie (1976:285)
claims that the body defiles the land physically through decay and symbolically
because the land belongs to God.

[128] Allen 1990:208; Block 1998:470. Cf. Wevers 1969:205. Against Eisemann
1988:597–598.

[129] Such an association is made by Allen (1990:208).

In the present case Ezekiel may have extended his priestly concern for ritual purity.

Corpses can also defile a place of worship. This can be found in Ez 6:1–7. The text reports what God will do to the high places on the mountains of Israel. He is going to throw the slain in front of the idols and scatter the bones around the altars. Here purity vocabulary does not appear because the focus, as seen in Chapter Three, is on the violation of the covenant and God's subsequent execution of the covenant curses appropriate to this violation. But placing corpses and bones on the altars defiles them. A clearer case is Ez 9:7 where Yahweh commands six executioners to "defile the house (הבית) and fill the courts[130] with the slain". In this case, the temple is explicitly said to be defiled by the presence of corpses.[131] Outside Ezekiel, a similar case is found in 2 Kg 23:14, 16, 20 which expound Josiah's defilement of high places first mentioned in 2 Kg 23:8. Noting that bones themselves are a source of defilement (Nu 19:18), Josiah's actions of scattering human bones on the sites[132] and burning bones on the altar (v.16) result in defilement (cf. 1 Kg 13:2). If impurity has to do with death as some claim,[133] then corpses and bones defile precisely because they are associated with death. And as such, they represent exactly the opposite of what the temple is meant to do— to bring life.[134] Thus, Ezekiel follows the tradition in holding that corpses or bones can defile the temple.

3.1.3. *Menses*

The root of נִדָּה is taken to be either נדד or נדה which share the common meaning "chase away, expel",[135] or from נדד which has the basic meaning of distancing oneself from something disgusting and abhorrent.[136] The word נִדָּה occurs five times in Ezekiel. The meaning

---

[130] The LXX has "the streets" (τὰς ὁδοὺς), which may be an error inspired by 11:6. See Cooke (1936:110), Allen (1994:123).

[131] One may ask if the defilement also comes from the action of killing itself. Cf. 2 Kg 11:15.

[132] This is already an act of defilement. See Long (1991:275). Cf. Robinson 1976:222.

[133] See Section 2.4.2. above.

[134] Lundquist (1983:212) suggests that the temple is associated with "abundance and prosperity". Note that in Ez 47:1–12 it is from the temple that the life-giving water flows.

[135] Milgrom and Wright 1986.

[136] Greenberg 1995:76.

of menstrual impurity is found in 22:10. The apposition אשה נדה in 18:6 seems to give an extended meaning of "menstruant".[137] It is known that the mentrual blood is a source of ritual impurity and any contact with it will contract impurity (Lev 15:19–24). In particular, a man should not have sexual intercourse with a menstruant (Lev 18:19). This prohibition recurs in Ez 18:6 and 22:10.

In Ez 7:19, 20 the word probably refers to something unclean in general,[138] but the idea of abhorrence is also present.[139] When under siege, silver and gold, which cannot buy the people food, are regarded as abhorrent, something from which to be set apart (7:19). The interpretation of 7:20 can take two directions. First, צבי עדיו may be taken as an allusion to the temple[140] with the suffix referring to Yahweh.[141] As such this verse refers to the making of idols in the temple (בו). Yahweh reacts to this by turning it—a collective form for the idols—into an unclean thing for the people. Second, the suffix of צבי עדיו may refer to the silver or, collectively, the gold and silver in v.19,[142] or the people collectively.[143] In either case, the beautiful ornaments were made from the gold and silver by which (בו) images are then made. Thus, it is also the gold and silver (as in v.19) which God will turn into an unclean thing. The second interpretation is preferred. First, it is odd to introduce the temple in v.20 with the phrase צבי עדיו without first naming the temple. Second, it is difficult to take the singular suffix of צבי עדיו to refer to Yahweh since he is not mentioned in the immediate context. Rather, since in v.19 silver and gold are taken as a unit (cf. היה, יוכל) and the people are referred to in the plural (cf. ישליכו, ישבעו, ימלאו and suffix ־ם), the singular suffix refers to gold and silver as a whole. Thus, it is the silver and gold which Yahweh turns into נדה, something unclean

---

[137] Greenberg 1995:75.

[138] E.g. Toy 1899:10; Herrmann 1924:50; Fisch 1950:38; Milgrom and Wright 1986:252. It is difficult to see why Cooke (1936:82) refers נדה to the "defilement of idolatry".

[139] Allen 1994:110.

[140] This interpretation is found in the Targum, which is followed by Rashi and Kimhi. See Levey (1987:35, n.12 to Ez 7). A contemporary follower is Block (1997:265).

[141] Block 1997:262n.106.

[142] Toy 1899:10; Cooke 1936:82; Aalders 1955:146; Wevers 1969:64–65; Zimmerli 1979:199; Allen 1994:102.

[143] Keil 1876a:107; Fisch 1950:38. Cf. Eichrodt 1970:98; Brownlee 1986:111; Greenberg 1983a:153.

and abhorrent. This affirms that the concern here has more to do with ritual impurity than moral impurity.

In 36:17 נדה is used in a simile. We will deal with the text in the following chapter, but its reference to a menstrual state is not to be doubted.

3.2. *Moral Impurity*

An examination of the moral impurity found in Ezekiel can be carried out from different perspectives. First, one can consider the subject of a defiling action. It could be Israel in general, some groups of Israelites, a foreign nation, or even God himself. Second, one can examine what kinds of action are said to produce moral impurity. Third, one can consider the object affected by the defiling action which could be the Israelites themselves, a foreign nation, God, the sanctuary, or the land. These three questions can, *mutatis mutandis*, be applied to moral purity. In the following discussion, we will approach our subject from the third perspective. This is not entirely arbitrary. First, the subject of a defiling action is mostly the Israelites, considered collectively as a whole, a sub-group, an individual member, or personified. Hence, a classification of the subjects involved may not be too illuminating. Second, it is important to know what/who is affected. This, as we will see in the following chapter, is significant for the idea of retribution. Third, the kinds of action causing moral impurity will not be ignored but will be indicated in the following.

Before we proceed further, it should be pointed out that different stems of טמא are used in Ezekiel to nuance the idea of defilement. The qal form is intransitive and denotes a condition which is either general or attained. The most common function of the piel form in Ezekiel is factitive, i.e., "it designates without regard to the process the bringing about of the state depicted by an adjective".[144] That is to say, it stresses the bringing about of the impure state.[145] The niphal form, which is normally the passive or reflexive of the qal, is here the passive or reflexive of the piel form.[146] It is not always

---

[144] W.-O'C. §24.1h. Their discussion is strongly influenced by Jenni (1968). See also J.-M. §52d.

[145] In contrast, the piel of טמא in Leviticus is mostly declarative-estimative, i.e., to declare someone to be in the impure state (e.g. Lev 13:3, 8, 11, 15, 20). For this use, see Jenni (1968:40–43), GKC §52g, J.-M. §52d, W.-O'C. §24.2fg.

[146] Siebesma 1991:51. Cf. BDB 379.

easy to determine whether it is passive or reflexive. The hitpael form[147] is primarily the reflexive of the piel,[148] and as such it is also factitive,[149] but it can also have the passive meaning.[150] Its relation to the niphal is difficult to determine. In Ezekiel, while the niphal of טמא is used only in the perfect apart from 20:30,31 where we have the participial form, the hitpael appears only in the imperfect. This phenomenon, however, is not restricted to Ezekiel. In the whole MT, the niphal of טמא occurs 16 times in the perfect and twice as a participle while all 13 occurrences of the hitpael form are in the imperfect. Commenting on this case, Bergsträßer holds that the niphal-perfect and hitpael-imperfect supplement each other to form a paradigm.[151] Thus, the niphal and hitpael forms of טמא are considered to be similar in meaning.[152]

3.2.1. *Sanctuary*

In Ezekiel the Jerusalem temple or sanctuary is said to be defiled explicitly in cases in which the piel of טמא is used, although some other implicit cases can be detected. The first case is found in Ez 5:11a in which Jerusalem is accused of defiling Yahweh's sanctuary (מקדש) with all her detestable things (שקוצים)[153] and all her abominations (תועבת). The word שקוצים occurs eight times and only in the plural in Ezekiel;[154] four times it is used with תועבת.[155] Its cognate שֶׁקֶץ occurs predominantly in Leviticus,[156] referring to animals that Israelites should abhor or find detestable.[157] This detestable

---

[147] The pual is used once in Ez 4:14 as a participle.

[148] GKC §54d; J.-M. §53i; W.-O'C. §26.2a.

[149] W.-O'C. §26.2b.

[150] J.-M. §53i. But Siebesma (1991:167) remarks that the hitpael only rarely has a passive meaning.

[151] Bergsträßer 1929:90. His opinion is followed by W.-O'C. §23.6.4a. Siebesma (1991:169) lists more verbs possessing this property.

[152] Lev 18:24 is an example in which both the hitpael and niphal forms are used without any difference in meaning (W.-O'C. §23.6.4a). Hartley's translation of the niphal as if it were a qal is incorrect (1992:281). See also Lev 11:43.

[153] The phrase בכל־שקוציך ו is not rendered in the LXX. But its combination with "abominations" occurs at 11:18, 21. This could be the result of homoioteleuton (Block 1997:205).

[154] 5:11; 7:20; 11:18, 21; 20:7, 8, 30; 37:23.

[155] 5:11; 7:20; 11:18, 21. Elsewhere only in 2 Kg 23:13; Jer 16:18. Cf. Dt 7:25–26; Jer 32:34–35.

[156] E.g. Lev 7:21; 11:10, 11, 12. Also Is 66:17; Ez 8:10.

[157] Budd 1996:166. But whether detestable animals are clean is controversial. See Milgrom (1992).

dimension may also have been retained in the word שִׁקּוּצִים, which refers mostly to foreign gods or idols, especially in Deuteronomy and Kings.[158] This is probably its meaning here, but one may ask whether the detestable idols themselves can defile the sanctuary. In Lev 19:4 and 26:1–2 idols are proscribed but not described as impure. Ezekiel's contemporary Jeremiah accuses the Israelites twice of setting up idols (שִׁקּוּצִים) in God's temple to defile it (7:30; 32:34). The ל-infinitive לְטַמְּאוֹ in Jer 7:30; 32:34 signifies either purpose or consecration. In either case, it is the whole action of setting the idols in the temple, not the idols themselves, that causes the defilement.[159] It is probably the same in Ezekiel.

The word תּוֹעֵבָה refers to something "which is excluded by its very nature, that which seems dangerous or sinister".[160] Its reference ranges from antisocial behaviour to pagan worship.[161] In the cultic realm, it refers to either cultic practices or objects which have no proper place in the cult.[162] In Ezekiel it often refers to cultic offences.[163] In Ez 5:11 it probably refers to the cultic practices more than abominable objects[164] because in 5:9 the same word is used as a keyword to sum up the misbehaviour of Jerusalem listed in 5:6–7. In the present context, the abominable practice is related to idols. The connection between abominable acts and their defiling power echoes the priestly texts.[165] In particular, Lev 20:3 relates the Molech cult to defilement of the sanctuary.[166] Another reference is 2 Chr 36:14 where performing the abominable acts of the nations will result in defiling God's temple.

In light of this we may consider the abominations in Ez 8:3–17. In a vision, Ezekiel is brought to Jerusalem where he is told four times (vv.6, 9, 13, 15) to witness the (great) abominations committed

[158] E.g. Dt 29:16; 1 Kg 11:5, 7; 2 Kg 23:13, 24. See von Orelli (1888:26) and Paschen (1970:66).

[159] Against Amorim (1985:334), Wright (1987:283–284).

[160] Gerstenberger 1997:1429.

[161] Grisanti 1996:315.

[162] The meaning "die fremden Götter und ihre Kultbilder" proposed by Paschen (1970:67) is too restricted.

[163] Hossfeld 1977:112; Zimmerli 1979:190; Ohnesorge 1991:39. For a more detailed study, see Sedlmeier (1990:203–211).

[164] See the translations in Allen (1994:48), Pohlmann (1996:80), Block (1997:205). Against Greenberg 1983a:100.

[165] Cf. Allen 1994:75. But Krüger (1989:84) links this passage to the Deuteronom(ist)ic literature.

[166] Note the use of לְמַעַן in Lev 20:3 as indicating result. See Brongers (1973:89).

within it. It is not our purpose to examine in detail the four abominations described or whether the description is anachronistic.[167] The text shows an inward movement from the north gateway of the city wall to the inner court of the temple.[168] As the prophet moves inward, he sees greater abominations. As there is an increasing degree of holiness from the outside to the inside of the temple,[169] the abominations are therefore more and more defiling. This section differs from other passages on the idolatry of Israelites in that the nature of the offence is more explicitly stated. The first one, the image of jealousy (v.3), is generally recognised to refer to the Canaanite goddess Asherah.[170] The second abomination refers to the seventy elders' offering of incense in a room full of detestable animals and idols in relief (vv.10–11). The offence consists not only in that the animals and idols are worshipped, but also in that they violate the requirement that only the Aaronites can offer incense (Nu 16:40). The third refers probably to the enacting of rites surrounding the goddess Tammuz by professional cultic personnel (v.14).[171] As the climax of the series, the last abomination, which takes place within the temple somewhere between the porch and altar, is the most defiling. The description points to worship in the sun cult. By turning their backs to the temple of Yahweh, these worshippers express a gesture of rejection of the Yahwistic cult in favour of another deity.[172] In this account the Israelites, whether the leaders or the common people, are accused of idolatry which consists in worshipping deities other than Yahweh. According to Faur, idolatry can take two forms: the worshipping of pagan gods on the one hand and worshipping God with unprescribed ritual on the other.[173] While 5:11 and 8:3–17

---

[167] For a review, see Ackerman (1992:47–51), Allen (1994:141), Duguid (1994:65–67).

[168] This represents the viewpoint of Wevers (1969:67), Carley (1974:52–54), Zimmerli (1979:236–237), Vogt (1981:42–45), Ackerman (1992:54–55) and Allen (1994:139–141).

[169] For this, see Jenson (1992:89–93).

[170] Eichrodt 1970:122–123; Carley 1974:53; Craigie 1983a:57; Greenberg 1983a:168; Blenkinsopp 1990:54; Ackerman 1992:61–62; Allen 1994:142. For a different opinion, see Day (1992:486).

[171] Dijkstra 1996:97–104. Noting that the Tammuz cult is a fertility cult, Siedlecki interestingly points out that this abomination reflects a conflict between male and female power regarding procreation (1991:38).

[172] Ackerman 1992:98; Allen 1994:145; Dijkstra 1996:106; against Taylor (1993:148–158) who argues for a syncretistic solar-Yahwistic rite.

[173] Faur 1978:13–14. For a recent discussion on the various types of idolatry, see Halbertal and Margalit (1994:236–240).

belong to the former form, 6:1–7 which refers to worship on the high places and is hence illegitimate belongs to the second form. There is no doubt that these acts are seen as defiling the temple.

Another case of clearly defiling the sanctuary appears in Ez 23:38 which belongs to an indictment of Oholah and Oholibah (23:36–45). In v.37 they are accused of adultery with idols (גלולים) and blood-guilt by offering their children to the idols as food. When they do this to God, they defile God's sanctuary (v.38). The word גלולים occurs 39 times in Ezekiel in a variety of contexts.[174] Basically it refers to pagan idols[175] and is used in polemics against the idols.[176] It is closely related to impurity,[177] and often linked to the defilement of the people. More on this will be said below. The idea of offering children to idols, the male images (16:17), as food recalls Ez 16:20–21. Both passages contain features pertaining to the Molech cult.[178] Here the Molech cult is linked to adultery. This, as noted in Chapter Two, is common in the OT. As to the defilement of the sanctuary by the Molech cult, a parallel can be found in Lev 20:3. Thus, Ezekiel is in the priestly tradition in this particular aspect.[179]

To conclude, firstly, according to Ezekiel, God's sanctuary is defiled by improper actions rather than by objects themselves. Secondly, these actions, when performed by the people (basically referred to as from Jerusalem or as Jerusalem personified), can be summed up by the word "idolatry". The two forms of idolatry suggested by Faur are found in Ezekiel and they are both defiling. In the following chapter we will explore further the connection between idolatry and defilement of temple and its relation to retribution.

3.2.2. *Land*

The idea of the defilement of land appears just a few times in Ezekiel, but it plays a significant role in Ezekiel's theology of retribution. It is found in Ez 36:17–18, and only the piel form of טמא is used. These verses belong to the section 36:16–38 which is concerned with the future salvation of Israel. While vv.17–19 speaks of the uncleanness

---

[174] Bodi 1993:491–508.

[175] And therefore it does not refer to "a sin of idolatry" as Preuß claims (1978:2).

[176] This observation holds good for the MT. The LXX has different renderings which do not always have a negative connotation. See Kennedy (1994:203–204).

[177] Preuß 1978:3; Bodi 1993:509–510.

[178] Heider 1985:365–368; Day 1989:15.

[179] Milgrom would probably specify that priestly tradition to be H (cf. 1991:49).

of Israel which has a counterpart in vv.24–32 on future purification, vv.20–21 is concerned with the profanation of Yahweh's holy name which is rectified in vv.22–23.[180]

Vv.17–18 can be translated as: "Son of man, the house of Israel, while dwelling on their land,[181] defiled it by their way and their deeds; like the impurity of menstruation was their way before me. Then I poured out my wrath upon them[182] on account of the blood which they poured upon the land, and by their idols they defiled it". In v.17 the land (אדמה) is said to be defiled by Israel's general conduct and particular acts (דרך ועלילות). The combination "conduct and particular acts" is generic but always negative in Ezekiel.[183] It is elaborated in v.18 as bloodshed and idolatry which are denounced elsewhere in Ezekiel (e.g. 22:3, 6; 23:37).[184] What is not clear is whether bloodshed in this case has to do with social violence or idolatry. In view of the occurrence of the pair elsewhere in Ezekiel (e.g. 22:4), the former is more probable.[185] V.18 repeats again that Israel defiles the land (ארץ) by their idols, meaning the worship of the idols.[186]

Another reference is found in Ez 22:24 where the land is described as "not purified" (לא מטהרה).[187] According to Greenberg, the passive construction (pual participle) implies "failure, or lack, of efforts to purify".[188] There is no purification of the land. The implication is that the land is unclean. The cause of this uncleanness is detailed in vv.25–29 which includes the misconduct of every group of the leaders: the princes are charged with bloodshed and robbery; the

---

[180] For this chiastic structure, see Parunak (1978:472), Allen (1990:177). Cf. Maarsingh 1991:65.

[181] The participle ישבים indicates a circumstantial clause. E.g. Cooke 1936:395; Hossfeld 1977:290; Allen 1990:175; Greenberg 1997:727; Block 1998:343.

[182] The rest of this verse is not represented in LXX. This may be a later elaboration. See Allen (1990:176), Greenberg (1997:728).

[183] 14:22, 23; 20:43, 44; 24:14; 36:19.

[184] Kutsko (2000:74) interestingly argues that the prohibitions against bloodshed and idolatry go back to the idea that humanity is created in the image of God.

[185] Keil 1876b:107; Fisch 1950:242; Hossfeld 1977:304; Alexander 1986:920; Tidiman 1987:143; Blenkinsopp 1990:165; Maarsingh 1991:66; Ohnesorge 1991:263n.252; against Kraetzschmar 1900:103; Haag 1943:22; Block 1998:347.

[186] Cf. Levey 1987:101.

[187] The LXX renders it as οὐ βρεχομένη "not rained on", reflecting לא מטרה. This is adopted by Zimmerli (1979:465), Allen (1990:32). However, the idea of cleansing is found in the preceding section 22:17–22. See Bodi (1991:111), Block (1997:723), Greenberg (1997:460).

[188] Greenberg 1997:460.

priests violate the law and make no distinction between the holy and profane, the clean and unclean; the officials are again charged with bloodshed and dishonest gain; the prophets tell no truth; and the people of the land (i.e., the nobility) practise extortion and oppression. All these wrongdoings of the leadership cause the defilement of the land.

The metaphor in 24:1–14 names Jerusalem as "a city of blood" and compares it to a copper pot with חלאה. According to v.11, חלאה is an unclean substance inside the pot that will be consumed by overheating. Since copper does not rust, the word probably refers to "encrusted residue of cooked matter stuck to the inside of the pot".[189] This encrusted impurity is immediately equated to the blood-guilt in v.7.[190] If the pot represents the city, the meat the inhabitants, and the impurity the bloodguilt, then the impurity of the pot caused by the meat stands for the city's impurity of bloodguilt caused by the inhabitants. The verb "to purify" (טהר piel) is used to denote God's cleansing of this impurity, but it is to no avail (vv.12–13; cf. v.6). Therefore, the city has not been cleansed and will be clean (טהר qal) no more until a more drastic action of God is executed. Although this passage speaks not of the defilement of a land but of a city, its inclusion here is not inappropriate. We may compare this passage to 22:24 where there is no purification of the land. Both texts present a gloomy picture of the land/Jerusalem: it is not clean, and it refuses to be cleansed.

In the priestly texts, the land is defiled by illicit sexual relations (Lev 18), the Molech cult (Lev 18:21), and murder (Nu 35:34). The last passage lays down that bloodshed, which defiles the land, should be avoided because God dwells in the land. God's presence in the land demands that the land be clean.[191] The indwelling of God in the land can also be found in Ezekiel. In a salvation oracle Yahweh promises to dwell among the people (37:27). The presence of his glory in Jerusalem before its departure demonstrates that he dwelt among the people. More definitely, Yahweh is in the midst of the

---

[189] Greenberg 1997:499. See also Wevers (1969:141), Cooper (1994:236), NIV's "encrusted" or "deposit". Against Cooke's (1936:267) and Zimmerli's (1979:494) "rust". Block's (1997:778) understanding of it as meat is unfounded in view of v.6 where it is distinguished from the meat.

[190] Cooke 1936:267; Brownlee 1972:25; Greenberg 1997:504.

[191] See further Joosten (1996:176–180).

people on earth at the time of Israel's disaster (35:10). Several times
the land of Israel is referred to as his land (36:5, 20; 38:16). Thus,
it is probable that as in the priestly texts Ezekiel correlates Yahweh's
dwelling in the land with the requirement that the land be clean.
Elsewhere the land is defiled by hanging overnight a criminal's corpse
(Dt 21:23) and idolatry (Jer 2:7). If we take into account the phrase
חנף הארץ, we have Nu 35:33 (murder), Ps 106:38 (children sacrificed
to idols), Is 24:5 (violation of laws and statutes and breaking of
covenant), Jer 3:1 (marriage of a divorced woman); 3:2 (whoredom
and wickedness); 3:9 (idolatry). Thus, Ezekiel's attribution of bloodshed and idolatry (as a generalisation of the Molech cult) as causes
for the defilement of the land is in line with the priestly tradition.

3.2.3. *People*

The impurity language in Ezekiel is frequently concerned with the
defilement of the people. It is in this case that the qal, niphal, piel
and hitpael forms of טמא are used. The piel forms are often used
in relation to sexual defilement, the concern of which is not ritual
but moral. In 18:6, 11, 15 a man defiling his neighbour's wife is a
criterion for his unrighteousness. This idea of defilement is less concerned with ritual defilement as a result of sexual intercourse,[192] and
more with moral defilement due to adultery.[193] In particular, 18:6b
seems to be an abbreviated reversed form of Lev 18:19–20, concerning both adultery and sexual relationship with a menstruant. As
a formal criterion for unrighteousness, the prohibition applies not
just to the people in Jerusalem, but to any single Israelite, or a generation of Israelites,[194] or even a future generation of Israelites.[195] In
fact, the Jerusalemites[196] are indicted for committing such an offence
in 33:26. It also appears in the judgement of Jerusalem but without
actually using the word טמא (22:11aα: "each one commits abomination with his neighbour's wife"). The piel is also used in a case

---

[192] Against Cooke 1936:198; Zimmerli 1979:380.

[193] Keil 1876a:250; Fisch 1950:109; Greenberg 1983a:329; Allen 1994:274; Block
1997:571.

[194] Joyce (1989:46–47) argues that the legal language in Ez 18 is reapplied on a
communal or national level.

[195] See the discussion in Matties (1990:159–196).

[196] The accused is actually called "the inhabitants of these waste places in the
land of Israel" (33:24). That it refers to the Jerusalemites is held by Greenberg
(1997:684).

of incest in 22:11aβ where one is accused of defiling his daughter-in-law. The parallel phrase in 22:11b may point to the defiling nature of another crime of incest: one violates (ענה) his sister. Another use of the piel related to sex is found in 23:17 where the Babylonians are said to defile Oholibah. Within Ez 23 Oholibah (as a byname for Jerusalem) is depicted as a married woman, and hence her defilement is a result of adultery.

While adultery and incest are sexual misconduct prohibited both in the Decalogue (Ex 20:14; Dt 5:18) and the priestly texts (e.g. Lev 18:6–16, 20), it is never said that the man defiles (טמא, piel) the woman with whom he commits the offence. For example, in Lev 18:20, where the man who commits adultery with his kinsman's wife is said to become defiled with her (לטמאה־בה, qal), no defilement of the woman is explicitly mentioned. Similarly, in Nu 5:13 the married woman who commits adultery is said to defile herself (נטמאה, niphal). In cases like these, the emphasis is put on the offender him/herself. That is to say, the one who commits adultery will bring him/herself into a dangerous state, namely, defilement. The point is to warn the people not to commit such an offence. In contrast, Ezekiel underlines the responsibility of the people for bringing about defilement not only on himself, but also on the others. Even if the offender does not care about his own condition, he should know that the offence brings defilement to the other person.

There are two more uses of the piel. Its use in Ez 20:26 is unique in the MT in that Yahweh is the subject of the verb טמא (piel) with the second generation in the wilderness as object. Contrary to most translations, which take the piel of טמא as factitive in meaning,[197] it is better to take it as declarative-estimative in meaning.[198] Thus, the text reads "I declared them unclean . . . .". The reason for such a declaration is based on their behaviour stated in v.26aβ. The phrase בהעביר כל־פטר רחם points to the practice of the Molech cult, especially when it is read with v.31.[199] The people's action is sometimes

---

[197] Keil 1876a:271; Ewald 1880:104; Smend 1880:132; Toy 1899:32; Kraetzschmar 1900:173; Herrmann 1924:120; Cooke 1936:218; Fisch 1950:126; Noordtzij 1957:215; Zimmerli 1979:401; Greenberg 1983a:361; Dijkstra 1986:193; Ohnesorge 1991:178; Block 1997:634. Or, less strongly as "I let them be defiled" (Davidson 1916:156; NIV). Cf. Allen 1990:2.

[198] Sedlmeier 1990:283.

[199] Heider 1985:371.

seen as a result of following[200] or misinterpreting[201] the no-good laws in 20:25. The assumption is that the people now obey these no-good laws, but this is not clear in the text. Moreover, the people are never said to have followed any of God's laws in Ez 20 (but only their fathers' as in 20:18). It is equally mistaken to claim that God demands the people to sacrifice their firstborn.[202] Rather, God declares them unclean when they perform this idolatrous act. In the two previous occurrences of טמא (hitpael) in Ez 20, God commands the first and second generations not to defile themselves with the idols (vv.7, 18), but they do not heed his commands. They do defile themselves with idols. Thus, this declaration forms a suitable conclusion to these commands. They are now formally declared unclean by God. His purpose is not, as some claim, to desolate them,[203] but to appal them[204] so that they will know he is Yahweh.

The last use of the piel form is found in 37:23. However, the use here is anomalous because it has no direct object. Thus, it is often translated as if it were a reflexive[205] or a passive.[206] The MT reads יִטַּמְּאוּ. While the consonants can be vocalised as a niphal (יִטָּמְאוּ), this would contradict the general pattern found in the MT that the niphal of טמא is used only in the perfect (except Ez 20:30, 31 where we have the participial form). It is therefore better to repoint it as a hitpael (יִטַּמְּאוּ).[207] This brings it in line with other hitpael uses in Ezekiel which will be dealt with shortly.

---

[200] Davidson 1916:156; Greenberg 1983a:368–369; Dijkstra 1986:202; Ohnesorge 1991:178; Eslinger 1998:108.

[201] Wevers 1969:118; Zimmerli 1979:411; Heider 1985:372; Allen 1990:12. Various interpretations have been offered to explain this difficult passage. See Block (1997:639) for a summary. For its *Wirkungsgeschichte* in ancient Judaism and early Christianity, see van der Horst (1992).

[202] As Block (1997:637) claims.

[203] Greenberg 1983a:369; Heider 1985:372n.738; Allen 1990:2; Block 1997:634.

[204] אשמם (v.26bα) is taken to mean "I might horrify them". E.g. Kraetzschmar 1900:173; Herrmann 1924:120; Cooke 1936:219; van den Born 1954:126; Zimmerli 1979:401; Vogt 1981:125; RSV; NRSV; NIV. Cf. Ez 32:10. Moreover, the idea that God does not actually destroy them is a motif in vv.3–29. Four times the Israelites are said to rebel against God or disobey his statutes (vv.8a, 13a, 16, 21a), and four times it is mentioned that God refrains from destroying them (vv.8b–9, 13b–14, 17, 21b–22).

[205] Keil 1876b:130; Kraetzschmar 1900:253; Herrmann 1924:234; Bertholet 1936:128; Cooke 1936:402; Schumpp 1942:186; Fisch 1950:251; Zimmerli 1983:270; Dijkstra 1989:136; Allen 1990:189; Block 1998:407; NRSV; NIV.

[206] Greenberg 1997:752.

[207] *BHS* apparatus.

The qal forms are found in 22:3, 4 (Jerusalem) and 23:17 (Oholibah). In the first two cases Jerusalem is indicted for both social offences (i.e., bloodshed) and cultic offences (i.e., idolatry). But the fact that she is in a state of uncleanness (hence the use of qal) is attributed only to the making of idols. This is made clear both in 22:3 where she is charged with making idols for her[208] so that she becomes unclean (לטמאה), and in 22:4. In both cases, bloodshed is also mentioned but not linked to impurity.[209] In v.5 the same distinction continues: she is said to have an impure name (טמאת השם) and is full of tumult (רבת המהומה). The first designation shows that Jerusalem is well-known for her uncleanness while the second probably refers to her social disorder (cf. Am 3:9).[210] It is important to note that at the beginning of the accusation in Ez 22, the impure state of Jerusalem is stressed. In 23:17, after it is said that the Babylonians defile (piel) Oholibah, she is said to be in an impure state (qal). This combination underlines more the uncleanness of Oholibah than that of the Babylonians.

The hitpael forms appear in 14:11; 20:7, 18 and 37:23 (after emendation). This form is basically reflexive and factitive. In 14:1–11 Yahweh gives a harsh reply to the elders among the exiles because they are charged with "bringing up their idols on their heart and placing a stumbling block of their iniquity before them". The phrase (ה)עלה על-לב refers to thinking.[211] The people are accused of thinking of the idols. The expression מכשול עון is unique to Ezekiel. In its six occurrences it is closely connected to idols.[212] In 14:11 one goal of God's punishment is that the house of Israel will never defile themselves with all their transgressions (כל-פשעיהם) which, in this case, refer to idolatry.[213] In the future, the house of Israel will not bring themselves any more into a state of defilement through idolatry, but in the present they are. A combination of transgression and idolatry is also found in 37:23a although there they may not be

---

[208] The Hebrew עליה means "on behalf of". E.g. BDB 754; Allen 1990:31; Block 1997:703. Cf. Zimmerli 1979:452.

[209] Against Block 1997:705.

[210] Zimmerli 1979:457; Allen 1990:30; Greenberg 1997:453.

[211] BDB 749; Allen 1994:192. Against Schoneveld (1969). But see Nay (1999:200–203) for a detailed discussion.

[212] Taylor 1969:126; Duguid 1994:117; Stevenson 1996:73. Its association with idols is therefore closer than Block thinks (1997:146–147).

[213] Cf. Ohnesorge 1991:113n.122.

equivalent. But again, it refers to a future situation in which the
Israelites will not defile themselves with idols and transgressions. The
basis for this is that God will cleanse them (v.23b, טהר piel). In 20:7
Yahweh commands the first generation of Israelites not to defile
themselves by the Egyptian idols.[214] The same command is repeated
in 20:18 for the second generation, although in both cases the command falls on deaf ears.

The niphal forms appear in 20:30, 31, 43; 23:7, 13, 30. As mentioned above, the niphal-perfect forms a paradigm with the hitpael-
imperfect and is therefore reflexive and factitive in meaning in these
cases.[215] The niphal participle of טמא is only found in 20:30 and 31.
In these verses, God first asks the exiles, the addressees of Ezekiel
(20:1), if they are defiling themselves in the way of their fathers and
then proceeds to answer affirmatively that they are defiling themselves with their idols. In v.31 the Molech cult is mentioned, referring
back to v.26. Later in a salvation oracle concerning the future of
the Israelites, they will remember the ways and deeds by which they
defile themselves on the land of Israel to which Yahweh will bring
them from among the nations (20:43). In the context of the chapter,
the defilement here refers to the result of idolatry as in 20:7, 18.

Ez 23:7a describes how Oholah (i.e., Samaria) bestows her harlotry to the choicest Assyrian men. Then in 23:7b בכל־גלוליהם is
apposed to and defines more clearly בכל אשר־עגנה.[216] That is, all
that she lusts after (עגב) are their idols (i.e., the Assyrian's idols),[217]
and it is with these idols that she defiles herself. Her sister, Oholibah
(i.e., Jerusalem), follows suit and is even worse. In 23:13 Oholibah
defiles herself in the same way as her sister, meaning, with the idols
of the Assyrians, although this is not mentioned explicitly. She is
indeed worse than Oholah because she even defiles herself with the
idols of the nations, not just Assyria (23:30). Throughout Ez 23:1–35

---

[214] Jenni (1992:145) claims that ב in 20:7, 18 is *beth instrumenti*. Thus, both verses
refer to people that defile themselves by means of idols.
[215] Cf. the translations of Zimmerli, Greenberg, Allen, and NRSV.
[216] Keil 1876a:324; Smend 1880:158; van den Born 1954:146. The addition of
"and" between these phrases overlooks the apposition between them (e.g. Dijkstra
1986:232; Einheitsübersetzung). Some others render 23:7b as "she defiled herself
with all the idols of all those after whom she lusted" (e.g. Kraetzschmar 1900:189;
Herrmann 1924:140; Zimmerli 1979:472). In this case the suffix of "idols" refers
to all after whom she lusted.
[217] Fisch 1950:151; Greenberg 1997:476.

a distinction between defilement as a result of adultery and that of idolatry is made. In the first case, the piel forms of טמא are used (23:17) whereas in the second case the niphal forms are used (vv. 7, 13, 30). Moreover, the verbs זנה and its cognates are used only to describe Oholah/Oholibah's relationship with the nations, but never with the idols. It is only in v.37 that נאף is used to characterise the relationship of Oholah or Oholibah with the idols.

The self-defilement of the people with idols or iniquities (עון) is further seen in the salvation oracle in 36:16–38, especially in vv.25, 29, 33. The first half of v.25 speaks of God sprinkling clean water upon the house of Israel so that they shall become clean. Then in v.25b God will purify (טהר piel) the people from their uncleanness and from their idols.[218] The "uncleanness" in v.29 has no reference but echoes the conduct of the people in v.17. Lastly in v.33 God will cleanse the people from their iniquities. These verses suggest that the people are defiled with their idols and iniquities, and in the future God will purify them from this defilement.

Surprisingly, a person's defilement with idols is not very prominent elsewhere in the OT. In Lev 18:24 and 30 the Israelites are asked not to defile themselves (hitpael) with the list of prohibitions in 18:2–23, including sacrifices to Molech. Again in Lev 18:24 the nations defile themselves (niphal) precisely in these ways. Jer 2:23 makes a parallel between Israel's not defiling itself (niphal) and its not going after the Baals. That is to say, by committing idolatry in following the Baals Israel defiles itself. Ps 106:39 links defilement (qal) more explicitly with idols in general and sacrifice of children in particular (vv.36–38). Lastly, one may refer to Gen 35:1–4. In this passage Jacob is summoned by God to go to Bethel and make an altar there. Before he starts the journey, he commands his household to put away the foreign gods and purify themselves. Later Jacob hides these gods under an oak tree. Although the meaning of these actions admits of different interpretations, the connection between the presence of foreign gods and the need for purification seems certain.[219] We can perhaps also mention Lev 19:31 where consulting

---

[218] Different from the accentuation of the MT, the LXX links v.25bαβ to v.25a and adds a copula to v.25bγ to make it an independent clause, and the NRSV connects v.25a to v.25bα.

[219] For a recent interpretation of this passage, see Pagolu (1998:231–241).

mediums and wizards will result in defilement. Thus, Ezekiel's concern with defilement with idols is much more emphatic than the rest of the OT.

Some conclusions can be drawn. First, the piel form of טמא with a human as subject is factitive in meaning, referring to the case when a man defiles a woman by illicit sexual intercourse. In these cases, the emphasis is on the power of the act to defile. In its only occurrence with Yahweh as subject (20:26), it is declarative in meaning. Second, the qal, niphal and hitpael forms are employed when the defilement of a person is connected with idols. The only exception is 23:17 where the qal is used for defilement by illicit sex, but it appears after the piel form in the same verse. The reflexive niphal and hitpael point out that the agent of defilement is the subject itself. In these cases, the emphasis is on the subjects themselves who bring about the state of defilement upon themselves with idols. Idols themselves are never the subject of טמא (piel), and are therefore never said to defile. Third, not only the past and present Israel/Jerusalem but also the present generation of exiles are characterised by defilement with idols. It is only in the future that Israel will be free from such a defilement (14:11; 36:25; 37:23).

3.2.4. God's Holy Name

Within the OT, defilement of God's holy name is found only in Ez 43:7–8. Elsewhere his name is said to be profaned rather than defiled.[220] This passage seems to say that impurity is caused by the proximity of graves of the kings to the temple. Various meanings are given to the word פגר. First, following a lead from Ugaritic, Neiman suggests the meaning "stele".[221] Second, Ebach argues that it means offering for the dead.[222] Third, it refers to a corpse[223] or its extended meaning "idol".[224] In view of its use elsewhere in the OT,[225] the last meaning is most probable. Thus, the point is that the kings are buried too close to the temple. Moreover, v.8 seems to point to

---

[220] The LXX here twice renders טמא by βεβηλόω which normally translates חלל, whereas the regular rendering for טמא is μιαίνω. See Amorim (1985:194n.1).

[221] Neiman (1948), followed by Zimmerli (1983:417), Allen (1990:238), Duguid (1994:41).

[222] Ebach (1971), followed by Dijkstra (1989:164), Block (1998:575).

[223] Most commentaries; Wright 1987:124; Bloch-Smith 1992:116.

[224] Keil 1876b:281. Cf. "lifeless idols" in NIV.

[225] Wright 1987:123–124.

the infringement of sacred space by the people. This recalls texts like 2 Kg 11 where the temple forms part of the royal palace complex. These actions are termed "abominations" by which the people and the former kings defile God's holy name. However, when observed closely, it seems that the concern here is more the temple than the name of God. Not only does the section 43:6–9 form part of the temple tour, vv.7–8 speak about the temple. So, it may be possible that here God's holy name is a designation of the temple,[226] although we must admit that this designation is never found elsewhere in Ezekiel.[227]

4. *Profanation and Sanctification in Ezekiel*

In the last section we noted that Ezekiel has a great concern with impurity, especially moral impurity. Belonging also to the related concepts of holiness are the polar concepts of profanation and sanctification. Since these concepts are less related to our concern, we will only refer to this briefly.

Regarding profanation, that which can be profaned includes the sancta (e.g. 7:21; 22:26), the sanctuary (e.g. with Yahweh as subject: 24:21; with a human subject: 23:38; 44:7), the Sabbaths (e.g. 20:13, 16, 21, 24; 22:8; 23:38), God's holy name (e.g. 20:9, 14, 22, 39; 36:20, 21, 22, 23; 39:7), and even God himself (e.g. 13:19; 22:26). Regarding sanctification, note firstly that the noun קֹדֶשׁ, which occurs 57 times in Ezekiel, is mostly in construct with another noun and so functions as an adjective. These include "holy name" (e.g. 20:39; 36:20), "holy mountain" (e.g. 20:40; 28:14), "Holy of Holies" (e.g. 41:4; 42:13; 48:12), "holy chambers" (e.g. 42:13; 4:19; 46:19), "holy garments" (42:14), and "holy portion" (e.g. 45:1, 4). Secondly, it is also used in its absolute form to refer to holy things (e.g. 20:40; 22:8), offerings (e.g. 36:38),[228] holy place (e.g. 41:21; 42:14), and holiness in opposition to the common (e.g. 22:26; 42:20; 44:23). The verb קָדֵשׁ mostly has Yahweh as subject, with exceptions in 20:20 and Ez 40–48.[229] The object of the verb includes the Israelites (e.g.

---

[226] Amorim 1985:195; Wright 1987:123; Bloch-Smith 1992:119.
[227] Cf. Ez 22:5 where טֻמְאַת הַשֵּׁם is a designation of Jerusalem.
[228] For this understanding, see Greenberg (1997:727).
[229] Against Joyce (1989:104) who says that the subject is "invariably Yahweh himself".

20:12; 37:28), Yahweh himself (e.g. 20:41; 38:23) and Yahweh's name (e.g. 36:23).

The above consideration is extremely brief. Details such as what sorts of actions are involved and in what contexts the profanation or sanctification takes place are omitted. It is not our purpose to delve into it. We may note that just as in the case of purity and impurity in which Israel's past is characterised as a period of defilement and its future as a period that presupposes purification, Israel's past is also characterised as a period in which Yahweh's name and sanctuary are profaned and its future is characterised as a period of sanctification of Yahweh's name and sanctuary.[230]

5. *Conclusion*

This chapter has examined the idea of purity and impurity in Ezekiel to provide the basis for the investigation of the relation between impurity and retribution in the following chapter. We started with a general discussion on the holiness word group, paying particular attention to purity/impurity. There are three types of impurity: permanent, ritual and moral. Of particular importance is the last type, although Ezekiel is concerned with ritual impurity. He takes care to ensure that food prepared in exile is not defiling or at least not repulsive. He follows the tradition of regarding scattering bones around places of worship as a way of defiling the places. His preoccupation with the impurity of corpses, which are able to defile even the land, exceeds the priestly concern as shown, for instance, in Leviticus. But the main concern for Ezekiel remains moral impurity.

In the priestly texts, moral impurity is caused by sexual sins, the Molech cult, illicit divination, deliberately eating sacrifices while impure, and bloodshed. Some of these are found in Ezekiel. While in the priestly texts offenders of sexual sins are often said to defile themselves, in Ezekiel it is often the male who is said to defile the female by those sins. The stress is not on warning people not to commit those sins as in Leviticus, but on showing the devastating effect such an offence has on other people. While sexual sin is mainly responsible for the defilement of the land (followed by an exile) in

---

[230] Luc (1983) provides a study in this direction which, however, suffers many imprecisions.

the priestly texts (e.g. Lev 18), its importance in Ezekiel in the defilement of land is of less significance, but not totally absent. Bloodshed does play a role in defiling the land (e.g. 24:1–14) in Ezekiel as in Nu 35:33–34, but the overwhelming concern of Ezekiel is idolatry.

There are basically two types of idolatry: worship of pagan gods and worship of Yahweh with unprescribed rituals. Both types are denounced in Ezekiel. The defiling power of idolatry is immense. It can defile the sanctuary, the land and the idolaters themselves. This defilement is actually caused by the act of idolatry, but not the idols themselves. Idolatry also leads to the profanation of the Sabbath and God's holy name. The practice of idolatry breaks every taboo and is seen as the sin *par excellence* in Ezekiel. In the reconstructed *past* of Israel (Ez 20), Israel as a nation is characterised by idolatry and self-defilement. In the *present* generation, whether in Jerusalem (e.g. 5:11) or in exile (e.g. 14:11), Israel is so portrayed as well. Idolatry is committed by Israel not only across *time* but also *space*. The whole history of Israel is actually a history of idolatry and hence a history of moral defilement. Only the future Israel will not be defiled by idolatry because of a cleansing performed by Yahweh (e.g. 36:25, 29). If the "old" Israel is characterised by their moral impurity, the "new" Israel is characterised by moral purity which can only be attained by Yahweh's cleansing action.

The presence of Yahweh in the sanctuary and the land requires them to be pure. But the land refuses to be cleansed and the sanctuary is defiled by illicit worship. That Ezekiel has great concern for the purity of the land is further noted by his extension of the priestly cultic impurity in allowing corpses to defile the land. The land should not be defiled by any cultic impurity or moral impurity. While the cultic defilement of the land (by the corpses) can be removed by human agents (39:11–15), the desolate situation of the land as a result of the moral defilement can only be healed by Yahweh himself (cf. 36:33–36). The sanctuary, being the abode of Yahweh, is defiled by idolatry. The temple vision Ez 8–11 expresses this concern and also a partial resolution of the problem as we will see in the following chapter. Incidentally, we note that Ezekiel's demand that the whole land be pure should be put side by side with his idea that not the whole land is holy. The city area is explicitly referred to as profane or common (48:15).

Generally speaking, the history of Israel can be perceived from two perspectives. It can first be seen as a history of moving from defilement to purification. While moral defilement is caused by human misconduct, its purification goes beyond the human level and requires a cleansing from Yahweh. Israel's history can also be seen as a history of moving from profanation of Yahweh's name and sanctuary to their sanctification. Again, while the profanation is caused by human failure, the reverse process of sanctification can only be done by Yahweh alone. The history of Israel is characterised by the two poles: human failure and divine reparation.

CHAPTER FIVE

IMPURITY AND RETRIBUTION (II)

1. *Introduction*

In the previous chapter we presented a basic understanding of the idea of holiness and purity in the OT in general and in Ezekiel in particular. The objective of this chapter is to examine how this idea is related to retribution. It will be demonstrated that the relation between an action and its consequence does not always operate under the juridical paradigm as misdeed and punishment according to law but can also be seen as under the paradigm of pollution and its resolution. This paradigm can be found in Leviticus with respect to ritual and moral impurity. Leviticus is concerned not only with the difference between pure and impure, but also with the restriction of impurity, the disposal of impurity,[1] and purification. With respect to moral impurity, the idea of pollution and its resolution by the disposal of impurity and purification can be found in Ezekiel. We have seen in Chapter Four that Ezekiel often views offences in terms of the purity/impurity category. It is not that he is mostly concerned with sacral offences and neglects social or moral offences,[2] but that he interprets the latter also by using the language of purity/impurity. If cultic, social and moral offences defile the offenders, the temple and the land, then the defilement has to be dealt with, either by disposing of the sources of impurity or by some sort of purification. That is to say, the action of producing moral impurity has a consequence of removing (the source of) this impurity. The underlying principle governing the act-consequence connection is therefore that impurity demands a resolution. Retribution, from this perspective, can be interpreted as an effort to check the spread of impurity.

In this chapter, we will first examine the temple vision in Ez 8–11. It will be argued that the slaughter in Ez 9 and the throwing of burning coals over the city Jerusalem in Ez 10 are acts of removing

---

[1] For a thorough discussion of this theme, see Wright (1987).
[2] As claimed by von Rad (1965:224).

impurity and cleansing. After that we will examine the close relationship between impurity and the land. We will demonstrate that
impurity leads to the denial of access to the land, the dispossession
of the land, and the departure from the land. That is to say, exile
is a means to remove impurity from the land.

2. *The Temple Vision in Ez 8–11*

2.1. *Introductory Remarks*

Ez 8–11 is the second and also the second longest vision of Ezekiel.[3]
In the present form the vision is taken as a literary whole with a
chiastic framework:[4]

A	8:1a	earthly context of the vision: date, location, exile elders as audience
B	8:1b	beginning of the vision: descent of Yahweh's hand upon the prophet
C	8:3b	translocation of the prophet: from Babylon to Jerusalem
[D	8:4–11:23	the vision]
C'	11:24a	translocation of the prophet: from Jerusalem to Babylon
B'	11:24b	end of the vision: ascent of the vision from the prophet
A'	11:25	earthly context of the vision: report to the exiles

The vision proper, which lies between 8:4 and 11:23, comprises several parts. The first part 8:4–18 consists of an account of four cultic abominations (vv.4–6, 7–13, 14–15, 16–17) and Yahweh's response
to them (v.18). Some common formal elements run through these
abominations:[5] (1) location (vv.3b, 7a, 14a, 16aα); (2) the command
to see (vv.5a, 9); (3) description of the abomination introduced by
והנה (vv.5b, 10–11, 14b, 16aβb) and participants (vv.11, 14b, 16aβ);
(4) a question about the prophet's seeing introduced by בן־אדם (vv.6a,
12, 15a, 17a); and (5) a transitional note that worse will be seen
(vv.6bβ, 13b, 15b).

The second part (Ez 9) follows up Yahweh's response to the abominations in 8:18. Some interconnections between Ez 8 and 9 can be

---

[3] Against Vawter and Hoppe (1991:63) who claim that this is the longest.
[4] Greenberg 1983a:192; but compare Parunak (1978:67). See also Hossfeld
(1986:156–157), Allen (1994:129–130) and Block (1997:272).
[5] Horst (1953:342–344), modified by Allen (1994:130).

detected:[6] (1) the phrase "loud voice" (8:18; 9:1); (2) the expression of mercilessness (8:18; 9:5, 10); (3) lawlessness of the land (8:17; 9:9) and abominations (8:6 etc.; 9:4); (4) the claim of the people (8:12; 9:9); and (5) the reference to worshippers (8:16–17; 9:6).[7] Within chapter 9, Allen discovers the following structure:[8] (1) summons of the agents: A1: vv.1–2aα; B1: v.2aβb; (2) two commands to the agents: B2: vv.3b–4; A2: vv.5–7; (3) Ezekiel's intercession and Yahweh's response: A3: vv.8–10; B3: v.11. Note that while all the A sections deal with destruction, the B sections concern the sparing of lives.

In the third part (Ez 10), several themes are interwoven together: the burning of Jerusalem, the departure of the glory of Yahweh, and the description of the cherubim and wheels. A command to spread burning coals over the city Jerusalem is found in 10:1–3 and 6–7. The departure of the glory of Yahweh is mentioned in 10:4, which first appears in essentially the same form in 9:3a, then continues in 10:18–19 and culminates in 11:22–23. The description of the cherubim is found in 10:5, 8–17, 20–22. This mixture of themes is often attributed to redactional activity. Various attempts have been made to identify the different layers of the text and its relation to Ez 1.[9]

The fourth part (11:1–13) continues the vision within the temple precinct. It has the form of a disputation. Graffy structures the text as: introduction (v.2), quotation (v.3), preparatory remarks (vv.4–6), a first refutation (vv.7–10), and a second refutation (vv.11–12).[10] In view of Murray's modification of the form,[11] Allen proposes the following: thesis (v.3aβb), dispute (v.6) and counterthesis (vv.7–11).[12] The thesis is put in the form of a quotation from the officials of the people. The dispute in v.6 then provides the reason for the invalidity of the thesis. Finally, the counterthesis (vv.7–11) expands the dispute and at the same time serves as an announcement of punishment introduced by לכן. The whole disputation is framed by a reference to Pelatiah (vv.1, 13). There are some connections with the preceding chapters: (1) the transportation of the prophet to the east gate

---

[6] Greenberg 1983a:193.
[7] Allen 1994:130.
[8] Allen 1994:130.
[9] E.g. Sprank and Wiese 1926:1–74; Schmidt 1950:83–90; Horst 1953; Balla 1958:325–326; Houk 1971; Hossfeld 1986, 1987.
[10] Graffy 1984:42–47.
[11] Murray 1987:99.
[12] Allen (1994:131), modified by Block (1997:330).

of the temple (11:1) follows up the movement of Yahweh's glory in
10:19; (2) the slain are found in both 11:6 and 9:7; (3) there is a
reference to 25 men in both 11:1 and 8:16; (4) the accusation in
11:6 resembles 9:9;[13] and (5) the prophet makes a similar intercession in 9:8 and 11:13.[14]

The last part (11:14–23) comprises a response to Ezekiel's intercession (11:13) in 11:14–21, and the conclusion to the departure of Yahweh's glory in 11:22–23. Graffy's opinion that vv.14–17
form a disputation[15] is modified by Allen: thesis (v.15), dispute (v.16)
and counterthesis (vv.17–20) which also serves as a proclamation of
salvation.[16]

There is no doubt that Ez 8–11 has undergone some redactional
changes which may be attributed to either Ezekiel himself or his dis-
ciples. It is not our purpose here to contribute to this discussion.
Our focus will be on deciphering the principle underlying the deed-
consequence nexus when the deeds are morally defiling.

2.2. *Disposal of Impurity*

2.2.1. *Introduction*

Ez 8–11 contains different themes including the cultic abominations
(Ez 8), the command to kill (Ez 9), the scattering of burning coals
over the city (Ez 10), and the departure of Yahweh's glory from the
city (Ez 9–11). Because of this multiplicity of themes, Ez 8–11 denies
exegetes a satisfactory interpretation which can accommodate all
these motifs. The task of the exegete becomes even more daunting
when the complexity of the growth of text is taken into consideration. Our main concern is Ez 9 and 10.

A common interpretation is to view Ez 9 and 10 as two acts of
judgement or punishment of God on the people for their idolatrous
abominations mentioned in Ez 8. Take Ewald as an example. After
discussing the four abominations in Ez 8, he states that the threat
in 8:18 is executed in a twofold manner, the slaughter in Ez 9 and
the burning of the city in Ez 10:1–8, holding that the latter is already
described in Ez 4–5.[17] In this understanding, the abominations done

---

[13] Greenberg 1983a:194.
[14] Block 1997:329.
[15] Graffy 1984:47–52.
[16] Allen 1994:131.
[17] Ewald 1880:58–63.

(Ez 8) are just like any death-incurring sins. Thus, the punishment for those who committed these offences is death. While Ewald conceives the burning of the city Jerusalem in 10:1–7 as an allusion to the siege and subsequent destruction of the city by Babylon, no such allusion is found for the slaughter in Ez 9.[18]

Ewald finds many supporters with his opinion that Ez 9:1–10:7 contains two divine punishments which realise the threat in 8:18.[19] However, in cases where some scholars take 8:1–9:11 and 10:1–7 as separate units, the destruction of the city can no longer be taken as a punishment for the offences done in Ez 8.[20]

2.2.2. *Defilement of Temple*

We have mentioned in the previous chapter that some offences defile the temple. Since this theme is of some importance in Ez 8–11, we will probe into it more. We will rely on Milgrom who provides an interesting exposition on this topic.

One must start with Milgrom's understanding of the הַחַטָּאת. According to him, the word is a piel derivative, and therefore it carries the meaning of the piel form of חטא, meaning "to cleanse, expurgate, decontaminate".[21] Hence, it should be rendered as "purification offering" rather than "sin offering".

If that is the case, then what is the object of this purification? Note that the purification offering is used in cases of severe ritual impurity (e.g. leprosy and bodily discharges: Lev 12–15) or commission of some inadvertent offences (e.g. Lev 4). First of all, ritual impurity is usually cleansed by ablution (e.g. Lev 15:8). Thus, the purification offering does not seem to purify the person concerned in cases of severe ritual impurity. And in cases of inadvertent offences, the inadvertent offenders are never called impure and therefore require no ablution. What they need is forgiveness, as the formula "the priest shall perform the purgation rite . . . that he/they may be

---

[18] Cf. Blenkinsopp 1990:59. Allen (1994:167) states that both events in Ez 9 and 10 anticipate what the Babylonians will do to the city in 587.

[19] E.g. Smend 1880:55; Bertholet 1897:50; Davidson 1916:60, 64; Kraetzschmar 1900:97, 104; Herrmann 1924:63; Zimmerli 1979:253; Vogt 1981:46; Greenberg 1983a:192; Allen 1994:146, 150; Biggs 1996:28, 30.

[20] Fohrer 1955:48; Balla 1958:325–326. They, however, do not accept the whole of the two units as authentic. Some other scholars do not say explicitly that Ez 10 contains another divine punishment. E.g. Blenkinsopp 1990:59.

[21] Milgrom 1971:237.

forgiven" clearly shows (Lev 4:20, 26, 31, 35). Again, the purification offering does not cleanse the inadvertent offenders.

To determine the object of the purification by this offering, we have to note how blood is used. In Lev 8:15 Moses took the blood of the purification offering and "put some on each of the horns of the altar, purifying the altar". Thus, the חַטָּאת blood is the purifying agent. Moreover, this blood is never applied to a person but only to the sanctuary.[22] A consideration of the prepositions used with כִּפֶּר is useful. According to Milgrom, in the context of purification offering, כִּפֶּר means only "purge", as is shown by its parallel usage with טִהַר or חִטֵּא (e.g. Lev 14:48, 52, 58).[23] With a non-human object, כִּפֶּר takes the preposition עַל, בְּ or a direct object (e.g. Lev 16:16, 20) and this must be understood literally. With a human object, the prepositions עַל (referring to persons other than the subject) or בַּעַד (referring to the subject himself), which signify "on behalf of" (e.g. Lev 16:6, 24, 30, 33), are used.[24] The point is that the purification rite is not performed on the offerer but on his behalf. These arguments demonstrate that the object of purification in this rite is that which receives the blood, namely, the sanctuary and its sancta.

If the sanctuary and its sancta are to be cleansed, it means that they must first be defiled by either the severe ritual impurity of the people concerned or the inadvertent offences. Apart from these, other offences as mentioned in the last chapter can also defile the sanctuary (e.g. the Molech cult in Lev 20:3), but that does not mean that all these acts defile the sanctuary to the same extent. There is a gradation in the polluting power of these acts. Mainly on the basis of Lev 4 and 16, Milgrom distinguishes three grades:[25] (1) The individual's severe physical impurity and inadvertent offences defile the sacrificial altar (in the courtyard) which is cleansed by daubing the חַטָּאת blood on its horns (Lev 4:25, 30; 9:9). (2) The inadvertent offences of the high priest or the whole congregation pollute the shrine which is then cleansed by sprinkling blood seven times in front of the curtain (פרכת) and putting blood on the horns of the incense altar (Lev 4:5–7, 16–18). (3) Unrepented sins are able to pollute not just the sacrificial altar and the shrine, but also the ady-

---

[22] Milgrom 1976b:391.
[23] Milgrom 1991:1079.
[24] Milgrom 1976b:391.
[25] Milgrom 1991:257.

tum. The cleansing has to wait until the Day of Atonement (or Purgation). It consists of two steps: the cleansing of the adytum of the wanton sins, and the cleansing of the shrine and sacrificial altar. Thus, "the graded purgations of the sanctuary lead to the conclusion that the severity of the sin or impurity varies in direct relation to the depth of its penetration into the sanctuary".[26]

For Milgrom the importance of purging the sanctuary lies in the postulate that "the God of Israel will not abide in a polluted sanctuary".[27] God will tolerate only a certain degree of impurity. The impurity can build up to such a point that God will leave the sanctuary, leaving the people to their doom. This, claims Milgrom, is what is depicted in Ez 8–11.[28] The importance of the purification offering is not for the atonement of the offerer, but for the purgation of the sanctuary so that God will remain in it.[29] For our purposes, Milgrom's contribution lies in pointing out the relation between the types of offences and their different degrees of pollution of the sanctuary.[30] But it remains to be seen how the conceptual framework of impurity works behind the slaughter and the burning of the city.

2.2.3. *The Slaughter in Ez 9*

We have mentioned above that most scholars agree that both the slaughter in Ez 9 and the burning of the city in Ez 10 are punishments for the cultic offences indicated in Ez 8. In some cases, these punishments are taken as an actualisation of the threat in 8:18. This may well be true, but in this and the next sections we would like to probe further to find if these two acts have any connection with the idea of impurity. We will argue that the slaughter can be seen

---

[26] Milgrom 1991:257.

[27] Milgrom 1991:258.

[28] Milgrom 1991:258; cf. Milgrom 1976b:397n.27. Whether this is true needs further proof. Of importance is the exegesis of Ez 8:6.

[29] Milgrom and Levine dispute the exact nature of sin and purification. Levine argues that impurity is an actualised form of evil forces (1974:77–78) and blood is used in sacrifice for apotropaic purposes. Blood is offered to "the demonic forces who accept it in lieu of God's 'life', so to speak, and depart . . ." (1974:78). But for Milgrom, one major contribution of the priestly theology is that "man is demonized" (1976b:397). A human person creates impurity, and the purpose of the sacrificial blood of the purification offering is to purge this impurity from the sanctuary and its sancta. The debate depends at least partly on how one interprets the magical language involved. See also Kaminsky's comments (1995:90n.68).

[30] For a critique of Milgrom's position, see Gammie (1989:37–41) and Maccoby (1999:165–181). See also Milgrom's rejoinder (2000a) to Maccoby.

as a case of the כרת penalty which can be taken further as a means of disposal of impurity.

2.2.3.1. *The כרת Penalty in General*

The formula ונכרתה הנפש ההוא מעמיה (Lev 7:20) with its variations are used to refer to the כרת penalty. Within the Pentateuch, the niphal and hiphil forms of כרת are found, but only the hiphil forms exist outside the Pentateuch. According to Good, the original form is probably the niphal with the hiphil its derivative.[31] The passive niphal form probably indicates that the ultimate agent of the penalty is God himself.[32] Wold classifies those offences which deserve the כרת penalty into six groups.[33] Milgrom modifies Wold's scheme into five groups with a total of 19 offences within the Pentateuch.[34] They are as follows.

(1) Violations against sacred time such as a failure to observe the Passover (Nu 9:13) or working on Sabbath (Ex 31:14).
(2) Violations against sacred substance such as eating blood (Lev 7:27), eating sacrificial suet (Lev 7:25), or blasphemy (Nu 15:30–31; cf. Lev 24:15).
(3) Failure to perform purification rituals such as neglecting circumcision (Gen 17:14) or neglecting purification after contamination by a corpse (Nu 19:13, 20).
(4) Illicit worship such as worshipping Molech (Lev 20:2–5) or sacrificing animals outside the authorised sanctuary (Lev 17:9).
(5) Illicit sexual relations (Lev 18:6–23, 29).

The precise nature of the כרת penalty is controversial. The main interpretations are: (1) the death penalty executed by human hand (e.g. Ex 31:14),[35] (2) excommunication from one's people or cultic community (e.g. Lev 20:17),[36] (3) premature death (e.g. Lev 17:10),[37] (4) childlessness and/or extirpation of descendants (e.g. Lev 20:2–5),[38]

---

[31] Good 1983:86. Cf. Zimmerli 1954:18; Knohl 1995:88.
[32] Hartley 1992:100. But see Zimmerli (1954:18), in reference to Nu 4:18.
[33] Wold 1979:3–24.
[34] Milgrom 1991:458.
[35] Good 1983:87; Hasel 1995:348. This option is rejected by Budd (1996:122).
[36] Zimmerli 1954:16, 18; von Rad 1962:264n.182; Hasel 1995:348.
[37] Tsevat 1961:197–201; Weinfeld 1972:242; Wenham 1979:241, 285; Greenberg 1983a:250; Horbury 1985:31–34; Levine 1989:241; Milgrom 1991:459; Hasel 1995:348. Cf. Joosten 1996:80.
[38] Wold 1979; Wright 1987:164n.2; Levine 1989:241.

and (5) misfortunes beyond death.[39] It is not our purpose here to determine which interpretation is most likely. Some scholars like Weinfeld and Milgrom make a distinction between sacral laws (*fas*) and civil laws (*jus*). The כרת penalty, so they argue, is for offences against sacral laws and as such the offences are punishable only by God himself. In this understanding, they reject associating human execution with the כרת penalty.[40] A case in point is Lev 20:2–5. For Milgrom, vv.2–3 show that the כרת penalty is different from the human execution by stoning, and hence the כרת penalty must refer to something else.[41] But for Good, vv.4–5, which point out that God himself will act in case of the non-compliance of the community, prove simply that in vv.2–3 the actions of the community to execute the offender "express the will of God and are therefore appropriated by him as though his own".[42] This exchange between scholars raises questions. On the one hand, should one interpret passages involving human and divine actions as expressing different actions or the same action from different perspectives? On the other hand, is the strict dichotomy between *fas* and *jus* sustainable?[43] On the whole, we think Hasel is fair to claim that the כרת penalty does not have only one meaning.[44] In a few cases, it can refer to the community's action of "cutting off" the offender. But in most cases, especially when the offences are committed in secrecy and judicial intervention is difficult if not impossible, God himself will execute the punishment which often results in premature death and the termination of the offender's line.

2.2.3.2. *The כרת Penalty in Ezekiel*

In Ezekiel, the divine כרת penalty is found in 13 cases. In six cases it is applied to foreign nations:[45] Ammon (25:7), Edom (25:13), Philistia (25:16), Egypt (29:8; 30:15) and Seir (35:7). In three cases it is applied to a hypothetical country: 14:13, 17, 19. It is directed three other

---

[39] Wenham 1979:241; Good 1983:88; Milgrom 1991:460.
[40] Cf. Zimmerli 1954:18.
[41] Milgrom 1991:460.
[42] Good 1983:88.
[43] Similarly, Kaminsky (1995:76–78) questions Milgrom's treatment of the Achan incident (Josh 7).
[44] Hasel 1995:348.
[45] This can also be found in Isaiah (14:22), Jeremiah (47:4; 48:2) and the minor prophets (e.g. Am 1:5; Ob 14; Zech 9:6).

times to Jerusalem: 14:21; 21:8, 9.[46] And finally, it is applied once to people who commit idolatry in 14:8. The כרת penalty is applied to Ammon, Edom, Philistia and Seir because of their attack on Israel. In these cases, כרת is used in parallel to אבד (25:7, 16) and שׁמד (25:7; 35:7; cf. 14:8–9), or נתן חרבה (25:13), referring to complete destruction. The penalty is applied to Egypt because of Pharaoh's claim to be divine, and it again refers to the desolation of land. Thus, Ezekiel not only nationalises the כרת penalty as Wold claims,[47] but he also has a different set of criteria for applying it to the foreign nations. However, the basis on which it is applied in 14:12–23 to the hypothetical country, which probably refers to Israel,[48] and in 14:8, can be found among the 19 offences in the Pentateuch as listed by Milgrom. The charge of acting faithlessly (מעל) against God in 14:12–23, referring basically to sancta trespass and oath violation, belongs to Milgrom's category (2) above. The charge of idolatry in 14:8 belongs to Milgrom's category (4) above. In 14:12–23 the penalty amounts to the destruction of both human beings and animals, although the destruction need not be total (cf. 14:22).

In addition to the above, some other cases can be taken as a כרת penalty without using the word כרת.[49] One example is from 5:11: "because you have defiled my sanctuary by all your detestable objects and all your abominations, I on my part will shear (נרע),[50] ...". Then 5:12 goes on to describe the three ways by which all the idolaters will be shorn. An obvious connection with 14:8 is that idolatry is singled out as the reason for the penalty. Wold provides another example.[51] The offences of Oholah and Oholibah are described in

---

[46] Also to Israel in 1 Kg 9:7; Hos 8:4.

[47] Wold 1979:22.

[48] See Chapter Three Section 4.2.

[49] Outside Ezekiel, the incidents of Uzzah (2 Sam 6:5–8), Nadab and Abihu (Lev 10:1–2) and Korah (Nu 16–17) are sometimes cited as cases where the כרת penalty is applied without using the word כרת. See Levine (1989:242).

[50] The Vulgate and Targum read as if it were אגדע "I will cut down", adopted by RSV and NRSV. The LXX and Syriac reflect אגעל "I will abhor" (e.g. Lamparter 1986:54; *BHS* apparatus). Block (1997:205n.40) thinks that this emendation is unlikely because Ezekiel does not use this verb in relation to God. Fairbairn (1855:70–71), Wevers (1969:58), Haik (1980:64) and Alexander (1986:773) take נרע to mean "to withdraw", referring to Yahweh's withdrawing his protective presence. According to Allen (1994:53n.11c), the absolute use of נרע has its primary meaning "to diminish, restrain", but its meaning of "to shear" can be found in Is 15:2; Jer 48:37. This meaning suits best the sign action of "cutting hairs". Cf. Pohlmann 1996:80.

[51] Wold 1979:21.

23:38–39 as idolatry and bloodshed, the defilement of the sanctuary and violation of Sabbaths. In return, they will be stoned and all their sons and daughters killed (23:47). A comparison with Lev 20:2–3 is useful. The description of the offences of Oholah and Oholibah resembles that of the offering of children to Molech which is precisely the subject matter of Lev 20:2–3. The punishment by stoning (רגם אבן) is found in both passages. Lastly, the כרת penalty as extinction in Lev 20:3 is also found in Ez 23:47.

For Ezekiel, within Israel the כרת penalty is applied, most clearly of all, to people who commit idolatry (14:8). Given that, it is not unreasonable to interpret the slaughter in Ez 9 as a case of the כרת penalty. Firstly, the abominations in Ez 8, which range from worship outside the sanctuary (v.5), to the worship of idols in secrecy (vv.7–12), and to open worship of another deity (vv.14, 16), can definitely be labelled as idolatry. Moreover, the כרת penalty serves as the sanction against idol worship in secrecy.[52] On the other hand, that the worship of another deity can be as open as described implies that one cannot rely on the judicial system to carry out the death penalty. In this case, again, the כרת penalty is the only option. One can compare this with Lev 20:4–5 which indicates that when the public deliberately turns a blind eye to the Molech offence, God himself will enact the כרת penalty. Secondly, the slaughter is clearly God-inflicted. The actual killing is mediated by six agents who are in no way ordinary humans, but "a squad of supernatural destroyers",[53] sometimes called "angels".[54] Their action is under God's direct command, and as such their action can be seen as God's own. Thirdly, the extent of the slaughter, which covers not just those who committed the various abominations,[55] but also others including the children, corresponds to the nature of the כרת penalty as extinction. Again we can compare the extent of the penalty mentioned in Lev 20:5 where not just the offender of the Molech cult, but also his family or clan (משפחה) and his associates are subjected to the penalty.

---

[52] Wenham 1979:241; Milgrom 1991:460.
[53] Allen 1994:146.
[54] E.g. Steinmann 1953:64; May 1956:111; Bunn 1971:257; Block 1997:304.
[55] Allen (1994:149) argues that the commands to kill "fan out and encompass in reverse the four groups who had engaged in shocking rites in chap. 8".

2.2.3.3. *The* כרת *Penalty as Control of Impurity*

Having argued that the slaughter in Ez 9 is to be understood as a
כרת penalty, we may pursue the question of the relationship between
the כרת penalty and the idea of impurity. Ritual impurities are easily acquired in daily life and are sometimes even a necessary part
of it (e.g. handling of corpses). They are tolerated[56] and removed by
appropriate rituals. But actions incurring the כרת penalty are not so.
These actions deliberately violate the divine distinction of what is
pure and impure, sacred and profane, and are sometimes crimes
against the social order (e.g. incestuous sexual relations). These actions,
if unrepented, will, according to Milgrom, be most defiling and pollute the adytum of the sanctuary whose purification comes only
through the sacrifice on the Day of Purgation.[57] The כרת penalty is
invoked to guard against these types of offences. Thus, we may say
that the כרת penalty is employed as a means to permanently remove
the source of this most grievously defiling impurity.

Wright provides a useful exposition on this idea. He holds that
ritual and moral impurities are not separated, but are interconnected
and can be graded on a spectrum. Ritual impurities can be graded
from two perspectives. The first is taken "along the lines of the presence or lack of sacrificial requirements and corresponding loci of
pollution".[58] For example, an abnormal sexual discharge or a confirmed
case of leprosy defiles not only the person concerned but also the
sacrificial altar. While ablution cleanses the impurity of the person,
a purification offering is needed to cleanse the altar. Other ritual
impurities require no sacrifice and only ablution (e.g. impurity resulting from sexual intercourse). The other way of grading ritual impurities is to consider their communicability. While every bearer of
impurity is restricted from contact with the sanctuary and the sancta,
only the bearer of communicable impurity is restricted regarding
his/her place of habitation.[59] Restriction is needed lest the communicable impurity may contaminate other persons or things within the
habitation. Thus, although these ritual impurities are tolerated and

---

[56] This is Wright's terminology (e.g. 1991:151).
[57] Milgrom 1976b:393. On the idea that repentance converts some of these
offences into inadvertent ones which defile the sanctuary less, see Milgrom
(1976a:108–121).
[58] Wright 1991:155.
[59] Wright 1991:157. For more details, see Wright (1987:163–228).

sometimes necessary, they are not allowed to remain unchecked. Impurities must be taken care of and rid from the environment. Ablution, sacrifices and restriction in habitation are different means to achieve this aim.

Moral impurities are phenomenologically connected to ritual impurities. In terms of sacrifice and the loci of pollution, moral impurities are more polluting for they defile not just the sacrificial altar but also the adytum which can only be cleansed on the Day of Purgation. In terms of restriction and communicability, if the offence is connected to ritual impurity (e.g. refusal to undergo purification after being contaminated by a corpse), then the usual restriction applies. Otherwise, the כרת penalty applies. Therefore, as we move from ritual to moral impurities, we can see gradations in terms of sacrifice, loci of pollution, and restriction.

If the purification rituals and restriction rules regarding the ritual impurities are taken as the means for controlling and removing ritually impure items, then we can infer that the כרת penalty regarding moral impurities serves the same end, that is, the control and removal of morally impure items.[60] While a person's ritual impurity can be removed by ablution and waiting over a period of time and the person him/herself be restricted in habitation, there is no similar control applied to moral impurity. The only way to remove moral impurity resulting from unrepented sins is to remove its source, that is, to remove the person concerned by the כרת penalty. While it is correct to claim that the כרת penalty is used by God to *punish* the offenders, it also serves as a means to restrict and remove the more polluting moral impurities. The concern is not just to punish, but to maintain a pure, cleansed environment. If any act incurring ritual impurity meets with a reaction aiming at removing the impurity or at purification, the same applies to acts incurring moral impurity. Only this time the כרת penalty is used instead of, for instance, ablution.

In the context of Ez 9, the כרת penalty is first applied within the temple precinct. God's command to the executioners to defile the temple may be odd in view of the sanctity he requires, but this command serves a twofold purpose. First, it makes clear that the temple is not an asylum. One cannot claim protection by staying in the temple (as in the case of Adonijah in 1 Kg 1:49–53).[61] If the people

---

[60] Cf. Weinfeld 1972:243.
[61] Heinisch 1923:60; Noordtzij 1957:110; Eichrodt 1970:132; Carley 1974:59;

commit idolatry in the holiest place of all, there they will be purged. Second, the command can be seen as a license to kill. The temple has already been polluted by the people. Hence, the executioners should not allow the concern for defilement to deter them from carrying out the command.[62] The כרת penalty is needed to remove the source of the more defiling moral impurity. In this connection, we may consider Ez 23 again. We mentioned above that both Oholah and Oholibah are said to defile the sanctuary (23:38) by idolatry and bloodshed,[63] and because of that they will suffer the כרת penalty (23:47). In this case, the כרת penalty can be seen also as a means to remove the source of impurity.[64]

2.2.4. *The Burning of the City in Ez 10*

After the slaughter, Yahweh commands in Ez 10 the seventh man to take some coals from among the cherubim and scatter them over the city Jerusalem. This action, as mentioned above, is often taken as a punishment. We will argue, however, that it is also at the same time an act of purgation and purification. This understanding arises from the dual function of fire as an agent of both punishment and purification.

2.2.4.1. *Fire as an Agent of Punishment*

In connection with God, fire often appears as a means of punishment. Perhaps the most famous example is that God rains fire and brimstone upon Sodom and Gomorrah so that all the inhabitants and what grows on the ground are destroyed (Gen 19:24–25). Reference to this incident as an antecedent has been made by some interpreters of Ez 10.[65] Another example is that God sends fire to

---

Eisemann 1988:177; Allen 1994:149 (comparing 1 Kg 1:50–53; 2:28–34; 11:15); Lind 1996:82.

[62]This idea can be traced back to Radak, noted in Eisemann (1988:178). See also Heinisch (1923:54), Fisch (1950:49), Aalders (1955:175), Greenberg (1983a:178), Klein (1988:59), Breuer (1993:64), Allen (1994:149), Block (1997:308).

[63] Zimmerli (1979:491) states that in contrast to Ez 16, Ez 23:38 speaks of offences against holiness. In addition, note that the impurity language pervades Ez 23 but not Ez 16. This may reflect different emphases. In Ez 16 the metaphor of covenant dominates and governs the development of the chapter, but in Ez 23 the idea of impurity predominates.

[64] Incidentally, Krašovec (1994:61–63) suggests that the punishment in the cases of Molech worship (Lev 20:1–5) and the Korah incident (Nu 16–17) is "purification" and "cleansing". Both, as mentioned in Note 49 above, are cases of the כרת penalty.

[65] Bertholet 1897:54; Kraetzschmar 1900:104; Noordtzij 1957:114; Allen 1994:151.

consume Nadab and Abihu for offering illegitimate fire before him (Lev 10:1–2). A third example is that some complaining Israelites are consumed by fire from God in the wilderness (Nu 11:1). This theme of God sending fire to destroy is found prominently in Amos.[66]

2.2.4.2. *Fire as an Agent of Purification*

Apart from being an agent of punishment, fire is also an agent of purification. As such it basically appears in two contexts. First, it is used in metallurgical description as a means for purification. Second, it is used to cleanse metal utensils from corpse contamination. Some examples may be cited for the first case. In Jer 6:27–30, God assigns Jeremiah to test the people and the process is described in metallurgical terms. The process described is that of refining silver by using lead as a flux.[67] The aim in heating is to melt the lead so that it can carry away the impurities from the silver. In this case, even though the bellows are fully blown, the heat fails to smelt the ore and the silver is not extracted from its impurity. It is therefore called "rejected silver". Similarly, the wickedness of the people is too great to be purified. God will reject them like "rejected silver". The same image is also used in Is 1:22, 25; 48:10; Zech 13:9 and Mal 3:2–3. In these cases, fire is seen as a means to purify the silver.[68]

We may consider two passages from Ezekiel. The first one is Ez 22:17–22 which, according to some, is dependent on Jer 6:27–30 and Is 1:22, 25.[69] Unlike both of these passages, Ez 22:17–22 is concerned with the smelting but not the refining process.[70] In the smelting process, the lead ore, which may contain a small percentage of silver, is melted in a crucible so that the dross will be left behind and removed. In v.18 Yahweh declares that the people are the dross;[71]

---

[66] E.g. 1:4, 7, 10, 12, 14; 2:2, 5.

[67] Thompson 1980:266–267; Holladay (1986:232), who offers a concise summary of the process involved on pp. 230–232.

[68] Regarding these passages, Miller (1982:39) suggests that the "metaphor of the refining fire that purifies" is used. He further points out that the fire here is "the refining fire, not the devouring fire".

[69] Burrows 1925:10; Fohrer 1952:137.

[70] Cooke 1936:242; Allen 1990:38.

[71] In v.18 the *qere* לסיג is adopted. The meaning of the word סיג is not clear. In some cases it means litharge, an alloy of lead and silver (e.g. Is 1:22, 25). In other cases, it refers to the dross, the impurities alone (e.g. Prov 25:4). In the present Ezekielian passage, the transposition of כסף after כלם in v.18 as suggested by *BHS* and others (e.g. Herrmann 1924:136; NRSV; Einheitsübersetzung) favours the first

thus the result of the smelting is mentioned before the process.[72] While one may expect the following verses to talk about the refining process, they return to the theme of smelting. The three steps of gathering of crude material into a crucible, blowing the fire to heat it up, and the melting of the material are repeated in v.20a. Like these steps,[73] the people will be gathered to Jerusalem, the fire of the wrath from God will be blown upon them and they will melt (vv.20b–22a). In this case, Jerusalem is like the crucible with the people as the crude material which after melting becomes only the dross without any silver.[74] The emphasis of the passage is placed on the melting of the people,[75] but the use of the metallurgical images does point to the use of fire not just for destruction, but also for purification,[76] only that this time no positive result is obtained.

Another example in Ezekiel can be found in 24.3–14 which is divided into vv.3–5, 6–8, and 9–14. Vv.3–5 may be a cooking song[77] one sings when preparing meals.[78] This is followed by two interpretations in vv.6–8 and 9–14, both introduced by לכן, then the messenger formula and the phrase הוי עיר הדמים ("woe to the bloody city"). In the first interpretation, Jerusalem is identified as the pot (סיר). The idea of חלאה ("filth")[79] is introduced in v.6. This filth is then immediately identified with the bloodguilt in v.7[80] and later called impurity (טמאה) in v.11. In this first interpretation, the filth remains in the pot (v.6). How it should be treated is the concern of the second interpretation. Logs are piled up to make the fire stronger (v.10). The pot is burned so that (למען) it may glow and the filth in

---

option. However, there is no compelling reason to do so, and the MT taken as it is favours the second option (e.g. Greenberg 1997:458).

[72] Greenberg (1997:459) remarks that the result of smelting is taken here as the ground for the melting process.

[73] Some scholars follow the versions in postulating an initial כ before קבצת in v.20a. Its omission is explained as due to either euphony (Keil 1876a:315) or a pseudohaplography after מ (Allen 1990:32). Greenberg (1997:459) argues that the comparative function of the noun phrase is implicit and requires no such a preposition. Cf. Block 1997:715n.9.

[74] Against Stalker (1968:188) who interprets Jerusalem also as dross.

[75] Note the multiple use of נתך in vv.20 (2x), 21, 22.

[76] Cf. Lind's "fire of purification" (1996:189) and Clements's "[f]ires of purification and cleansing" (1996:103).

[77] Brownlee 1972:24; Lind 1996:206. Cf. Greenberg 1997:505.

[78] Kelso (1945:391) suggests that it may refer to sacrificial meals on the basis of the word סיר ("caldron") which also occurs in 2 Chr 35:13.

[79] For its meaning, see Chapter Four Section 3.2.2.

[80] Cooke 1936:267; Brownlee 1972:25; Greenberg 1997:504.

it may melt and be consumed (v.11).[81] Then v.12 picks up the theme of vv.6 and 11 again. V.12a may speak of the frustrated effort to get rid of the filth.[82] V.12bα repeats the same idea in v.6 that the filth is not out of the pot. Lastly, the verbless clause in v.12bβ, which reads literally "in fire her filth",[83] can be seen as a recapitulation of v.11. If the filth does not go out of the pot after all the efforts, it is hoped that the fire will bring it out.[84] The meaning of the clause can be clarified by adding a verb like "to go", that is, "in fire her filth will go". The whole idea is repeated in v.13, but now the signifier gives way to the signified. Yahweh again addresses to the city, the "filth (of the pot)" is now replaced by "lewdly uncleanness". For our purposes, it suffices to note that fire is used here as a means to remove impurity. While it may be destructive, it is also purgative.[85]

We may now consider the use of fire as a means of purification for vessels contaminated by corpses. This appears in the OT only in Nu 31:21–24, but this purification ritual can be found in other ancient Near Eastern cultures. It is possible that Israel borrowed this from the Babylonian.[86] The regulation is introduced by Eleazar and called "the statute of the law" (חקת התורה). This label occurs elsewhere

---

[81] Against Kelso (1945:391–392), Kraeling (1966:475) and Brownlee (1972:26), who hold that the purpose is to melt down the pot itself.

[82] The meaning of the text תאנים הלאת, which is absent in the LXX, is most uncertain. It is often taken as a dittography of הלאתה תתם at the end of v.11, and therefore deleted by Herrmann (1924:148), van den Born (1954:155), Wevers (1969:142), Zimmerli (1979:495–496). It is retained by Kraetzschmar (1900:196–197), Allen (1990:55), Greenberg (1997:502), Block (1997:768). The translation "in vain I have wearied myself" in RSV and NRSV accepts the emendation הנם נלאתי of BHK, followed by Ziegler (1948:79). Some render the text as "it/she/he has frustrated all efforts". E.g. Keil 1876a:342; Ewald 1880:127; Aalders 1955:390; Allen 1990:53; Greenberg 1997:496; RV; NIV. This is accepted here.

[83] The LXX reads באש as if it were בוש. Some scholars delete either this clause or only הלאתה as a gloss. E.g. Toy 1899:41; Herrmann 1924:148; Bertholet 1936:86; van den Born 1954:155; Allen 1990:53 (who, however, retains it in his earlier article 1987:410). For those who delete only הלאתה, they usually render v.12b as "its thick filth does not go out from it by fire" (e.g. Herrmann 1924:148; Bertholet 1936:86; van den Born 1954:155; Auvray 1957:95). However, this contradicts vv.11, 13. Moreover, the LXX attests to the clause. Some repoint באש as the noun בּאָש "stench" (e.g. Hitzig 1847:183; Fisch 1950:164; Noordtzij 1957:254). There is, however, no compelling reason to alter the MT.

[84] Keil 1876a:347; Davidson 1916:192; Aalders 1955:391; Block 1997:781; Greenberg 1997:502.

[85] Cf. Greenberg 1997:505. While Allen (1990:60) states that "cleansing is an ironic metaphor for destruction", we underline the dual function of fire—to destroy and to cleanse.

[86] Budd 1984:331.

only in Nu 19:2 which introduces the ritual of the red heifer for the purification of corpse-contamination. Some similarities between Nu 19 and 31 show not only that these two chapters are related, but also that Nu 31 presupposes Nu 19.[87] In Nu 19, while a corpse-contaminated person has to undergo both the sprinkling of the water of purgation (מי נדה) on the third and seventh days, followed by bathing and laundering on the seventh day (vv.18–19), an object receives only the sprinkling of water (v.18). Nu 31:21–24 supplements the rules on cleansing objects.[88] Inflammable objects made of gold, silver, copper, iron, tin and lead, taken as booty and corpse-contaminated, are to pass through fire, and then they will be clean (וטהר) (vv.22–23aα). However, these objects also need to be purified by the water of purgation (v.23aβ),[89] which, presumably, takes place before the passing through of fire.[90] Flammable objects have to pass through water (v.23b). Thus, this twofold purification process for objects parallels the ritual for purification of corpse-contaminated persons in Nu 19. But why is fire required instead of simply water? Wright argues that since contamination by a corpse is more serious and communicable, a more powerful means of purification, i.e., fire, is needed.[91]

Although water is the usual agent of purification, our discussion above shows that fire can also be an agent of purification. As such, it is usually applied to vessels which can withstand fire such as the crucible used for smelting (Jer 6:27–30; Ez 22:17–22), or the pot for cooking (Ez 24:3–14) or metallic vessels (Nu 31:21–24). Fire is used in extreme cases such as when every other means fail (Ez 24:11–13) or in the case of corpse-contamination (Nu 31:21–24). The purifying power of fire lies in its ability to destroy impurities.[92] Thus, fire possesses the ambivalent dual function of destruction and purgation.

---

[87] Wright 1985:214–215; 1987:170.

[88] Wright 1987:170n.15.

[89] Wright 1985:219. Cf. translations of Milgrom (1990b:261) and Ashley (1993:584–585).

[90] Wright 1985:222.

[91] Wright 1985:222–223. Wright (1985:222n.24) suggests without further elaboration that the theme of purification by fire also occur in our two Ezekiel passages examined above.

[92] Cf. Is 4:4, which, however, does not use the same vocabulary.

2.2.4.3. *Purification in Ez 10*

The command to scatter coals taken from among the cherubim over the city Jerusalem, is often taken as a punishment, that is, destruction and consumption of the city.[93] This action is often compared to the burning of Sodom and Gomorrah in Gen 19.[94] This may be true, but we will argue that the element of purification is present in this scene. If the slaughter in Ez 9 can be seen not just as a punishment, but also as the removal or disposal of impurity, then it would not be surprising if the same idea is found in Ez 10.[95]

First, the seventh man, in his appearance in Ez 9, is to mark with a sign those who moan and groan for the abominations so that they will not be killed by the other six executioners. His task is therefore not one of destruction, but protection or salvation. This points to the possibility that his action in Ez 10 is not simply negative, i.e., the destruction of Jerusalem.[96]

Second, the text clearly distinguishes him from the other six executioners by stressing that he is dressed in linen (הבדים) (9:2, 3, 11; 10:2, 6, 7). Linen, as noted by many, is used to make the dress of a priest (Ex 28:42; 39:28; Lev 6:3; 16:4, 23, 32), and is also taken as the dress of a heavenly figure in Daniel (10:5; 12:6, 7). This seventh man, functioning as a priestly figure,[97] is going to scatter burning coals over Jerusalem. The verb זרק ("to scatter, sprinkle"), when used with a priest, occurs basically in two contexts. The first is the sprinkling of blood against the sides of the altar in a sacrifice (e.g. Lev 1:5, 11; 3:2, 8, 13; 7:2, 14; 2 Kg 16:15; 2 Chr 29:22; 30:16).[98] This action, according to Milgrom, is to purify the altar.[99] The second is the sprinkling of the water of purgation (מי נדה) on objects or persons who are corpse-contaminated (Nu 19:13, 20; cf. Nu 19:18;

---

[93] Keil 1876a:137; Smend 1880:59; Toy 1899:114; Heinisch 1923:61; Schumpp 1942:56; van den Born 1954:68; Wevers 1969:66; Eichrodt 1970:134; Carley 1974:61; Zimmerli 1979:251; Greenberg 1983a:181; Maarsingh 1985:127; Stuart 1989:97; Biggs 1996:30; Lind 1996:83.

[94] Bertholet 1897:54; Kraetzschmar 1900:104; Cooke 1936:112; Noordtzij 1957:114; Taylor 1969:106; Eisemann 1988:182; Klein 1988:60; Allen 1994:151.

[95] Cf. Cooper (1994:131), who says that the city is purged in judgement.

[96] Herrmann 1924:66; Brunner 1969a:115. Cf. Mosis 1978:98.

[97] Steinmann 1953:65; Fuhs 1984:56–57; Andrew 1985:49; Duguid 1994:124; 1999:134.

[98] Cf. van den Born (1954:69), who claims that זרק in P and Ugarit is a technical term for the splashing of blood on the altar.

[99] See Section 2.2.2 above.

31:23). Again, the action concerns purification. The verb זרק occurs
three times in Ezekiel (10:2; 36:25; 43:18). In 36:25 it speaks of God
sprinkling clean water on the people to cleanse them, and 43:18
speaks of dashing blood against the altar. Thus, on the one hand,
the combination of a priestly figure together with the action of scattering or sprinkling gives a picture of purification,[100] and on the other
hand, the use of זרק elsewhere in Ezekiel supports the view that
purification is intended here in Ez 10.

Third, what is to be thrown upon Jerusalem are burning coals
(נחלי־אש). The exact expression occurs only five times in the Bible.
In 2 Sam 22:13 (//Ps 18:13) and Ez 1:13 it is connected with theo-
phany.[101] In Lev 16:12 it refers to burning coals from the sacrificial
altar. Therefore, as such the term is neutral. Although coals or fire
are sometimes associated with punishment,[102] they can in some cases
relate to purification. The classic example is Is 6:6–7 which is cited
by scholars either for or against the view that purification is intended
in Ez 10.[103] There are indeed some obvious reasons for *not* including Is 6:6–7 in the current discussion. In terms of genre, the Isaian
passage is part of a call vision which Ez 10 is not. There the prophet
is cleansed before his commission but such a theme is not present
here. There the burning coal[104] is taken from the altar of incense
but not here. Lastly, there Isaiah is cleansed of his sin[105] but here,
as we shall point out, the city is cleansed from impurity. The importance then of Is 6:6–7 for Ez 10 lies in indicating that burning coals
can have the connotation of purification.[106]

As we have argued above,[107] fire need not be seen solely as an
agent of punishment. It is also a purifying agent. In Ez 22 and 24,

---

[100] Cf. Houk 1971:53.

[101] Fuhs 1977:464.

[102] Fuhs 1977:463–464.

[103] Those who hold that Is 6:6 depicts a different situation and therefore cannot
be used as a support include Currey (1882:51), Bertholet (1897:54), Herrmann
(1924:66), Fohrer (1955:56), Noordtzij (1957:114), Carley (1974:61), Maarsingh
(1985:127), Lind (1996:83). Those who claim the relevance of Is 6:6 include Brunner
(1969a:115), Houk (1971:53–54), Fuhs (1984:57), Alexander (1986:78).

[104] The LXX's rendition of רצפה is ἄνθραξ, the same as that for נחלי־אש in
Lev 16:12. Cf. Kaiser 1972:81; Wildberger 1991:250.

[105] Note the words עון and חטאת in Is 6:7. See also Kaiser (1972:81), Wildberger
(1991:270).

[106] Fisch 1950:51. Hals (1989:63) points out the dual role of fire from Yahweh:
to cleanse and to kill.

[107] See Section 2.2.4.2.

Jerusalem is likened to a crucible or pot to which fire is applied in order to get rid of impurity. In particular, it is said explicitly that coals (נחלת) are used to heat up the pot in 24:11. In these cases, the impurity is either the dross (Ez 22) or the filth (Ez 24), and it signifies the impurity resulting from idolatry or bloodshed. In Ezekiel the idea that Jerusalem is like a vessel is further found in the immediate context of Ez 10, i.e., Ez 11:1–13.[108] While it is true that there is no fire mentioned in 11:1–13, the sudden death of Pelatiah reminds us of the כרת punishment inflicted by God (v.13). This resembles the slaughter in Ez 9 in that in both cases, the כרת punishment is followed by Ezekiel's concern for the remnant of Israel. Thus, one should not be surprised that in Ez 10 Jerusalem is conceived of as a pot to which burning coals are applied.

This leads to the question of what is to be cleansed in Ez 10. There are two options. The first is to conceive along the lines of Nu 31:21–24 that the severity of corpse-contamination requires the metallic vessels to be cleansed by fire. After the slaughter in the city in Ez 9, the city, conceived of as a metallic pot, is therefore corpse-contaminated. Thus, the command in Ez 10 to scatter burning coals over the city in order to cleanse it from this impurity cannot come at a more appropriate time. The second option, which is more probable, is to take the cue from within Ezekiel. The impurity discussed in Ez 22 or 24 is caused by idolatry or bloodshed. As we have pointed out in the last chapter, these acts can defile the temple and the land. The abominations described in Ez 8 would certainly defile the sanctuary and the land. They are, therefore, in need of purification.[109] Since those who deliberately refuse to undergo purification after being corpse-contaminated and those who commit idolatry suffer the same כרת penalty (Nu 19:20; Lev 20:2–5), it is reasonable to assume that both acts have a similar degree of defilement and therefore require a similar degree of purification. Hence, purification by fire seems appropriate. Incidentally, we note that in the metaphors

---

[108] Actually, in Ezekiel the word סיר occurs only in chapters 11 and 24.

[109] Brunner (1969a:115) suggests that God may purify the place for his future return. Houk (1971:53) holds that the coals are "signs of purification". But his discussion is quite unclear. At one place he says that the coals are used to mark the foreheads of the faithful so as to protect them (1971:53–54), and elsewhere he claims that both the temple and city have been purified (1971:53). Moreover, his reasoning is based on a certain dissection of the text. Fuhs (1984:57), following Houk, holds that in the original composition the coals are means of purification as in Is 6, but in the present form they represent the destruction of the city.

in Ez 22 and 24, fire is also used appropriately to remove impurity
not only on the level of the signifier, but also on the level of the
signified.

2.3. *Summary*

In this section we have attempted to explain the various themes of
Ez 8–11 by employing the concept of impurity. We have tried to
go beyond the usual framework of sin and judgement employed to
explain these themes. We suggested that the slaughter in Ez 9 and
the burning of Jerusalem in Ez 10 which are usually understood simply as punishment are dominated by the idea of impurity and its
resolution. The abominations performed by the Israelites as described
in Ez 8 are most defiling, rendering not just the offenders but also
the temple and the city impure. The slaughter of the offenders in
Ez 9 can be seen as a case of the כרת penalty, which is a way to
dispose of impurity, especially when the offence is done in secret or
when the community fails to carry out appropriate measures to control the offence. The scattering of burning coals over the city means
not simply to destroy but also to purify.[110] This, as we have said,
has to do with the ambivalent nature of fire which purifies by destroying the impurities. If the above observation has some force, then the
idea of purity provides a better perspective to look at the text. From
this point of view, we observe a *broad* chiastic structure of Ez 8–11:

A	Ez 8	abominations defiling the temple and land
B	Ez 9	כרת penalty and the removal of impurity
C	Ez 10	fire and the removal of impurity
B'	Ez 11:1–13	כרת penalty and the removal of impurity
A'	Ez 11:14–21	reversal: removal of abominations from the land

Running through these sections is the idea of the appearance and
departure of Yahweh's glory.

3. *Impurity and the Land*

3.1. *Introduction*

In this section we will discuss the relationship between impurity and
the land. The first idea to be examined is related to the exile. As

---

[110] See Note 92 above.

pointed out in Chapter Three the exile is seen as a punishment for violating the covenant. Here we look at it from a different perspective. We have noted that Ezekiel interprets the various kinds of offences in terms of the purity language. This also applies to the exile. Thus, the exile is seen as a means of removing impurity from the land. A related theme is that impurity would lead to the dispossession of the land lest the land be defiled. This idea finds confirmation by looking at its converse, i.e., entering or possessing the land requires the people to be clean. This takes two forms. First, re-entering or returning to the land requires purification from past impurity. Second, those who defile themselves will not be allowed to enter the land in the first place. While the first form speaks of a future event, the second form traces back to a historical past re-interpreted from this perspective. In this understanding, Ezekiel uses the pollution theory to interpret not only "the disturbance and dislocation created by the experience of exile",[111] but also the (future) resolution of this exile.

3.2. *Exile as Removal of Impurity*

3.2.1. *Ez 36:16–38*

The word reception formula at 36:16 demarcates the beginning of a new literary unit which ends at 36:38. The three messenger formulae in vv.22, 33 and 37 indicate the start of three oracles: vv.22–32, 33–36 and 37–38. The recognition formula at v.23 indicates a minor break within vv.22–32. The oracle vv.22–32 has an inclusion "it is not for your sake that I am about to act" in vv.22 and 32. While the oracles vv.17–21, 37–38 speak of the Israelites in the third person, they are addressed in the second person in vv.22–32, 33–36. In terms of content, some suggest a chiastic structure for vv.17–32:[112] A (vv.17–19): impurity of people and land; B (vv.20–21): profanation of Yahweh's name; B' (vv.22–23): reversal of profanation of Yahweh's name; A' (vv.24–32): reversal of impurity of people and land.

Hossfeld may be right in pointing out that even though the recognition formula is often extended by the use of ‏ב‎ plus an infinitive construct, the extension is never separated from the recognition formula by the divine speech formula ("says the Lord Yahweh"). Thus,

---

[111] Budd 1996:37.
[112] See Chapter Four Note 180.

he suggests that the infinitive construct in v.23bβ marks the beginning but not the end of a section.[113] If that is the case, then v.23bβ
forms a transition from vv.22–23bα to vv.24–32.[114] Actually, it is
better to read v.23bβ with v.24 which negates v.20b and therefore
forms a conclusion to the reversal of the profanation.

Within vv.25–32, vv.25–28, 29–32 are two sections of parallel
structures: (A) Yahweh's cleansing action (vv.25, 29a); (B) a further
action of Yahweh (vv.26–27, 29b–30); (C) a consequence for the people (vv.28, 31–32). A similar structure can also be found for vv.33–38:
A: v.33a; B: vv.33b–37; C: v.38. While vv.25–28 deal with the inner
renewal of the people, vv.29–32 are concerned with the fertility of
the land, and vv.33–38 the rehabitation of cities and increase in pop-
ulation (by using the sheep metaphor).

The concern of this section is with vv.17–19, which deal with the
relationship between land, impurity and exile. In the last chapter we
pointed out that offences such as bloodshed and idolatry can defile
the land. In the course of that discussion, we came across the present
text. Now we will first elaborate a little more on the phrase כטמאת הנדה
and then discuss the relationship between exile and impurity.

In v.17b Ezekiel compares the "way" of the people with טמאת הנדה.[115]
The word הנדה is generally taken to mean the menstrual state[116]
rather than the menstruous woman.[117] The impurity element of menstruation is not used to illustrate the state of the land as claimed by
Block,[118] but the impropriety of the people's conduct. In Lev 15:19–24
regulations for a menstruant are laid down. Since the source of impurity is not the menstruant herself but the menstrual blood,[119] care
must be taken not to touch anything on which she lies or sits lest
there is a contact with the blood.[120] For Ezekiel, the people's behav-

---

[113] Hossfeld 1977:288–289.
[114] We are aware of the textual problem concerning 36:23bβ–38 which is absent
in LXX[967] and the Old Latin Codex Wirceburgensis, but it is not our purpose to
examine this issue here. For a discussion of this problem, see Filson (1943), Bogaert
(1978), Lust (1981a), Spottorno (1981), McGregor (1985:190–191), Allen (1990:177–178),
Ohnesorge (1991:203–207), Greenberg (1997:738–740) and Block (1998:337–343).
[115] This expression occurs otherwise only in Lev 15:26.
[116] Zimmerli 1983:241; Milgrom and Wright 1986:252; Dijkstra 1989:123; Allen
1990:175; Block 1998:343; Klee 1998:107n.25.
[117] Keil 1876b:106; Greenberg 1997:727–8. Cf. LXX and Targum.
[118] Block (1998:346), who holds that the feminine gender of אדמה fits this figure
of speech.
[119] Klee 1998:63.
[120] See the detailed discussion in Klee (1998:45–52, 63).

iour is like menstrual impurity, i.e., the menstrual blood. When they dwell (יֵשֵׁב) on the land, they defile the land (36:17a), just as a menstruant renders unclean that on which she sits (יֵשֵׁב) (Lev 15:20b). Hence, one may write the following:

> the Israelites :: a menstruant
> their conduct :: menstrual blood
> defile the land on which they dwell (יֵשֵׁב) :: defiles that on which she sits (יֵשֵׁב)

The analogy is an apt one[121] except that one is concerned with moral impurity and the other ritual impurity.[122] Even though a menstruant cannot control her menstrual blood, she is expected to be careful with it in order to confine the spread of impurity. But the people, who should be able to control their conduct and behaviour, simply allow their action to defile the land.[123] In response to that, God scatters them among the nations. The point, however, is not the scattering itself, but the going out from the land. By sending the people into exile, God disposes of the source of impurity and separates the impurity from the land. The removal of this source of impurity does not imply that the land will thereby be cleansed[124] but only that the land will not be defiled further. Some Jewish exegetes maintain the analogy and interpret God's action as that of a husband who puts away his menstruous wife in the days of her impurity, but draws her near when she becomes pure again.[125] This interpretation is right in taking uncleanness as temporary but not in understanding the way of cleansing. While the menstruant has to wait for seven days and take a bath and hence be clean, the people who are exiled have to be cleansed by an external agent, namely, God himself.[126]

---

[121] Thus, נדה is not "simply . . . a generic term for pollution" (Galambush 1992:146). Cf. Ezr 9:11 which relates the נדה land with the נדה of the people.

[122] Against Wevers 1969:191.

[123] Against Blenkinsopp (1990:165), who suggests that the primary concern is the defilement of the sanctuary, and only then the land.

[124] As claimed by Feinberg (1969:208), Ohnesorge (1991:263), Lind (1996:290).

[125] Fisch 1950:242; Breuer 1993:317; Greenberg 1997:728, referring to Kimchi. Cf. Eisemann 1988:554. This provides a better analogy than Klee (1998:108), who says that "[j]ust as a menstruant is careful to remove her menstrual items from her living quarters, so God will remove those people from the land", thus comparing God to the menstruant!

[126] Apart from Ez 36:17, the imagery of a menstruant is also used in Lam 1 for Jerusalem. See especially vv.9 and 17. According to Hunter (1996:129), the sins of people and their consequent unclean state is an important theme in Lamentations.

A similar idea linking pollution of the land and exile can be found in Lev 18:24–30 which forms the parenetic conclusion to its preceding sexual laws.[127] Cross-references between Lev 18:24–30 and Ez 36:17–19 are sometimes made by commentators on either text.[128] The priestly text exhibits a universalising view that the Canaanites can also defile themselves by those immoral acts mentioned in Lev 18:6–23.[129] Their acts also cause the land to become unclean. With Yahweh administering the emetic the land then vomits out its inhabitants.[130] The land is personified as a pure body distinct from its inhabitants and vomits out that which causes impurity. It may imply that by throwing out the impurities, the land will eventually recover.[131] The picture portrayed is that before the entry of the Israelites into the land, it has already been cleared of the source of impurities, i.e., the nations. And in order to stay in the land, the Israelites have to keep the regulations so as not to defile themselves and the land. This understanding challenges the idea that an organic unity exists between the people and the land.[132] In fact, the Israelites are not necessarily bound to the land. If the land did vomit out its former inhabitants because of their impurity, the land can do the same to the Israelites (Lev 18:28). The Israelites have no special privilege to claim the land.[133] Although this seems to portray a relationship involving only the land and the people,[134] this is not the case since the role of Yahweh is clearly mentioned in both vv.24 and 25. A similar idea is found in Lev 20:22–26. This passage also talks about the land vomiting people out from it, but it also contains the idea, lacking in Lev 18:24–30, that Israel is separated by God from the other nations. This idea of separation, which dominates this passage, is expressed through the distinction between clean and unclean animals. The Israelites have to keep the distinction so that they will not defile themselves and be vomited out from the land.

---

[127] Hartley 1992:285.

[128] E.g. Ziegler 1948:108; Eichrodt 1970:494; Porter 1976:150; Allen 1990:178; Blenkinsopp 1990:165.

[129] Budd 1996:262.

[130] Hartley (1992:298) further suggests that the emetic can be drought or plague or war. See also Frymer-Kensky (1983:413n.7).

[131] Hartley 1992:298.

[132] See further Joosten (1996:153–154).

[133] A similar idea is found in Dt 9:4–5, without using the priestly categories of purity/impurity.

[134] So Eichrodt 1970:494.

The above-mentioned Leviticus texts give weight to understanding the exile in Ez 36:17–19 as the removal of impurities. Frymer-Kensky makes a comparison between the exile and the flood. In an earlier article she argues that the flood is not simply a means of destruction, but also of purging the pollution that humankind has brought to the earth while allowing for a remnant.[135] In a later article she seeks to demonstrate that this idea also applies to the exile. She first points out the various offences which can pollute the land. Then by drawing texts from Isaiah, Jeremiah and Ezekiel, she suggests that the destruction of the land is expressed with flood terminology such as "violence" (חמס), "end" (קץ) and the marking on the forehead. The point is that the exile, like the flood, is a way to deal with the pollution of the land. Its purpose is, again, not simply destruction, but purgation so that there will be a remnant to start all over again.[136] Although Frymer-Kensky's argument is questionable at some points,[137] her general observation that exile serves as a means of removing impurities is correct.

What remains unclear in her argument is the exact object of cleansing in the flood/exile. Does the flood/exile cleanse the earth? In the case of the flood, her answer is yes. She holds that the flood is used to "physically erase everything from the earth" so that it will be "a clean, well-washed one".[138] But in the case of exile, she seems to answer negatively. She holds that as "the impure individual becomes pure after a set period of time even without purification rituals, so too time can eliminate the impurity of the land".[139] Her first statement is incorrect. For example, both men and women need ablution after intercourse. Although ablution is not mentioned explicitly as necessary for women after the period of menstrual impurity, it is generally recognised that such is required.[140] The truthfulness of her second statement requires further substantiation.[141] At present it suffices

---

[135] Frymer-Kensky 1977:150–154.

[136] Frymer-Kensky 1983:409–411.

[137] It is dubious, for instance, whether the idea of "the land is full of violence" is related only to the flood, and the marking of the forehead in Ezekiel and of Cain represents flood terminology.

[138] Frymer-Kensky 1977:153.

[139] Frymer-Kensky 1983:411–412. Cf. Milgrom (2000b:1404): "Israel's polluted land is purified by time".

[140] Wright 1987:185n.38; Milgrom 1991:934.

[141] In Ez 36:29–30 and 33–36, Yahweh's cleansing of the people is followed by

to note that in Ezekiel, the exile represents the removal of that which causes pollution to the land, namely, the people.

3.2.2. *Ez 22:15 and Ez 39:23–24*

Our understanding above can be further substantiated. First, there is a passage in Ezekiel which escapes Frymer-Kensky's notice, namely, 22:15. Ez 22 is a chapter replete with impurity vocabulary. Jerusalem is first accused of shedding blood and defiling herself with idols (vv.1–5). Then a more detailed description of her offences is given (vv.6–12), followed by God's reaction (vv.13–16). The text of v.15 reads:

והפיצותי אותך בגוים	v.15aα	and I will scatter you among the nations,
וזריתיך בארצות	v.15aβ	and I will disperse you among the countries,
והתמתי טמאתך ממך	v.15b	and I will finish your uncleanness from you.

The two clauses in v.15a occur frequently in Ezekiel and require no special comment. For our purpose, it suffices to note that the feminine singular suffixes in v.15a refer to the Jerusalemites even though grammatically speaking they refer to the city itself.[142] Of special relevance to us is v.15b. The question lies in whether the second person feminine singular suffix refers also to the inhabitants as in v.15a[143] or back to the city.[144] If the former is the case, then the exile is seen as a means of purifying the people. If the latter is the case, then the exile is a means to rid Jerusalem of impurity. There are some reasons to support the latter option. First, although the reference to the inhabitants gives a consistent reading for v.15, it is then inconsistent with v.16 in which the referent is the city.[145] Second, note that the combination תמם and טמאה occurs only in Ez 22:15 within the Bible, but a comparison with 24:11 is illuminating. There the

---

his rejuvenating the land, making it fertile and habitable again. This action may indicate a reversal of the effect brought about by defilement. If so, it is Yahweh himself who "cleanses" the land. But Ez 11:18 hints at the role of a human agent to remove detestable things from the land.

[142] When the זרה-פוץ pair is used elsewhere in Ezekiel, the objects are always explicitly people: 12:15; 20:23; 29:12; 30:23, 26; 36:19.

[143] Redpath 1907:112; Ziegler 1948:69; Fisch 1950:146; Stalker 1968:186; Feinberg 1969:128; Cooper 1994:221; Biggs 1996:67; Duguid 1999:287.

[144] Herrmann 1924:138; Fohrer 1955:128; Wevers 1969:130; Zimmerli 1979:459; Maarsingh 1988:121; Allen 1990:37; Greenberg 1997:457, 466; Block 1998:713.

[145] Greenberg 1997:457.

qal of חמם is used with הלאה as the subject parallel to טמאה. In that case, fire is applied to Jerusalem as a pot to melt down the impurity so that the filth may vanish. The concern there is to put an end to the impurity in Jerusalem. The use here may also have the same meaning, i.e., removing impurity from Jerusalem. Third, in the immediate context of 22:15, i.e., 22:17–22, the house of Israel is likened to dross which is gathered into the crucible Jerusalem to be smelted. Again, it is the people who are regarded as the impurity to be removed from Jerusalem. If that is the case, then 22:15 provides another indication that exile is a means of removing impurity. That is to say, the nexus offence-exile is operated under the principle of impurity—removal of impurity.

We may also consider 39:23–24. The text speaks explicitly of Israel's exile (גלו) because of their iniquity. This is interpreted as God's turning his face from them and handing them over to their enemies. In this way, God deals with them כטמאתם. The preposition כ is variously rendered as "gemäß",[146] "nach",[147] "wie . . . es verdienten",[148] "as . . . warranted",[149] "according to".[150] Some of these imply that God's action is like the Israelites' action, and some state explicitly that the Israelites' action deserves God's action. Jenni classifies this case under the rubric of "Vergeltung nach Anlaß".[151] He explains that: "Die Veranlassung zu vergeltendem Handeln wird durch כ in Verbindung mit einem sehr allgemeinen Ausdruck für Handeln . . . angegeben, der sehr oft eine Wertung beinhaltet".[152] If this is the case, then God's action is occasioned by the impurity of the people. That is to say, the people's impurity is a cause for God's sending them into exile. One may also take this action of God as the removal of impurity from his land.

---

[146] Kraetzschmar 1900:261; Herrmann 1924:242.

[147] Ziegler 1948:117; Fohrer 1955:218.

[148] Einheitsübersetzung. Cf. Auvray (1957:149): "je les ai traités comme le méritaient leurs souillures . . .".

[149] Allen 1990:199.

[150] Toy 1899:70; Cooke 1936:422; Fisch 1950:264; Eichrodt 1970:517; Zimmerli 1983:294; Eisemann 1988:601; Breuer 1993:351; Block 1998:478; NRSV; NIV. Cf. Dijkstra's "overeenkomstig" (1989:143).

[151] Jenni 1994: 99.

[152] Jenni 1994: 100.

3.3. *Impurity and the Dispossession of the Land*

Related to the idea that exile is the removal of impurity is that impurity leads to the dispossession of the land. This is found in Ez 33:23–29. This passage is a disputation speech consisting of the thesis in v.24, dispute in vv.25–26 and counterthesis in vv.27–29.[153] The words "inhabitants of these ruins" (v.24) point to a post-587 BCE situation.[154] Those who escaped the two exiles are now claiming that the land is for them to possess on the basis of a tradition that Abraham was promised the possession of the land even though he was alone (Gen 15; cf. Is 51:2). Now that they are many, they argue that the land is given to them as a possession. The niphal נִתְּנָה, as in 11:15, implies that it is God who gives the land to them.[155] Ezekiel disputes this thesis by referring to their conduct in two triads, each ending in the rhetorical question "will you possess the land?" (vv.25–26). That their conduct leads to the dispossession of the land is readily pointed out by most commentators, but why this is the case is not attended to. Their misconduct includes: eating "on the blood",[156] lifting up eyes to the idols, shedding blood, relying on the sword,[157] committing abominations, and defiling a neighbour's wife. Note that the first two items are of the same nature, referring to idolatry.[158]

---

[153] Murray (1987:103–104), followed by Allen (1990:151) and Block (1998:261).

[154] Greenberg 1997:684; Block 1998:258.

[155] Graffy 1984:79.

[156] This is a literal rendering of the Hebrew עַל־הַדָּם תֹּאכֵלוּ. The LXX omits the dispute in vv.25aβ–26 probably due to homoioteleuton (Zimmerli 1983:195; Maarsingh 1991:19). A first group of commentators emends the text to עַל־הֶהָרִים on the basis of the fact that that phrase appears in Ezekiel and also precedes "lift up eyes to the idols" in 18:6, 15. E.g. Cornill 1886:396; Kraetzschmar 1900:240; Fohrer 1955:187; Wevers 1969:180; Dijkstra 1989:102. Cf. Cooke 1936:371; Eichrodt 1970:460–461; Greenberg 1997:684. However, there is no textual support for this emendation. A second group interprets עַל as "with" and hence the phrase as "you eat (flesh) with blood (on it)". E.g. Keil 1876b:75; Redpath 1907:182; Davidson 1916:267; Herrmann 1924:212; Bertholet 1936:16; Cooke 1936:371; Fisch 1950:226; van den Born 1954:199; Aalders 1957:153; Eichrodt 1970:460; Zimmerli 1983:195; Allen 1990:149; Maarsingh 1991:18–19; Block 1998:257. A third group holds that taking עַל as "with" does not solve the problematic passage 1 Sam 14:32–34 in which the phrase is also found. Instead, they maintain the general meaning of עַל as "on" and take Lev 19:26 as the point of departure for interpreting the phrase. Grintz (1970/71:84–90) argues that "eating on the blood" in Lev 19:26a is explained by its following sentence "do not practise augury or witchcraft". This interpretation can also be applied to the case of 1 Sam 14. Thus, the phrase is a reference to worshipping demons.

[157] Cf. *HALAT* 795; Allen 1990:149.

[158] See Note 156.

The fourth item, although separated from the third one in the first triad, probably reflects the same charge as the third one.[159] The phrase "commit abomination" can refer to idolatry (e.g. 8:9), but in 22:11 it refers to sexual immorality. This may be its sense here.[160] There is no doubt that the misconduct of the people defiles not only themselves but also the land. This conduct which defiles the land causes their dispossession of the land. To avoid the land from being polluted, not only can they not possess the land, but they will also be eradicated from the land (v.27).

3.4. *Purification and Return to the Land*

3.4.1. *Ez 36:16–38*

The above interpretation of exile as a means to remove impurity can be buttressed by looking at its converse: the return to the land requires purification. This idea is found most clearly in 36:25, 29 and 33. First, the clause טהורים מים עליכם וזרקתי ("I will sprinkle upon you clean water") in v.25a is doubly unique in the OT. Only here is Yahweh the subject of the verb זרק and the expression טהורים מים is also unique. The closest parallel to the clause in terms of phraseology is Nu 19:13, 20: עליו לא־זרק נדה מי. The context is the ritual of the red heifer. The ashes of a burnt unblemished red heifer are used to produce the water of purgation (נדה מי) which is for cleansing those who are corpse-contaminated. Corpse contamination is a serious pollution and any corpse-contaminated person who does not undergo purification defiles the tabernacle and will incur the כרת penalty. The association between Ez 36:25 and Nu 19:13, 20 is made via the word נדה which is used to describe the behaviour of the people (Ez 36:17).[161] In fact, the Targum to Ez 36:25 makes the association explicit: "you had been purified by the waters of sprinkling and by the ashes of the heifer sin-offering".[162] If this allusion is intended, then it points to the severity of the people's impurity. The result of God's sprinkling the clean water on the people (Ez 36:25) is that the people shall be clean (טהר qal).

This action of God in v.25a is further explained in v.25b as an action of cleansing the people from all their uncleannesses and all

[159] Greenberg 1997:685. Cf. Keil 1876b:75.
[160] Greenberg 1997:685.
[161] Hossfeld 1977:315.
[162] Levey 1987:101–102.

their idols.[163] The plural form טמאות is attested in the OT only at Lev 16:16, 19 and Ez 36:25, 29. This may point to a connection with Lev 16 which is concerned with the Day of Purgation.[164] On that day the sacrificial blood purges impurities from the sanctuary and the scapegoat removes Israel's iniquities (Lev 16:16, 21–22).[165] Although the word "impurities" in Lev 16:16 refers not just to ritual impurities, but also to moral impurities,[166] in the context of Ez 36, it probably refers only to moral impurities.[167] If this is the case, then the cleansing action is not ritual in nature as some claim,[168] but an act to cleanse offences and the moral impurity generated.[169] If the purification carried out by a human priest does away with ritual impurity, purification executed by God rids the human person of moral impurity.[170] In the past the people can rely on the priest to purge their serious offences and impurities on the Day of Purgation, but this is no longer the case since, firstly, the priests themselves do not perform the priestly duty of distinguishing the pure from impure, and the holy from profane (22:26), and secondly, the possibility that the people will defile the land again needs to be eliminated completely by an action of God. After this cleansing and the implanting of a new spirit and new heart, the people can then dwell on their land (v.28).[171]

Ez 36:29 speaks of God saving (והושעתי) the people from uncleanness (טמאות). The verb ישע is rare in Ezekiel, found only in 34:22; 36:29 and 37:23. Its combination with uncleanness is unique in the OT. This verse is probably a repeat of the idea in v.25, referring to God's cleansing,[172] although the use of הושיע מן, which usually

---

[163] Not all scholars follow the Masoretic accentuation. See, for example, NRSV, Ohnesorge (1991:216), Breuer (1993:319–320).

[164] Suggested by Haag (1943:38), followed by Zimmerli (1983:249) and Greenberg (1997:730). Hossfeld (1977:316) avers that the plural is used in parallel to the plural form גלולים.

[165] Milgrom 1991:1033–1034, 1043.

[166] Milgrom 1991:1033.

[167] Against Sawyer and Fabry (1990:456), who claim ritual impurity.

[168] E.g. Zimmerli 1983:249; Fuhs 1988:205; Cooper 1994:316.

[169] Hitzig 1847:284; Smend 1880:274; Aalders 1955:190; Fohrer 1955:204; Eichrodt 1970:497–498; Hossfeld 1977:316–317; Blenkinsopp 1990:167; Ohnesorge 1991:268; Block 1998:354–355.

[170] Ohnesorge 1991:268.

[171] Ziegler (1948:109) suggests that the cleansing takes place *before* entering into the land.

[172] Sawyer and Fabry 1990:456. Against Keil 1876b:112.

means deliverance from a person under some power,[173] hypostasises the uncleanness. Ez 36:33a again uses the verb "to cleanse", but now with the object "your iniquities" (עונותיכם). This combination is rare, found again only in Jer 33:8 in an oracle of restoration.[174] This certainly recalls Ez 36:25, and also the removal of iniquities on the Day of Purgation in Lev 16. Again, it is after this cleansing that the land becomes habitable, and that the people can live on the land again (vv.33b, 38).

3.4.2. *Ez 37:21–23 and Ez 11:18*

The idea that the return to the land requires purification appears also in Ez 37:21–23. V.21 speaks of gathering and bringing the people of Israel to their land, using basically the same vocabulary as 36:24 but with some variations in phraseology. This is followed by the theme of the unification of the two kingdoms which is the main concern of 37:15–28. Then the people will not defile themselves again with their idols and transgressions (v.23a). God will save them from their apostasies[175] and cleanse them. In this case, entering the land is followed by the cleansing of the people. But unlike 36:26–27, where the Israelites are guarded from further defilement by the implant of a new heart and a new spirit, here in 37:23 it is stated simply that they will never defile themselves again. The texts 37:21–23 and 36:24–25 demonstrate the link between the requirement to be clean and the (re-)entrance into the land. This supports the correlation between defilement and exile from the land, based on the principle that impurity requires a resolution.

While some texts speak of the purification of the people as they re-enter the land, some other texts point to their removal of detestable things and abominations as they enter the land. This idea appears in 11:18. The pericope 11:14–21 is a disputation speech dealing with a conflict between those remaining in the land and the exiles regarding the possession of the land. The Jerusalemites argue that since the exiles are far from the land,[176] the land is given to them as a

---

[173] Block 1998:357.

[174] But compare Lev 16:30; Ps 51:4; Prov 20:9.

[175] The Hebrew מושבתיהם, meaning "dwelling places", is probably a metathetical error for משובתיהם, with support from LXX (ἀνομιῶν) and Symmachus, also in accordance with some scholars: Zimmerli 1983:270; Allen 1990:190; Ohnesorge 1991:346n.38; Greenberg 1997:756; Block 1998:407.

[176] For a wordplay on the legal and ordinary meaning of רחק in this case, see Cross (1996:320).

possession (v.15). In reply, God promises to be a sanctuary in a small measure to the exiles (v.16).[177] He further promises to gather them from the nations and give them the land. Instead of the usual הביא clause, where God is said to bring them to the land (e.g. 34:13; 36:24; 37:21), here it is said that they go to the land, and remove from it all its detestable things and abominations. Unlike 36:24–25 there is no mention of the cleansing of the people as they enter the land since their self-defilement is not stated explicitly. But the idea of defilement by detestable things forms the background within the immediate context of Ez 8–10 and the broader context within Ezekiel. The detestable things and abominations are that with which the people defile the sanctuary (5:11) and themselves (cf. 20:7, 8; 37:23), and also the land. Thus, the removal of detestable things and abominations by the people implies the removal of that with which they defile the land. Although the reason why God removed them from the land and scattered them among the nations is not given explicitly within this pericope, Ez 8–10 and 11:18 do point to the defilement of the people as the reason. That those who will possess the land will remove detestable things from the land implies that those who remain in the land are not able to possess it because they have no intention to remove those things and to refrain from defilement. This understanding is stated explicitly in 33:23–29. Defilement implies the dispossession of the land, as we have seen above.

3.5. *Impurity and Non-Entrance to the Land*

If passages like 36:16–38 refer to a future event in which re-entering the land requires purification, then 20:5–26 refers to a historical past which is re-interpreted from this perspective. The connection between these two passages is more than incidental. Regarding Ez 36:16–38, Rendtorff argues that it can "only be understood as a deliberate continuation and development of chap. 20".[178] In 20:8, 13, 21, Yahweh mentions that "I would pour out my wrath upon them", and its fulfilment is found in 36:18 ("I poured out my wrath upon them"). Moreover, the threat of dispersion in 20:23 is seen as realised in

---

[177] For a recent discussion of 11:16, see Joyce (1996:50–56).
[178] Rendtorff 1993:193. Cf. Greenberg 1983a:384. This contradicts Krüger's opinion that Ez 20 takes over and develops the argumentation of Ez 36:16–38 (1989:257n.258).

36:19 by using the same wording. Other links include the profanation of the divine name and defilement.[179] Apart from these, we may
add that there is also a link between the people's impurity and the
land in Ez 20.

Ez 20:5–26 depicts a history of Israel which is full of tension and
conflict. It is a history dependent not just upon the actions of Israel,
but also upon Yahweh's care for his name.[180] Our concern is with
the relationship between entering the land and defilement. If 11:18
attests that God's bringing the Israelites to the land in the future
implies that they will remove the detestable things and idols, then
20:5–26 shows that God's refusal in the past to bring them to the
land has to do with their unwillingness to cast these things away.
The land is first mentioned in v.6. When God chose Israel while
they were still in Egypt, he raised his hand to them to bring them
(להוציאם) out of the land of Egypt to (אל) a land that he had searched
out (תור) for them. This is followed by a command that the people
should renounce detestable things and not defile themselves with the
idols of Egypt. According to Ezekiel, the gods of Egypt are not gods
but idols[181] which must be cast away. To be a people of Yahweh, Israel has to cut their ties with Egypt by forsaking the idols of
Egypt. Note that in v.6, entering the land is not indicated by the
verb הביא but only the preposition אל. The verb הביא is employed
in v.10 to refer to the entrance into the wilderness. Thus, Sedlmeier
is right to claim that v.6 does not underscore the entrance into the
land as such. Rather, it "will . . . JHWHs Absicht, das Volk aus der
Lebenswelt Ägypten herauszuführen, betonen und den neuen von
JHWH ausgesuchten Lebensraum in seinem Wert vorstellen".[182] There
is no mention of the gift of the land in v.6 as in v.15.[183] But Sedlmeier claims too much when he states that "[d]as Hineinbringen ins
Land ist somit von Anfang an nicht intendiert, vielmehr nur das

---

[179] Rendtorff 1993:192. Boadt (1990:13) provides more links but some are problematic. For example, he avers that one reason why God poured out his wrath on
the people (20:8, 21; 36:18) is because they had profaned his holy name (20:9;
36:21)!
[180] Hattori (1974) calls this God's dilemma.
[181] Kutsko (2000:35–39) points out the omission of the word אלהים in Ezekiel in
referring to pagan gods or divine images. For Ezekiel, they are not worthy to be
called "gods", but only גלולים, i.e., "idols" or "shit-gods". See Kutsko (1998) for
the gist of his book.
[182] Sedlmeier 1990:219.
[183] Sedlmeier 1990:247.

Hineinbringen in den Zwischenbereich מדבר".[184] V.6 clearly attests
such an intention, and if it were otherwise, it would be difficult to
explain why Yahweh searched out (תור) a land for Israel. The verb
תור, apart from referring to the spying of the land before the Israelites
entered it (Nu 13), is used of God (or the ark) searching for a place
for them to rest (or camp) in the wilderness (Nu 10:33; Dt 1:33).
Its usage implies God's leading them to a right place. Although there
may be a difference between "leading" and "bringing", it should not
be overstated in this case.

The failure of the people to follow the command did not seem
to alter completely God's intention. He still led them out of Egypt,
but he brought them (ואבאם) to the wilderness (v.10) where he gave
them his statutes and ordinances, and sanctified them with his Sabbaths. But the Israelites rejected the former and profaned the latter.
It is at this point that Yahweh raised his hand to them to show that
he would not bring them (הביא אותם) to the land which he had given
them[185] (v.15). The reason for this decision of God is then given in
v.16 which culminates in the phrase "for their heart habitually[186]
went after their idols". This indicates the relationship between entering the land and idolatry. By defiling themselves with the idols of
Egypt, the Israelites forfeit their chance to enter the land. Being
unclean is therefore incompatible with entering the land. That is to
say, being pure from idolatry is a prerequisite for entering the land.
This understanding helps to explain God's reaction in v.10. The
defilement of the Israelites while they were still in Egypt did not
deter God from bringing them out of Egypt, nor to the wilderness.
Actually by doing so God removed them from those idols of Egypt
with which they defiled themselves. But instead of entering the land,
they were brought to the wilderness. There they were sanctified, but
they defiled themselves again and God determined that they would
not be brought into the land. The second generation in the wilderness was again given a chance to cleanse themselves, but again they
defiled themselves with the idols of their fathers (v.24). This time,
God not only would not bring them into the land, he would also

---

[184] Sedlmeier 1990:247n.88.
[185] MT lacks להם which is found in some other Hebrew manuscripts and attested
in LXX. Zimmerli (1979:400–401) avers that נתתי might have replaced the original תרתי.
[186] Note the use of the participle הלך after a series of qatal forms in v.16.

scatter and disperse them among the nations to move them further away from the land. In Ez 20:5–26 we see again a close relationship between the land and the defilement of the people. In this reconstructed history of Israel, the defilement of the people contributes directly to their not being brought to the land. The reason, we aver, has to do with the defilement of the land.

3.6. *Summary*

In this section we have examined the various relationships between impurity and the land. The most important is that exile, the removal from the land to other nations, is a reaction to the defilement of the land. The exile serves as a removal of the source of defilement from the land so that the land will not be polluted any more. Thus, the exile is interpreted from the perspective that impurity demands a resolution. In connection with this understanding, the re-entering into the land as a future event demands some sort of purification— either the people are purified by God as they enter the land, or the people themselves have to remove that with which they defile themselves. The point is that the land should not be defiled again when the people re-enter the land. Related to this is the idea that those who defile themselves and the land are not allowed to possess the land. The land is reserved only for those who are clean. The historical past of Israel is similarly re-interpreted from this perspective. If the future re-entering the land requires purification, then this should also apply to the first entrance into the land. The first generation of Israelites defiled themselves already in Egypt and were brought not into the land but to the wilderness. The second generation did the same and would be dispersed among the nations. To enter and possess the land the people need to be clean and not to defile the land. Even if in their defilement they can enter the land they will not be able to possess it or stay in it. If they are not purified, eventually they will go out of the land. In this understanding, the purity of the land forms the focus of the whole of Israel's history—from the reconstructed past to the present exile, and from the present exile to the future return to the land. The past defiled Israel is not allowed to enter the land lest she defiles it. Her impurity is barred from the land. The present defiled Israel is exiled from the land so that she as the source of impurity is removed from the land. The future Israel who will return to the land will have to be cleansed

and will also be responsible for removing that with which she has
defiled herself in the past.

4. *Conclusion*

In this chapter we have examined the relationship between impurity and retribution. The focus is not on demonstrating that offences
which produce moral impurity will be recompensed. That hardly
needs to be proved. Our concern is to determine the underlying
principle governing the connection between morally defiling actions
and their recompense.

The present chapter focuses on both the temple and the land since
they are two essential elements for the existence of the Israelite
nation. Our study shows that in Ez 8–9 those who defile the temple by idolatry will suffer the כרת penalty. Based on a study by
Wright in which he shows that "tolerated" impurities are phenomenologically continuous with moral impurities, the כרת penalty can
be seen as a means to remove the source of moral impurity just as
ablution and confinement are required to purify ritual impurities.
The idolaters who defile the temple are therefore removed to avoid
further pollution of the temple. This consideration shows that the
people's deed and its consequence are related and this relation is
expressed in the principle that impurity demands a resolution which,
in this case, is the permanent disposal of the source of impurity.
Noting that fire can be an agent of purification as shown in metallurgical descriptions and cleansing of corpse-contaminated metallic
vessels, we argue that the burning in Ez 10 is to be understood as
purification of Jerusalem, conceived of as a pot contaminated by the
offences of the people (and by the corpses). Again, in this case the
people's deed and its consequence are related and interpreted by
the principle that impurity requires a resolution which refers to purifying the impurities.

We have also discussed the importance of the purity of the land
and its role in the "history" of Israel. In the reconstructed past, the
first self-defiling generation of Israelites is not allowed to enter the
land but only stays in the wilderness. The second generation would
be removed even further away from the land by being scattered
among the nations. The present generation has to go out of the land
because of their defiling actions. In the future, as Israelites re-enter

the land they will be cleansed and they will have to remove the detestable things with which they defiled themselves in the past. The possibility that they will defile the land again is eliminated. Thus, the emphasis is not just on the purity of the people as such, but how this affects the land which in turn affects the status of the people. These all serve to prove the point that exile is used as a means to remove impurity from the land. Again, the deed-consequence nexus is interpreted from the principle that impurity demands a resolution which, in this case, refers to the temporal removal of the source of impurity from the land. Once cleansed, they are allowed to return to the land.

From the above consideration of the defilement of the temple/land and its purification, we can see that the "history" of Israel revolves around the principle that impurity demands its resolution. This principle governs the deed-consequence nexus and differs from the juridical point of view which sees misdeeds and sins as requiring punishment according to pre-conceived norms of action. The idea that impurity demands a resolution smacks not of a forensic flavour as does the juridical perspective. While the covenantal ideas we discussed in Chapters Two and Three are more limited to the world of Israel, the concept of impurity and purification is broader and exists in the ANE world.[187] A yet more general principle will be examined in the next chapter.

---

[187] See, for instance, van der Toorn (1985:27–29), Wright (1987) and Wilson (1994).

CHAPTER SIX

POETIC JUSTICE

1. *Introduction*

In previous chapters we examined the relation between offence and its consequence from the perspectives of covenant/law and purity. This chapter continues the examination. There are cases in Ezekiel (and other parts of the OT) where the punishment bears correspondences or likenesses to the offence. Such correspondences or likenesses can take many forms. Consider, for example, Ez 36:6–7, which deals with the sin and punishment of foreign nations. As Israel has suffered the insult of its surrounding nations (v.6: יען כלמת גוים נשאתם), in return God will make sure that the nations themselves will suffer insult (v.7: המה כלמתם ישאו). In this case, the nations will suffer what they have inflicted upon Israel. What they have done will be done to them. The consequence the nations bear is like the deed they committed, and this likeness or correspondence is forged by using the same verb נשא and the same noun כלמה. This phenomenon of correspondences between a misdeed and its recompense has been pointed out by some biblical scholars.[1] A more thorough study is done by Miller. Although the title of his book is *Sin and Judgment in the Prophets,* he deals with only three passages from Ezekiel, Ez 27–28; 35:14–15; 36:6–7 (our example above) which are all related to foreign nations. We will in the following sections examine passages pertaining to *Israel* which exhibit correspondences between its offence and punishment. Thus, this chapter will supplement Miller's interesting study. We will first examine the notion of "poetic justice" which is often used to denote this phenomenon of correspondences. Then we will focus on some passages from Ezekiel relating to the sin and punishment of Israel. After that, we will examine expressions like "I will bring their deeds upon their head", which suggest a certain correspondence between the people's deeds and Yahweh's punishment.

---

[1] Wolff 1934:27–28; Fichtner 1949; Lohfink 1961; Westermann 1967:160–161; Janzen 1972:35–38; Zimmerli 1974.

2. *The Meaning of "Poetic Justice"*

In a study on the "Poetry of Poetic Justice", Lichtenstein does not explicitly define "poetic justice", but he holds that there is a poetic character in divine retribution which "often exhibits a measure for measure correspondence between a crime and its punishment" and his aim is to examine imagery related to "the notion of poetic justice".[2] Thus, for Lichtenstein poetic justice is related first of all to divine retribution, and, secondly, designates a special form of divine retribution in which the punishment has what we may call a talionic relationship with the crime. In an article entitled "Natural Law and Poetic Justice in the Old Testament", Barton holds that "poetic justice" refers to cases where "a divine judgment is declared in a way that stresses its *appropriateness* to the sin which has called it down".[3] Instead of Lichtenstein's "correspondence", Barton uses "appropriateness" to designate the relationship between the misdeed and its recompense. While Lichtenstein's aim is to exhibit the poetic character of divine retribution, Barton's concern is to detect behind texts displaying poetic justice the idea of natural law. Common to them are the ideas that poetic justice deals with divine retribution, and more specifically, with sin and its recompense. Miller's study mentioned above focuses on the correspondences between sin and punishment in the prophets. He identifies three sources or settings for this correspondence: poetic justice, covenant and curses, and talionic style or thinking.[4] For him, poetic justice is basically a literary device found in different genres such as myths, fairy stories and legends,[5] and it is created through metaphor, simile and paronomasia.[6] Thus, both Miller and Lichtenstein emphasise that poetic justice is a literary technique used to depict a certain correspondence between a misdeed and its recompense. The ways that these three scholars use "poetic justice" have similarities and differences. It is worthwhile to see how the term is used in literary studies.

The term "poetical justice" was first coined by Thomas Rymer in

---

[2] Lichtenstein 1973:255.
[3] Barton 1979:9 (his italics).
[4] Miller 1982:98–110.
[5] Miller 1982:98.
[6] Miller 1982:115.

1678[7] in his *Tragedies of the Last Age*.[8] Its variant, "poetic justice",
which was first devised by Dryden, has been used synonymously with
"poetical justice" until now.[9] Although Rymer's use of the term is
rather vague and restricted only to punishment, Zach detects in it
three basic meanings: (1) "ausgezirkelt gerechte Bestrafung"; (2) "iro-
nisch angemessene Bestrafung"; and (3) "strengere Bestrafung, als es
das Vergehen verdient".[10] Some of these meanings, as we will see
immediately, survive to this day. As the point of departure for considering its use in current literature, we follow Zach's procedure in
giving a list of definitions found in dictionaries:[11]

> An ideal distribution of rewards and punishments such as common in
> some poetry and fiction. (1)

> The ideal justice in distribution of rewards and punishments supposed
> to befit a poem or other work of imagination. (2)

> A situation in which someone is made to suffer for something bad
> they have done, in a way that seems perfectly suitable or right. (3)

> An outcome of a fictitious or real situation in which vice is punished
> and virtue is rewarded usually in a manner peculiarly or ironically
> appropriate to the particular situation. (4)

> The morally reassuring allocation of happy and unhappy fates to the
> virtuous and the vicious characters respectively, usually at the end of
> a narrative or dramatic work ... such justice is 'poetic', then, in the
> sense that it occurs more often in the fictional plots of plays than in
> real life. ... In a slightly different but commonly used sense, the term
> may also refer to a strikingly appropriate reward or punishment, usu-
> ally a 'fitting retribution' by which a villain is ruined by some process
> of his own making. (5)

> There are 2 related though clearly distinguishable meanings attached
> to the term. The literary scholar uses it to refer to the doctrine that

---

[7] In his study devoted to the idea of "poetic justice", surprisingly Zach gives the
year 1677 (1986:25).
[8] Zach 1986:25; Cuddon 1992:724.
[9] Zach 1986:25.
[10] Zach 1986:30.
[11] (1) *Random House Dictionary* 1493; (2) *OED* (8:326) which uses "poetical justice"
instead; (3) *Longman Dictionary* 1085; (4) *Webster's* 2:1749; (5) Baldick 1990:172; (6)
Shipley 1955:311; (7) von Wilpert 1989:692. This list differs slightly from Zach's
(1986:28).

all conflicts between good and evil, whether in the drama, the epic,
or the novel, must be concluded with the reward of the virtuous and
the punishment of the evil. . . . To the non-literary scholar, or a lay
person, poetic justice means a reward or a punishment (more frequently the latter) which is somehow peculiarly appropriate to the good
deed or the crime; it may be of a sort that occurs rarely in life; but
it is gratifyingly concrete, and it somehow ironically "fits the crime"
as when a villain is overwhelmed by the catastrophe he had planned
for others. (6)

"Poetische Gerechtigkeit", der in der Dictung oft erscheinende, in der
Wirklichkeit vermißte Kausalzusammenhang von Schuld und Strafe. . . . (7)

From these definitions, several observations can be made. First, the
term "poetic justice" is often taken as a literary device used in literature (1, 2, 5, 6, 7) and it rarely relates to a real life situation (4, 6).
Second, it includes both reward and punishment (1, 2, 4, 5, 6),
although it can be associated with only the latter (3, 7). Third, it
has two related meanings not always noted (5, 6), and more often
only one is mentioned (1, 2, 3, 4). Its first meaning is the ideal distribution of justice with regard to reward and punishment, usually
mentioned at the end of a work. Its second meaning emphasises the
ironic aspect or appropriateness of the reward or, more often, the
punishment. Both of these meanings were already recognised by
Rymer. In particular, Shipley (6) specifically mentions that these two
different meanings are adopted by literary and non-literary scholars
respectively. The latter more often than the former uses the term to
refer to the ironic aspect of the appropriate punishment or reward.[12]
This seems to be the case for the three biblical scholars Lichtenstein,
Barton and Miller mentioned above. However, it is not clear if these
two meanings can be separated completely. While it is true to say
that ideal distribution of justice does not necessarily imply that there
is any ironic aspect in the retribution, the latter seems to imply the
former. By saying that there is an ironic or peculiarly appropriate
retribution, it is implied that the good person will be appropriately
rewarded and the bad one appropriately punished. Having a "strik-
ingly appropriate" reward or punishment points to the idea of distributive justice. In comparison to these two basic meanings, the idea
that poetic justice denotes the causal relationship between sin and

---

[12] Zach (1986:32–33) attributes the dominance of the first meaning among literary scholars to its popularisation by Addison in 1711.

punishment is rather rare (7),[13] and it is, according to Zach, not taken up in modern English.[14] This meaning is not to be found in Rymer's usage of the term, and his third understanding of poetic justice as a punishment more severe than deserved does not seem to survive in modern English.

This discussion shows that the term "poetic justice" has a broader meaning in literary studies than in biblical studies. In the latter, the term is restricted to the appropriateness or correspondence between an offence and its recompense. In this chapter we will adopt this more restricted meaning. The causal relationship between sin and punishment in poetic justice, which is kept by some German but not English literary critics,[15] requires further clarification since its meaning may admit of different interpretations.

3. *Poetic Justice in Ezekiel*

3.1. *Ez 5:5–17*

In the symbolic action in Ez 5:1–4 Ezekiel cuts and divides his hair into three parts which are then burned, cut with a sword, and scattered to the wind. Then an interpretation of this symbolic act is given in 5:5–17.[16] Vv.5–6, introduced by the messenger formula, form an accusation of Jerusalem. Then in vv.7–10 the first interpretation of the symbolic act, introduced by לכן and the messenger formula, is given in the form of an oracle of judgement. A second interpretation, vv.11–13, is put in the form of a proof saying. This is followed by two further oracles, vv.14–15 and vv.16–17, with the form of an announcement of punishment and ended with the asseveration formula.[17]

In the first interpretation, the word יען in v.7 introduces the accusation:

---

[13] Drescher (1979:367) also holds that poetic justice is that which "den Kausalzusammenhang von Schuld u. Sühne erfaßt".

[14] Zach 1986:34.

[15] Zach 1986:34.

[16] Hals 1989:29; Allen 1994:56. Some scholars prefer to take Ez 4–5 as composed of two parts. The first part consists of commands to perform symbolic acts and the second part a series of oracular materials commenting on the previous acts. See, for example, Cooke (1936:58), Zimmerli (1979:154, 174), Greenberg (1983a: 117–119).

[17] Hals 1989:29–30; Allen 1994:55–56.

v.7aα   הֲמֻנְכֶם מִן־הַגּוֹיִם אֲשֶׁר סְבִיבוֹתֵיכֶם
v.7aβ   בְּחֻקּוֹתַי לֹא הֲלַכְתֶּם
v.7aγ   וְאֶת־מִשְׁפָּטַי לוֹא עֲשִׂיתֶם
v.7b   וּכְמִשְׁפְּטֵי הַגּוֹיִם אֲשֶׁר סְבִיבוֹתֵיכֶם [18]לֹא עֲשִׂיתֶם

The punishment, which is then introduced by לָכֵן in v.8, is preceded
by the challenge-to-duel formula הִנְנִי עָלַיִךְ,[19] and the expression גַּם־אָנִי
which is typical of announcement of punishment and expressing correspondence especially in retribution.[20] Then in v.8b we have:

v.8b   וְעָשִׂיתִי בְתוֹכֵךְ [21]מִשְׁפָּטִים לְעֵינֵי הַגּוֹיִם

---

[18] There are two options concerning the word לֹא. The first option is to delete
it because: (1) about 30 Hebrew manuscripts and the Peshitta lack the word: Bertholet
1936:20; Fohrer 1955:33; (2) a comparison with 11:12, which does not have the
word, points to its absence: Hitzig 1847:38; van den Born 1954:46; Pohlmann
1996:79n.231; *BHS* apparatus. This option is also adopted by RSV and NRSV.
The second option is to keep it because: (1) textually speaking, the MT is supported by the LXX (except LXX[311, 613]) and Targum; (2) the idea that Israel is
worse than the nations is not foreign to the OT in general or Ezekiel in particular: Bertholet 1897:31 (citing Ez 16 and 23); Kraetzschmar 1900:58 (citing Ez 3:6–7;
16:47 and Jer 2:10–11); Greenberg 1983a:112–113; (3) that Israel is worse than the
nations is found in the context of v.7, i.e., in v.6: Aalders 1955:115; Allen 1994:52,
74; (4) the omission is probably a harmonisation with 11:12: Keil 1876a:89; Herrmann
1924:30; Zimmerli 1979:151; Allen 1994:52; (5) from a stylistic point of view,
Greenberg (1983a:113) holds that the double negative of the divine act (לֹא עֲשָׂה) in
v.9 parallels the double negative of the human act (לֹא עֲשָׂה) in v.7. This is followed
by Brownlee (1986:88) and Allen (1994:52). We may add that the double negative
of the human act in v.7 is contrasted with the double positive divine act in vv.8–9.
The second option is also held by Lofthouse (1907:82), Davidson (1916:41), Heinisch
(1923:47), Schumpp (1942:32), Wevers (1969:58), Eichrodt (1970:79). On the whole,
the MT is preferred on both external and internal grounds.
[19] Humbert 1933.
[20] BDB 169.
[21] Some scholars propose to emend מִשְׁפָּטִים to שְׁפָטִים because (1) the latter word
is more common for "judgement" in Ezekiel (e.g. Ez 5:10,15; 11:9; 16:41; 28:22,
26; 30:19): Bertholet 1987:32; Cooke 1936:66; Zimmerli 1979:151; Brownlee 1986:88;
(2) the former word is more likely to be a mechanical assimilation to the word in
v.7: Brownlee 1986:88; Allen 1994:53; (3) the LXX attests the latter word: Fohrer
1955:33. This proposal is also accepted by Bertholet (1936:20), van den Born
(1954:46), Wevers (1969:58). Against (1), we may point out that the expression
עָשָׂה מִשְׁפָּט can have the meaning "to execute judgement" both outside Ezekiel (e.g.
Ps 9:17; 119:84; cf. Jer 51:9) and inside Ezekiel (39:21). Thus, its being less common in Ezekiel does not mean that it has to be emended here. Cf. Pohlmann
1996:80n.233. Against (2), some scholars hold that the MT exhibits a wordplay
with v.7 where the word means "ordinances" while here it means "judgements".
E.g. Bertholet (1897:32), who nevertheless proposes to change it; Kraetzschmar
1900:59; Aalders 1955:116; Greenberg 1983a:113; Maarsingh 1985:64; Block 1997:202.
See also Liedke (1971:73–100) and Bovati (1994:208–211) for a discussion on the
various meanings of מִשְׁפָּט. Against (3), Fohrer's argument is weak, as noted in Allen

By comparing v.7αγb and v.8b, we can detect some correspondences in the use of עשה and משפטים: the judgements (משפטים) God is going to do (עשה) correspond to the ordinances (משפטים) of God and the nations, which the people failed to do (לא עשה). But strictly speaking, it is incorrect to say that there is a correspondence between the offence and punishment as such, as claimed, for instance, by Greenberg,[22] because the actual punishment of being killed by pestilence, famine and sword does not have any correspondence to the crime of not obeying Yahweh's ordinances. So the correspondence is on the lexical level, not on the level of content. Apart from these correspondences, in both cases the nations play a role. In v.7 the ordinances of the nations serve as a reference point for the behaviour of the Jerusalemites, and in v.8 the nations are taken as witnesses for God's punishing action. In both cases, the nations are involved, although not directly, in the interaction between God and Jerusalem.

Correspondences between sin and punishment go beyond lexical similarities. Since what Jerusalem has done is worse than the nations (vv.6, 7aα, 7b), what Yahweh is going to do to it will be something unlike what he has done before and what he will do in the future. This is stated in v.9a. In this case, the extent of punishment corresponds to the extent of the offence.[23]

Related to this is another correspondence. Before the punishment, Jerusalem was placed amidst the nations (v.5). This implies that Jerusalem has occupied a prestigious position with respect to the nations, and one may even detect a sense of divine election.[24] But God's punishment will turn it into desolation (חרבה) and a reproach (חרפה) among the nations around it (בגוים אשר סביבותיך) (v.14). Note that there is a wordplay between the final condition of Jerusalem as חרבה and חרפה on the one hand and the means to bring about this (i.e., דבר, רעב and חרב) on the other hand. Jerusalem is further char-

---

(1994:53). Others who keep the MT include Heinisch (1923:47), BDB (1048). Thus, there is no compelling reason to emend the MT.

[22] Greenberg 1983a:113.

[23] Cf. Taylor (1969:86), who remarks that "unparalleled sin demands unparalleled punishment".

[24] Keil 1876a:88; Herrmann 1924:39; Wevers 1969:58; Zimmerli 1979:174; Fuhs 1984:37; Allen 1994:72; Block 1997:197–198. Greenberg (1983a:110) suggests that בתוך הגוים only means that Jerusalem is put among the nations as an equal, citing 19:2, 6; 31:14, 18 as support. However, the context, which points to a comparison between Israel and the nations through the threefold use of the comparative מן, renders Greenberg's interpretation less likely.

acterised as a taunt (נדופה), a warning (מוסר) and a horror (משמה) to its surrounding nations (לגוים אשר סביבותיך) (v.15).[25] Although both before and after the punishment Jerusalem remains situated amidst the nations—note the use of the prepositions ב for Jerusalem and סביב for the nations in vv.14–15—the prestigious position which it enjoyed before is now revoked. Jerusalem is now physically seen by all passers-by as only a desolation and is deemed by the nations to be a taunt and horror. Once it fails to perform what is required of it in its prestigious position, this position is removed and Jerusalem becomes nothing among the nations.

Three different types of correspondences can be detected in this pericope. The first type involves the use of identical words for the offence and the punishment. The second type is less on the lexical level, but pertains to the extent of the offence and the punishment—both are unusual and extreme. The third type, which contains some lexical connections, deals with the initial and final conditions of Jerusalem—they are just the opposite. Although it is true to say that there is a casual relationship between the offence and the punishment in these cases, it is a relationship that is definitely mediated by Yahweh whose powerful "I" dominates all the descriptions of the punishments issued from him.

3.2. *Ez 6:1–14*

Ez 6 has been discussed above in connection with covenant and retribution. Here we will focus on the correspondences between sin and punishment. Idolatry is indisputably the offence committed by the people as stated explicitly in 6:9 ("their whoring heart which turned away[26] from me and their wanton eyes whoring after their idols") and 6:13 ("they offered pleasing odour to all their idols"). The punishment announced in 6:3–6 targets this idolatry. First, Yahweh will bring an end to the places where idolatry is committed. The high places (במות) will be destroyed (v.3; cf. v.6). Second, the means of

---

[25] The LXX reads differently in vv.14–15. Since the textual problems do not affect our argument, a detailed discussion of them is forgone here. For a careful treatment see Allen (1994:53–54).

[26] Whether אשר־סר should be deleted in accordance with the LXX is of no direct relevance to us. It is deleted by Herrmann (1924:42), Bertholet (1936:22), Cooke (1936:74), Fohrer (1955:37), Wevers (1969:60), Zimmerli (1979:180) and Allen (1994:83). It is retained by Greenberg (1983a:134), Block (1997:230).

worship will be demolished. The altars and the chapels will be desolated and cut down (vv.4, 6). In addition, the altars will be dese-
crated by scattering bones around them (v.5). Third, the idols
themselves will be broken (v.6). Fourth, even the idolaters themselves
will be slain and thrown before the idols (vv.4, 5, 7). These gestures
show that the idols are impotent to protect not only themselves, but
also their worshippers.[27]

Apart from these, the extent of the idolatry corresponds to that
of Yahweh's punishment. First, the abomination of the people is
qualified by "all" (כל) (v.9). Second, in v.13b the altars are said to
be found everywhere, again, by using the word כל: on *every* high
hill, on *every* mountain top, under *every* green tree and under *every*
leafy oak. An intensification can be seen by this fivefold use of כל
to qualify both the locations and the idols. In response to this,
Yahweh's punishment is equally comprehensive. First, total destruction is expressed by means of paronomasia: שממה ומשמה (v.14aβ).
Second, this destruction is applied everywhere, indicated by "all" (כל)
their settlements" and "from the wilderness to Riblah", i.e., from
the north to the south (v.14aγ). This extensive punishment is earlier
indicated in v.12 by the use of the meristic "far" (רחוק) and "near"
(קרוב), hinting at the comprehensiveness of the punishment. Since
this twofold distinction does not work well with the three means of
punishment (in v.11), a third category is added: "those who are left
and spared".[28] The point is to emphasise the totality of punishment.
Thus, although no lexical links can be found, the extensiveness of
the punishment clearly corresponds to the extensiveness of the idolatry. In sum, the lexical link between sin and punishment is limited
only to the word "idols" (גלולים), but the correspondences in the various aspects involved in idolatry are prominent (i.e., the locale, cultic paraphernalia, idols and worshippers, and Yahweh's dealing with
them). It should be noted that all these happen at the places where
the idolatry is committed. Thus, Fohrer captures it well by saying
that "der Ort der Schuld wird derjenige des Gerichts".[29]

---

[27] Cf. Joash's challenge in Jdg 6:31.
[28] The Hebrew word והנשאר is absent in LXX. By reference to Is 49:6 it is often
regarded as secondary or a gloss to explain the word והנצור which follows it. E.g.
Hitzig 1847:43; Herrmann 1924:42; Bertholet 1936:22; Fohrer 1955:39; Wevers
1969:61; Zimmerli 1979:181. However, Allen (1994:83) rightly explains the pairs of
words as "he who is left over (from the pestilence) and he who is preserved (from
the sword)".
[29] Fohrer 1955:38.

3.3. *Ez 7:20–21*

The offence of the people lies in that they take pride in the ornaments made from gold and silver, and by which they made images of abomination. In return (note the use of עַל־כֵּן), Yahweh will make the silver and gold into something unclean and abhorrent (נִדָּה). This is achieved by handing it over to strangers as booty and letting them profane it (v.21). By making (עָשָׂה) images from gold and silver, the people think that they are making something holy and venerable, but by delivering it to strangers as a booty and allowing them to treat it as common, Yahweh is making it into (נָתַן לְ) the opposite, something profane and unsuitable for worship. Thus, the punishment is appropriate to the crime in that it frustrates the very purpose of the crime. What is meant for veneration is made unvenerable for the people. Since the people misused what was originally precious, Yahweh will render it useless for them.

3.4. *Ez 11:1–13*

The section Ez 11:1–13, which is part of the temple vision Ez 8–11, is framed by the reference to Pelatiah (vv.1, 13). According to Allen, the main oracle (vv.2–12) has the form of a disputation and a proof saying. The tripartite structure of the disputation is: thesis (v.3aβb), dispute (v.6) and counterthesis (vv.7–11).[30] In this case, the dispute forms the accusation, and the counterthesis the judgement. The recognition formula in vv.10b and 12aα, which is a part of the proof saying, plays no role in the structure of the disputation.

In the vision, this event takes place at the east gate of the temple where Ezekiel sees 25 men. He identifies two of them as the officials of the people (שָׂרֵי הָעָם). In v.2 these people are characterised as those who "devise iniquity and give wicked counsel in this city". The word עֵצָה ("counsel") occurs again only in Ezekiel at 7:26, associated with the function of the elder. It is thus probable that the other 23 people are elders. The quotation in v.3 has two parts:

לֹא בְקָרוֹב בְּנוֹת בָּתִּים	v.3aβ	It is not near to build houses,
הִיא הַסִּיר וַאֲנַחְנוּ הַבָּשָׂר	v.3b	it is the pot and we are the flesh.

The ambiguity of both parts has led to a variety of interpretations. V.3aβ is particularly difficult since it is not taken up again in the

---

[30] Allen (1994:131), followed by Block (1997:330).

following oracle. It can be seen as a statement as given above, a question,[31] or a command.[32] "To build houses"[33] can mean literally the physical construction of houses, or metaphorically the continuation of family lines (e.g. Dt 25:9; Ru 4:11). The word בקרוב can be taken either in a temporal sense, or a spatial sense.[34] In v.3b the "it" has its antecedent in v.2, referring to "this city", that is, Jerusalem. There are basically two interpretations of the image. First, as the pot protects the meat inside it from insects, etc., so the city protects the people from being harmed. Second, since only the choice meat is to be put in the pot, the officials are claiming that they are the elite of the society in contrast to other groups of people who could be either the exiles or those who are less privileged socially. Exegetes usually base their decision partly upon the interpretation of vv.6–8. Generally speaking, two main positions can be discerned.

The first is to take the accusation as pertaining to civil matters. The point of departure is to compare the present text with Mic 2:1–2 through the common expression חשב(·)ם אָוֶן ("those who devise iniquity") which is found only in these two texts in the OT.[35] In Mic 2:1–2, those who devise iniquity are the powerful people who covet other people's property—fields, houses and inheritance—and seize them from their owners. When applied to the present text, the officials are powerful people who take away the property of the less-privileged people. In this case, v.3aβ is often taken as a statement and בקרוב in a temporal sense. Thus, for them there is no urgency to build houses for they can easily seize them from the poor.[36] They are therefore the choice meat in the pot, i.e., Jerusalem. They deserve to be there whereas the poor do not. This is the meaning of v.3b. To support this interpretation the "slain" in v.6 are normally taken as the civilians who are victims of biased judicial decision.[37] That is to say, the officials are accused of gaining profit at the expense of the poor.[38] One problem with this interpretation is how satisfacto-

---

[31] Eichrodt 1970:107; Graffy 1984:43; Brownlee 1986:154; NIV. Cf. LXX.

[32] Horst 1953:340.

[33] Steinmann (1953:61) is unique in emending בתים to במות ("hauts-lieux").

[34] Cf. the ברחוק in Ps 10:1.

[35] Cf. Ps 36:5.

[36] Fohrer 1955:60; Greenberg 1983a:187; Fuhs 1984:60; Ohnesorge 1991:69; Allen 1994:160; Block 1997:333.

[37] This is usually based on Eissfeldt (1950). But see Kraetzschmar (1900:118).

[38] Cf. Ez 22:27 where the officials (שרים) are said to destroy lives for dishonest gain.

rily to incorporate v.8 into this line of thinking. For example, Allen interprets the sword in v.8 as referring to "the fall of Jerusalem at the hands of the Babylonians", which is sent by Yahweh to carry out his "moral retribution".[39] But this understanding of the sword apparently has no connection with his interpretation of vv.2–3. Greenberg's opinion that the officials are afraid of the sword because of their "bad conscience" is even more far-fetched.[40]

The second position is to take the accusation as pertaining to political matters. This position takes seriously the expression הַיֹּעֲצִים עֵצַת־רָע בָּעִיר הַזֹּאת ("those who give wicked counsel in this city"). At that time, the sort of wicked counsel that could be given in Jerusalem probably refers to the counsel of the officials and the elders who proposed an anti-Babylonian policy.[41] In this case, v.3aβ can mean that there is no time to build the houses since all the resources must be used to fortify the city (cf. Is 9:9).[42] Or, it can be a complacent remark, meaning "we have plenty of time to build up the houses".[43] Thus, the pot-meat image in v.3b underlines the idea of protection.[44] The argument is that "we do not have to worry about the Babylonians, since Jerusalem, being the chosen city of Yahweh, can protect us". The slain in v.6 refer to the political opponents killed by the anti-Babylonian regime (cf. Jer 41–42).[45] This anti-Babylonian group is certainly afraid of the sword, referring to the war which ensued from

---

[39] Allen 1994:162.

[40] Greenberg 1983a:188.

[41] Eichrodt's opinion (1970:135) that this group has a consistent pro-Babylon policy is untenable because Ezekiel, who himself argues strongly that Babylon is an agent of Yahweh's punishment and that Judah must submit to Babylon (e.g. Ez 17), would hardly call such a policy "wicked counsel". See also Pohlmann's comment (1996:162).

[42] Fisch 1950:57; Taylor 1969:109; Greenberg 1983a:187; Cooper 1994:140; Clements 1996:46; Pohlmann 1996:164; Block 1997:333.

[43] Graffy 1984:43–44.

[44] Keil 1876a:145; Bertholet 1897:61; Kraetzschmar 1900:116; Cooke 1936:122; Feinberg 1969:63; Eichrodt 1970:137; Carley 1974:67; Graffy 1984:44; Andrew 1985:54; Cooper 1994:140; Duguid 1994:116; Block 1997:332 (pot as a storage vessel).

[45] Cooke 1936:122; Fisch 1950:58; Pohlmann 1996:164. The opinion that the slain refer to future victims of war because of the bad counsel, held by Horst (1953:341), Wevers (1969:77), Zimmerli (1979:259), Stuart (1989:101) and Clements (1996:47), cannot be accepted because vv.6–7 indicate not only that the killing has already happened, but also that it is the group of elders and officials who killed and placed the victims within the city. In this connection we may mention the purely conjectural emendation of Bertholet (1936:34) who changes the second person plural verbal forms in vv.6–7 to first person singular (with Yahweh as subject).

their decision. Thus, this line of thinking, which incorporates well
vv.8–10, referring to the attack of the Babylonians and the subsequent exile and execution, is to be preferred.

This passage is built upon the themes of (i) סיר ("pot") and בשר
("meat") with each word occurring three times (vv.3, 7, 11); (ii) being
inside or outside the city, expressed in a variety of ways including
the use of the prepositions ב, בתוך and מתוך; and (iii) sword and
judgement. These three themes are intertwined and can be found
in both sin and punishment.

First, the pot-meat theme. The group claims that the city is the
pot, and they are the meat (v.3). As a pot protects the meat inside
it, so the city will protect the group inside it. In response to this,
Yahweh announces a first twist in v.7a. In v.6, this group of people is accused of having multiplied their slain (הרביתם חלליכם) *in* this
city (העיר הזאת) which obviously refers back to the city already mentioned in vv.2 and 3. Verse 7a follows up the lead in v.6. Having
murdered them *in* the city, the group further placed them *in the midst*
of it (בתוכה). Now being in the city conceived as the pot, the slain
thus by definition constitute the meat in the pot (v.7a). This is empha-
sised in the Hebrew by the use of the personal pronoun: המה הבשר.
They, the slain, are the meat and the city is the pot. This sets up
a contrast to the claim of the group: אנחנו הבשר. This also hints that
by committing the killing, the group's identification with the meat
in the metaphor is undermined.[46] This first twist denies only implicitly that the group is the meat as they claimed, and introduces a
second group of people, the slain, who cannot protect themselves
and are therefore murdered and declares them to be the meat by
virtue of the action of their murderers who placed them inside the
city. The second twist comes at v.11 where Yahweh states that "it
will not become your pot, and you will not[47] become meat inside

---

[46] By comparing with Mic 3:2–3, some scholars (e.g. Greenberg 1983a:187–188;
cf. Keil 1876a:147) hold that the slain are being treated by their murderers as meat
in a caldron. If that is the case, the murderers attribute to the slain the status of
being meat (in the pot) by committing this offence and thereby forfeit their own
status.

[47] The MT does not have the second negation which is supplied in the LXX.
Following the suggestion of GKC §152z or J.-M. §160q, many commentators hold
that the first לא performs double duty (e.g. Kraetzschmar 1900:118; Herrmann
1924:57; van den Born 1954:74; Aalders 1955:194; Zimmerli 1979:229; Greenberg
1983a:188; Allen 1994:127; Pohlmann 1996:127). Cooke (1936:127) denies that but
insists that a second לא should be supplied. Fisch's interpretation (1950:59) that

it"". That is, the city will not protect the group, and they will not
be the meat in it because, as said in vv.7 and 9, they will be taken
out of the city. Once out of the city, they are by default not meat
any more. This second twist explicitly denies the group's claim to
be meat. If the first twist allows the first half of their claim (i.e.,
"this city is the pot") to remain unchallenged and denies only the
second half (i.e., "we are the meat"), then the second twist denies
the group from identifying both the city as the pot and themselves
as meat in the pot. This forms a final and complete refutation to
the group's claim.

Second, the theme of inside and outside. We have mentioned
above that being inside the city is the criterion for claiming to be
meat. The idea of inside and outside in this passage is mostly related
to the 25 men. This group is devising iniquity and giving wicked
counsel *in* (ב) the city. They have killed many *in* (ב) the city and
placed them *in the midst* of it (בתוכה). As a result, they will be taken
(הוציא) *out* of it (מתוכה). Thus, "inside" is not contrasted with the
"surroundings" (expressed by the preposition סביב), but with "from/out
of inside" (מתוכה). Not only will they be out of the city, they will
be taken to the Israelite border (נבול ישראל)[48]—the furthest place

---

"after their flight from the city they would be the *flesh* which fell . . ." is simply self-
contradictory. Graffy (1984:46–47) argues against the consensus. He holds that
Ezekiel declares the people to be meat, but the meat of the slain in line with v.7.
His interpretation fails to see that to be meat it has to be inside the pot, and he
takes no notice of the rhetorical effect of vv.6–7. Block (1997:336) opines that the
people will be meat in the pot because the pot now has not the connotation of
protection (as in v.3) but that of cooking. However, this change is nowhere evident
in the text. Both Block and Graffy fail to resolve the tension their opinion has with
vv.7 and 9 where the people are said to be taken out of the city (although Graffy
[1984:47n.70] acknowledges the problem).
    [48] Most scholars (e.g. Herrmann 1924:57; Cooke 1936:123; Auvray 1957:48;
Zimmerli 1979:229; Greenberg 1983a:185; Pohlmann 1996:127) claim that על-נבול
ישראל (vv.10, 11) means "on Israelite border". Others disagree. Graffy (1984:46),
followed by Allen (1994:162) (cf. Block 1997:337), holds that נבול ישראל refers not
to the border, but the territory of Israel, claiming that they base this observation
on Ottoson's view (1977:365) that נבול ישראל does not refer to the border of Israel
apart from 2 Kg 14:25. Allen further claims that על-נבול ישראל is a shortened variant of בכל-נבול ישראל which means "in all the Israelite territory". However, Ottoson
does not discuss the expression על-נבול ישראל and his observation is inconclusive
because one should also consider the preposition that goes with the word נבול rather
than just the expression itself. When prefixed by ב, the expression בנבול refers to
the territory of whatever is in construct with it (Num 33:44; Dt 2:4; Jos 24:30;
Jdg 2:9; 11:18; 1 Sam 7:13; 10:2). This is also the same for the prefix בכל (Jdg 19:29;
1 Sam 11:3, 7; 27:1; 2 Sam 21:5; 1 Kg 1:3; 2 Kg 10:32; 1 Chr 21:12). But in the
case of על, (i) in the sense of "on/at", the expression refers to the *border* of whatever

from the city[49]—and there Yahweh will judge them. This group commits wicked actions within the city and they claim to be protected
by the city by staying in it. In response to this claim, Yahweh
announces that they will be taken out of city, to the border of Israel
which is furthest from the city. While they killed many in the city,
it is outside the city that the sword will come upon them. While
they placed the slain in the city, it is outside the city that they themselves will fall by the sword. Following their own logic, once outside
the city they cannot be the meat and thus have no protection which
they eagerly want.

Third, the theme of sword and judgement. The people are afraid
of the sword (i.e., the war). In response to this, Yahweh himself will
bring the sword upon them. This in itself does not necessarily imply
the death of the people, but only that they will be thrown into war.
But vv.9–10 quickly supply the frightful news. Instead of staying
safely within the city, they will be taken out of it and handed over
to the foreigners, that is, the Babylonians, who will execute judgement upon them. If that still leaves them a faint hope of survival
(as those who survived the first attack in 597 BCE), this is shattered
immediately—for by the sword they will fall. It is noteworthy to
point out that in all three clauses (vv.8a, 8bα and v.10aα) wherein
the word "sword" (חרב) is found, it always occupies the first position: it is the sword which they fear, it is the sword which Yahweh
will bring to them, and it is by the sword that they will fall. One
can hardly miss the prominence which Ezekiel gives to the word
"sword". Foreigners judging the people is finely paralleled by Yahweh
judging them on the border (vv.10, 11).[50] While v.9 indicates that it
is the foreigners who will execute judgement on the people, vv.10
and 11 claim that it is Yahweh who judges the people. While v.8

---

is in construct with it outside Ezekiel (Nu 20:23; 22:36; Jos 19:2), (ii) in the sense
of "adjoining to", it probably refers to territory (Jos 18:5; Ez 48:2, 3, 4, 5, 6, 7,
8, 24, 25, 26, 27, 28; Jl 4:6), (iii) in the sense of "against", it refers to territory
(Zep 2:8). In Ez 11:10, our observation above justifies rendering the expression as
"at the border of Israel". Similarly, noting the frequent interchange between על
and אל in Ezekiel, Ez 11:11 should be interpreted in the same way. Note that
Rogerson (1999) recently questions whether there was such a strict distinction between
boundary and territory.

[49] Greenberg (1983a:188) remarks that the Israelite border represents the "extrem-
ity of the expulsion".

[50] This interpretation follows the Masoretic accentuation. Auvray (1957:48) is
alone in holding otherwise: "Vous tomberez par l'épée sur le territoire d'Israël, . . .".

says that it is Yahweh who will bring the sword to the people, vv.9 and 10 suggest that the people will actually fall at human hands. From this, the idea that there is synergism between human action and divine action comes to the fore. The sword is Yahweh's agent to carry out his purpose and the foreigners are his agents to execute his judgement.

In this passage there are a number of correspondences between sin and judgement which include lexical links such as "pot", "meat" and "sword". These links show that the punishment is not only related to the sin, but also appropriate to it. Apart from lexical links, the rhetorical effect produced by the theme inside and outside also serves to foster a link between sin and punishment. Punishment is thereby seen as a reversal of the offence and therefore fit for it.

3.5. *Ez 12:17–20*

Ez 12:17–20 is a sign act related to the one in Ez 4:10–16. After the word reception formula in v.17, Yahweh's instruction for the prophet to act is given in v.18. Then the addressees are introduced in v.19aα, followed by the interpretation of the sign act in vv.19aβ–20 which is in the form of a bipartite proof saying.[51]

Although the prophet acts out the instruction (i.e., to eat bread while quaking and drink water with trembling and anxiety) before his fellow exiles and explains that to them,[52] his sign act is basically about[53] the inhabitants of Jerusalem on the land of Israel. Of special relevance to us is vv.19aβ–20a: "They shall eat their bread with anxiety and drink their water with trembling, so that[54] its[55] land will

---

[51] Hals 1989:79.

[52] The people of the land (עַם הָאָרֶץ), Ezekiel's addressees, probably refers to his fellow exiles (e.g. Fisch 1950:67; Carley 1974:77; Greenberg 1983a:223; Allen 1994: 183; Block 1997:382; against Cooke 1936:133; Ziegler 1948:39). It is not necessary to take the reference to people living on the land of Israel because Ezekiel uses the designation in different ways. For a discussion, see Greenberg (1983a:223) and Maarsingh (1985:160).

[53] The Hebrew אמר ל means "to speak of". E.g. Zimmerli 1979:276; Greenberg 1983a:222; Allen 1994:171, 174; Pohlmann 1996:172; Block 1997:380.

[54] The word לְמַעַן admits of different possibilities. First, it can have the final sense, indicating a purpose. E.g. Smend 1880:71; Toy 1899:17; Kraetzschmar 1900:128; Herrmann 1924:75; Cooke 1936:133; Schumpp 1942:66; Fisch 1950:67; van den Born 1954:80; Aalders 1955:212; Auvray 1957:52; Zimmerli 1979:276; Maarsingh 1985:160; Brownlee 1986:177; Breuer 1993:85. Second, it can have the consecutive sense, indicating result. E.g. Greenberg 1983a:223; Block 1997:380. Third, it may indicate a cause, meaning "because". E.g. Hitzig 1847:84; Keil 1876a:161;

be stripped[56] of all it contains because of the violence of all those inhabiting in it. And the inhabited cities shall be in ruins and the land shall be a desolation." Here the offence of the people is violence (חמס). Violence is an offence with which Ezekiel charges the people several times (7:11, 23; 8:17; 45:9). In response to this offence, the punishment will be twofold, corresponding to the two aspects of the offence (i.e., the inhabitants and the city/land).

Firstly, the offenders are characterised as "inhabitants (ישבים) of Jerusalem". The significance of this can be seen by comparing it with 7:23 and 8:17. In these two texts, the city/land is also said to be "full of violence" (מלא חמס). However, in 7:23 there is no explicit reference to the offenders and in 8:17 the offenders are simply called "house of Judah". In the present text, the idea of inhabitant is related to the punishment of *depopulation*. This is found first in v.19bα: Jerusalem in which the people dwell will be stripped of its content. That is to say, the inhabitants are no longer inhabitants of the city. If the land is filled with violence, then this violence will lead to the emptying of what fills the land. The wordplay on ישב, חמס, and מלא seems deliberate. The idea also appears in v.20a, where the cities which will become ruins are qualified by the word "inhabited"

Fohrer 1955:65; Eisemann 1988:211. Cf. Allen 1994:174. It is difficult to decide between the final and consecutive meanings, but with a finite verb following it, it is more likely that it has the final sense. For this, see Brongers (1973:89–91). One can also compare its use in 4:17 which, as we have argued, also has a final sense. Although the meaning of "because", or rather, "on account of", is listed in BDB (775), a review of the examples given shows that in these cases למען is unanimously followed by a noun or with personal suffixes. The present case does not seem to fit this category.

[55] There are three interpretative options for אדצה: (1) keep the MT reading and interpret it as Jerusalem's vicinity. E.g. Keil 1876a:161; Kraetzschmar 1900:128; Fisch 1950:67; Aalders 1955:213; Greenberg 1983a:223; Allen 1994:174; Block 1997:380; (2) emend it to "(the) land" in line with the LXX. E.g. Smend 1880:71; Cornill 1886:244; Toy 1899:17; Bertholet 1936:44; Pohlmann 1996:172; (3) emend it to "their land" in line with some Hebrew manuscripts. E.g. Ehrlich 1912:42; Herrmann 1924:75; Cooke 1936:133; van den Born 1954:80; Fohrer 1955:65; Zimmerli 1979:276; Brownlee 1986:177. In our opinion, the first interpretation makes sense and there is no need for emendation.

[56] There are three interpretative options for ממלאה: (1) interpret the מן as privative in meaning as in the case of Ez 32:15. E.g. Keil 1876a:161; Cornill 1886:244; Toy 1899:17; Kraetzschmar 1900:128; Schumpp 1942:66; Aalders 1955:213; Carley 1974:77; Zimmerli 1979:276; Allen 1994:174; Pohlmann 1996:172; Block 1997:380 (comparing with 32:15); (2) interpret the מן as causal as in v.19bβ (in this case what fills the city is violence). E.g. Greenberg 1983a:224; (3) emend the text to ומלאה ("and its fullness"). E.g. LXX; Herrmann 1924:75; Bertholet 1936:44. In view of Ez 32:15, the first option is most probable.

(הנושבות). The then inhabited cities will be depopulated. The inhabitants will be no more. We may compare this with 4:17 where the lack of food and water would eventually lead to the people wasting away. That is to say, those who used to inhabit in the land/city are no longer able to do so because of their sin and thus are no longer inhabitants of the land/city.

Secondly, the land/city in which the people dwell will be desolated. While v.19bα is concerned only with the desolation of Jerusalem and its vicinity, v.20a extends the desolation to all cities and the whole land. Not only are the land and cities depopulated, they will become ruins and a waste.[57] Thus, the land will become uninhabitable. In this passage, the correspondences between sin and punishment show that the latter will undermine the status of the offenders as being inhabitants of the land and also destroy the location of the offence.

When commenting on Hos 4:1–3 where similar ideas are found, Wolff argues that "the judgment results not from the direct actions of Yahweh himself, but from 'an organic structure of order,' 'a sphere in which one's actions have fateful consequences' which Yahweh puts into effect".[58] His opinion is definitely influenced by Koch. Wolff's comment may also be applied to our text here since in it Yahweh's action on the people and the land/cities is nowhere to be found. However, it is difficult to prove that Wolff's idea is true. In our text here, the recognition formula which concludes the passage points out the importance of what precedes it. The ways in which the inhabitants and the land/cities fare are clearly related to God and are indeed for the purpose of arriving at a knowledge of God. If that is true, one may wonder whether an immanent-causal understanding of the events correctly portrays what Ezekiel has in mind. In fact, one may claim that the correspondences between sin and punishment depicted are used not only to "underscore the fact that Yahweh will punish when Israel has sinned"[59] but also to stress that his punishment is just and appropriate.

---

[57] According to Ehrlich (1909:101), the verb שׁמם (hiphil) with a locality as object refers less to destruction and more the doing away with the inhabitants. Although we have only its cognate noun שׁממה here, the same connotation may still be present.

[58] Wolff 1974:68.

[59] Miller 1982:11.

3.6. *Ez 12:21–25*

Ez 12:21–25 is a disputation speech comprising three elements: thesis (v.22b), counterthesis (v.23bβ) and dispute (vv.24–25aα).[60] It is concluded by a recapitulation of the counterthesis and the concluding formula. Although it is not clear if the thesis and the counterthesis can be labelled as sin and punishment respectively, the correspondences between them are difficult to miss.

In v.22 the quotation is called a מָשָׁל which probably means that it is a well established proverb.[61] In view of the "in Israel" (בְיִשְׂרָאֵל) in v.23, the proverb should be taken as one current *in* the land of Israel but not *about* the land of Israel (עַל־אַדְמַת יִשְׂרָאֵל) (v.22).[62] The proverb says:

> יַאַרְכוּ הַיָּמִים וְאָבַד כָּל־חָזוֹן   The days are prolonged and every vision
>   comes to nothing

It echoes the opinion of those remaining in Israel that many days have passed but the prophecy of disasters has never come true.[63] The proverb actually denies the fulfilment of *every* vision. God responds with a counter-proverb (v.23bβ):

> קָרְבוּ הַיָּמִים וּדְבַר כָּל־חָזוֹן   The days and the content of every vision are
>   approaching

The counter-proverb takes over the words "days" and "every vision" from the quotation and changes the rest of it. There are two changes: first, the word יַאַרְכוּ of the proverb is replaced by קָרְבוּ; second, the word וְאָבַד is omitted and וּדְבַר[64] is added in construct with "every vision". Thus, the phrase "the content of every vision" becomes the second subject of קָרְבוּ. In the first change, the yiqtol form having

---

[60] Allen 1994:194.
[61] Block 1997:387. Referring to quotations, the word also appears in Ezekiel at 18:2, 3.
[62] Ziegler 1948:39; Zimmerli 1979:279; Greenberg 1983a:226; Graffy 1984:53; Block 1997:386; against Allen 1994:185; Pohlmann 1996:172.
[63] Greenberg 1983a:230; Graffy 1984:54.
[64] Some propose to emend וּדְבַר to: (1) וּבָא: Cornill 1886:244; Herrmann 1924:78; (2) וְעָבַר: Ewald 1880:74; (3) וְנֶבַר: cf. Heinisch 1923:70 ("eintreffen"); Bertholet 1936:44; Ziegler 1948:40; Fohrer 1955:67; (3) וּמֵהֵר: Kraetzschmar 1900:129. But the MT is supported by the LXX. Its reading is kept by, for example, Ehrlich (1912:40), Cooke (1936:136), Aalders (1955:215), van den Born (1954:81), Zimmerli (1979:279), Greenberg (1983a:226), Graffy (1984:55), Allen (1994:187), Pohlmann (1996:172), Block (1997:389n.28).

a durative sense[65] is replaced by the qatal form denoting an action performed at the moment of utterance or in the very near future.[66] Thus, the opposition is brought about not just by using a verb of opposite meaning, but also by the form of the verb. The second change introduces the word דָּבָר, which with its cognate verb dominates v.25. The contrast brought about by this change is discussed below.

The dispute comprises two כִּי-clauses. The first one is negative, stating that there will be no more empty visions[67] and flattering divinations (v.24). The second one is positive, stressing that Yahweh will speak and whatever he speaks will be done (v.25aα).[68] The *idem per idem* construction in v.25aα underscores that *everything* that God says will be realised.[69] These two clauses further bring out the contrast between the proverb and the counter-proverb. The negative clause characterises "every vision" as "every empty vision" (כָל־חֲזוֹן שָׁוְא), thus giving a negative connotation to כָל־חֲזוֹן in the proverb. This partly concedes the claim of the quotation.[70] It is true to say that empty visions, and only empty visions, will not come true. The positive clause immediately underlines that Yahweh's word, that which he speaks, will be done (וְיַעֲשֶׂה). In v.25b, it is Yahweh himself who will execute his word. Thus, v.25 provides a positive understanding of דבר. The second half of Yahweh's counter-proverb is actually saying "every vision's content, as far as it is from me, is approaching". The whole dispute is recaptured in v.25aβbα where the idea of imminence is repeated by using the phrases "there will be no more delay" (לֹא תִמָּשֵׁךְ עוֹד) and "in your days".

Thus, the correspondences between the thesis and the counterthesis are lexical and connotative. The counterthesis links lexically to the thesis by repeating the words הַיָּמִים and כָל־חֲזוֹן from the thesis, and by using קָרְבוּ as an opposite to יַאֲרִכוּ. Although linked lexically,

---

[65] For this use, see J.-M. §113f.

[66] For this understanding, see J.-M. §112fg. Cf. "in your days" (בִּימֵיכֶם) in v.25, which implies a sense of imminence. For the switch from yiqtol to qatal form, see also Graffy (1984:55), Allen (1994:198), Block (1997:389n.28).

[67] This follows the MT vocalisation. If the absolute form חָזוֹן attested in some manuscripts is accepted, then שָׁוְא should be taken as a predicate, i.e., "every vision is empty". For this understanding, see Ehrlich (1912:42–43), Allen (1994:187). Cf. Greenberg 1983a:228.

[68] The syntax of the text is difficult. For a discussion, see Zimmerli (1979:279–280), Allen (1994:188), Block (1997:391). However, the main thrust of the text is clear.

[69] Ogden 1992:112. For a definition of the construction, see p. 107.

[70] Graffy 1984:55.

there is a difference in the connotation between כל־חזון and דבר
כל־חזון. By means of these similarities and differences, the counterthesis is constructed as a complete rejection and reversal of the
thesis. If those who say the proverb could be said to commit an
offence, then the punishment is not simply to put an end to the
proverb, but to replace it with a counter-proverb with a totally opposite content.

3.7. *Ez 12:26–28*

Ez 12:26–28 is a disputation speech having a thesis (v.27aβb), a
counterthesis (v.28aβ) and a dispute (v.28bα). It is introduced by the
word reception formula (v.26) and concluded with the concluding
formula (v.28bβ). The thesis in the form of a quotation clearly has
a chiastic structure:

החזון אשר־הוא חזה לימים רבים	The vision he sees is for many days,
ולעתים רחוקות הוא נבא	and for far-off times he prophesies.

In contrast to 12:21–25, this saying is not about visions in general,
but those of Ezekiel, as indicated by the twofold use of הוא. And it
is not about unfulfilled visions, but those which are only concerned
with[71] the future and therefore will be fulfilled in the distant future
as underscored by the chiastic structure which has a temporal element at its centre. In the counterthesis, Yahweh identifies his words
with Ezekiel's vision and prophecy by using "all my words" (כל־דברי),[72]
and there is a denial of any further delay of all Yahweh's words.[73]
This constitutes a direct refutation of the thesis. The argument used
to support the counterthesis is the affirmation that the word spoken
by Yahweh will be fulfilled. Although it is not clear if the quotation
is about Ezekiel's prophecy of salvation[74] or destruction,[75] the coun-

---

[71] The ל of both לימים רבים and לעתים רחוקות marks the topic of discussion. See
W.-O'C. §11.2.10g.

[72] Allen (1994:200) takes "my words" as a challenge to the "he" in the thesis.

[73] This understanding follows the Masoretic accentuation. Taking the major dis-
junction at עוד, some scholars leave the verb תמשך to stand by itself, thus in parallel to v.25. See, for example, Ehrlich (1912:43), Bertholet (1936:44), Ziegler
(1948:40), Greenberg (1983a:229). But the LXX indirectly reflects the Masoretic
accentuation by rendering תמשך as the plural μηκύνωσιν, and it is possible to have
a feminine singular verb for a plural subject (e.g. GKC §145k). See, for example,
Cooke (1936:137), Zimmerli (1979:283), Allen (1994:188).

[74] Graffy 1984:57.

[75] Greenberg 1983a:231; Allen 1994:200; Block 1997:392.

terthesis captures the tone of the thesis well and refutes it directly.
For the thesis to have any force, it is necessary that Ezekiel's prophecy
be fulfilled only in the very distant future. But the immediacy and
certainty of the fulfilment of God's word stressed by the counterthesis
takes away the force of the thesis. Thus, the counterthesis forms a
fitting response to the thesis.

3.8. *Ez 13:10–16*

Introduced by the word reception formula, 13:1–16 is an oracle
against the male false prophets. The first part, vv.3–9, is a woe oracle in the form of a tripartite proof saying concerning false prophecies and visions. It starts with a series of accusations (vv.3b–7). The
word "therefore" introduces a summary of the accusation (v.8). This
is followed by an announcement of punishment (v.9a) and concluded
with the recognition formula (v.9b). Without a proper introduction,
the second part of the oracle, vv.10–16, is a tripartite proof saying
concerning the false proclamation of peace. The accusation is introduced by "because" (יען וביען) (v.10).[76] The punishment anticipated
in vv.11–12 appears in vv.13–14bα, followed by the recognition formula in v.14bβ. V.15 then provides a summary statement. An overall conclusion to the whole oracle is found in v.16 which contains
elements from both parts, namely, "visions" and "peace".[77] We will
deal only with the second part of the oracle.

In this oracle, the prophets are accused of leading the people astray
by proclaiming the false message of peace when there is no peace
(v.10a). This charge resembles similar accusations made by Jeremiah
of the Jerusalem prophets (e.g. Jer 6:14; 8:11; 23:17). It is then
expressed by means of a metaphor. The people build a loose wall
of unmortared stones,[78] but the prophets come and smear untempered

---

[76] Talmon and Fishbane (1975/76:133), followed by Greenberg (1983a:241), suggest that the first part ends in v.10a. But Ez 36:3 shows that יען ביען can introduce an oracle. See Aalders (1955:225), Allen (1994:189).

[77] These form-critical observations are based on Hals (1989:84–86) and Allen
(1994:194). Parunak (1978:26) points out some chiastic features of vv.10–16: v.10a//v.16,
vv.10b–11a//vv.14–15, v.11b//v.13, and v.12 forms the centre. Tidiman's chiastic
structure is less convincing (1985:188).

[78] The Hebrew חַיִץ is a hapax. Ehrlich (1912:45) argues on the basis of its use
in Mishnah that it refers to a loose wall. This is followed, for example, by Herrmann
(1924:79), Fisch (1950:71), Greenberg (1983a:237), Allen (1994:202) and Duguid
(1994:94). Cf. Block 1997:406n.69.

plaster[79] on it. Thus, the prophets cover the wall with plaster which does not really work, giving the impression that the wall is solid and good (i.e., קִיר) instead of revealing its weakness.

The metaphor continues in vv.11–12. Those who did the plastering are first told that the wall will fall (v.11aβ). Then vv.11b–12, which read "there is flooding rain,[80] and you, hailstones fall,[81] and (you) tempestuous wind burst forth. And behold, the wall falls, will you not be asked, where is the plaster which you smeared?", anticipate the fall of the wall and the uselessness of the plaster. But at this stage, nothing about the plasterers themselves is in view. In v.13 the three meteorological phenomena recur in a slightly different order: tempestuous wind, flooding rain and hailstones. They are all respectively qualified by an element of (God's) anger: "in my wrath" (בְחֵמָתִי), "in my anger" (בְאַפִּי) and "in wrath" (בְחֵמָה). Although only the tempestuous wind is said to be brought about by Yahweh, there is no doubt that the other two are also of divine origin. The purpose of this is to bring destruction. V.14a makes that clear. The wall which the plasterers have worked on will be broken down and torn to the ground so that its foundation will be revealed. So far only the wall is singled out for Yahweh's action. But v.15 goes further. Not only the wall but also the plasterers are the target of Yahweh's destructive action in anger, so that at the end Yahweh can say, "There is no wall, and there are no plasterers." In v.14bα the feminine verbal form and suffix cannot refer to the wall (קִיר) which is

---

[79] The word תָּפֵל refers to plaster without the necessary ingredients. See Greenberg (1983a:237) and Block (1997:406–407). But Propp (1990:408) holds that this understanding is too literal and prefers to render it as "hogwash", i.e., "nonsense".

[80] Some scholars turn the MT into a conditional by adding a ו to היה in view of the LXX (e.g. Herrmann 1924:80; Zimmerli 1979:287; Greenberg 1983a:233, 238; Allen 1994:186, 189–190; Pohlmann 1996:185; Block 1997:397). Some emend it to read יהיה in view of v.13 (e.g. Toy 1899:18; Cooke 1936:144). And some change it to the conditional particle הֵן (e.g. Kraetzschmar 1900:134). Aalders (1955:227) rightly argues that there is no need to make any emendation for the change between qatal and yiqtol forms in a sentence is entirely possible as Ps 2:1–2 testifies.

[81] The Hebrew וְאַתֵּנָה is difficult. Our translation follows those who keep the MT and render both תִּפֹּלְנָה and תְבַקֵּעַ as second person (e.g. Keil 1876a:166; Aalders 1955:228; Eisemann 1988:221; Breuer 1993:94; cf. Greenberg 1983a:233). Some propose וְאַתֵּנָה according to the LXX (e.g. Toy 1899:18; Herrmann 1924:80; Schumpp 1942:71; cf. Greenberg 1983a:238; NIV). Others prefer to delete the word (e.g. Heinisch 1923:72; Cooke 1936:144; Ziegler 1948:41; Allen 1994:190), taking it as a dittography with וְאֶבְנֵי (e.g. Auvray 1957:54; Zimmerli 1979:287; Block 1997:397).

masculine. Jerusalem is probably referred to (cf. v.16).[82] When Jerusalem falls, "you", the false prophets, will perish within it.

The basic correspondence between the offence and the punishment revolves around the word "wall". The word "wall" (קִיר) used
in the metaphor is associated with the city wall (e.g. 12:12). In the
metaphor, the offence lies in covering up a loose wall with plaster
which does not work so as to give it an impression of strength. In
reality, the prophets by their proclamation of peace give the people
a false sense of the security of the city Jerusalem. Correspondingly,
in the metaphor the punishment is to tear down the wall and lay
bare its foundation so that one can see that the wall is unstable and
the plaster useless, and in reality the city wall of Jerusalem will be
broken down and the message of the prophets shown to be false. In
this understanding, the punishment is appropriate to the offence in
the sense that the former frustrates the intention of the latter, making the latter a futile exercise. That is to say, the covering up will
not work. What is concealed will be revealed. In this sense, the pair
of verbs נלה-טוח are opposites characterising the offence and the punishment respectively. An ironic element of the punishment is that
the prophets who claim that the Jerusalem wall will stand actually
perish when it falls. That is to say, Jerusalem, the object of their
lies, is also the means of their punishment.

3.9. *Ez 13:17–23*

Ez 13:17–23 presents an oracle against the prophetesses[83] for prac-
tising sorcery. It is first introduced with a command to perform a
hostile gesture and the messenger formula in vv.17–18aα. Then there
is a woe-oracle in the form of a tripartite proof saying: accusation
in vv.18aγ–19, announcement of punishment in vv.20–21a, and the
recognition formula in v.21b. This is followed by another tripartite
proof saying: accusation in v.22, announcement of punishment in
v.23abα, and the recognition formula in v.23bβ.

In contrast to the male prophets who are more concerned with
public affairs (13:2–16), the text suggests that the female prophets

---

[82] E.g. Aalders 1955:229; Greenberg 1983a:238; Allen 1994:190; Pohlmann 1996:
185n.895; Block 1997:398n.35.
[83] The circumlocution בנות עמך המתנבאות may be a sign of disdain. See Pohlmann
(1996:192n.934).

have a private ministry, dealing with those who come to them pri-
vately. It is possible that these prophetesses are involved in some
sort of black magic or necromancy.[84] The exact procedure of the
prophetesses' divination cannot be determined from the text. The
word כסת, which appears only in Ez 13:18, 20, probably refers to
bands used in magical contexts.[85] It has been suggested that these
bands are to be tied to the wrists of the prophetesses,[86] or to the
people,[87] or to an image of the victim.[88] Since in v.20 Yahweh will
tear these bands from the prophetesses' arms,[89] it is more probable
that they are worn by the prophetesses themselves. They also put
מספחה on the head. The word occurs only in Ez 13:18, 21. It probably refers to a veil or shawl which is used to cover the head[90] of
the prophetess in view of v.21. V.18b speaks of them entrapping
other people and maintaining their own lives. The phrase "entrap
the person" (צוד נפש) is found again only in Prov 6:26 where it may
refer to the seduction of the gullible.[91] This could well be its meaning here. By using the bands and veils as some sort of divinatory
paraphernalia, the prophetesses deceive the gullible among the people.

Their divination probably involves invoking Yahweh,[92] for otherwise the name of other gods would probably be indicated.[93] In this
way they profane Yahweh (v.19a) by downgrading him as if he is a
puppet they can manipulate at will. It is possible that the barley and
bread are involved in the ritual, as offerings that accompany the div-

---

[84] Korpel 1996:109.
[85] Cooke 1936:145; Saggs 1974:5; Duguid 1994:96; Jeffers 1996:94; Korpel
1996:102; Block 1997:413.
[86] Dumermuth 1963:228; Greenberg 1983a:239; Block 1997:413.
[87] Cooke 1936:145; Eichrodt 1970:169; Allen 1994:204.
[88] Saggs (1974:5), followed by Jeffers (1996:94).
[89] For זרועתיכם, one may expect to have a feminine suffix instead of a masculine one (or a third person masculine plural suffix as in *BHS* apparatus). Other similar cases can be found in this passage: בכובם (v.19), אתם (v.20), אתם (v.20), and
מספחתיכם (v.21). Regarding this, Rooker (1990:78–81) points out the tendency of
late Biblical Hebrew to replace feminine forms by masculine ones. This is adopted
by Block (1997:412n.19) who produces more examples of late Biblical Hebrew in
this passage.
[90] Allen 1994:191; Pohlmann 1996:185. Cf. Greenberg's "rags" (1983a:239).
[91] Greenberg 1983a:240; Pohlmann 1996:192n.938.
[92] Kraetzschmar 1900:136; Cooke 1936:147; Eichrodt 1970:171; Zimmerli 1979:297;
Greenberg 1983a:240; Andrew 1985:67; Allen 1994:204; Pohlmann 1996:193; Block
1997:416.
[93] Pohlmann (1996:193), citing Jer 23:13 and 2 Kg 1:2 as examples.

ination (v.19a).[94] While their act may give the impression that their divination is an inquiry made to Yahweh, it is in fact only an imitation of a real consultation of Yahweh.[95] They prophesy only out of their hearts (v.17) and what they see is only emptiness (v.23). The charge that they put to death those who should not die and keep alive those who should not live (v.19a) probably refers to their telling lies (v.19b), giving unfavourable or favourable messages[96] to those who do not deserve them. Thus, they dishearten the righteous and strengthen the wicked (v.22). The language of life and death, and righteous and wicked recalls the role of Ezekiel as a watchman (3:17–21; 33:7–9). What they do amounts to usurping the privilege of the prophetic or priestly role to announce life and death, and abuse it.[97]

In response to their offence, Yahweh first announces that he will remove the bands and veils from them (vv.20a, 21aα). Note that while the prophetesses sew (תפר) the bands to the wrists, Yahweh will tear them away (קרע). The word קרע is chosen appropriately because it is the opposite of תפר, as Ecc 3:7 clearly shows. The correspondence between the offence and the punishment is made obvious not just by employing the same direct object ("bands", "veils"), but also by the choice of the pair of opposite verbs תפר-קרע. That is to say, what was used for plying their trade is removed. The punishment is appropriate to the offence because the means by which the offence is carried out is eliminated.

Secondly, by performing that counteraction Yahweh further negates the prophetesses' action. Like the last case, the objects of the prophetesses' and Yahweh's actions are the same, namely, the people, who are designated similarly in the prophetesses' action (נפשות or עמי or הנפשות לעמי) and in Yahweh's counteraction (נפשות or עמי). And again the actions are opposite. While the prophetesses hunted (צוד: vv.18, 20b) the people so that they became a prey (מצודה: v.21aγ), Yahweh

---

[94] Cooke 1936:147; van den Born 1954:87; Taylor 1969:125; Greenberg 1983a:240; Korpel 1996:103; Pohlmann 1996:193; Block 1997:416. Other OT parallels pointed out include Nu 5:15 and Lev 2:5. This use of ב can also be found in Jer 16:18; Ez 20:39; 22:16; 36:20. Some other scholars take it as a payment by the clients. E.g. Kraetzschmar 1900:136; Fisch 1950:73; Zimmerli 1979:297; Jenni 1992:152; Allen 1994:204; Duguid 1994:97; Jeffers 1996:95.

[95] Cf. Pohlmann 1996:193.

[96] Jeffers 1996:93.

[97] Hossfeld and Meyer 1973:133; Greenberg 1983a:244; Pohlmann 1996:194.

will deliver or release (שָׁלַח: v.20b; הִצִּיל: v.21) them so that they are free (פְּרֻחוֹת: v.20a).[98] Instead of *in* the hand of the prophetesses (בְּידכֶן: v.21aγ), the people will be *out* of their hand (מִידְכֶן: vv.21aβ, 23bα). In this case, the punishment is appropriate to the offence in that the former reverses the result of the latter.

Regarding the fate of the prophetesses themselves, it appears that nothing concrete has been indicated.[99] They themselves are not the target of God's punishment and hence the punishment is lighter than expected.[100] However, two observations can be made. First, the punishment that the prophetesses will no longer see empty visions and practise divination means that they will no longer be able to function as they used to. If their designation as הַמִּתְנַבְּאוֹת מִלִּבְּהֶן ("prophesying from their heart") represents what they are, then the punishment is a denial of their very essence. It is a refutation of their being. Second, if Ezekiel as a watchman has to bear the consequence for not giving warning to the wicked so that they can repent, the same can perhaps be said of the prophetesses who, instead of warning, have actually encouraged the wicked so that they do not repent and save their own lives.[101] Having done that, one cannot expect that the prophetesses can secure their own lives.

3.10. *Ez 16:1–43*

We have dealt with this passage in some detail in Chapter Two. Here it suffices to list some correspondences between sin and punishment found in the text. First, while the woman is charged with bribing all her lovers (כָּל־מְאַהֲבִים) to have sex with (בּוֹא אֶל) her "from all around" (מִסָּבִיב) (v.33b), her husband will gather all her lovers (כָּל־מְאַהֲבִים) to come against (עַל) her "from all around" (מִסָּבִיב) (v.37). In both cases, the woman's and her husband's actions have the same object, namely, all her lovers who are from the same whereabouts. The difference lies in what the lovers do to the woman expressed by a different preposition(al phrase): בּוֹא אֶל and עַל. Interestingly, the prepositions אֶל and עַל are very often used interchangeably in

---

[98] The word לְפָרֵחַ is difficult. BDB (827) lists only Ez 13:20 for the meaning "to fly" for פָּרַח. Block (1997:411n.13), following Brownlee (1986:194), treats the participle more verbally, i.e., as "for flying".

[99] Pohlmann 1996:194.

[100] Taylor 1969:125.

[101] Duguid 1994:97, 101.

Ezekiel. In this case the correspondence between sin and punishment is created by lexical similarities and contrast. The punishment is appropriate to the crime in that the agents of the offence happen also to be the agents of punishment.

Second, she is accused of revealing her nakedness (נלה ערוה) to her lovers (v.36a),[102] and in return her husband will reveal her nakedness (נלה ערוה) to her lovers (v.37bβ). While the former action represents an offence of the woman, namely, adultery, the latter action is a symbolic act of punishment for adulterers. In the former case, her lovers are those with whom she commits adultery, but in the latter case, her lovers become the witnesses of her punishment. In this case, the punishment corresponds to the sin in that the same action is done to the woman, but by different agents and with opposite meaning.

Third, the woman is charged with not remembering the days of her youth when she was "naked and bared" (ערם ועריה) (v.22bα; cf. v.7) and when she was "wallowing in blood" (v.22bβ; cf. v.6). Corresponding to her first situation, the husband will let her lovers strip her of her garments and take away her beautiful objects and leave her "naked and bared" (עידם ועריה) (v.39). The combination ע(י)רם ועריה occurs only in Ez 16:7, 22, 39; 23:29 within the OT. It is first found in v.7 to describe the situation of the baby girl and then in v.22 in the indictment. Its appearance in v.39 is significant for it clearly refers back to its previous two occurrences. If the woman's root offence lies in her not remembering that she was "naked and bared", then the punishment aims at bringing her back to this status and helping her to recall this lost memory. In this case, through lexical links the punishment is shown to be appropriate to the offence by correcting the offence. Corresponding to her second situation, the husband will turn her into "a bloody victim of wrath and jealousy" (v.38b), which probably refers to execution. The lexical link between the punishment and the offence is the word "blood" (דם). Again, if she forgets that she was in blood in her youth, then the punishment brings back this memory to her.[103] The offence will

---

[102] The text actually reads ותגלה ערותך. But this undoubtedly refers to her exposing her nakedness. We may compare this with v.25 where she is said to part her legs to every passer-by. In this case, her action is done in public. This corresponds to her punishment, i.e., being exposed naked before witnesses.

[103] Cf. Fishbane (1984:138): "a poetic reprise of her bloody origins".

be rectified by the punishment.[104] The reference to "blood" in the punishment is also related to the woman's offence of shedding blood (v.38; cf. v.36). By shedding blood, she is turned into blood.

Fourth, in the early description of the sins of the woman in vv.16–18 she is said to abuse the garments and jewellery by making idols out of them. Correspondingly, these will be taken away (v.39a). The punishment is fitting in that it removes the instrument of the offence, the means by which the offence is committed. Similarly, while the woman builds a brothel (גב) and booth (רמה) for her prostitution (vv.24–25, 31), the punishment inflicted upon her will include the breaking down of the brothel and the pulling down of the booths (v.39a). Again, the punishment corresponds to the offence in that the former destroys the instrument by which the latter is committed.

Lastly, the idea of publicity plays a role in both sin and punishment. This is first found in v.14 in a positive sense. The name of the woman is spread among the nations because of her beauty. She was famous but not notorious. But that is quickly given a negative twist. In v.15 she plays the whore because of her name, and she pours out her whorings on *every* passer-by (כל־עובר). Her whoring has become a public event and becomes worse. In vv.24–25 she builds brothels and booths *everywhere* (כל־ראש דרך, כל־רחוב) and she spreads her feet to *every* passer-by (כל־עובר). The idea of committing the offence publicly comes to the fore. Corresponding to this, the punishment is done in the public. Not only is the woman stripped naked before her former lovers (v.37), other punishments are executed "before the eyes of many women" (לעיני נשים רבות) (v.41). She who offended publicly will be shamed and punished publicly.

In this passage, the correspondence between sin and punishment is forged mostly by means of lexical links and the idea of reversal. Thus, the punishment inflicted is deemed appropriate to the sin. The reversal of the offence includes the turning back of the lovers against the woman, the removal of the means by which she commits her offence, and the bringing back of the lost memory which is her root offence.

---

[104] Note also that there is a shift in the connotation of "blood" from vv.6 and 9 to vv.36 and 38. According to Klee (1998:104n.20), "blood" as blood from birth and menstruation in vv.6 and 9 connotes life whereas "blood" as blood shed in murder and death penalty in vv.36 and 38 connotes death.

3.11. *Ez 34:7–10*

The passage 34:7–10 is part of Ez 34 which is an oracle of salvation built on the metaphor of shepherd and sheep. The structure of Ez 34 has been discussed above and need not be repeated here.[105] Here we are concerned with vv.7–10, focusing on the correspondences between the offence of the shepherds and their punishment.

The summary of indictment in v.8 gives the following accusations:

(1) my flock has become spoil, and my flock has become food (אכלה) for all the animals of the field for there is no shepherd,
(2) and my shepherds have not looked for (דרש) my flock,
(3) and the shepherds have tended (רעה) themselves,
(4) and my sheep they have not tended.

In the indictment, those who bear the title "shepherd" (רעה) are basically accused of not living up to their title. That is to say, they do not perform what is required and expected of a shepherd. They do not look for any lost sheep, and they do not protect the flock and so it becomes spoil and food for the wild animals. Moreover, they tend themselves instead of tending the sheep. The way in which they tend themselves is not mentioned here but found in v.3: "you eat the fat, you clothe with the wool, you slaughter the fatlings". Thus, not only do they not perform what a shepherd should do, they also make use of their position as shepherd to exploit the flock. Thus, although they are called "shepherds", there is in fact no shepherd (אין רעה).

In response to this, Yahweh announces the following (v.10):

(1) I will ask for (דרש) my flock from their hand,
(2) I will stop them from tending (רעה) my flock,[106]
(3) and no longer will the shepherds tend themselves,
(4) and I will rescue my flock from their mouths, and it shall not become their food (אכלה).

Since the shepherds did not look for (דרש) the flock, Yahweh demands (דרש) the flock from them. Yahweh holds the shepherds responsible

---

[105] See Chapter Three Section 5.1.
[106] The LXX reads "my flock" for the MT צאן. It is possible that the MT drops the י by pseudohaplography with the following ו. E.g. Zimmerli 1983:205; Allen 1994:157; Block 1997:279.

for the flock. The correspondence stresses that the shepherds' failure to דרש is repaid with Yahweh's דרש.[107] When v.8 (and v.5) is compared with v.10, we notice that the behaviour of the shepherds is like that of the wild animals preying on the flock. But the shepherds can no longer tend themselves because Yahweh will deliver the flock from them so that they can no more take the flock as food. Although Yahweh does not claim that he is a shepherd in this passage, what he does is exactly what one expects of a shepherd. By demonstrating what a real shepherd should do, Yahweh reveals the false claims of the shepherds. Since they were not really tending the flock, Yahweh will stop them from having the title "shepherd". They cannot claim to tend Yahweh's flock anymore.

Thus, the correspondences between sin and punishment revolve basically around the verb רעה, with דרש and אכלה also playing a part. What is directly under attack is the office of a shepherd. If the shepherds take advantage of their office and exploit the flock, then they will be removed from their office and so can exploit no more. If a רעה is stopped from tending the flock, then he is reduced to nothing at all. The job will be taken up by someone else—in this case, Yahweh—and this is the theme of vv.11–16.

4. *Poetic Justice*, Lex Talionis, *and Justice*

Our discussion above shows that punishment is related to the offence in that the punishment is like the sin by incorporating some elements of the offence. This likeness or correspondence between the offence and punishment is forged by different means: the repetition of the same verb and/or the same agents in both the offence and punishment; the indication that both the offence and punishment are of the same (outrageous) extent; the punishment consists in removing or destroying the means of committing the offence, or removing the offender from her/his office of which s/he takes advantage to commit an offence, or reversing the intention or result of the offence. Through these correspondences, the punishment is made to look like the offence. The principle, which works behind these texts displaying poetic justice, is "like for like". The punishment should

---

[107] Cf. Jer 23:2 where the shepherds' failure to פקד the flock is repaid with Yahweh's action to פקד.

be like the offence although how this "likeness" is to be realised
varies in individual cases.[108]

This principle of "like for like" is vague and general yet also deep,
fundamental and pervasive in human civilisation.[109] One of its actualisations is found in the *lex talionis*. The literature on *lex talionis* is
legion[110] and it is not our objective here to contribute to the current debate.[111] Regarding the terminology, the Latin word "talio"
originally means "die gleiche Wiedervergeltung eines empfangenen
Schadens am Körper".[112] In the OT, Ex 21:24; Lev 24:19–20 and
Dt 19:21 are the only three passages displaying this idea of "talion".
It was only in the seventh century CE that it acquired the definition
"talio est similitudo vindictae, ut taliter quis patiatur, ut fecit".[113]
Nowadays, the word "talion" has a broader reference which includes:
(1) punishment of a bodily part which is used directly in the offence;
(2) punishment by the same means which the offender used in the
crime; (3) punishment determined according to the motivating force
which forms the basis of the crime.[114] As such, it is sometimes called
"spiegelnden Strafen".[115] One should note that "mirror punishments"
in their various forms are not simply literary products but can actually be found not only in ancient law codes such as the Code of
Hammurapi and Assyrian laws, but also in the Pentateuchal laws
(e.g. Dt 25:11).[116] While "mirror punishments" are rightly distinguished from the actual talion as claimed by some scholars,[117] it is
also justified to describe these punishments as having talionic features

---

[108] While this principle of "like for like" forms the background for God's action,
in *Wisdom of Solomon* it is made the object of one's knowledge. See Amir (1992:38–39).

[109] Henberg 1990:43–55.

[110] E.g. Alt (1934), Daube (1947:102–153), Weismann (1972), Frymer-Kensky
(1980).

[111] According to Huffmon (1992:321–322), the current debate on *lex talionis* and
biblical material is centred upon two issues: (1) whether it is actually practised or
a principle guarding against excessive punishment; (2) the relationship between talion and pecuniary compensation. For a summary of various options, see Westbrook
(1988:41–47). See also Martin-Achard (1989) for an overview of some recent literature, and Otto (1991) for a recent discussion.

[112] Jüngling 1984:3.

[113] Herdlitczka 1932:2069. He also provides a historical development of the meaning of "talio" in antiquity. A summary of his article is given by Jüngling (1984:3–4).

[114] Herdlitczka 1932:2069.

[115] Brunner 1892:589; Weissmann 1972:337; Jüngling 1984:4. Cf. Miller's "'mirror' punishment" (1982:104).

[116] For examples, see Miller (1982:105–110).

[117] E.g. Jüngling 1984:4.

or talionic in nature. Regarding the correspondences between sin
and punishment in Ezekiel, it is unlikely that they can be found in
the Pentateuchal laws or any other ancient law codes, but their sharing the same form as the "mirror punishments" implies that they
can equally be said to be talionic.

In the original understanding of talion an offender suffers the same
bodily harm s/he inflicted on the victim. The presupposition is that
justice is done if the punishment is the same as the crime. In the
broadened sense of the *lex talionis*, or the "mirror punishment", the
presupposition of justice is that the punishment should in some way
be like or commensurate with the offence. Thus, by positing correspondences between sin and punishment, Ezekiel is able not only to
provide a stronger link between the two, but also to appeal to the
presupposition that there is justice when punishment is like the sin.

Commenting on poetic justice texts, Barton, following Scharbert,
holds that they show that God's "punishment is understood in terms
of 'a sense of justice which demands an appropriate "reward" for a
good or evil deed'".[118] Justice is done when the punishment is appropriate to the crime. In these texts, this notion of "appropriateness" is expressed by means of "correspondences" between sin and
punishment which can take different forms. That is to say, when a
punishment corresponds to a sin, it is appropriate. And since the
punishment is appropriate, justice is done. Thus, these correspondences between sin and punishment point to "a concept of *retributive
justice*".[119]

5. *Poetic Justice and Dynamistic Thought*

In connection with this type of sin-punishment relationship, it is
sometimes said that it expresses what some would call "dynamistic
thought". For example, Koch considers Hos 4:4–6 as exhibiting "the
view that actions have built-in consequences".[120] That is to say, "[t]he
one who does something will passively experience the consequences
of what was actively set in motion".[121] In discussing dynamistic thought

---

[118] Barton 1979:12.
[119] Miller 1982:134 (his italics).
[120] Koch 1983:66–67.
[121] Koch 1983:66.

in the prophets, Tucker suggests that when the prophets see the punishment as corresponding to the sin and express that in rhetorical patterns they are assuming that "there is justice built in the very structure of reality".[122] He cites, for example, Is 1:19–20; Hos 8:7; and Hos 10:12–13. Some comments on these claims are in order.

First, Miller points out that some texts utilised by Koch (and therefore Tucker) to support his idea are actually more concerned with the *correspondences* between an action and its consequence than simply the *consequence* of the action.[123] Take Hos 4:4–6 as an example. There the punishments are generally described and their correspondences to the offences clearly show a talionic emphasis. The text indeed speaks of consequences, but the stress is on correspondences. The point is to show that there is justice in the punishments.

Second, even if an offence does work itself out to its inevitable consequences, this does not mean that the consequences have to be like it.[124] In other words, the fact that there are correspondences between the offence and its consequence does not support the idea that this consequence is actually an inevitable outgrowth of the offence. Further argument is needed to show that this is in fact the case. On the other hand, Miller notes that the correspondence pattern "serves to sharpen or heighten the relation between sin and punishment when the *Tun-Ergehen Zusammenhang* is not clearly evident and even when it is".[125] This observation is pertinent to the question of how we know that this event is the consequence of that action done previously. How can we be sure that that the man falling into the pit he dug is the consequence of his digging the pit (e.g. Prov 26:27)? The answer is "we do not know". Saying that his falling into the pit is a consequence of his digging is actually forged by the correspondence pattern. Far from concluding from the correspondence pattern that the text implies dynamistic thought, the correspondence pattern highlights the *certainty* that sin will be punished.[126]

Third, Koch in his mechanistic understanding[127] of sin and consequence uses words like "inevitable" or "pre-determined" to describe

---

[122] Tucker 1997:385.
[123] Miller 1982:122.
[124] Miller 1982:122.
[125] Miller 1982:137.
[126] Cf. Janowski 1994:261.
[127] Koch later revokes this idea (1962:398).

the consequence.[128] Congenial to this is especially the use of nature
metaphors (e.g. Hos 8:7).[129] This use of nature metaphors and the
idea of inevitability have the important implication that one should
be able to determine the consequence on the basis of the sin. When
one sows an orange seed, one expects to get an orange tree and
nothing else. When a person walks on hot coals it is expected that
his feet will be scorched (Prov 6:28). But this feature cannot be found
in those sin-punishment relations where correspondences play an
important role.

Our discussion above shows that there are different ways to forge
the correspondence between different sins and their punishments.
We can even conceive different punishments corresponding to the
same offence. For example, in the case of Ez 13:10–16 the punishment for the false prophets could be that they become dumb so that
they will not be able to speak any more false message. The correspondence between the sin and its punishment in this hypothetical
case is clear. Or in Ez 13:17–23 it is not necessary that the bands
and veils used by the prophetesses be torn away from their arms.
God can equally inflict upon the prophetesses the punishment that
their arms will be chopped off. This punishment corresponds to the
crime in that the means of their crime is destroyed. Or in Ez 34:7–10
the punishment could be that although the shepherds feed on the
flock they will never be sated (cf. Hos 4:10aα). This punishment corresponds to the crime in that it renders futile the intention of the
crime. There is, therefore, some arbitrariness in the type of correspondences forged between a sin and its punishment. However, in
spite of these actual or possible variations in the correspondence pattern between sin and punishment, these correspondences all serve to
convey the point that the punishment is appropriate to the crime.
This particular punishment is appropriate to and fits this particular
crime. The punishment is justified and just because it fits the crime.[130]
This idea exhibits the moral character of Yahweh who is just in
dealing with people, giving them what befits their conduct.

If, corresponding to an offence, different possible punishments can
be conceived, each corresponding to different aspects of the sin, then

---

[128] E.g. Koch 1983:48, 74.
[129] Koch 1983:61. According to Barton (1979:10), Koch's thesis is also derived
from texts dealing with poetic justice.
[130] For a discussion of the idea of justice as fittingness, see Cupit (1996).

the particular punishment announced for a sin *cannot* be *the* inevitable outcome of the sin. It is but one of the many possible punishments chosen in that particular context for that particular sin. Thus, the fact that there are various correspondence patterns between sin and punishment cannot be used to support the dynamistic viewpoint. Rather, it proves exactly the opposite. That is, the punishment which corresponds to the sin is *not* the inevitable outgrowth of the sin. Rather, that one particular punishment is announced instead of another implies that there is some arbitrariness, or more positively, a choice. Despite the arbitrariness, the point is that the punishment, being appropriate to the sin, is just. Thus, while Barton is certainly right to claim that passages displaying poetic justice concern "not the mechanics of retribution, but the moral character of the God" who is "consistent and rational in his dealings with men" and "makes the punishment fit the crime",[131] one can go further and claim that these passages actually refute the idea of mechanistic retribution.

Fourth, it is interesting to note that the discussion of Tucker and Koch makes no reference whatsoever to Ezekiel. This is perhaps not accidental. In Ezekiel the divine "I" comes to the fore.[132] In the above eleven cases in which poetic justice can be detected, in almost all the cases (the possible exception is 12:17–20) Yahweh himself announces and inflicts the punishment. In these cases there is no hint whatsoever suggesting dynamistic thought. It is Yahweh who discloses the sort of correspondence a punishment has with the sin and it is he himself who will carry out the punishment. Only in three cases (7:20–21; 11:1–13; 16:1–43) do we find any human agent involved in the execution of the punishment. The theocentric view characteristic of Ezekiel[133] renders dynamistic thought less likely. Furthermore, in the opinion of Koch and Tucker, the passive formulation of a punishment, as for example in Is 1:20, implies there is no divine involvement and therefore hints at dynamistic thought.[134] We have already commented on this.[135] In the case of Ezekiel the only passive formulation is found in 12:25a and 28b where it is said

---

[131] Barton 1979:12.
[132] Cf. Reventlow (1960:324–325), who speaks of the prominence of the divine "I" in Ezekiel.
[133] For an exposition of this theme, see Joyce (1989:89–105).
[134] Tucker 1997:383.
[135] See Chapter One Section 4.

that Yahweh's word "will be done" (וְיָעֶשָׂה). Even then, in 12:25b it
is said immediately and explicitly that Yahweh himself will do it
(וְעָשִׂיתִיו). It is made clear that Yahweh himself fulfils his word, not
that the divine word realises itself. The prominence of this divine
persona in Ezekiel may account for the non-inclusion of Ezekiel in
Koch's or Tucker's study.

6. *Expressions Suggesting Correspondences between Sin and Punishment*

In this section we will examine three expressions relating punishment to sin. The first expression, "I will put your way(s) on your
head", may suggest that the punishment afflicted on the offender is
nothing but the offence itself. It resembles "I will visit/punish (פקד)
upon him his ways" as found in Hos 4:9b, which Koch argues is
indicative of dynamistic thought where Yahweh's action is limited to
"setting in motion the consequences of a human action".[136] Miller,
however, argues that one should not fail to consider Hos 4:9a which
underscores a comparison correspondence.[137] We will examine the
meaning and function of this expression. The second expression under
consideration is "I will judge (שׁפט) you according to your way(s)".
The language of judgement clearly points to intervention by an external agent in the correlation between sin and punishment. The third
expression is "I will do as you have done". The importance of these
latter two phrases is that they point to a certain correlation between
the punishment and the offence. This supplements our discussion of
correspondences between sin and punishment above.

6.1. *"I will put your way(s) on your head"*

In Ezekiel there is a phrase which seems to imply that the punishment is nothing but the offence. We shall call this the requital formula for the sake of convenience.[138] Its various forms are given below:

Type A		
	דרכם בראשם נתתי	9:10
	דרכם בראשם נתתי	11:21
	דרכך בראש נתתי	16:43
	דרכם בראשם נתתי	22:31

---

[136] Koch 1983:67. See also Wolff (1974:83) and Jeremias (1983:67).
[137] Miller 1982:122.
[138] This terminology is borrowed from Hals (1989:68).

Type B	דרכיך עליך אתן	7:4
Type C	אלתי... וברית׳... ונתתיו בראשו	17:19
Type D	ונתתי עליך את כל־תועבתיך	7:3
	ונתתי עליך את כל־תועבתיך	7:8
	ונתנו זמחכנה עליכן	23:49
Type E	כדרכיך עליך אתן	7:9

In Type A, the phrase is formed by the verb נתן with the direct
object דרך and indirect object ראש prefixed by the preposition ב.
Outside Ezekiel it occurs only in 1 Kg 8:32 (//2 Chr 6:23) (לתת דרכו
בראשו). In all these cases, the subject of נתן is always Yahweh. Type
B, found only in Ezekiel, replaces בראש in Type A with the preposition על with a personal suffix.[139] Type C, also found only in Ezekiel,
replaces דרך in Type A with other substantives. Type D is a mixture of Type B and Type C, found also outside Ezekiel.[140] The last
one, Type E, is close to Type B.[141] In Type E, the subject of נתן is
Yahweh, and its object is not stated explicitly but qualified by a
prepositional phrase composed of כ prefixed to a noun (phrase). In
contrast to Ezekiel, the use of the שוב (hiphil) in Type C is more
common elsewhere.[142] Another variation of this is the use of על or
אל instead of ב.[143] One may add further the formula "his blood is
on him/his head" which according to some scholars has a similar
meaning.[144] In Ezekiel, this "blood restriction formula"[145] appears in
18:13 and 33:4, 5.[146]

A quick overview of these types of formula shows that it is composed of three elements. The first element is the verb נתן that almost
always has Yahweh as the subject. The second element is either the
direct object of נתן or an expression introduced by כ which qualifies
the verb. The third element is the indirect object of נתן which is
prefixed by ב or על or ל.

---

[139] Cf. Hos 4:9.

[140] E.g. Jer 26:15; Jon 1:14.

[141] A similar form is found in 1 Kg 8:39 (= 2 Chr 6:30); Jer 17:10; 32:19:
ונתת לאיש ככל־דרכיו. Cf. Ps 20:5; 28:4. With שלם, see Jb 34:11; Ps 62:13; Jer 25:14;
Lam 3:64; with השיב, see Prov 24:12, 19; with פקד, see Hos 12:3.

[142] Nu 5:7; Jdg 9:57; 1 Sam 25:39; 1 Kg 2:44; Ps 7:17; Jl 4:4, 7; Ob 15. Cf.
1 Kg 2:33 (qal of שוב).

[143] For על, see 1 Kg 2:32; cf. Est 9:25 (qal of שוב). For אל, see Neh 3:36.

[144] Babut 1986:476. See below for a refutation of this claim.

[145] This terminology is borrowed from Hals (1989:119).

[146] For a list of this formula outside Ezekiel, see Babut (1986:474).

Some observations on these types of formula can be made. The first observation concerns the context of the formula. Regarding Type A, the formula serves as a conclusion to either an indictment (9:10; 11:21) or an announcement of judgement (16:43; 22:31). As such it forms the conclusion of the judgement process. The formulae in the other types are also found in oracles of judgement. Moreover, these formulae all appear in the immediate context of judgement wherein the verb שפט ("to judge") is found. Thus, these formulae form a part of the judgement proceeding.

The second observation pertains to the first element. In Type A, the translations of the four cases are not consistent regarding the tense used. For instance, the NRSV renders 9:10 and 11:21 in the future tense ("I will bring . . .") but 16:43 and 22:31 in the present perfect ("I have returned . . .").[147] It is not clear if the different contexts warrant such different renderings. In these cases, it is perhaps best to take נתתי as a performative perfect,[148] an action performed at the moment of speaking or in the immediate future.[149] In the other types, the wᵉqatal or the yiqtol forms are often rendered as future, referring to an action in the immediate future.

The third observation pertains to the second element of the formula. Regarding Types A and B, the second element is the noun דרך ("way") which has a personal suffix. In 9:9 the Israelites ("the house of Israel and Judah") are accused of bloodshed and perversity. In response to this, God declares that there will be no mercy (9:10a), followed by the requital formula (9:10b). The accusation does not specify any offence but provides only a general description of the misconduct. In 11:21 the accusation points to idolatry,[150] but its contrast with "following the statutes and keeping the ordinances of God" (v.20) suggests a more general negative description of the people concerned. This is different from Ez 16 where the crime of the woman is specified as adultery and bloodshed (v.38). These crimes, especially adultery, are not isolated incidents but offences which characterise the conduct of the woman.[151] Lastly, in the accusation of

---

[147] Without listing all the differences, we note that the present, present perfect/past or the future tenses have been used in rendering each of these four cases.

[148] Allen 1994:123, 129, 231.

[149] J.-M. §112fg; cf. W.-O'C. §30.5.1d and n.17.

[150] Allen 1994:166.

[151] Note the use of the participle זונה (v.30) to characterise the woman after the verb זנה is used to describe her activity (vv.15, 16, 17, 26, 28).

the four classes of people in 22:25–29, their conduct, which is often contradictory to how they are supposed to act, is also depicted in a rather generalised way. For example, the job of the priests is to differentiate clean from unclean, but they are not doing so (v.26). The prophets are supposed to speak what Yahweh commands them to speak, but instead they see false visions and tell lies (v.27). In other words, their offence lies in acting contrary to what their office requires. After the indictment or judgement, God pronounces the requital formula. The point of this consideration is that the word דרך used in the requital formula does not refer to any specific action of the people, but to their general conduct or way of life. For this use of דרך in Ezekiel, one may consider 7:4, 9 where it again denotes the general conduct of the people.

In the most detailed study of the word דרך published so far, Zehnder distinguishes four semantic groups (with further subdivisions) of the word: concrete spatial usage; movement related; (morally assessed) life style; and journey through life.[152] Without going into detail, he classifies the above cases as belonging to the group "Conduct/Way of Life" ("Lebenswandel")[153] which our observation above confirms. Of special relevance to us is his comparison between sentences involving this use of דרך and those without.[154] Consider for example the following two sentences:

(a) "I do not like your actions/deeds" and
(b) "I do not like your ways".

Some differences between them can be noted:

(1) In (a) the actions as far as they are expressed by a verb are temporally defined, but the temporal element is dropped in (b).
(2) While in (a) the action is a self-contained unit having a beginning and an end, in (b) the actions are not considered as individual units but a collective whole ("kollectiver Plural").
(3) While an individual action is connected with a pinnacle of action, the way as a totality of actions understood as a unity is more concerned with a certainty of direction ("Richtungsbestimmtheit").

---

[152] Zehnder 1999:296. Cf. Aitken 1998:28–29.
[153] Zehnder 1999:326.
[154] The following is based on Zehnder (1999:476–478).

(4) In using "way/s" the inchoative aspect of an action is dropped
    whereas the final aspect passes on from the individual action to
    the totality of action now understood as a unity.

In this understanding, the use of "way" represents an abstraction
and generalisation from individual actions. The word characterises
the conduct of the person concerned. It says more about the character than any individual action of the person. The temporal start-
ing and ending points of each individual action are not important.
What is significant is the direction the "way" is going. How this
direction is evaluated can only be determined from the context. One
implication of this consideration is that the requital formula and similar sayings cannot be used by Koch to support his idea of a dynamistic
worldview. In his argument he underscores *an action* as such: in performing an act, the act remains as a physical spatial substance in
the world which he calls "schicksalwirkende Tatsphäre".[155] By using
the word דרך as a metaphor for the conduct or character of a person, the requital formula and similar sayings (e.g. Prov 28:10)[156] say
nothing about any particular action and its consequence as such.
The concern is more with character than actions.[157]

Regarding Type C, the second element is אלה וברית which is
clearly not general but refers to a specific action of Zedekiah, namely,
the oath he takes in making the covenant with Nebuchadnezzar.
Regarding Type D, in 7:3 and 7:8 the second element כל־תועבת
does not, again, refer to any specific action but is used as a term
to characterise negatively the behaviour of Israel. Its use as a parallel to דרכים in its context confirms this. In 23:49 זמה refers to the
adultery and bloodshed of the woman. From the context, we know
that the rather specific reference of the second element in 17:19 and
23:49 leads to a rather specific reference to the punishment concerned. This has been dealt with in previous chapters.

The fourth observation is related to the third element, בראש (Types
A and C) or עליך (Types B, D and E). Except in 16:43, בראש always
has a personal suffix. Whether 16:43 should be emended is of no
special importance since the context clearly shows that it refers to
the head of the woman (Jerusalem). The word ראש is often used

---

[155] Koch 1962:398. Cf. Koch 1983:65.
[156] Used by Koch (1983:59).
[157] Cf. Boström 1990:138.

pars pro toto for the ethically responsible person,[158] and the preposition ב indicates localisation.[159] Thus, the reference of בראש is "on the head", that is, "on the person". As for its meaning, Rabinowitz, comparing with Egyptian and Aramaic sources, argues that it means "*on the responsibility* or *liability of* ".[160] Some take up this idea and render the formula as "I held them responsible for their behaviour".[161] Regarding Types B, D and E, Maon holds that the simplest Hebrew expression for the idea of responsibility is the use of the preposition על followed by the person concerned or a member of the body (e.g. ראש) or possessions.[162] Babut, however, argues that the idea of responsibility is foreign to the formula. His argument is based on an analysis of the various types of the formula (given above) in 2 Sam 16:8; 1 Kg 2:32, 33, 37, 44. By comparing 1 Kg 2:37 and 44, he holds that the formulae "your blood will be on your head" and "Yahweh will bring back your wickedness on your head" have the same meaning. By considering 1 Kg 2:33, he concludes that the formula should not involve the idea of responsibility since Joab's descendants are not responsible for Joab's killing.[163] Hence, he holds that the formula should mean "(faire) subir (à quelqu'un) les conséquences d'un crime".[164] It is not clear, however, that the two formulae in 1 Kg 2:37 and 44 have the same meaning.[165] Moreover, the idea of corporate responsibility, which seems to be denied by Babut, should not be dismissed from a proper interpretation of 1 Kg 2:33.[166]

Bovati's study on the legal process in the Hebrew Bible sheds more light on the requital formula. According to him, formulae of

---

[158] Beuken and Dahman 1993:275.

[159] Jenni 1992:193.

[160] Rabinowitz 1957:399 (his italics). See also Rabinowitz (1959:210).

[161] E.g. Allen 1990:31 (regarding Ez 22:31); cf. Breuer 1993:41.

[162] Maon 1985:357. He finds similar expressions in Ugaritic, Aramaic and Phoenician.

[163] Babut 1986:479.

[164] Babut (1986:479), followed by Mulder (1990:113).

[165] The "blood restriction formula" is first of all found in Leviticus (20:9, 11–13, 16, 27). It clearly belongs to the legal sphere, and more specifically, is employed in the sentence (Bovati 1994:359). As such, it establishes that the accused is guilty (Bovati 1994:359; Budd 1996:292; Gerlemann 1997:338). A consequence of this is that it also exonerates the bloodguilt of the executioner (Zimmerli 1979:384; Hartley 1992:339; Allen 1994:276; Gerlemann 1997:338). Regarding its use in Ez 18:13, Matties (1990:78) goes as far as to say that it "absolve[s] Yahweh of responsibility for the consequences of the sinner's actions". If that is the case, then the meaning of the formula proposed by Babut is too limited.

[166] For a recent discussion, see Kaminsky (1995:104 and n.32).

the above types belong to the last stage of juridical procedures in ancient Israel, namely, the execution of the verdict.[167] This is to be distinguished from the sentencing.[168] Regarding this, he makes a distinction between two cases, one emphasising the aspect of punishment and the other retribution.[169] The specificity of the second case is that the

> "retributive" nature of punishment brings out the link between crime (or innocence) and punishment (or acquittal/favourable decree) in such a way that the justice of the judgment appears obvious: anyone who has done evil (in the sense of having transgressed the law and committed a crime) is made to undergo . . . proportionate suffering; those who have not done evil have their right satisfied, are repaid for any injury received, and have the exercise of their liberty guaranteed.[170]

According to him, the formulae under consideration belong to the second case, i.e., they are more concerned with retribution. He also notes that the formula is composed of three elements and his discussion is more general. The first element is a verb, especially נתן, שוב (hiphil) and שלם (piel), which expresses the idea of "giving" or "handing over". The second element is a complement which is the direct object of the verb. It admits of two basic forms: (1) the object of the verb means "behaviour" or "conduct" (cf. Ez 9:10); or a variant of this in which the complement consists of the preposition כ prefixed to a noun phrase (cf. Ez 7:9); (2) the object of the verb means "recompense" so that the phrase formed by the verb plus the object expressed "what is already contained in the verb itself, but leaving unspecified the reason for the retribution" (e.g. Ps 28:4b).

---

[167] Bovati 1994:373–380. Although he has not dealt specifically with Ezekiel, some considerations from Ezekiel confirm his opinion. For instance, in Ez 7:3 and 8 the "judgement" in the sense of passing on a sentence (against Greenberg [1983a:147] and Brownlee [1986:104] who render שפט as "to punish") is followed by the formula which speaks of punitive consequences. This is also true for Ez 16:49 (with judgement found in 16:38) and 23:49 (with judgement found in 23:45). It is interesting to note that only in case of Ez 23:43–49 are all the judges and the executioners of the sentence human.

[168] Bovati 1994:371–372. He notes that the "blood restriction formula" is better relegated to the stage of sentencing (1994:359). In this sense the formula underlines the guilt and the responsibility of the person concerned (cf. Boecker 1964:138–139; Matties 1990:78). This shows that one should not (as Babut does) confuse the blood restriction formula with the requital formula which emphasises the punishment or retribution inflicted.

[169] Bovati 1994:374.

[170] Bovati 1994:376–377.

The third element is a reference to the guilty/innocent accused. It is always a prepositional phrase usually with the preposition עַל, לְ or בְּ which either prefixes a noun representing the person (e.g. רֹאשׁ, חֵיק) or has a personal suffix.[171]

From the above, note first that the formula has a legal function, namely, to designate the execution of the sentence or the verdict. As such it can be rendered as "I am imposing (the penalty of) your conduct (etc.) on you".[172] Secondly, the second element, which often generally denotes behaviour or conduct, or specifically some offensive action, points out the reason for the punishment. Hence, thirdly, by incorporating this second element, the formula emphasises the idea of retribution more than punishment, or more specifically, the idea of proportionate suffering. This is connected with poetic justice which holds that a punishment is commensurate to the offence and hence is just and justified, although this formula lacks the specificity found in poetic justice. If this is the case, then both (a) the claim that this formula shows that acts "boomerang" back to the actor,[173] an idea going back to Koch, and (b) Koch's extrapolation from the formula that the role of God is that of a midwife who completes what is already in action, are in need of correction. Regarding the first claim, the point of the formula is to indicate that just punishment is imposed on the offender. Regarding the second point, the fact that human persons and not Yahweh are the subject of the formula in Ez 23:49 renders Koch's understanding problematic. Fourthly, the executioner of the punishment is usually God himself (except in 23:49). He is the one who imposes the punishment on the accused who has now been declared guilty with an announcement of punishment. This has to do with the reason that God alone brings just judgement.[174]

6.2. *"I will judge you according to your way(s)"*

The formula "I will judge you according to your way(s)" occurs *only* in Ezekiel:

---

[171] Bovati 1994:378–379.
[172] Cf. Greenberg 1983a:147; *HALOT* 734 (on Ez 7:3).
[173] E.g. Brownlee 1986:106, 165; Lind 1996:83. See also Zimmerli (1979:204), Allen (1994:107).
[174] Cf. Bovati 1994:379.

7:3 וּשְׁפַטְתִּיךְ כִּדְרָכָיִךְ

7:8 וּשְׁפַטְתִּיךְ כִּדְרָכָיִךְ

18:30 אִישׁ כִּדְרָכָיו אֶשְׁפֹּט אֶתְכֶם

24:14 כִּדְרָכַיִךְ וְכַעֲלִילוֹתַיִךְ שְׁפָטוּךְ

33:20 אִישׁ כִּדְרָכָיו אֶשְׁפֹּט אֶתְכֶם

36:19 כְּדַרְכָּם וְכַעֲלִילוֹתָם שְׁפַטְתִּים

The formula has three components: (1) the verb שׁפט with Yahweh
as subject;[175] (2) the object of the verb expressed either as a separate pronoun or as a suffix to the verb; and (3) a prepositional phrase
qualifying the verb.

The verb שׁפט admits of different meanings.[176] It can mean "to
govern" (e.g. Gen 19:9). More relevant to us is the meaning "to
judge". In a situation where right and wrong are not clearly distinguished the act of judging may be required to decide and separate
them (e.g. Dt 25:1). This can be seen, for instance, in the expression שׁפט בֵּין . . . וּבֵין (e.g. Gen 16:5; Ez 34:20; cf. Ez 34:17, 22). When
judging someone in the right, שׁפט has the nuance of "to defend, to
save, to vindicate".[177] But for the guilty, "the action by which a judge
decrees a punitive sanction is also expressed by the verb . . .".[178] Thus,
שׁפט means the handing down of a sentence of punishment.[179] This
seems to be the meaning of the verb in our cases above.[180] In these
cases, the emphasis is not on deciding whether someone has done
good or evil since the contexts clearly indicate that there is a guilty

---

[175] The only exception is the MT of 24:14. Some emend the text to שְׁפַטְתִּיךְ or
אֶשְׁפֹּט (e.g. Toy 1899:41; Schumpp 1942:126; Eichrodt 1970:335; Dijkstra 1989:14;
Einheitsübersetzung) on (1) textual grounds: with many manuscripts and the versions (e.g. Ehrlich 1912:96; Herrmann 1924:148; Bertholet 1936:86; Cooke 1936:269;
Fohrer 1955:139; Wevers 1969:142; Zimmerli 1979:496; Block 1997:769); (2) internal grounds such as its use elsewhere in Ezekiel (e.g. Fohrer 1955:139; Zimmerli
1979:496; Block 1997:769) or that it fits the context better (e.g. Cooke 1936:269;
Zimmerli 1979:496; Greenberg 1997:503). But others keep the MT (e.g. Kraetzschmar
1900:197; Ziegler 1948:76; van den Born 1954:156; Auvray 1957:95), holding that
(1) it is the harder reading (Allen 1990:55; Greenberg 1997:503); and (2) there is
an interchange between God and his earthly executioners (e.g. Aalders 1955:392;
Maarsingh 1988:151; Greenberg 1997:503). In favour of the emendation, we note
that, unlike other passages, the interchange of God and human is too abrupt here.
Moreover, the emendation fits the context well after a series of actions with Yahweh
as the subject.

[176] For a brief discussion, see Liedke (1971:62–73), Niehr (1995).

[177] Bovati 1994:202–205.

[178] Bovati 1994:205.

[179] Liedke 1971:72.

[180] Liedke 1971:72; Bovati 1994:206n.92.

party, but on the delivering of a sentence of punishment whose content is not always made explicit. In the above cases, the objects of שׁפט, the recipients of the sentence, are "the land of Israel" (7:3, 8), "the house of Israel" (18:30; 33:20; 36:19), and "Jerusalem" (24:14).

That the sentence delivered is not arbitrary is shown by the use of a qualifying prepositional phrase. It is the syntagm דרך + כ with a personal suffix, and in two cases with an additional וכעלילות[181] with the same personal suffix which agrees with the object of the verb. In these cases, the word דרך refers to the general conduct of the people[182] and some implications of this use have already been mentioned above. Regarding the use of the preposition כ, two observations can be made. First, according to Jenni, all the above six uses belong to the class "Vergeltung nach Anlaß". For Jenni, "Die Veranlassung zu vergeltendem Handeln wird durch כ in Verbindung mit einem sehr allgemeinen Ausdruck für Handeln ... angegeben, der sehr oft eine Wertung beinhaltet".[183] That is to say, the דרכ(ים) ("way/s") is the reason for the sentence. It is because of the conduct of the people that God delivers his sentence.[184] While this formula certainly assumes that one's conduct is related to one's recompense, it also clearly shows the role of Yahweh as a judge who delivers his sentence after deliberation. The recompense is not automatic as suggested by Koch. Apart from being a reason for the sentence, the relation between the sentence and the people's conduct is further qualified by the preposition כ. This leads to our second observation.

In the above cases, the preposition כ is usually rendered as "according to",[185] "entsprechend/gemäß/nach",[186] "overeenkomstig/naar gelang van".[187] In these cases the meaning of "according to" is not "as stated by someone" as in "according to A it means ...", but "in a manner or degree that is in proportion to (something)" as in "salary according to experience".[188] In this sense, the sentence delivered is

---

[181] The pair עלילה-דרך occurs only in Ezekiel (14:22, 23; 20:43, 44; 24:14; 36:17, 19), referring to the conduct of the Israelites. Cf. Ps 103:7.
[182] Zehnder 1999:326.
[183] Jenni 1994:100.
[184] Cf. Ez 14:22–23.
[185] E.g. Greenberg 1983a:142; Block 1997:247.
[186] E.g. Herrmann 1924:46; Pohlmann 1996:111, 258.
[187] E.g. Noordtzij 1957:85; Dijkstra 1986:75, 178.
[188] Burchfield 1998:15; cf. *NSOED* 1:15 ("in a manner consistent with or a degree proportioned to").

not random but is limited by what is attached to the preposition, in this case, דרכ(ים) ("way/s"). The sentence is decided in proportion to the ways of the people and is appropriate to their conduct. By saying that the announced punishment is made according to something, it suggests that there is a scale against which the punishment is measured and this scale is nothing other than the conduct of the people itself. This seems to be an apologetic statement countering any possible complaint of injustice. Beneath this idea of justice or fairness is the presupposition, which the prophet assumes to be accepted universally, that to take one's conduct as the measuring rod for one's recompense is just. At a time when the Israelites were questioning if the exile was a fair punishment, Ezekiel reacted by stressing that God's punishment was a just one. The fact that this formula is found only in the Book of Ezekiel testifies that the prophet took seriously the justice of God and hence the responsibility of the people.

Like the requital formula, this formula underlines the relationship between punishment and offence. Since this formula occurs in contexts which have no reference to any specific offensive action (with the possible exception of 24:14 where bloodshed is mentioned), it takes on the character of a principle which is even more general than the requital formula. The formula does not indicate exactly what sentence is delivered in this or that case but only that the punishment is dependent on the offence. Apart from saying that the conduct of a person is the reason for his/her recompense, it expresses the general principle that the conduct of a person is the measure against which the punishment is issued.[189] This idea reflects the general principle of "like for like" which underlies poetic justice. They all have the same implication that punishment corresponding to the offence of the people is just.

---

[189] This differs in emphasis from the phrase שפט במשפטים which is found only in Ezekiel within the OT (7:27; 23:24; 44:24). According to Jenni (1992:148–149), the preposition ב is *beth normae*, i.e., that which is prefixed by ב is a norm or measure for some action (cf. BDB 90). Thus, the phrase can be rendered as "to judge by/in accord with/on the basis of ordinances". See also the translations by Cooke (1936:85), Greenberg (1983a:145, 1997:472), Allen (1990:42; 1994:99) and Block (1997:269). In these cases, the emphasis is put on using the ordinances of a certain group (Israel in 7:27; some foreign nations in 23:24; Yahweh in 44:24) as the point of reference for the judging action. As such, this phrase is less concerned with the conduct of the people than perhaps the authority and impartiality of the judging action.

6.3. *"I will do as you have done"*

The phrase "I will do[190] as you have done" (ועשיתי [Q] אותך כאשר עשית)
in this form occurs only at 16:59 in Ezekiel.[191] Similar forms can be
found in 7:27 (כטמאתם וכפשעיהם עשיתי) and 39:24 (מדרכם אעשה אותם
אתם).[192] These phrases say that Yahweh's action corresponds to what
others have done.

We will not repeat here what has been said regarding Ez 16:59–63
in Chapter Two. Note that what Jerusalem has done is to "despise
the oath by breaking the covenant" (v.59b). God's reaction has already
been mentioned in some detail in vv.35–43a. Jenni holds that the
meaning of כאשר here refers to "Vergeltung, wie veranlaßt".[193] Unlike
Ez 16:59, כאשר having this meaning can also be used in cases where
the same two agents are not found in both actions (e.g. Ru 1:8), or
the same verb is not used (e.g. Jdg 1:7). In cases where exactly the
same action is performed in both the offence and the punishment,
the *agens* of the offence becomes the *patiens* of the punishment. For
example, in Lev 24:19–20 the one who maims another will suffer
the same injury. Or in Jer 50:29 Babylon which has besieged other
cities and killed many will be besieged and have its inhabitants killed.
In Ez 16:59 by using the same verb (i.e., עשה) for the actions of
Jerusalem and God, the text says that God does the same as Jerusalem did in breaking the covenant. This may seem surprising but
from vv.35–43a what God as the husband would do (e.g. the withdrawal of gifts and protection) amounts to the breaking of the marriage covenant. Although the precise ways in which the woman
(Jerusalem) and the husband (God) break the covenant are different,
there is no doubt that both actions can be characterised as breaking the covenant. Thus, it is rightly said that the idea of *lex talionis*
is behind this formula.[194]

---

[190] Some scholars find the future sense in the weqatal form difficult. Ehrlich
(1912:61) proposes to change [Q]ועשיתי to לא אעשה. Cornill (1886:272), followed
by Kraetzschmar (1900:155), Cooke (1936:181) and Wevers (1969:103), drops the
ו, rendering it as "when I have done to you . . .". See also Schumpp (1942:86),
Brownlee (1986:242). Allen (1994:232) renders it as a question. Most scholars keep
the MT and render it as a statement.

[191] See also Lev 24:19, 20; Jdg 1:7; Ob 15.

[192] Cf. 35:11 (referring to Mount Seir: ועשיתי כאפך וכקנאתך אשר עשיתה).

[193] Jenni 1994:97.

[194] Smend 1880:105; Maarsingh 1988:30. Cf. Breuer 1993:132: "measure for
measure"; Block 1997:515: "principle of reciprocity".

Regarding 7:27 there are basically two interpretations of מִן in מִדַּרְכָּם.[195] The first is to take it as causal in meaning, "on account of, because of".[196] This use can also be found in Ez 35:11 (מִשִּׂנְאָתְךָ). Thus, in 7:27 God declares that his future punishing action is caused by the conduct of the people. The second is its usual meaning "from (among)".[197] In this case, God states that his action is actually derived or borrowed from the people's previous actions. God will act as the people have acted. Thus, the conduct of the people is not only the cause of God's response, but also the model for God's action. To decide between these options, note that the immediate context speaks of God judging on the basis of the people's ordinances (וּבְמִשְׁפְּטֵיהֶם אֶשְׁפְּטֵם).[198] Thus, the point of the text is not simply to state the reason for God's action, but to indicate that there is a reference point for God's action. Hence, the second meaning is preferred. Although it is not clear which action of the people would be borrowed by God when he acts, the text shows that God's punishment corresponds to the offence of the people.

Lastly, note that we have already dealt with 39:24 in the last chapter. It suffices here to stress, in line with what we have mentioned above in this chapter, that the action of God corresponds to the uncleanness and transgressions of the people.

7. *Conclusion*

In this chapter we have examined the relationship between offence and its consequence from the perspective of poetic justice. Passages displaying poetic justice show that the consequence is made to look like the offence by incorporating some features of the offence. That is to say, the consequence is related to the offence by being like the offence. Thus, the principle governing the transition from offence to its consequence is that of "like for like". This principle is general

---

[195] Some scholars emend the Hebrew to כְּדַרְכָּם according to the LXX. E.g. Cornill 1886:221; Toy 1899:10; Herrmann 1924:48; Ziegler 1948:28; Pohlmann 1996:113. Others claim that the מִן should be retained. See further below. But even if the emendation is allowed, it would not alter our overall argument that God's punishing action is like the offence of the people.

[196] E.g. Cooke 1936:88; Zimmerli 1979:200; Allen 1994:103; Block 1997:269. Cf. Smend 1880:47.

[197] E.g. Hitzig 1847:56; Keil 1876a:111; Aalders 1955:151; Fisch 1950:40; Greenberg 1983a:157, referring to BDB (579).

[198] For this phrase, see Note 189 above.

and can be actualised in various forms. In the case of Ezekiel, this "likeness" is forged by various means including the repetition of the same verb of action in both the offence and consequence, the repetition of the same agents, the use of the means for committing the offence in executing the consequence, the portrayal that the consequence is as outrageous as the act, or the consequence rendering the act futile. In these cases, it is mostly Yahweh and sometimes a human agent who carries out the punishment for the offence. In some cases, synergism between Yahweh and human agents can be seen. This principle of "like for like" as found in these cases is not forensic in nature, nor is it based on the principle that impurity demands a resolution.

Although the principle is general, it is fundamental and pervasive in human civilisation. It is sometimes actualised in the *lex talionis* or "mirror punishments" which can be said to have talionic features. The principle and its various actualisations appeal to the deep-rooted idea of retributive justice. That is to say, when a punishment inflicted on an offender is like the offence, there is retributive justice. Thus, by forging correspondences between punishment and offence, Ezekiel not only creates a link between these two, but also appeals to the fundamental idea that justice is done when punishment is like the offence. This provides a strong apologetic instrument to combat the complaint that Yahweh's punishment is not just.

The fact that the principle can be actualised in different ways provides a basis to refute a dynamistic understanding of retribution based on texts displaying poetic justice. That is to say, since an offence could have a variety of different consequences that all still bear similarities to the offence, it is not necessary that this particular deed must inevitably have that particular consequence. Thus, when viewing an offence, there is no way to know exactly what its corresponding punishment will be. Koch's argument of a mechanical connection or a nature-like relationship between sin and its recompense on the basis of poetic justice texts is untenable. These texts demonstrate, on the contrary, the indefensibility of dynamistic thought.

The idea that the punishment is like the offence is also found in various expressions. Three such expressions have been examined here. These expressions show in different ways not only that punishment is caused by the offence or conduct of the people, but more importantly that punishment is like the crime. What God will do corresponds to the offence of the people.

CHAPTER SEVEN

SUMMARY AND CONCLUSIONS

In this study we have examined the concept of retribution in Ezekiel by determining the underlying principles governing the transition from evil deed to its consequence. In Chapter One a review of past literature on the idea of retribution sets the stage for the study. Koch's article on retribution is taken as the point of departure. He claims that the OT depicts a mechanistic understanding of the connection between act and consequence and therefore retribution understood as a divine intervention according to predetermined norms is simply non-existent. This claim is challenged by many scholars whose studies either revise or refute Koch's argument. His claim suffers most under the considerations that linguistic structure does not necessarily reflect thought structure or reality, or that there are different stylistic uses of language, or that language does not simply have a descriptive function. Language does not necessarily re-present the mechanism of act and consequence. It can be poetic or rhetorical with an aim to convince the audience of the moral vision held by the speaker, or to highlight and even create the connection between act and consequence so as to put the justice of God into greater relief. What remains to be seen is whether retribution can be understood in simply juridical terms, and how retribution can be just (or punishment well-deserved). Taking cues from some studies on retribution, we attempted to show that the idea of retribution in its negative aspect with reference to Israel/Judah as depicted in Ezekiel is basically governed by three principles.

The first principle examined in Chapters Two and Three is that the act-consequence connection is governed by a juridical understanding, and in particular by the covenant. The basic idea of this principle is that the act-consequence connection is juridical in nature. The consequence of one's act is determined by an external agent according to agreed norms. Thus, while this principle certainly takes into consideration legal sanctions, it also includes the terms of a covenant as such. In Chapter Two we examined the word ברית ("covenant") in three passages in Ezekiel (Ez 16, 17, 20). In Ez 16 the word בְּרִית refers to a marriage covenant in the metaphor. Inherent in a marriage covenant are mutual obligations between the husband and the wife. While the man is obliged to provide food, clothes, oil and protection, the woman is expected to reciprocate by not abusing the property of her husband and by being loyal to him. However, the wife not only misused what the husband had given her to make images, she also sacrificed their children and committed harlotry with all passers-by. In response, the husband judged her as an adulteress and shedder of blood. The punishments that she would receive are those inflicted on an adulteress or a murderer. According to the marriage covenant, the husband divorced her by taking back what he had given her. And according to the sanctions for adultery (and murder), her brothels are destroyed and she is stoned and mutilated.

In Ez 17 the word בְּרִית primarily denotes a vassal treaty, namely, the one between Zedekiah and Nebuchadnezzar. This treaty was accompanied by an oath of Zedekiah to Yahweh, appealing to Yahweh as the witness and guarantor of the treaty. In a vassal treaty, the vassal is supposed to give up independence in external politics and pay a tribute. But Zedekiah violated the treaty by trying to secure military assistance from Egypt. Yahweh, being the guarantor of the vassal treaty, serves as a judge who delivers a verdict on Zedekiah in his absence. Moreover, what is to happen to Zedekiah as described in Ez 12 parallels the curses found in some ANE treaties which are imposed upon a person who breaches those treaties. Thus, Zedekiah who violated the treaty was punished according to its terms. The juridical tone rings loudly in this case. But Zedekiah violated more than just the vassal treaty. In revoking his treaty with Nebuchadnezzar, he was also despising the oath he took, thus breaking a covenant with Yahweh as well. This treason against Yahweh is repaid by punishment couched in the stereotypical language of "spreading of net and snare" which in Ezekiel refers to the divine punishment of rulers.

In Ez 20 the "rule of the covenant" (מִסְרַת בְּרִית) serves the same function as the statutes and ordinances in a covenant. Obedience to it is a criterion for whether a person keeps the covenant and hence for determining the fate of that person.

In Chapter Three we considered the theme of curses and blessings of a covenant and its use in Ezekiel. By comparing similar details between Ezekiel and Lev 26, we argued that Ezekiel used the covenantal framework of Lev 26 and the theme of curses and blessings

associated with it. The covenantal curses of Lev 26 were utilised
sometimes sporadically and sometimes quite extensively in Ezekiel in
terms of both the order and content of the curses. This use is most
prominent in Ez 4–6 and 14:12–23. In some cases, the curses are
seen as realised not only during the exile as in Lev 26, but already
during the siege of Jerusalem. In some other cases, Ezekiel intensified
the extent of the curses by adding the qualifier כל ("all, every"). In
these cases Ezekiel interpreted what happened to Judah/Jerusalem
as the actualisation of the curses, thus trying to convict the people
of their violation of the covenant. In other cases, the execution of
the curses simply serves as basic assumptions on which Ezekiel built
his argument to convince the people that they were responsible for
their plight. That Ezekiel used the covenantal framework of Lev 26
is further buttressed by his use of the blessings of Lev 26 in Ez 34
and 37 in connection with the covenant of peace. Differing from
Lev 26 where the blessings are conditional upon the obedience of
the people, the blessings in Ez 34 and 37 are delivered by God without regard to the behaviour of the people. In one case, it is even
said that God himself will guarantee the people's future obedience
of his statutes and ordinances, thus fulfilling the condition for his
blessings.

The second principle examined in Chapters Four and Five is that
impurity requires its resolution. Basic to this principle is the idea
that impurity should be confined or disposed. One way to do this
is to remove the source of impurity. Thus, the connection between
act and consequence is likened to the connection between the pro-
duction of impurity (i.e., the act) and the removal of (the source of)
impurity (i.e., the consequence). Being a priest, Ezekiel's use of the
priestly categories of purity/impurity to interpret the act-consequence
connection is not surprising. In Chapter Four we looked into the
idea of impurity in the OT in general and Ezekiel in particular. We
identified three types of impurities: permanent, ritual and moral.
While ritual impurity is the basic concern of Leviticus, Ezekiel was
preoccupied with moral impurity. The most fundamental cause of
moral impurity is idolatry which involves both the worship of idols
and the worship of Yahweh with unprescribed rituals. The defiling
power of idolatry is immense, capable of polluting the sanctuary, the
land and the idolaters themselves. It can also lead to the profanation of the Sabbath and Yahweh's holy name. The pollution of the
temple and the land, two fundamental elements in Yahwism, is therefore of great concern to Ezekiel.

In Chapter Five we investigated the relationship between impurity and retribution. Purity is the prime concern of the temple vision in Ez 8–11. There the main offence of the people is idolatry, resulting in the pollution of the temple. We argued that the slaughter in Ez 9 and the burning of the city Jerusalem in Ez 10 are responses to the pollution of the temple/city. The slaughter in Ez 9 can be seen as a כרת penalty, which in Ezekiel is applied most clearly to people who commit idolatry (14:8). It consists chiefly of the divine execution which results in premature death and termination of a person's line. The main purpose of the penalty is to control the spread of impurity especially when the social control of it is weak. It is a means to remove permanently the source of the most defiling impurity. Regarding the burning of Jerusalem in Ez 10, we noted first that fire is not just an agent of punishment, it is also an agent of purification. It is a means of purification used in metallurgical description and also in cleansing metal vessels from corpse-contamination. The metaphor of Jerusalem as a crucible to which fire is applied for purification purposes can be found in Ez 22 and 24. We demonstrated that the same idea also appears in Ez 10. Burning is a means to purify the city. Thus, the connection between the act of producing moral impurity and the consequence of being removed by the trk penalty and subjected to fire is governed by the principle that impurity demands its resolution.

For Ezekiel, the exile, the forced removal of the inhabitants from their land to other nations, is a reaction to the defilement of the land. The exile serves as a means to dispose from the land the source of defilement so that the land will not be polluted any more. The people who defiled the land were not able to possess the land. This concern for the purity of the land is also a theme in the reconstructed past history of Israel (Ez 20). There the first self-defiling generation was denied access to the land and the second generation would even be dispersed among the nations. In the future, the people will be cleansed as they re-enter the land. They must also remove from the land the idols with which they had defiled themselves. The emphasis is not simply on the purity of the people, but also on the purity of the land and this forms the focus of the history of Israel— from the reconstructed past to the present exile, and from the present exile to the future (re-)entering to the land.

The third principle governing the transition from act to consequence, examined in Chapter Six, is that the consequence is like the act by incorporating some features of the act. This is the principle

of "like for like". This "likeness" is forged by the repetition of the
same verb of action in both the act and the consequence, the repetition of the same agent(s), the use of the means for committing the
deed in executing the consequence, the portrayal of the consequence
as outrageous as the deed, or rendering the deed futile by the consequence. Texts having these features are said to display poetic justice. This principle is general and can be actualised in many different
ways such as the *lex talionis* in the legal domain. In this understanding,
the consequence is constructed in such a way so as to be appropriate to the act. Texts displaying poetic justice appeal to our sense of
retributive justice. Since there are different ways in which a consequence is made to look like the act, texts displaying poetic justice
speak against a mechanistic understanding of the act-consequence
connection. Some expressions such as "I will put your way(s) on your
head" are also illustrations of this principle of "like for like".

These three principles governing retribution are distinct from each
other. The principle that the act-consequence connection is governed
by a covenant is juridical in tone because it requires an external
agent to serve as the judge who deliberates on what should happen
to the actor according to some agreed norms. These norms can be
the terms of the covenant (in the sense of a marriage covenant, a
vassal treaty, or a covenant between Yahweh and Israel), or they
can be the curses or blessings which are part and parcel of a covenant.
The person who violates a covenant is subjected to the terms laid
down in the covenant. This legal understanding of retribution displays a distrust in the idea that the world is mechanistic in retribution, that the world in itself is self-regulating with respect to retribution,
and asks instead for the intervention of an external agent. In contrast to the first one, the principle that impurity demands a resolution does not carry a forensic flavour. It conjures up a picture totally
different from that of the first principle. Categories beyond legal
thinking are required to be able to conceive that an action can actually defile the people, the temple and the land. The resolution of
the impurity by means of the כרת penalty, or fire, or exile has a
logic of its own, but the idea that impurity should be dealt with is
not unique to Israel. The concept of impurity and purification also
existed in the ANE context. Being a priest, the categories of purity/
impurity and purification/defilement are congenial to Ezekiel and
are used by him to interpret the events happening around him, especially those connected with the temple and the land. Lastly, the prin-

ciple of "like for like", that the consequence of an action bears some similarities to the act, is the most general among the three principles examined. It is applicable to a variety of cases, including those not covered by both the first and second principles. Since it is so adaptable to different cases, it is at the same time vague and general. There is no way to tell which aspect of an act will be reflected in its consequence to make the latter appropriate to the former. How this "like for like" is conceived and actualised depends not only on cultural backgrounds but also on individual cases.[1]

That the act-consequence connection is governed by some principles serves as a response to the question of theodicy. Confronted with the people's claim that Yahweh is not just in dispensing what happened to them, Ezekiel in his oracles seeks to convict and convince. He attempts to convict the people of their guilt by reminding them that it is because of what they have done that these things are happening to them. There is a connection between their actions and the consequences they are now bearing and this is a connection of which they should all be aware. Their claim to be descendants of Abraham who possessed the land promised to him by God implies that they know they are in a covenantal relationship with Yahweh their God and also that their keeping or violating the covenant would result in the delivery of blessings or curses respectively. Again, they must have knowledge of the requirement to be clean and the rituals for purification. They are equally aware of the demand to be morally pure lest they defile themselves, the temple and the land. Lastly, the idea that "like for like", realised in concrete terms in a variety of ways, is deep, fundamental and pervasive in human civilisation. The point is that the people should acknowledge their responsibility in causing this present plight. Commenting on Isaiah's oracles of doom, Barton says that "das kommende Unheil . . . nicht als ganz und gar unverständliche Willkür Gottes, sondern als notwendige Folge der nationalen Sünden begreifbar wird".[2] This comment applies equally to Ezekiel. He, however, does more than convict. He also tries to convince the people that God is just in his actions. If God acts according to the terms of the covenant, and if he removes impurity as they are expected to with their ritual impurity, and if he

---

[1] Cf. Henberg 1990:62.
[2] Barton 1987:434.

repays like for the like, then God is just in how he acts. What he has inflicted upon the people cannot simply be an *emotive* reaction to the acts of the people, it is also a *calculated* reaction which ensures that the people bear a consequence appropriate to what they have done. The justice of Yahweh is the message of Ezekiel.[3] Although this message does not assuage the physical pain of the people, it can at least soothe the dejected mind of those who claim that "the way of the Lord is not according to the standard"[4] (18:25, 29).

The present consideration of these three principles demonstrates the inadequacy of both Koch and Horst because retribution is understood not as mechanistic, nor simply juridical in nature. Retribution is also conceived in purity categories and in terms of the general principle "like for like". This principle of "like for like" is of special importance. We have already mentioned in Chapter Six that it confutes the mechanistic idea, but it is also non-juridical in two senses. First, it is true that some laws found, for instance, in the Code of Hammurabi reflect this principle.[5] But the fact that a *specific* consequence is announced *ad hoc* for a *specific* offence[6] implies that the consequence for that offence *cannot* be described as meted out according to some pre-determined norms. Second, the particularity of the consequence for an offence implies that no universal application of that act-consequence connection is intended. This contradicts the intention of the universal application of laws in juridical thought.

The three principles under consideration have implications for the current discussion on corporate and individual retribution. It seems that whether corporate or individual retribution is in view depends partly on the principle and the imagery used. For example, in Ez 16 Jerusalem is conceived of as a woman and hence punishment is targeted on her as an individual only. One may also compare the more individualistic tone in Ez 20:32–38. This is different from the idea of moral impurity. Referring to the image of the smelting furnace in Is 1:21–26, Miller says that

---

[3] Cf. Fishbane 1984:147–148; Barton (1987:435): "Nicht moralische Erneuerung, sondern Verkündigung der Gottesgerechtigkeit war die Aufgabe der Propheten . . .".

[4] Delcor (1997), followed by Schenker (1981:458) and Lust (1987:135–136), argues for this meaning of תכן. See also BDB (1067).

[5] E.g. Miller 1982:106.

[6] Against Fishbane (1984:148) who claims that there is no "focused attempt in the Book of Ezekiel to correlate specific sins with specific judgments".

[s]uch an image also points to the communal character of the experience of judgment. Purification cannot take place here and there, removing the alloy or impurities while leaving the silver alone. The silver as a whole must go through the smelting furnace.[7]

Thus, it would be hard to avoid the idea of corporate retribution when this sort of imagery is used in Ezekiel. This also applies to the case of the impurity of the land. By considering the function of הרם Kaminsky argues that "the community as a whole was obligated to make every attempt possible to avoid polluting themselves or their land".[8] Ezekiel always conceives the offender as the whole community instead of individuals in connection with the defilement of the land. The point is that although impurity is basically an individual's, its ability to defile the sanctuary and land implies that its ramifications go beyond the individual to the communal level. Thus, the use of the principle that impurity requires a resolution usually gives a corporate view of retribution. Regarding the principle of "like for like", since it dictates that a punishment is appropriate to the offence, the bearer of the consequence is always limited to the offender, no matter whether the offender is considered as a group or as an individual. The principle of "like for like" enjoins, by its nature, individual retribution. This discussion here is rather brief but it aims at pointing out the relevance of the principles governing retribution in the discussion of individual or corporate retribution.[9]

The present study opens up some questions for further examination. One obvious question is whether the same principles, and if not, what others, can be found in other biblical books. The literature review in Chapter One shows that the principle of "like for like" features prominently in Proverbs (and also some prophetic books). This probably has to do with the general nature of the principle which allows it to better appeal to the common sensibility of the people and to apply to a wide variety of cases, especially those that cannot be dictated by law such as laziness. Does that also apply to the narrative sections of the Bible as found, for instance, in Judges, Kings, Esther?

---

[7] Miller 1982:39.
[8] Kaminsky 1995:89.
[9] One may also note that there are cases of vicarious substitutions which can be seen as an application of the principle "like for like". See the examples given by Miller (1982:107).

Within Ezekiel, we have mentioned briefly the relation between profanation and sanctification on the one hand, and the history of Israel on the other. This theme relates to the idea of retribution since the action and fate of Israel in its history are closely tied to the profanation and sanctification of Yahweh's name. Also related to the idea of holiness is its connection to building up one's status. Eilberg-Schwartz points to the difference between ascribed status and achieved status,[10] the former being status assigned to a person for what he/she is and the latter for what he/she does. While Eilberg-Schwartz's concern is more with impurity, his consideration can also apply, *mutatis mutandis*, to holiness. Duguid in his study has examined the past actions of the leaders of Israel and their future status as shown in the eschatological picture of Ez 40–48. How the different groups of people relate to the eschatological temple indicates their state of holiness (cf. Jenson's *Graded Holiness*) which is an achieved status related to their past actions. The change in the status of holiness of the people as a result of their actions is related to retribution. Thus, a combination of the perspectives proposed by these scholars may yield some interesting results regarding retribution.

---

[10] Eilberg-Schwartz 1990:196.

BIBLIOGRAPHY

Aalders, G. Ch.
    1955   *Ezechiël I*. COT. Kampen: Kok.
    1957   *Ezechiël II*. COT. Kampen: Kok.
Ackerman, Susan
    1992   *Under Every Green Tree: Popular Religion in Sixth-Century Judah*. HSM 46.
            Atlanta: Scholars.
Ackryod, Peter R.
    1968   *Exile and Restoration: A Study of Hebrew Thought of the Sixth Century B.C.* OTL.
            London: SCM.
Adler, Elaine J.
    1990   "The Background for the Metaphor of Covenant as Marriage in the
            Hebrew Bible." Ph.D. Dissertation, University of California, Berkeley.
Aitken, James K.
    1998   "דרך." In *Semantics of Ancient Hebrew*, ed. T. Muraoka, 11–37. ANS 6.
            Louvain: Peeters.
Allen, Leslie C.
    1987   "Ezekiel 24:3–14: A Rhetorical Perspective." *CBQ* 49:404–414.
    1990   *Ezekiel 20–48*. WBC 29. Dallas: Word Books.
    1994   *Ezekiel 1–19*. WBC 28. Dallas: Word Books.
Alexander, Ralph H.
    1986   "Ezekiel." In *The Expositor's Bible Commentary*, Vol.6, ed. Frank E. Gaebelein,
            735–996. Grand Rapids: Zondervan.
Alt, Albrecht
    1934   "Zur Talionsformel." In Koch 1972:407–411. [= Reprint of *ZAW* 11
            (1934) 303–305.]
Amir, Yehoshua
    1992   "Measure for Measure in Talmudic Literature and in Wisdom of Solomon."
            In Reventlow and Hoffman 1992:29–46.
Amorim, Nilton D.
    1985   "Desecration and Defilement in the Old Testament." Ph.D. Dissertation,
            Andrews University, Seventh-day Adventist Theological Seminary.
André, G.
    1990   "יסף." *TDOT* 6:121–127.
André, G. and H. Ringgren
    1986   "טמא." *TDOT* 5:330–342.
Andrew, Maurice E.
    1985   *Responsibility and Restoration: The Course of the Book of Ezekiel*. Dunedin:
            University of Otago.
Ashley, Timothy R.
    1993   *The Book of Numbers*. NICOT. Grand Rapids: Eerdmans.
Auvray, Paul.
    1957   *Ézéchiel*. SB. Paris: Cerf.
Averbeck, Richard E.
    1996a   "Clean and Unclean." *NIDOTTE* 4:477–486.
    1996b   "טמא" *NIDOTTE* 2:365–376.
Babut, Jean-Marc
    1986   "Que son sang soit sur sa tête!" *VT* 36:474–480.

Baldick, Chris
1990 *The Concise Oxford Dictionary of Literary Terms*. Oxford: Oxford University Press.
Balla, Emil
1958 *Die Botschaft der Propheten*. Ed. Georg Fohrer. Tübingen: Mohr.
Baltzer, Dieter
1971a *Ezechiel und Deuterojesaja: Berührungen in der Heilserwartung der beiden großen Exilspropheten*. BZAW 121. Berlin: de Gruyter.
1971b *The Covenant Formulary in Old Testament, Jewish, and Early Christian Writings*. Trans. David E. Green. Oxford: Blackwell. [= ET of *Das Bundesformular*. WMANT 4. Neukirchen: Neukirchener Verlag, 1960.]
1986 "Literarkritische und literarhistorische Anmerkungen zur Heilsprophetie im Ezechiel-Buch." In Lust 1986:166–181.
Barr, James
1961 *The Semantics of Biblical Language*. Oxford: Oxford University Press.
1972 "Semantics and Biblical Theology—A Contribution to the Discussion." In *Congress Volume, Uppsala 1971*, ed. G. W. Anderson *et al.*, 11–19. SVT 22. Leiden: Brill.
1977 "Some Semantic Notes on the Covenant." In *Beiträge zur alttestamentlichen Theologie: Festschrift für Walter Zimmerli zum 70. Geburtstag*, ed. Herbert Donner, Robert Hanhart and Rudolf Smend, 23–38. Göttingen: Vandenhoeck & Ruprecht.
Barth, Christoph
1977 "Ezechiel 37 als Einheit." In *Beiträge zur alttestamentlichen Theologie: Festschrift für Walter Zimmerli zum 70. Geburtstag*, ed. Herbert Donner, Robert Hanhart and Rudolf Smend, 39–52. Göttingen: Vandenhoeck & Ruprecht.
Barthélemy, Dominique
1992 *Critique textuelle de l'Ancien Testament*. Vol.3: *Ézéchiel, Daniel et les 12 Prophètes*. OBO 50/3. Göttingen: Vandenhoeck & Ruprecht.
Barton, John
1979 "Natural Law and Poetic Justice in the Old Testament." *JTS* 30:1–14.
1987 "Begründungsversuche der prophetischen Unheilsankündigung im Alten Testament." *EvTh* 47:427–435.
1998 *Ethics and the Old Testament*. London: SCM.
Batto, Bernard F.
1987 "The Covenant of Peace: A Neglected Ancient Near Eastern Motif." *CBQ* 49:187–211.
Baudissin, Wolf W.
1878 *Studien zur semitischen Religionsgeschichte*. Vol.2. Leipzig: Grunow.
Bauer, Johannes B.
1970 "Clean and Unclean." *EBT* 1:118–121.
Becker, Joachim
1971 *Der priestliche Prophet: Das Buch Ezechiel*. SKKAT 12. Stuttgart: Katholisches Bibelwerk.
1976 "Recensiones: Horacio Simian, *Die theologische Nachgeschichte der Prophetie Ezechiels*. Form- und traditionskritische Untersuchung zu Ez 6; 35; 36 (Forschung zur Bibel, 14)." *Biblica* 57:133–137.
Begg, Christopher T.
1986 "*Bᵉrit* in Ezekiel." In *Proceedings of the Ninth World Congress of Jewish Studies. Jerusalem, August 4–12, 1985*. Division A: *The Period of the Bible*, 77–84. Jerusalem: World Union of Jewish Studies.
Bergmann, J., H. Ringgren and B. Lang
1980 "זָבַח." *TDOT* 4:8–29.
Bergsträßer, G.
1929 *Hebräische Grammatik mit Benutzung der von E. Kautsch bearbeiten 28. Auflage von*

Wilhelm Gesenius' hebräischer Grammatik. II. Teil: *Verbum*. Leipzig: Hinrichs'sche Buchhandlung.

Bertholet, Alfred
  1897   *Das Buch Hesekiel*. KHCAT 12. Freiburg: Mohr.
  1901   *Leviticus*. KHCAT 3. Tübingen: Mohr.
  1936   (With Kurt Galling) *Hesekiel*. HBAT I,13. Tübingen: Mohr.

Bettenzoli, Giuseppe
  1979   *Geist der Heiligkeit: Traditionsgeschichtliche Untersuchung des* QDŠ-*Begriffes im Buch Ezechiel*. QS 8. Florence: University of Florence.

Beuken, W. A. M.
  1972   "Ez. 20: Thematiek en literaire vormgeving in onderling verband." *Bijdragen* 33:39–64.

Beuken, W. and U. Dahmen
  1993   "ראשׁ I." *TWAT* 7:271–284.

Biggs, Charles R.
  1996   *The Book of Ezekiel*. EpC. London: Epworth Press.

Bird, Phillis
  1989   "'To Play the Harlot': An Inquiry into an Old Testament Metaphor". In *Gender and Difference in Ancient Israel*, ed. Peggy L. Day, 75–94. Minneapolis: Fortress.

Blenkinsopp, Joseph
  1990   *Ezekiel*. IBCTP. Louisville: Knox.
  1995   *Wisdom and Law in the Old Testament*. Oxford: Oxford University Press.
  1996   "An Assessment of the Alleged Pre-Exilic Date of the Priestly Material in the Pentateuch." *ZAW* 108:495–518.

Bloch, Renée
  1955   "Ezéchiel XVI, exemple parfait du procédé midrashique dans la Bible." *Cahiers Sioniens* 9:193–223.

Bloch-Smith, Elizabeth
  1992   *Judahite Burial Practices and Beliefs about the Dead*. JSOTSS 123. Sheffield: JSOT.

Block, Daniel I.
  1997   *The Book of Ezekiel: Chapters 1–24*. NICOT. Grand Rapids: Eerdmans.
  1998   *The Book of Ezekiel: Chapters 25–48*. NICOT. Grand Rapids: Eerdmans.

Boadt, Lawrence
  1980   *Ezekiel's Oracles against Egypt: A Literary and Philological Study of Ezekiel 29–32*. BibOr 37. Rome: Biblical Institute.
  1986   "Rhetorical Strategies in Ezekiel's Oracles of Judgment." In Lust 1986: 182–200.
  1990   "The Function of the Salvation Oracles in Ezekiel 33 to 37." *HAR* 12:1–21.
  1992   "Ezekiel, Book of." *ABD* 2:711–722.

Bodi, Daniel
  1991   *The Book of Ezekiel and the Poem of Erra*. OBO 104. Freiburg, Schweiz: Universitätsverlag; Göttingen: Vandenhoeck & Ruprecht.
  1993   "Les *gillûlîm* chez Ezéchiel et dans l'Ancien Testament et les différentes pratiques cultuelles associées à ce terme." *RB* 100:481–510.

Boecker, Hans J.
  1964   *Redeformen des Rechtslebens im Alten Testament*. WMANT 14. Neukirchen-Vluyn: Neukirchener Verlag.

Bogaert, Pierre-Maurice
  1978   "Le témoignage de la Vetus Latina dans l'étude de la tradition des Septante Ézéchiel et Daniel dans le Papyrus 967." *Biblica* 59:384–395.

Boogaart, T. A.
  1985   "Stone for Stone: Retribution in the Story of Abimelech and Shechem", *JSOT* 32:45–56.

Boström, Lennart
    1990   *The God of the Sages: The Portrayal of God in the Book of Proverbs.* CBOT 29.
            Stockholm: Almqvist & Wiksell.
Bovati, Pietro
    1994   *Re-Establishing Justice: Legal Terms, Concepts and Procedures in the Hebrew Bible.*
            JSOTSS 105. Sheffield: Sheffield Academic Press.
Breuer, Joseph
    1993   *The Book of Yechezkel: Translation and Commentary.* New York: Philipp Feldheim.
            [= ET of *Das Buch Jecheskel übersetzt und erläutert.* Frankfurt: Sänger and
            Friedberg, 1921.]
Brewer, David I.
    1996   "Three Weddings and a Divorce: God's Covenant with Israel, Judah and
            the Church." *TynBul* 47:1–25.
Brichto, Hebert C.
    1963   *The Problem of "Curse" in the Hebrew Bible.* JBLMS 13. Philadelphia: SBL.
Brögelmann, Emil
    1935   *Der Gottesgedanke bei Ezechiel: Ein Beitrag zur biblischen Theologie des Alten
            Testament.* Hannover: Orientbuchhandlung Heinz Lafaire.
Brongers, H. A.
    1973   "Die Partikel לְמַעַן in der biblisch-hebräischen Sprachen." *OTS* 18:84–
            96.
Brownlee, William H.
    1972   "Ezekiel's Copper Caldron and Blood on the Rock (Chapter 24:1–14)."
            In *For Me to Live: Essays in Honor of James Leon Kelso*, ed. Robert A. Coughe-
            nour, 21–43. Cleveland: Dillon/Liederbach.
    1986   *Ezekiel 1–19.* WBC 28. Waco: Word.
Brunner, Heinrich
    1892   *Deutsche Rechtsgeschichte.* Vol.2. Leipzig: Duncker & Humblot.
Brunner, Robert
    1969a   *Das Buch Ezechiel.* Second Edition. Vol.1. ZB. Zürich: Zwingli.
    1969b   *Das Buch Ezechiel.* Second Edition. Vol.2. ZB. Zürich: Zwingli.
Büchler, Adolph
    1928   *Studies in Sin and Atonement in the Rabbinic Literature of the First Century.* London:
            Oxford University Press.
Budd, Philip J.
    1984   *Numbers.* WBC 5. Waco: Word.
    1989   "Holiness and Cult." In *The World of Ancient Israel: Sociological, Anthropological
            and Political Perspectives*, ed. Ronald E. Clements, 275–298. Cambridge:
            Cambridge University Press.
    1996   *Leviticus.* NCB. Grand Rapids: Eerdmans.
Bunn, John T.
    1971   "Ezekiel." In *Jeremiah-Daniel*, 223–371. BBC 6. Nashville: Broadman Press.
Burchfield, R. W.
    1998   *The New Fowler's Modern English Usage.* Third Edition. Oxford: Clarendon.
Burger, J. A.
    1989   "The Law of Yahweh, The Fear of Yahweh, and Retribution in the
            Wisdom Psalms." *OTE* 2:75–95.
Burrows, Millar
    1925   *The Literary Relations of Ezekiel.* Philadelphia: JPS.
Calvin, John
    1994   *Ezekiel I: Chapters 1–12.* Trans. D. Foxgrover and D. Martin. COTC 18.
            Grand Rapids: Eerdmans.
Campbell, Edward F.
    1975   *Ruth.* AB 7. Garden City: Doubleday.

Carley, Keith W.
   1974   *The Book of the Prophet Ezekiel*. CBC. London: Cambridge University Press.
   1975   *Ezekiel among the Prophets*. SBT 2,31. London: SCM.
Carpenter, Eugene and Michael A. Grisanti
   1996   "פֶּשַׁע." *NIDOTTE* 3:706–710.
Carroll, Michael P.
   1978   "One More Time: Leviticus Revisited." In *Anthropological Approaches to the Old Testament*, ed. Bernhard Lang, 117–126. London: SPCK, 1985. [= Reprint of *AES* 19 (1978) 339–346.]
Carroll, Robert P.
   1984   "Theodicy and the Community: The Text and Subtext of Jeremiah v 1–6." *OTS* 23:19–38.
   1986   *Jeremiah*. OTL. London: SCM.
   1992   "The Myth of the Empty Land." *Semeia* 59:79–93.
Charette, Blaine
   1992   *The Theme of Recompense in Matthew's Gospel*. JSNTSS 79. Sheffield: JSOT.
Clements, Ronald E.
   1970   "Leviticus." In *Leviticus-Ruth*, BBC 2, 1–73. London: Marshall, Morgan and Scott.
   1982   "The Ezekiel Tradition: Prophecy in a Time of Crisis." In *Israel's Prophetic Tradition: Essays in Honour of Peter R. Ackroyd*, ed. Richard Coggins, Anthony Phillips and Michael Knibb, 119–136. Cambridge: Cambridge University Press.
   1986   "The Chronology of Redaction in Ez 1–24." In Lust 1986:283–294.
   1993   "שׁחם." *TWAT* 7:1214–1218.
   1996   *Ezekiel*. WestBC. Louisville: Westminster John Knox Press.
Cody, Aelred
   1984   *Ezekiel with an Excursus on Old Testament Priesthood*. OTM 11. Wilmington: Glazier.
Coffman, James B. and Thelma B. Coffman
   1991   *Commentary on Ezekiel*. JBCOTC. Abilene: Abilene Christian University.
Cogan, Morton
   1968   "A Technical Term for Exposure." *JNES* 27:133–135.
Cooke, G. A.
   1936   *A Critical and Exegetical Commentary on the Book of Ezekiel*. ICC. Edinburgh: T. & T. Clark.
Cooper, Lamar E.
   1994   *Ezekiel*. NAC 17. Nashville: Broadman & Holman.
Cornill, Carl H.
   1886   *Das Buch des Propheten Ezechiel*. Leipzig: Hinrichs.
Cover, Robin C.
   1992   "Sin, Sinners (OT)." *ABD* 6:31–40.
Craigie, Peter C.
   1976   *The Book of Deuteronomy*. NICOT. Grand Rapids: Eerdmans.
   1983a   *Ezekiel*. DSB. Edinburgh: Saint Andrews.
   1983b   *Psalms 1–50*. WBC 19. Waco: Word.
Cross, Frank M.
   1996   "A Papyrus Recording a Divine Legal Decision and the Root *rhq* in Biblical and Near Eastern Legal Usage." In *Texts, Temples, and Traditions: A Tribute to Menahem Haran*, ed. Michael V. Fox *et al.*, 311–320. Winona Lake: Eisenbrauns.
Cuddon, J. A.
   1992   *The Penguin Dictionary of Literary Terms and Literary Theory*. Third Edition. London: Penguin.

Cupit, Geoffrey
    1996   *Justice as Fittingness*. Oxford: Clarendon.
Currey, G.
    1882   "Ezekiel." In *The Holy Bible with an Explanatory and Critical Commentary*, Vol.VI: *Ezekiel-Daniel-and the Minor Prophets*, ed. F. C. Cook, 1–209. London: John Murray.
Darr, Katheryn Pfisterer
    1994   "Ezekiel among the Critics." *CR:BS* 2:9–24.
Daube, David
    1947   *Studies in Biblical Law*. Cambridge: Cambridge University Press.
    1961   "Direct and Indirect Causation in Biblical Law." *VT* 11:246–269.
Davidson, A. B.
    1916   *The Book of the Prophet Ezekiel*. Revised by A. W. Streane. CBSC. Cambridge: Cambridge University Press.
Davies, Eryl W.
    1981   "Inheritance Rights and the Hebrew Levirate Marriage: Part 1." *VT* 31:138–144.
Davies, Graham I.
    1992   *Hosea*. NCB. Grand Rapids. Eerdmans.
Day, John
    1989   *Molech: A God of Human Sacrifice in the Old Testament*. UCOP 41. Cambridge: Cambridge University Press.
    1992   "Asherah." *ABD* 1:483–487.
Deist, F. E.
    1971   "The Punishment of the Disobedient Zedekiah." *JNSL* 1:71–72.
Delcor, M.
    1997   "תכן." *TLOT* 1422–1424.
Delkurt, Holger
    1993   *Ethische Einsichten in der alttestamentlichen Spruchweisheit*. BTSt 21. Neukirchen-Vluyn: Neukirchener Verlag.
Dempsey, Carol J.
    1998   "The 'Whore' of Ezekiel 16: The Impact and Ramifications of Gender-Specific Metaphors in Light of Biblical Law and Divine Judgment." In *Gender and Law in the Hebrew Bible and the Ancient Near East*, ed. Victor H. Matthews, Bernard M. Levinson and Tikva Frymer-Kensky, 57–78. JSOTSS 262. Sheffield: Sheffield Academic Press.
De Roche, M.
    1983   "Yahweh's *rîb* against Israel: A Reassessment of the So-called 'Prophetic Lawsuit' in the Preexilic Prophets." *JBL* 102:563–74.
Dijkstra, Meindert
    1986   *Ezechiël I: Een praktische bijbelverklaring*. TT. Kampen: Kok.
    1989   *Ezechiël II: Een praktische bijbelverklaring*. TT. Kampen: Kok.
    1996   "Goddess, Gods, Men and Women in Ezekiel 8." In *On Reading Prophetic Texts: Gender-Specific and Related Studies in Memory of Fokkelien van Dijk-Hemmes*, ed. Bob Becking and Meindert Dijkstra, 83–114. BIS 18. Leiden: Brill.
Dillard, Raymond B.
    1987   *2 Chronicles*. WBC 15. Waco: Word.
Dillmann, August and V. Ryssel
    1897   *Die Bücher Exodus und Leviticus*. Third Edition. KeHAT. Leipzig: Hirzel.
Dohman, C.
    1997   "מזבח." *TDOT* 8:209–225.
Döller, Johannes
    1917   *Die Reinheits- und Speisegesetz des Alten Testaments*. ATA 7.2–3. Münster: Aschendorffschen Verlagsbuchhandlung.

Dommershausen, W.
  1980 "חָלַל II." *TDOT* 4:417–421.
  1995 "כֵּן." *TDOT* 7:229–231.
Douglas, Mary
  1966 *Purity and Danger: An Analysis of Pollution and Taboo*. London: Routledge &
    Kegan Paul.
  1993 *In the Wilderness: The Doctrine of Defilement in the Book of Numbers*. JSOTSS
    159. Sheffield: Sheffield Academic Press.
  1996 "Sacred Contagion." In *Reading Leviticus: A Conversation with Mary Douglas*,
    ed. John F. A. Sawyer, 86–106. JSOTSS 227. Sheffield: Sheffield Acade-
    mic Press.
Drescher, Horst W.
  1979 *Lexicon der englischen Literatur*. Stuttgart: Kröner.
Drijvers, Han J. W.
  1988 "Aramaic *HMN* and Hebrew *HMN*: Their Meaning and Root." *JSS*
    33:165–180.
Driver, G. R.
  1935 "Studies in the Vocabulary of the Old Testament: VIII." *JTS* 36:293–301.
Driver, G. R. and John C. Miles
  1952 *The Babylonian Laws*. Vol.1. Oxford: Clarendon.
  1955 *The Babylonian Laws*. Vol.2. Oxford: Clarendon.
Driver, S. R.
  1902 *A Critical and Exegetical Commentary on the Book of Deuteronomy*. ICC. Edinburgh:
    T. & T. Clark.
Duguid, Iain M.
  1994 *Ezekiel and the Leaders of Israel*. SVT 56. Leiden: Brill.
  1999 *Ezekiel*. NIVAC. Grand Rapids: Zondervan.
Duhm, Bernhard
  1901 *Das Buch Jeremia*. KHCAT 11. Tübingen: Mohr.
Dumermuth, Fritz
  1963 "Zu Ez. XIII 18–21." *VT* 13:228–229.
Durlesser, James A.
  1987 "The Striking of the Ship of Tyre (Ezek 27): A Study of Rhetoric in
    Hebrew Allegory." *PEGLMBS* 7:79–93.
  1988 "The Rhetoric of Allegory in the Book of Ezekiel." Ph.D. Dissertation,
    Pittsburgh University.
Ebach, Jürgen H.
  1971 "*PGR* = (Toten-)Opfer? Ein Vorschlag zum Verständnis von Ez. 43, 7.
    9." *UF* 3:365–368.
Ehrlich, Arnold B.
  1909 *Randglossen zur hebräischen Bibel*. Vol.2: *Leviticus, Numeri, Deuteronomium*. Leipzig:
    Hinrichs'sche Buchhandlung.
  1912 *Randglossen zur hebräischen Bibel*. Vol.5: *Ezechiel und die kleinen Propheten*. Leipzig:
    Hinrichs'sche Buchhandlung.
Eichrodt, Walther
  1961 *Theology of the Old Testament*. Vol.1. OTL. London: SCM.
  1970 *Ezekiel*. OTL. Philadelphia: Westminster Press. [= ET of *Der Prophet Hesekiel
    übersetzt und erklärt*. ATD 22,1–2. Göttingen: Vandenhoeck & Ruprecht,
    1969².]
Eilberg-Schwartz, Howard
  1990 *The Savage in Judaism: Anthropology of Israelite Religion and Ancient Judaism*.
    Bloomington and Indianapolis: Indiana University Press.
Eisemann, Moshe
  1988 *Yechezkel—The Book of Ezekiel: A New Translation with a Commentary Anthologized*

from Talmudic, Midrashic, and Rabbinic Sources. Third Edition. ASTS. New
York: Mesorah.

Eising, H.
1980 "זָכַר." *TDOT* 4:64–82.

Eissfeldt, Otto
1936 "Hesekiel Kap.16 als Geschichtsquelle." *JPOS* 16:286–292.
1950 "Schwerterschlagene bei Hesekiel." In *Studies in Old Testament Prophecy:
Presented to Professor Theodore H. Robinson by the Society for Old Testament Study
on His Sixty-fifth Birthday,* ed. H. H. Rowley, 73–81. Edinburgh: T. & T.
Clark.

Elliger, Karl
1966 *Leviticus.* HBAT 1,4. Tübingen: Mohr.

Erlandsson, S.
1980 "זָנָה." *TDOT* 4:99–104.

Eslinger, Lyle
1998 "Ezekiel 20 and the Metaphor of Historical Teleology: Concepts of Biblical
History." *JSOT* 81:93–125.

Ewald, Georg H. A.
1880 *Commentary on the Prophets of the Old Testament.* Vol.IV: *Hézeqiél, "Yeraya,"*
xl.–lxvi. Trans. J. Frederick Smith. London: Williams and Norgate.

Fahlgren, K. Hj.
1932 *Sᵉdaka, nahestehende und entgegengesetzte Begriffe im Alten Testament.* Uppsala:
Almqvist & Wiksell.
1972 "Die Gegensätze von sᵉdaqa im Alten Testament." In Koch 1972:87–129.
[= Extracts of 1932.]

Fairbairn, Patrick
1855 *Commentary on Ezekiel.* Grand Rapids: Kregel, 1989. [= Reprint of *Ezekiel
and the Book of Prophecy: An Exposition.* Edinburgh: T. & T. Clark, 1855².]

Faur, José
1978 "The Biblical Idea of Idolatry." *JQR* 69:1–15.

Feinberg, Charles L.
1969 *The Prophecy of Ezekiel: The Glory of the Lord.* Chicago: Moody.

Feldman, Emanuel
1977 *Biblical and Post-Biblical Defilement and Mourning: Law as Theology.* New York:
Yeshiva University Press.

Fensham, F. C.
1962 "Maledictions and Benedictions in Ancient Near Eastern Vassal-Treaties
and the Old Testament." *ZAW* 74:1–9.
1963 "Common Trends in Curses of the Near Eastern Treaties and *Kudurru-*
Inscriptions Compared with the Maledictions of Amos and Isaiah." *ZAW*
75:155–175.
1987 "The Curse of the Dry Bones in Ezekiel 37:1–14 Changed to a Blessing
of Resurrection." *JNSL* 13:59–60.

Fichtner, Johannes
1949 "Jesaja unter den Weisen." *TLZ* 74:75–80.

Filson, F. V.
1943 "The Omission of Ezek. 12:26–28 and 36:23b-38 in Codex 967." *JBL*
62:27–32.

Fisch, S.
1950 *Ezekiel.* SonB. London: Soncino.

Fishbane, Michael
1984 "Sin and Judgment in the Prophecies of Ezekiel." *Interpretation* 38:131–150.
1985 *Biblical Interpretation in Ancient Israel.* Oxford: Clarendon.

Fitzgerald, A.
  1972   "The Mythological Background for the Presentation of Jerusalem as Queen
          and False Worship as Adultery in the OT." *CBQ* 34:403–416.
  1975   "*Bṭwlt* and *Bt* as Titles for Capital Cities." *CBQ* 37:167–183.
Fohrer, Georg
  1952   *Die Hauptprobleme des Buches Ezechiel.* BZAW 72. Berlin: Töpelmann.
  1955   (With Kurt Galling) *Ezechiel.* HBAT I,13. Tübingen: Mohr.
Friebel, Kelvin G.
  1999   *Jeremiah's and Ezekiel's Sign-Acts.* JSOTSS 283. Sheffield: Sheffield Academic
          Press.
Fritz, Volkmar
  1981   "Die Bedeutung von *ḥammān* im Hebräischen und von *ḥmn'* in den
          palmyrenischen Inschriften." *BN* 15:9–20.
Frymer-Kensky, Tikva
  1977   "The Atrahasis Epic and Its Significance for Our Understanding of Genesis
          1–9." *BA* 40:147–155.
  1980   "Tit for Tat: The Principle of Equal Retribution in Near Eastern and
          Biblical Law." *BA* 43:230–234.
  1983   "Pollution, Purification, and Purgation in Biblical Israel." In *The Word of
          the Lord Shall Go Forth: Essays in Honor of David N. Freedman in Celebration of
          His Sixtieth Birthday*, ed. Carol L. Meyers and M. O'Connor, 399–414.
          Winona Lake: Eisenbrauns.
  1989   "Law and Philosophy: The Case of Sex in the Bible." *Semeia* 45:89–
          102.
Füglister, Notker
  1977   "Sühne durch Blut. Zur Bedeutung von Leviticus 17,11." In *Studien zum
          Pentateuch: Walter Kornfeld zum 60. Geburtstag*, ed. Georg Braulik, 143–164.
          Wien: Herder.
Fuhs, Hans F.
  1977   "נחל." *TDOT* 2:461–465.
  1984   *Ezechiel 1–24.* NEB 7. Würzburg: Echter Verlag.
  1988   *Ezechiel II 25–48.* NEB 22. Würzburg: Echter Verlag.
Galambush, Julie
  1992   *Jerusalem in the Book of Ezekiel: The City as Yahweh's Wife.* SBLDS 130.
          Atlanta: Scholars.
Gammie, John G.
  1970   "The Theology of Retribution in the Book of Deuteronomy." *CBQ* 32:1–12.
  1989   *Holiness in Israel.* OBT. Minneapolis: Fortress.
Garscha, Jörg
  1974   *Studien zum Ezechielbuch. Eine redaktionskritische Untersuchung von Ez 1–39.* EHS
          23. Bern: Lang; Frankfurt: Lang.
Gerleman, Gillis
  1973   "Die Wurzel *šlm*." *ZAW* 85:1–14.
  1997   "דם." *TLOT* 337–339.
Gerstenberger, Erhard S.
  1965   *Wesen und Herkunft des "Apodiktischen Rechts".* WMANT 20. Neukirchen-Vluyn:
          Neukirchener Verlag.
  1996   *Leviticus: A Commentary.* OTL. Louisville, Knox. [= ET of *Das dritte Buch
          Mose: Leviticus.* ATD 6. Göttingen: Vandenhoeck & Ruprecht, 1993.]
  1997   "תעב." *TLOT* 1428–1431.
Gertner, M.
  1960   "The Masorah and the Levites: An Essay in the History of a Concept."
          VT 10:241–272.

Gispen, W. H.
1948 "The Distinction between Clean and Unclean." *OTS* 5:190–196.
Gleis, Matthias
1997 *Die Bamah*. BZAW 251. Berlin: de Gruyter.
Good, Edwin M.
1970 "Ezekiel's Ship: Some Extended Metaphors in the Old Testament." *Semitics* 1:79–103.
Good, Robert M.
1983 *The Sheep of His Pasture: A Study of the Hebrew Noun 'Am(m) and Its Semitic Cognates*. HSM 29. Chico: Scholars Press.
Graffy, Adrian
1984 *A Prophet Confronts His People: The Disputation Speech in the Prophets*. AnBib 104. Rome: Biblical Institute.
Grant, F. W. and J. Bloore
1931 *Ezekiel*. The Numerical Bible. New York: Loizeaux Brothers.
Gray, George B.
1903 *A Critical and Exegetical Commentary on Numbers*. ICC. Edinburgh: T. & T. Clark.
Gray, John
1977 *I & II Kings*. Third Edition. OTL. London: SCM.
1979 *The Biblical Doctrine of the Reign of God*. Edinburgh: T. & T. Clark.
Greenberg, Moshe
1983a *Ezekiel 1–20*. AB 22. New York: Doubleday.
1983b "*MSRT HBRYT*, 'The Obligation of the Covenant,' in Ezekiel 20:37." In *The Word of the Lord Shall Go Forth: Essays in Honor of David Noel Freedman in Celebration of His Sixtieth Birthday*, ed. Carol L. Meyers and M. O'Connor, 37–46. Winona Lake: Eisenbrauns.
1984 "The Design and Themes of Ezekiel's Program of Restoration." *Interpretation* 38:181–208.
1995 "The Etymology of נִדָּה '(Menstrual) Impurity'." In *Solving Riddles and Untying Knots: Biblical, Epigraphic, and Semitic Studies in Honor of Jonas C. Greenfield*, ed. Ziony Zevit, Seymour Gitin and Michael Sokoloff, 69–77. Winona Lake: Eisenbrauns.
1997 *Ezekiel 21–37*. AB 22A. New York: Doubleday.
Greenfield, Jonas C.
1958 "Lexicographical Notes I." *HUCA* 29:203–228.
Greengus, Samuel
1969 "The Old Babylonian Marriage Contracts." *JAOS* 89:505–532.
1992 "Law: Biblical and ANE Law." *ABD* 4:242–252.
Greenhill, William
1645–67 *An Exposition of Ezekiel*. Edinburgh: Banner of Truth Trust, 1994. [= Reprint of 1863 Nichol edition. First published in 1645–67.]
Grintz, Jehoshua M.
1970/71 "'Do Not Eat on the Blood': Reconsiderations in Setting and Dating of the Priestly Code." *ASTI* 8:78–105.
Grisanti, Michael A.
1996 "תעב." *NIDOTTE* 4:314–318.
Groß, Heinrich
1960 "Zur Wurzel zkr." *BZ* 4:227–237.
Gruenthaner, Michael J.
1942 "The Old Testament and Retribution in This Life." *CBQ* 4:101–110.
Grünwaldt, Klaus
1999 *Das Heiligkeitsgesetz Leviticus 17–26: Ursprüngliche Gestalt, Tradition und Theologie*. BZAW 271. Berlin: de Gruyter.

Gunkel, Herrmann
  1931   "Vergeltung: II. Im AT und im Judentum." *RGG*² 5:1529–1533.
Haag, Herbert
  1943   *Was lehrt die literarische Untersuchung des Ezechiel-Textes? Eine philologisch-theolo-gische Studie*. Freiburg: Universitätsbuchhandlung.
Haik, Peter R.
  1980   "The Holiness of God in the Thought of Ezekiel." Th.D. Dissertation, New Orleans Baptist Theological Seminary.
Halbertal, Moshe and Avishai Margalit
  1994   *Idolatry*. Trans. Naomi Goldblum. Cambridge: Harvard University Press.
Hall, Gary H.
  1996   "זנה." *NIDOTTE* 1:1122–1125.
Hals, Ronald M.
  1989   *Ezekiel*. FOTL 19. Grand Rapids: Eerdmans.
Hänel, Johannes
  1931   *Die Religion der Heiligkeit*. Gütersloh: Bertelsmann.
Haran, Mehahem
  1979   "The Law Code of Ezekiel XL–XLVIII and Its Relation to the Priestly School." *HUCA* 50:45–71.
Harrington, Hannak K.
  1993   *The Impurity Systems of Qumran and the Rabbis: Biblical Foundations*. SBLDS 143. Atlanta: Scholars.
Harrison, Ronald K.
  1980   *Leviticus*. TOTC. Downers Grove: Inter-Varsity.
Hartley, John E.
  1979   "Clean and Unclean." *ISBE* 1:718–723.
  1992   *Leviticus*. WBC 4. Dallas: Word.
Hasel, Gerhard F.
  1989   "פלט." *TWAT* 6:589–606.
  1995   "כָּרַת." *TDOT* 7:339–352.
Hattori, Yoshiaki
  1974   "Divine Dilemma in Ezekiel's View of the Exodus: An Exegetical Study of Ezekiel 20:5–29." In *The Law and the Prophets: Old Testament Studies Prepared in Honor of Oswald Thompson Allis*, ed. John H. Skilton, 413–424. N.p.: Presbyterian and Reformed Publishing Co.
Hausmann, Jutta
  1995   *Studien zum Menschenbild der älteren Weisheit (Spr 10ff.)*. FAT 7. Tübingen: Mohr.
Heider, G. C.
  1985   *The Cult of Molek: A Reassessment*. JSOTSS 43. Sheffield: JSOT.
Heinisch, Paul
  1923   *Das Buch Ezechiel*. HSAT VIII, 1. Bonn: Hanstein.
Hempel, Johannes
  1964   *Das Ethos des Alten Testaments*. BZAW 67. Second Edition. Berlin: Töpelmann.
Henberg, Marvin
  1990   *Retribution: Evil for Evil in Ethics, Law and Literature*. Philadelphia: Temple University.
Herdlitczka, A.
  1932   "Talio." *PRE*, Second Series, 4:2069–2077.
Herrmann, Johannes
  1924   *Ezechiel*. KAT XI. Leipzig: Deichestsche.
Herrmann, Siegfried
  1965   *Die prophetischen Heilserwartungen im Alten Testament*. BWANT 85. Stuttgart: Kohlhammer.

Herzog, Patricius
1923   *Die ethischen Anschauungen des Propheten Ezechiel.* ATA 9.2–3. Münster: Aschen-
        dorffschen Verlagsbuchhandlung.
Hillers, Delbert R.
1964   *Treaty-Curses and the Old Testament Prophets.* BibOr 16. Rome: Pontifical
        Biblical Institute.
1969   *Covenant: The History of a Biblical Idea.* Baltimore: John Hopkins University.
Hitzig, Ferdinand
1847   *Der Prophet Ezechiel.* KeHAT 8. Leipzig: Weidmann'sche Buchhandlung.
Hoffman, Yair
1992   "The Creativity of Theodicy." In Reventlow and Hoffman 1992:117–130.
Hoffmeier, J. K.
1986   "The Arm of God Versus the Arm of Pharao in the Exodus Narratives."
        Biblica 67:378–387.
Holladay, William L.
1961   "'On Every High Hill and under Every Green Tree'." *VT* 11:170–176.
1986   *Jeremiah 1.* Hermeneia. Minneapolis: Fortress.
Horbury, William
1985   "Extirpation and Excommunication." *VT* 35:13–38.
Horst, Friedrich
1953   "Exilsgemeinde und Jerusalem in Ez VIII–XI: Eine literarische Unter-
        suchung." *VT* 3:337–360.
1956   "Recht und Religion im Bereich des Alten Testaments." *EvTh* 16:49–75.
1962   "Vergeltung. II. Im AT." *RGG*[3] 6:1343–1346.
Hossfeld, Frank-Lothar
1977   *Untersuchungen zu Komposition und Theologie des Ezechielbuches.* FzB 20. Würzburg:
        Echter Verlag.
1986   "Die Tempelvision Ez 8–11 im Licht unterschiedlichen methodischer
        Zugänge." In Lust 1986:151–65.
1987   "Probleme einer ganzheitlichen Lektüre der Schrift dargestellt am Beispiel
        Ez 9–10." *TQ* 167:266–277.
Hossfeld, Frank-Lothar and Ivo Meyer
1973   *Prophet gegen Prophet: Eine Analyse der alttestamentlichen Texte zum Thema: Wahre
        und falsche Propheten.* BibB 9. Fribourg: Schweizerisches Katholisches
        Bibelwerk.
Houk, Cornelius B.
1971   "The Final Redaction of Ezekiel 10." *JBL* 90:42–54.
Houston, Walter
1993   *Purity and Monotheism: Clean and Unclean Animals in Biblical Law.* JSOTSS
        140. Sheffield: Sheffield Academic Press.
Hubbard, Robert L.
1980   "Dynamistic and Legal Language in Complaint Psalms." Ph.D. Disserta-
        tion, Claremont Graduate School.
1982a   "Dynamistic and Legal Processes in Psalm 7." *ZAW* 94:267–279.
1982b   "Is the 'Tatsphäre' always a sphere?" *JETS* 25:257–262.
1988   *The Book of Ruth.* NICOT. Grand Rapids: Eerdmans.
1997   "*Ganzheitsdenken* in the Book of Ruth." In Sun 1997:192–209.
Huffmon, H. B.
1992   "Lex Talionis." *ABD* 4:321–322.
Hugenberger, Gordon P.
1994   *Marriage as a Covenant: A Study of Biblical Law and Ethics Governing Marriage,
        Developed from the Perspective of Malachi.* SVT 52. Leiden: Brill.
Hulst, A. R.
1997   "שׁכן." *TLOT* 1327–1330.

Humbert, Paul
1933 "Die Herausforderungsformel ,hinnenî êkékâ'." *ZAW* 51:101–108.
1960 "Le substantif *toʿeba* et le verbe *tʿb* dans l'Ancien Testament." *ZAW* 72:217–237.
Hunn, Eugene
1979 "The Abominations of Leviticus Revisited: A Commentary on Anomaly in Symbolic Anthropology." In *Classifications in Their Social Context*, ed. Roy F. Ellen and David Reason, 103–116. London: Academic Press.
Hunter, Jannie
1996 *Faces of a Lamenting City: The Development and Coherence of the Book of Lamentations.* BEATAJ 39. Frankfurt: Lang.
Hurvitz, Avi
1982 *A Linguistic Study of the Relationship Between the Priestly Source and the Book of Ezekiel: A New Approach to an Old Problem.* CRB 20. Paris: Gabalda.
Jackson, Bernard S.
1975 *Essays in Jewish and Comparative Legal History.* SJLA 10. Leiden: Brill.
Jahn, Gustav
1905 *Das Buch Ezechiel auf Grund Der Septuaginta hergestalt.* Leipzig: Eduard Pfeiffer.
Janowski, Bernd
1994 "Die Tat kehrt zum Täter zurück: Offene Fragen in Umkreis des 'Tun-Ergehen-Zusammenhangs'." *ZTK* 91:247–271.
Janzen, Waldemar
1972 *Mourning Cry and Woe Oracle.* BZAW 125. Berlin: de Gruyter.
Japhet, Sara
1989 *The Ideology of the Book of Chronicles and Its Place in Biblical Thought.* BEATAJ 9. Frankfurt: Lang.
1993 *I & II Chronicles.* OTL. London: SCM.
Jarick, John
1986 "*Shalom* Refirmed: A Response to Gerleman's Theory." *LTJ* 20:2–9.
Jeffers, Ann
1996 *Magic and Divination in Ancient Palestine and Syria.* SHCANE 8. Leiden: Brill.
Jenni, Ernst
1968 *Das hebräische Piʿel: Syntaktisch-semasiologische Untersuchung einer Verbalform im Alten Testament.* Zurich: EVZ.
1992 *Die hebräischen Präpositionen.* Vol.1: *Die Präposition Beth.* Stuttgart: Kohlhammer.
1994 *Die hebräischen Präpositionen.* Vol.2: *Die Präposition Kaph.* Stuttgart: Kohlhammer.
1997 "עוֹלָם." *TLOT* 852–862.
Jenson, P. P.
1992 *Graded Holiness: A Key to the Priestly Conception of the World.* JSOTSS 106. Sheffield: JSOT.
Jeremias, Jörg
1983 *Der Prophet Hosea.* ATD 24,1. Göttingen: Vandenhoeck & Ruprecht.
Johnson, Aubrey R.
1949 *The Vitality of the Individual in the Thought of Ancient Israel.* Cardiff: University of Wales Press.
1961 *The One and the Many in the Israelites Conception of God.* Second Edition. Cardiff: University of Wales Press.
Johnstone, William
1986 "Guilt and Atonement: The Theme of 1 and 2 Chronicles." In *A Word in Season: Essays in Honour of William McKane*, ed. James D. Martin and Philip R. Davies, 113–138. JSOTSS 42. Sheffield: JSOT.
1996 "The Use of Leviticus in Chronicles." In *Reading Leviticus: A Conversation with Mary Douglas*, ed. John F. A. Sawyer, 243–255. JSOTSS 227. Sheffield: Sheffield Academic Press.

Joosten, Jan
    1996   *People and Land in the Holiness Code: An Exegetical Study of the Ideational Frame-work of the Law in Leviticus 17–26*. SVT 67. Leiden: Brill.
Joyce, Paul M.
    1989   *Divine Initiative and Human Response in Ezekiel*. JSOTSS 51. Sheffield: JSOT.
    1995   "Synchronic and Diachronic Perspectives on Ezekiel." In *Synchronic or Diachronic?: A Debate on Method in Old Testament Exegesis*, ed. Johannes C. de Moor, 115–128. *OTS* 34. Leiden: Brill.
    1996   "Dislocation and Adaptation in the Exilic Age and After." In *After the Exile: Essays in Honour of Rex Mason*, ed. John Barton and David J. Reimer, 45–58. Macon: Mercer University.
Jüngling, Hans-Winfried
    1984   "'Auge für Auge, Zahn für Zahn': Bemerkungen zu Sinn und Geltung der alttestamentlichen Talionsformeln." *ThPh* 59:1–38.
    1993   "Eid und Bund in Ez 16–17." In *Der neue Bund im Alten: Studien zur Bundes-theologie der beiden Testamente*, ed. Erich Zenger, 113–148. QD 146. Freiburg: Herder.
Kaiser, Otto
    1972   *Isaiah 1–12: A Commentary*. OTL. London: SCM.
Kalluveettil, Paul
    1982   *Declaration and Covenant: A Comprehensive Review of Covenant Formulae from the Old Testament and the Ancient Near East*. AnBib 88. Rome: Biblical Institute.
Kaminsky, Joel S.
    1995   *Corporate Responsibility in the Hebrew Bible*. JSOTSS 196. Sheffield: Sheffield Academic Press.
Kasher, Rimmon
    1998   "Anthropomorphism, Holiness and Cult: A New Look at Ezekiel 40–48." *ZAW* 110:192–208.
Kedar-Kopstein, B.
    1978   "דָּם." *TDOT* 3:234–250.
Keel, Othmar
    1994   *The Song of Songs*. CC. Minneapolis: Fortress.
Keil, Carl F.
    1876a   *Biblical Commentary on the Prophecies of Ezekiel*. Vol.1. Grand Rapids: Eerdmans, 1950. [= Reprint of *Biblical Commentary on the Prophecies of Ezekiel*. Trans. James Martin. Vol.1. Edinbrugh: T. & T. Clark, 1876.]
    1876b   *Biblical Commentary on the Prophecies of Ezekiel*. Vol.2. Grand Rapids: Eerdmans, 1950. [= Reprint of *Biblical Commentary on the Prophecies of Ezekiel*. Trans. James Martin. Vol.2. Edinbrugh: T. & T. Clark, 1876.]
Keller, Carl-A.
    1977   "Zum sogenannten Vergeltungsglauben im Proverbienbuch." In *Beiträge zur alttestamentlichen Theologie: Festschrift für Walter Zimmerli zum 70. Geburtstag*, ed. Herbert Donner, Robert Hanhart and Rudolf Smend, 223–238. Göttingen: Vandenhoeck & Ruprecht.
Kellermann, D.
    1986   "מִשְׁכָּן." *TWAT* 5:62–69.
Kelly, Brian E.
    1996   *Retribution and Eschatology in Chronicles*. JSOTSS 211. Sheffield: Sheffield Academic Press.
Kelso, J. L.
    1945   "Ezekiel's Parable of the Corroded Copper Caldron." *JBL* 64:391–393.
Kennedy, Charles A.
    1994   "The Semantic Field of the Term 'Idolatry'." In *Uncovering Ancient Stones:*

Essays in Memory of H. Neil Richardson, ed. Lewis M. Hopfe, 193–204. Winona Lake: Eisenbrauns.

Kilian, Rudolf
1963 *Literarkritische und formgeschichtliche Untersuchung des Heiligkeitsgesetzes.* BBB 19. Bonn: Hanstein.

Kiuchi, N.
1987 *The Purification Offering in the Priestly Literature: Its Meaning and Function.* JSOTSS 36. Sheffield: JSOT.

Klawans, Jonathan
1997 "The Impurity of Immorality in Ancient Judaism." *JJS* 48:1–16.

Klee, Deborah
1998 "Menstruation in the Hebrew Bible." Ph.D. Dissertation, Boston University.

Klein, Ralph W.
1979 *Israel in Exile: A Theological Intepretation.* OBT. Philadelphia: Fortress.
1988 *Ezekiel: The Prophet and His Message.* SPOT. Columbia: University of South Carolina.

Klostermann, A.
1877 "Ezechiel und das Heiligkeitsgesetz." In *Der Pentateuch: Beiträge zu seinem Verständnis und seiner Entstehungsgeschichte*, 368–418. Leipzig: Deichert'sche, 1893. [= Reprint of "Beiträge zur Entstehungsgeschichte des Pentateuchs." *ZLTK* 38 (1877) 401–445.]

Knierim, Rolf
1965 *Die Hauptbegriffe für Sünde im Alten Testament.* Gütersloh: Gerd Mohn.
1997a "מרד." *TLOT* 684–686.
1997b "פֶּשַׁע." *TLOT* 1033–1037.

Knohl, Israel
1995 *The Sanctuary of Silence: The Priestly Torah and the Holiness School.* Minneapolis: Fortress.

Koch, Klaus
1955 "Gibt es ein Vergeltungsdogma im Alten Testament?" *ZTK* 52:1–42.
1962 "Der Spruch 'Sein Blut bleibe auf seinem Haupt' und die israelitesche Auffassung vom vergossenen Blut." *VT* 12:396–416.
1972 (Ed.) *Um das Prinzip der Vergeltung in Religion und Recht des Alten Testament.* WdF 125. Darmstadt: Wissenschaftliche Buchgesellschaft.
1983 "Is There a Doctrine of Retribution in the Old Testament?" In *Theodicy in the Old Testament*, ed. James L. Crenshaw, 57–87. Philadelphia: Fortress. [= ET of 1955]

Koehler, Ludwig
1957 *Old Testament Theology.* Trans. A. S. Todd. London: Lutterworth. [= ET of *Theologie des Alten Testaments.* Tübingen: Mohr, 1953³.]

Koenen, Klaus
1994 *Heil den Gerechten—Unheil den Sündern!: Ein Beitrag zur Theologie der Prophetenbücher.* BZAW 229. Berlin: de Gruyter.

Korošec, Viktor
1931 *Hethitische Staatsverträge: Ein Beitrag zur ihrer juristischen Wertung.* Leipziger rechtswissenschaftliche Studien 60. Leipzig: Weicher.

Korpel, Marjo C. A.
1996 "Avian Spirits in Ugarit and in Ezekiel 13." In *Ugarit, Religion and Culture: Proceedings of the International Colloquium on Ugarit, Religion and Culture, Edinburgh, July 1994. Essays Presented in Honour of Professor John C. L. Gibson*, ed. N. Wyatt, W. G. E. Watson and J. B. Llyod, 99–113. UBL 12. Münster: Ugaritic-Verlag.

Kraeling, Emil G.
1966 *Commentary on the Prophets.* Vol.I: *Isaiah, Jeremiah, Ezekiel.* Camden: Nelson.

Kraetzschmar, Richard
  1900   *Das Buch Ezechiel.* HKAT III, 3/1. Göttingen: Vandenhoeck & Ruprecht.
Krašovec, Joze
  1983   *Antithetic Structure in Biblical Hebrew Poetry.* SVT 35. Leiden: Brill.
  1994   "Is There a Doctrine of 'Collective Retribution' in the Hebrew Bible?"
          HUCA 65:35–89.
  1999   *Reward, Punishment, and Forgiveness: The Thinking and Beliefs of Ancient Israel
          in the Light of Greek and Modern Views.* SVT 78. Leiden: Brill.
Kraus, Hans-Joachim
  1960   *Psalmen 1.* Neukirchen: Neukirchener Verlag.
Kruger, Paul A.
  1984   "The Hem of the Garment in Marriage. The Meaning of the Symbolic
          Gesture in Ruth 3:9 and Ezek 16:8." *JNSL* 12:79–86.
Krüger, Thomas
  1989   *Geschichtskonzepte im Ezechielbuch.* BZAW 180. Berlin: de Gruyter.
Kuntz, J. Kenneth
  1977   "The Retribution Motif in Psalmic Wisdom." *ZAW* 89:223–233.
Kutsch, Ernst
  1973   *Verheißung und Gesetz: Untersuchungen zum sogenannten "Bund" im Alten Testament.*
          BZAW 131. Berlin: de Gruyter.
  1997   "פרר." *TLOT* 1031–1032.
Kutsko, John F.
  1998   "Will the Real *selem 'elohim* Please Stand up? The Image of God in the Book
          of Ezekiel." In *SBL 1998 Seminar Papers,* 86–105. Atlanta: Scholars Press.
  2000   *Between Heaven and Earth: Divine Presence and Absence in the Book of Ezekiel.*
          BJS 7. Winona Lake: Eisenbrauns.
Laato, Antti
  1992   *Josiah and David Redivivus: The Historical Josiah and the Messianic Expectations
          of Exilic and Postexilic Times.* CBOT 33. Stockholm: Almqvist & Wiksell.
Lafont, Sophie
  1999   *Femmes, Droit et Justice dans l'Antiquité orientale: Contribution à l'étude du droit
          pénal au Proche-Orient ancien.* OBO 165. Göttingen: Vandenhoeck & Ruprecht.
Lamparter, Helmut
  1986   *Zum Wächter bestellt: Der Prophet Hesekiel.* Second Edition. BAT 21. Stuttgart:
          Calwer Verlag.
Lang, Bernhard
  1978   *Kein Aufstand in Jerusalem: Die Politik des Propheten Ezechiel.* SBB. Stuttgart:
          Katholisches Bibelwerk.
  1981   *Ezechiel: Der Prophet und das Buch.* EdF 153. Darmstadt: Wissenschaftliche
          Buchgesellschaft.
Levey, Samson H.
  1987   *The Targum of Ezekiel: Translated, with a Critical Introduction, Apparatus, and
          Notes.* The Aramaic Bible 13. Edinburgh: T. & T. Clark.
Levin, Christoph
  1985   *Die Verheißung des neuen Bundes in ihrem theologiegeschichtlichem Zusammenhang
          ausgelegt.* FRLANT 137. Göttingen: Vandenhoeck & Ruprecht.
Levine, Baruch A.
  1974   *In the Presence of the Lord: A Study of Cult and Some Cultic Terms in Ancient
          Israel.* SJLA 5. Leiden: Brill.
  1987a   "The Epilogue to the Holiness Code: A Priestly Statement on the Destiny
          of Israel." In *Judaic Perspectives on Ancient Israel,* ed. Jacob Neusner, Baruch
          A. Levine and Ernest S. Frerichs, 9–34. Philadelphia: Fortress.
  1987b   "The Language of Holiness: Perceptions of the Sacred in the Hebrew

Bible." In *Backgrounds for the Bible*, ed. Michael P. O'Connor and David
N. Freedman, 241–255. Winona Lake: Eisenbrauns.
1989   *Leviticus*. JPSTC. Philadelphia: JPS.
Levitt Kohn, Risa
1999   "Ezekiel, the Exile and the Torah." In *SBL 1999 Seminar Papers*, 501–526.
Atlanta: SBL.
Lichtenstein, Murray H.
1973   "The Poetry of Poetic Justice: A Comparative Study in Biblical Imagery."
JANES 5:255–265.
Liedke, Gerhard
1971   *Gestalt und Bezeichnung alttestamentlicher Rechtssätze: Eine formgeschichtlich-termi-
nologische Studie*. WMANT 39. Neukirchen-Vluyn: Neukirchener Verlag.
Lind, Millard C.
1996   *Ezekiel*. BCBC. Scottdale: Herald Press.
Lindars, Barnabas
1965   "Ezekiel and Individual Responsibility." *VT* 15:452–467.
Lofthouse, William F.
1907   *Ezekiel*. CB. London: Caxton.
Lohfink, Norbert
1961   "Zu Text und Form von Os 4,4–6." *Biblica* 42:303–332.
Long, Burke O.
1991   *2 Kings*. FOTL 10. Grand Rapids: Eerdmans.
Longman Dictionary of Contemporary English.
1995   Third Edition. Essex: Longman Group.
Luc, Alex
1983   "A Theology of Ezekiel: God's Name and Israel's History." *JETS*
26:137–143.
Lundquist, John M.
1983   "What is a Temple? A Preliminary Typology." In *The Quest for the Kingdom
of God: Studies in Honor of George E. Mendenhall*, ed. H. B. Hoffmon, F. A.
Spina and A. R. W. Green, 205–219. Winona Lake: Eisenbrauns.
Lust, Johan
1967   "Ez., XX, 4–26 une parodie de l'histoire religieuse d'Israel." *ETL*
43:488–527.
1981a   "Ezekiel 36–40 in the Oldest Greek Manuscript." *CBQ* 43:517–533.
1981b   "'Gathering and Return' in Jeremiah and Ezekiel." In *Le Livre de Jérémie*,
ed. P.-M. Bogaert, 119–142. BETL 54. Leuven: Leuven University.
1986   (Ed.) *Ezekiel and His Book: Textual and Literary Criticism and Their Interrelation*.
BETL 74. Leuven: Leuven University.
1987   "Ezechiel en de zure druiven." *Collationes* 17:131–138.
1994   "For I Lift up My Hand to Heaven and Swear: Deut 32:40." In *Studies
in Deuteronomy: In Honour of C. J. Labuschagne on the Occasion of His 65th
Birthday*, ed. F. García Martínez *et al.*, 155–164. SVT 53. Leiden: Brill.
Maag, Victor
1982   *Hiob: Wandlung und Verarbeitung des Problems in Novelle, Dialogdichtung und Spät-
fassungen*. FRLANT 128. Göttingen: Vandenhoeck & Ruprecht.
Maarsingh, B.
1985   *Ezechiël I*. POT. Nijkerk: Callenbach.
1988   *Ezechiël II*. POT. Nijkerk: Callenbach.
1991   *Ezechiël III*. POT. Nijkerk: Callenbach.
Maccoby, Hyam
1999   *Ritual and Morality: The Ritual Purity System and Its Place in Judaism*. Cambridge:
Cambridge University Press.

Maier, Christl
    1994   "Jerusalem als Ehebrecherin in Ezechiel 16: Zur Verwendung und Funktion
            einer biblischen Metapher." In *Feministische Hermeneutik und Erstes Testament:
            Analysen und Interpretationen*, by Hedwig Jahnow *et al.*, 85–105. Stuttgart:
            Kohlhammer.
Malul, Meir
    1990   "Adoption of Foundlings in the Bible and Mesopotamian Documents: A
            Study of Some Legal Metaphors in Ezekiel 16.1–7." *JSOT* 46:97–126.
Maon, Pierre
    1985   "Responsabilité." *DBSup* 10:357–365.
Marin-Achard, Robert
    1989   "Etude critique: Récentes travaux sur la loi du talion selon l'Ancien
            Testament: ouvrages et articles cités." *RHPR* 69:173–188.
Matties, Gordon H.
    1990   *Ezekiel 18 and the Rhetoric of Moral Discourse*. SBLDS 126. Atlanta: Scholars.
May, Herbert G.
    1956   "The Book of Ezekiel." In *Interpreter's Bible*, vol.6: *Lamentations, Ezekiel, Daniel,
            Twelve Prophets*, 39–338. New York: Abingdon Press.
    1961   "Individual Responsibility and Retribution." *HUCA* 32:107–120.
Mayes, Andrew D. H.
    1979   *Deuteronomy*. NCB. London: Marshall, Morgan & Scott.
Mayo, Jim
    1973   "Covenant Theology in Ezekiel." *Restoration Quarterly* 16:23–31.
McCarthy, Dennis J.
    1981   *Treaty and Covenant: A Study in Form in the Ancient Oriental Documents and in
            Old Testament*. Second Edition. AnBib 21A. Rome: Biblical Institute.
McGregor, Leslie J.
    1985   *The Greek Text of Ezekiel: An Examination of Its Homogeneity*. SCS 18. Atlanta:
            Scholars.
McKane, William
    1970   *Proverbs: A New Approach*. OTL. London: SCM.
McKeating, Henry
    1979   "Sanctions against Adultery in Ancient Israelite Society, with Some
            Reflections on Methodology in the Study of Old Testament Ethics." *JSOT*
            11:57–72.
    1993   *Ezekiel*. OTG. Sheffield: Sheffield Academic Press.
Mein, Andrew
    1996   "Ezekiel and the Ethics of Exile." Ph.D. Dissertation, Oxford University.
Mendenhall, George E.
    1954   "Covenant Forms in Israelite Tradition." *BA* 17:50–76.
    1955   *Law and Covenant in Israel and the Ancient Near East*. Pittsburgh: Biblical
            Colloquium.
    1960   "The Relation of the Individual to Political Society in Ancient Israel." In
            Biblical Studies in Memory of H. C. Alleman, ed. J. M. Meyers, 89–108. Locust
            Valley: J. J. Augustin.
    1962   "Covenant." *IDB* 1:714–723.
Meyer, Rudolf and Friedrich Hauck
    1965   "καθαρός κτλ." *TDNT* 3:413–431.
Miao, Albert W. T.
    1998   "The Concept of Holiness in the Book of Ezekiel." Ph.D. Dissertation,
            University of Cambridge.
Milgrom, Jacob
    1963   "The Biblical Diet Laws as an Ethical System." *Interpretation* 17:288–301.

1970   *Studies in Levitical Terminology. I. The Encroacher and the Levite: The Term*
        'Aboda. Berkeley: University of California Press.
1971   "Sin-Offering or Purification-Offering?" *VT* 21:237–239.
1976a   *Cult and Conscience: The* Asham *and the Priestly Doctrine of Repentance.* SJLA
        18. Leiden: Brill.
1976b   "Israel's Sanctuary: The Priestly 'Picture of Dorian Gray'." *RB* 83:390–399.
1989   "Rationale for Cultic Law: The Case of Impurity." *Semeia* 45:103–109.
1990a   "Ethics and Ritual: The Foundations of the Biblical Dietary Laws." In
        Religion and Law: Biblical-Judaic and Islamic Perspectives, ed. Edwin B. Firmage,
        Bernard G. Weiss and John W. Welch, 159–191. Winona Lake: Eisenbrauns.
1990b   *Numbers.* JPSTC. Philadelphia: JPS.
1991   *Leviticus 1–16.* AB 3. New York: Doubleday.
1992   "Two Biblical Hebrew Priestly Terms: *Šeqes* And *Tame'*." *Maarav* 8:107–116.
1997   "Leviticus 26 and Ezekiel." In *The Quest for Context and Meaning: Studies in*
        Biblical Intertextuality in Honor of James A. Sanders, ed. Craig A. Evans and
        Shemaryahu Talmon, 57–62. BIS 28. Leiden: Brill.
2000a   "Impurity is Miasma: A Response to Hyam Maccoby." *JBL* 119:729–733.
2000b   *Leviticus 17–22.* AB 3A. New York: Doubleday.
Milgrom, Jacob and David P. Wright
1986   "נִדָּה." *TWAT* 5:250–253.
Miller, John W.
1955   *Das Verhältnis Jeremias und Hesekiels sprachlich und theologisch untersucht met beson-*
        derer Berücksichtugung der Prosareden Jeremias. GTB 28. Assen: Van Gorcum.
Miller, Patrick D., Jr.
1978   *Genesis 1–11: Studies in Structure and Theme.* JSOTSS 8. Sheffield: JSOT.
1982   *Sin and Judgment in the Prophets: A Stylistic and Theological Analysis.* SBLMS
        27. Chico: Scholars.
1984   "Sin and Judgment in Jeremiah 34:17–19." *JBL* 103/4:611–613.
Mills, Mary E.
1998   *Images of God in the Old Testament.* London: Cassell.
Mosis, Rudolf
1978   *Das Buch Ezechiel.* Vol.1: *Kap. 1,1–20,44.* GS 8/1. Düsseldorf: Patmos.
Muilenburg, J.
1962   "Holiness." *IDB* 2:616–625.
Mulder, M. J.
1990   "1 Koningen 8:31 en 32." *JNSL* 16:107–114.
Müller, H.-P.
1997   "קדשׁ." *TLOT* 1103–1118.
Muraoka, T.
1985   *Emphatic Words and Structures in Biblical Hebrew.* Jerusalem: Magnes.
Murphy, Roland E.
1990   *The Song of Songs.* Hermeneia. Minneapolis: Fortress.
Murray, D. F.
1987   "The Rhetoric of Disputation: Re-examination of a Prophetic Genre."
        JSOT 38:95–121.
Nay, Reto
1999   *Jahwe im Dialog: Kommunikationsanalytische Untersuchung von Ez 14,1–11 unter*
        Berücksichtigung des dialogischen Rahmens in Ez 8–11 und Ez 20. AnBib 141.
        Rome: Pontifical Biblical Institute.
Neiman, David
1948   "*PGR*: A Canaanite Cult-Object in the Old Testament." *JBL* 67:55–60.
Neusner, Jacob
1973   *The Idea of Purity in Ancient Judaism.* SJLA 1. Leiden: Brill.

Newsom, Carol A.
 1984 "A Maker of Metaphors—Ezekiel's Oracles Against Tyre." *Interpretation* 38:151–164.
Newton, Michael
 1985 *The Concept of Purity at Qumran and in the Letters of Paul.* SNTSMS 53. Cambridge: Cambridge University Press.
Neyrey, Jerome H.
 1988 "Unclean, Common, Polluted, and Taboo: A Short Reading Guide." *Forum* 4:72–82.
Nicholson, Ernest W.
 1986 *God and His People: Covenant and Theology in the Old Testament.* Oxford: Clarendon.
Niehr, H.
 1995 "שָׁפַט." *TWAT* 8:420–428.
Nielsen, Kirsten
 1985 "Le choix contre le droit dans le livre de Ruth. De l'aire de battage au tribunal." *VT* 35:201–212.
 1986 *Incense in Ancient Israel.* SVT 38. Leiden: Brill.
Noordtzij, A.
 1957 *De Profeet Ezechiël.* KVHS. Vol.1. Second Edition. Kampen: Kok.
Noth, Martin
 1966 "The Laws in the Pentateuch: Their Assumptions and Meaning." In *The Laws in the Pentateuch and Other Studies*, 1–107. Trans. D. R. Ap-Thomas. Edinburgh: Oliver & Boyd. [= ET of *Die Gesetz im Pentateuch (Ihre Voraussetzungen und ihr Sinn)*. Halle: Niemeyer, 1940.]
Ogden, G. S.
 1992 "*Idem per idem*: Its Use and Meaning." *JSOT* 53:107–120.
Ohnesorge, Stefan
 1991 *Jahwe gestaltet sein Volk neu: Zur Sicht der Zukunft Israels nach Ez 11,14–21; 20,1–44; 36,16–38; 37,1–14.15–28.* FzB 64. Würzburg: Echter Verlag.
Otto, Eckart
 1991 "Zur Geschichte des Talions im Alten Orient und Israel." In *Ernten, was man sät: Festschrift für Klaus Koch zu seinem 65. Geburtstag*, ed. Dwight R. Daniels, Uwe Gleßmer and Martin Rösel, 101–130. Neukirchen-Vluyn: Neukirchener Verlag.
Ottoson, Magnus
 1977 "גְּבוּל." *TDOT* 2:361–366.
Pagolu, Augustine
 1998 *The Religion of the Patriarchs.* JSOTSS 277. Sheffield: Sheffield Academic Press.
Parpola, S. and K. Watanabe
 1988 *Neo-Assyrian Treaties and Loyalty Oaths.* Helsinki: Helsinki University.
Parunak, Henry van Dyke
 1978 "Structural Studies in Ezekiel." Ph.D. Dissertation, Harvard University.
 1980 "The Literary Architecture of Ezekiel's *Mar'ôt 'elohîm*." *JBL* 99:61–74.
Paschen, Wilfried
 1970 *Rein und Unrein: Untersuchung zur biblischen Wortgeschichte.* SANT 24. Munich: Kösel.
Paton, Lewis B.
 1896 "The Holiness-Code and Ezekiel." *PRR* 7:98–115.
Paul, Shalom M.
 1970 *Studies in the Book of the Covenant in the Light of Cuneiform and Biblical Law.* SVT 18. Leiden: Brill.
 1990 "Biblical Analogues to Middle Assyrian Law." In *Religion and Law: Biblical-Judaic and Islamic Perspectives*, ed. Edwin B. Firmage, Bernard G. Weiss and John W. Welch, 333–350. Winona Lake: Eisenbrauns.

Pau, E.
1960/61   "Studien zum Vergeltungsproblem der Psalmen." *SBFLA* 11:56–112.
Peels, Hendrik G. L.
1995   *The Vengeance of God: The Meaning of the Root NQM and the Function of the
          NQM-Texts in the Context of Divine Revelation in the Old Testament.* OTS 31.
          Leiden: Brill.
Perles, Felix
1911/12   "A Miscellany of Lexical and Textual Notes on the Bible." *JQR* 2:97–132.
Phillips, Anthony
1980   "Uncovering the Father's Skirt." *VT* 30:38–43.
Plöger, Josef G.
1967   *Literarkritische, formgeschichtliche und stilkritische Untersuchungen zum Deuteronomium.*
          BBB 26. Bonn: Hanstein.
Podella, Thomas
1997   "Reinheit." *TRE* 28:473–483.
Pohlmann, Karl-Friedrich
1992   *Ezechielstudien: Zur Redaktionsgeschichte des Buches und zur Frage nach den
          ältesten Texten.* BZAW 202. Berlin: de Gruyter.
1996   *Der Prophet Hesekiel (Ezechiel): Kapitel 1–19.* ATD 22,1. Göttingen: Van-
          denhoeck & Ruprecht.
Pope, Marvin H.
1977   *Song of Songs.* AB 7C. Garden City: Doubleday.
1995   "Mixed Marriage Metaphor in Ezekiel 16." In *Fortunate the Eyes That
          See: Essays in Honor of David Noel Freedman in Celebration of His Seventieth
          Birthday,* ed. Astrid B. Beck *et al.,* 384–399. Grand Rapids: Eerdmans.
Porter, J. R.
1965   "The Legal Aspects of the Concept of 'Corporate Responsibility' in
          the Old Testament." *VT* 15:361–380.
1976   *Leviticus.* CBC. Cambrige: Cambridge University Press.
Preuß, H. D.
1978   "גלולים." *TDOT* 3:1–5.
Procksch, Otto
1964   "ἅγιος κτλ. C. The History of the Term in the OT." *TDNT* 1:91–97.
Propp, William H.
1990   "The Meaning of *Tapel* in Ezekiel." *ZAW* 102:404–408.
Rabinowitz, Jacob J.
1957   "Demotic Papyri of the Ptolemaic Period and Jewish Sources." *VT*
          7:398–400.
1959   "An Additional Note on בראש." *VT* 9:209–210.
Raitt, Thomas M.
1977   *A Theology of Exile: Judgment/Deliverance in Jeremiah and Ezekiel.* Philadelphia:
          Fortress.
Random House Dictionary of the English Language.
1987   Second Edition. New York: Random House.
Rankin, O. S.
1936   *Israel's Wisdom Literature: Its Bearing on Theology and the History of Religion.*
          Edinburgh: T. & T. Clark.
Redpath, Henry A.
1907   *The Book of the Prophet Ezekiel.* WestC. London: Methuen & Co.
Renaud, Bernard
1986   "L'alliance éternelle d'Ez 16,59–63 et l'alliance nouvelle de Jér 31:31–34."
          In Lust 1986:335–339.
Rendtorff, Rolf
1993   "Ezekiel 20 and 36:16ff. in the Framework of the Composition of the
          Book." In *Canon and Theology,* 190–195. OBT. Minneapolis: Fortress.

[= ET of "Ez 20 und 36,16ff im Rahmen der Komposition des Buches Ezechiel." In Lust 1986:260–265.]

Renner, J. T. E.
1985   "Thoughts of Peace and Not of War." *LTJ* 19:65–72.

Renz, Thomas
1999   *The Rhetorical Function of the Book of Ezekiel.* SVT 76. Leiden: Brill.

Reventlow, Henning G.
1959   "Die Völker als Jahwes Zeugen bei Ezechiel." *ZAW* 71:33–43.
1960   "Sein Blut komme über sein Haupt." *VT* 10:311–327.
1961   *Das Heiligkeitsgesetz formgeschichtlich untersucht.* Neukirchen: Neukirchener Verlag.
1962   *Wächter über Israel: Ezechiel und seine Tradition.* BZAW 82. Berlin: Töpelmann.

Reventlow, Henning G. and Yair Hoffman
1992   (Ed.) *Justice and Righteousness: Biblical Themes and Their Influence.* JSOTSS 137. Sheffield: JSOT.

Ringgren, Helmer
1948   *The Prophetical Conception of Holiness.* UUÅ 12. Uppsala: A.-B. Lundequistska Bokhandeln.
1997   "מָעַל." *TDOT* 8:460–463.

Robinson, H. Wheeler
1911   *The Christian Doctrine of Man.* Edinburgh: T. & T. Clark.
1936   "The Hebrew Conception of Corporate Personality." In 1981:25–44. [= Reprint of *Werden und Wesen des Alten Testaments: Vorträge gehalten auf der Internationalen Tagung alttestamentlicher Forscher zu Göttingen vom 4.–10. September 1935*, 49–62. BZAW 66. Berlin: Töpelmann, 1936.]
1937   "The Group and the Individual in Israel." In 1981:45–60. [= Reprint of *The Individual in East and West*, ed. Ernest R. Hughes. London: Oxford University Press, 1937.]
1981   *Corporate Personality in Ancient Israel.* Second Edition. Edinburgh: T. & T. Clark.

Robinson, J.
1976   *The Second Book of Kings.* CBC. Cambridge: Cambridge University Press.

Rogerson, John W.
1970   "The Hebrew Conception of Corporate Personality: A Re-examination." *JTS* 21:1–16.
1977   "The Old Testament View of Nature: Some Preliminary Questions." *OTS* 20:67–84.
1978   *Anthropology and the Old Testament.* Sheffield: JSOT, 1984. [= Reprint of *Anthropology and the Old Testament.* Oxford: Blackwell, 1978.]
1999   "Frontiers and Borders in the Old Testament." In *In Search of True Wisdom: Essays in Old Testament Interpretation in Honour of Ronald E. Clements*, ed. Edward Ball, 116–126. JSOTSS 300. Sheffield: Sheffield Academic Press.

Rooker, Mark F.
1990   *Biblical Hebrew in Transition: The Language of the Book of Ezekiel.* JSOTSS 90. Sheffield: JSOT.

Roth, Martha T.
1989   *Babylonian Marriage Agreements: 7th–3rd Centuries B.C.* AOAT 222. Kevelaer: Butzon & Bercker; Neukirchen-Vluyn: Neukirchener Verlag.

Rudolph, Wilhelm
1958   *Jeremia.* HBAT 1,12. Tübingen: Mohn.
1971   *Joel-Amos-Obadja-Jona.* KAT XIII/2. Gütersloh: Mohn.

Ruppert, L.
1989   "פרר." *TWAT* 6:773–780.

Ruprecht, E.
1997   "פלט." *TLOT* 986–990.

Saggs, H. W. F.
    1974   "External Souls in the Old Testament." *JSS* 19:1–12.
Sanmartin-Ascaso, J.
    1978   "דּוֹד." *TDOT* 3:143–156.
Sasson, Jack M.
    1989   *Ruth: A New Translation with a Philological Commentary and a Formalist-Folklorist Interpretation.* Second Edition. The Biblical Seminar. Sheffield; JSOT.
Sauer, G.
    1997   "קִנְאָה." *TLOT* 1145–1147.
Sawyer, J. F. and H.-J. Fabry
    1990   "יֵשַׁע." *TDOT* 6:441–463.
Scharbert, Josef
    1960   "Das Verbum PQD in der Theologie des Alten Testaments." In Koch 1972:278–299. [= Reprint of *BZ* 4 (1960) 209–226.]
    1961   "SLM im Alten Testament." In Koch 1972:300–324. [= Reprint of *Lex tua veritas. Festschrift für Hubert Junker zur Vollendung des 70. Lebensjahres am 8. Aug. 1961. Dargeboten von Kollegen, Freunden und Schülern*, ed. Heinrich Gross and Franz Mussner, 209–229. Trier: Paulinus Verlag, 1961.]
    1977   "אָלָה." *TDOT* 1:261–266.
Schenker, Adrian
    1981   "Saure Trauben ohne stumpfe Zaehne: Bedeutung und Tragweite von Ez 18 und 33.10–20 oder ein Kapitel alttestamentlicher Moraltheologie." In *Mélanges Dominique Barthélemy: Etudes bibliques offertes a l'occasion de son 60° anniversaire*, ed. Pierre Casetti, Othmar Keel and Adrian Schenker, 449–470. OBO 38. Göttingen: Vandenhoeck & Ruprecht.
Schmidt, Martin A.
    1950   "Zur Komposition des Buches Hesekiel." *TZ* 6:81–98.
Schoneveld, J.
    1969   "Ezekiel xiv 1–8." *OTS* 15:193–204.
Schoors, Anton
    1973   *I am God Your Saviour: A Form-Critical Study of the Main Genres in Is. XL–LV.* SVT 24. Leiden: Brill.
Schottroff, Willy
    1964   *"Gedenken" im Alten Orient und im Alten Testament: Die Wurzel zakar im semitischen Sprachkreis.* WMANT 15. Neukirchen-Vluyn: Neukirchener Verlag.
    1997   "זכר." *TLOT* 381–388.
Schultz, Richard
    1996   "שׁפט." *NIDOTTE* 4:213–220.
Schumpp, Meinrad
    1942   *Das Buch Ezechiel.* HBK X/1. Freiburg: Herders.
Schwienhorst, L.
    1998   "מָרַד." *TDOT* 9:1–5.
Sedlmeier, Franz
    1990   *Studien zu Komposition und Theologie von Ezechiel 20.* SBB 21. Stuttgart: Katholisches Bibelwerk.
Seebass, H.
    1989   "פֶּשַׁע." *TWAT* 6:791–810.
Shipley, Joseph T.
    1955   (Ed.) *Dictionary of World Literary Terms: Criticism, Forms, Technique.* London: George Allen & Unwin.
Siebesma, P. A.
    1991   *The Function of the Niph'al in Biblical Hebrew in Relation to Other Passive-Reflexive Verbal Stems and to the Pu'al and Hoph'al in Particular.* SSN 28. Assen: Van Gorcum.

Siedlecki, Armin
  1991   "Purity and Power: A Rhetorical Study of the Ideology of Purity and Defilement in the Book of Ezekiel." M.A. Thesis, Wilfrid Laurier University.
Simian, Horacio
  1974   *Die theologische Nachgeschichte der Prophetie Ezechiels: Form- und traditionskritische Untersuchung zu Ez 6; 35; 36.* FzB 14. Würzburg: Echter Verlag.
Skinner, John
  1895   *The Book of Ezekiel.* ExpB. London: Hodder & Stoughton.
Smend, Rudolf
  1880   *Der Prophet Ezechiel.* Second Edition. KeHAT 8. Leipzig: Hirzel.
Smith, Daniel L.
  1989   *The Religion of the Landless: The Social Context of the Babylonian Exile.* Bloomington: Meyer-Stone Books.
Smith, William Robertson
  1894   *The Religion of the Semites: The Fundamental Institutions.* London: Black.
Snaith, Norman H.
  1944   *The Distinctive Ideas of the Old Testament.* London: Epworth.
  1969   *Leviticus and Numbers.* NCB. London: Nelson.
Söderblom, Nathan
  1913   "Holiness (General and Primitive)." *ERE* 6:731–741.
Soggin, J. A.
  1997a   "מֶלֶךְ." *TLOT* 672–680.
  1997b   "רעה." *TLOT* 1246–1248.
Soler, Jean
  1979   "The Semiotics of Food in the Bible." In *Food and Drink in History: Selections from the Annales Economies, Societés, Civilisations,* Vol.V, ed. Robert Forster and Orest Ranum, 126–138. Baltimore: Johns Hopkins University Press.
Soulen, Richard N.
  1981   *Handbook of Biblical Criticism.* Second Edition. Atlanta: Knox.
Sperber, Alexander
  1962   (Ed.) *The Bible in Aramaic Based on Old Manuscripts and Printed Texts.* Vol.III: *The Latter Prophets According to Targum Jonathan.* Leiden: Brill.
Spottorno, M. V.
  1981   "La omisión de Ez. 36.23b-38 y la transposición de capitulos en el papiro 967." *Emerita* 50:93–99.
Sprank, Siegfried and Kurt Wiese
  1926   *Studien zu Ezechiel und dem Buch der Richter.* BWANT 40. Stuttgart: Kohlhammer.
Stade, Bernhard
  1905   *Biblische Theologie des Alten Testaments.* Vol.1. Tübingen: Mohr.
Stalker, D. M. G.
  1968   *Ezekiel: Introduction and Commentary.* TBC. London: SCM Press.
Steck, Odil H.
  1989   "Zion als Gelände und Gestalt: Überlegungen zur Wahrnehmung Jerusalems als Stadt und Frau im Alten Testament." *ZTK* 86:261–281.
Steingrimsson, S.
  1980   "זמם." *TDOT* 4:87–90.
Steinmann, Jean
  1953   *Le prophète Ézéchiel et les débuts de l'Exil.* LD 13. Paris: Cerf.
Stendebach, F. J.
  1995   "שָׁלוֹם." *TWAT* 8:12–46.
Stevenson, Kalinda R.
  1996   *The Vision of Transformation: The Territorial Rhetoric of Ezekiel 40–48.* SBLDS 154. Atlanta: Scholars.

Stienstra, Nelly
  1993   *YHWH is the Husband of His People: Analysis of a Biblical Metaphor with Special Reference to Translation*. Kampen: Kok Pharos.
Stuart, Douglas
  1989   *Ezekiel*. CCSOT 18. Dallas: Word.
Sun, Henry T. C.
  1992   "Holiness Code." *ABD* 3:254–257.
  1997   *et al.* (Ed.) *Problems in Biblical Theology: Essays in Honor of Rolf Knierim*. Grand Rapids: Eerdmans.
Swanepoel, M. G.
  1993   "Ezekiel 16: Abandoned Child, Bride Adorned Or Unfaithful Wife?" In *Among the Prophets: Language, Image and Structure in the Prophetic Writings*, ed. Philip R. Davies and David J. A. Clines, 84–104. JSOTSS 144. Sheffield: JSOT.
Talmon, Shemaryahu
  1978   "הר." *TDOT* 3:427–447.
  1997   "מדבר." *TDOT* 8:87–118.
Talmon, Shemaryahu and Michael Fishbane
  1975/76   "The Structuring of Biblical Books: Studies in the Book of Ezekiel." *ASTI* 10:129–153.
Taylor, John B.
  1969   *Ezekiel: An Introduction and Commentary*. TOTC. Leicester: Inter-Varsity.
Taylor, J. Glen
  1993   *Yahweh and the Sun: Biblical and Archaeological Evidence for Sun Worship in Ancient Israel*. JSOTSS 111. Sheffield: JSOT.
Thiel, Winfried
  1970   "*HEFER BᴱRȋT*: Zum Bundbrechen im Alten Testament." *VT* 20:214–229.
Thompson, J. A.
  1980   *The Book of Jeremiah*. NICOT. Grand Rapids: Eerdmans.
Tidiman, Brian
  1985   *Le Livre d'Ezéchiel*. Vol.1. CEB 4. Vaux-sur-Seine: EDIFAC.
  1987   *Le Livre d'Ezéchiel*. Vol.2. CEB 6. Vaux-sur-Seine: EDIFAC.
Tigay, Jeffrey H.
  1996   *Deuteronomy*. JPSTC. Philadelphia: JPS.
Toombs, L. E.
  1962   "Clean and Unclean." *IDB* 1:641–648.
Towner, W. S.
  1971   "Retributional Theology in the Apocalyptic Setting." *USQR* 26:203–214.
  1976   "Retribution." In *IDB*, Supp. Vol., ed. Keith Crim, 742–744. Nashville: Abingdon.
Toy, C. H.
  1899   *The Book of the Prophet Ezekiel*. London: James Clarke & Co.
Tromp, N.
  1986   "The Paradox of Ezekiel's Prophetic Mission. Towards a Semiotic Approach of Ezekiel 3,22–27." In Lust 1986:201–213.
Tsevat, Matitiahu
  1959   "The Neo-Assyrian and Neo-Babylonian Vassal Oaths and the Prophet Ezekiel." *JBL* 78:199–204.
  1961   "Studies in the Book of Samuel. I: Interpetation of I Sam. 2:27–36." *HUCA* 32:191–216.
Tucker, Gene M.
  1965   "Covenant Forms and Contract Forms." *VT* 15:487–503.
  1997   "Sin and 'Judgment' in the Prophets." In Sun 1997:373–388.

Tuell, Steven S.
 1992   *The Law of the Temple in Ezekiel 40–48.* HSM 49. Atlanta: Scholars Press.
Tullock, John H.
 1994   "Retribution." In *The Lutterworth Dictionary of the Bible,* ed. Watson E. Mills,
       757–758. Third Edition. Cambridge: Lutterworth.
Uehlinger, Christoph
 1987   "'Zeichne eine Stadt . . . und belagere sie!' Bild und Wort in einer
       Zeichenhandlung Ezechiels gegen Jerusalem (Ez 4f)." In *Jerusalem: Texts-
       Bilder-Steine, in Namen von Mitgliedern und Freunden des Biblischen Instituts der
       Universität Freiburg Schweiz zum 100. Geburtstag von Hildi + Othmar Keel-Leu,*
       ed. Max Küchler and Christoph Uehlinger, 111–200. NTOA 6. Freiburg:
       Universitätsverlag.
Uffenheimer, Benjamin
 1992   "Theodicy and Ethics in the Prophecy of Ezekiel." In Reventlow and
       Hoffman 1992:200–227.
Van den Born, A.
 1954   *Ezechiël.* BOT. Roermond: J. J. Romen & Zonen.
Van der Horst, Pieter W.
 1992   "I Gave Them Laws That Were Not Good." In *Sacred History and Sacred
       Texts in Early Judaism: A Symposium in Honour of A. S. van der Woude,* ed. Jan
       N. Bremmer and Florentino García Martínez, 94–118. CBET 5. Kampen:
       Kok Pharos.
Van der Toorn, Karel
 1985   *Sin and Sanction in Israel and Mesopotamia: A Comparative Study.* SSN 22.
       Assen/Maastricht: Van Gorcum.
van Oyen, Hendrik
 1967   *Ethik des Alten Testaments.* Gütersloh: Mohn.
Vawter, Bruce and Leslie J. Hoppe
 1991   *A New Heart: A Commentary on the Book of Ezekiel.* ITC. Grand Rapids:
       Eerdmans.
Viberg, Åke
 1992   *Symbols of Law: A Contextual Analysis of Legal Symbolic Acts in the Old Testament.*
       CBOT 34. Stockholm: Almqvist & Wiksell.
Vieweyer, Dieter
 1993   *Die literarischen Beziehungen zwischen den Bücher Jeremia und Ezechiel.* BEATAJ
       26. Frankfurt: Lang.
Vogt, Ernst
 1981   *Untersuchungen zum Buch Ezechiel.* AnBib 95. Rome: Biblical Institute.
Von Orelli, C.
 1888   *Das Buch Ezechiel und die zwölf kleinen Propheten.* KKHS A5. Nördlingen:
       Verlag der C. H. Beck'schen Buchhandlung.
Von Rad, Gerhard
 1962   *Old Testament Theology.* Trans. D. M. G. Stalker. Vol.1. Edinburgh: Oliver
       and Boyd. [= ET of *Theologie des Alten Testaments.* Vol.1. Munich: Chr.
       Kaiser Verlag, 1957.]
 1965   *Old Testament Theology.* Trans. D. M. G. Stalker. Vol.2. Edinburgh: Oliver
       and Boyd. [= ET of *Theologie des Alten Testaments.* Vol.2. Munich: Chr.
       Kaiser Verlag, 1960.]
 1972   *Wisdom in Israel.* Nashville: Abingdon. [= ET of *Weisheit in Israel.* Neukirchen-
       Vluyn: Neukirchener Verlag, 1970.]
 1977   "εἰρήνη κτλ. B. שָׁלוֹם in the OT." *TDNT* 2:402–406.
Von Wilpert, Gero
 1989   *Sachwörterbuch der Literatur.* Seventh Edition. Stuttgart: Kröner.

Wächter, L.
1967   *Der Tod im Alten Testament*. Stuttgart: Calwer.
Webster's Third International Dictionary.
1961   Springfield: Merriam.
Weinfeld, Moshe
1972   *Deuteronomy and the Deuteronomic School*. Oxford: Clarendon.
1977   "בְּרִית." *TDOT* 2:253–279.
Weiser, Artur
1955   *Das Buch des Propheten Jeremia, Kap. 25:15–52:34*. ATD 21. Göttingen:
        Vandenhoeck & Ruprecht.
1962   *The Psalms*. OTL. London: SCM.
Weismann, Jakob
1972   "Talion und öffentliche Strafe im mosaischen Rechte." In Koch 1972:325–
        406.
Wells, Jo Bailey
2000   *God's Holy People: A Theme in Biblical Theology*. JSOTSS 305. Sheffield:
        Sheffield Academic Press.
Wenham, Gordon J.
1979   *The Book of Leviticus*. NICOT. Grand Rapids: Eerdmans.
1983   "Why Does Sexual Intercourse Defile (Lev 15 18)?" *ZAW* 95:432–434.
1997   *Numbers*. OTG. Sheffield: Sheffield Academic Press.
Westbrook, Raymond
1988   *Studies in Biblical and Cuneiform Law*. CRB 26. Paris: Gabalda.
1990   "Adultery in Ancient Near Eastern Law." *RB* 97:542–580.
1991   *Property and the Family in Biblical Law*. JSOTSS 113. Sheffield: Sheffield
        Academic Press.
Westermann, Claus
1967   *Basic Forms of Prophetic Speech*. Trans. Hugh C. White. London: Lutterworth.
1991   *Prophetic Oracles of Salvation in the Old Testament*. Edinburgh: T. & T. Clark.
Wevers, John W.
1969   *Ezekiel*. NCB. Grand Rapids: Eerdmans, 1982. [= Reprint of *Ezekiel*.
        London: Thomas Nelson and Sons, 1969.]
Wildberger, Hans
1991   *Isaiah 1–12: A Commentary*. CC. Minneapolis: Fortress.
Williamson, Hugh G. M.
1982   *1 and 2 Chronicles*. NCB. Grand Rapids: Eerdmans.
Willmes, Bernd
1984   *Die sogenannte Hirtenallegorie Ez 34: Studien zum Bild des Hirten im Alten Testament*.
        BBET 19. Frankfurt: Lang.
1986   "Differenzierende Prophezeiungen in Ez 34." In Lust 1986:248–254.
Wilson, E. Jan
1994   *"Holiness" and "Purity" in Mesopotamia*. AOAT 237. Kevelaer: Butzon &
        Bercker.
Wold, D. J.
1979   "The *Kareth* Penalty in P: Rationale and Cases." In *SBL Seminar Papers
        1979*, ed. P. J. Achtemeier, 1–46. Missoula: Scholars.
Wolff, Hans W.
1934   "Die Begründungen der prophetischen Heils- und Unheilssprüche." *ZAW*
        11:1–22.
1974   *Hosea*. Trans. Gary Stansell. Hermeneia. Philadelphia: Fortress. [= ET of
        Dodekapropheten 1 Hosea. BKAT XIV/1. Neukirchen-Vluyn: Neukirchener
        Verlag, 1965.]
Wood, A. S.
1975   "Holiness." *ZPEB* 3:173–183.

Woudstra, Marten H.
  1971   "The Everlasting Covenant in Ezekiel 16:59–63." *CTJ* 6:22–48.
Wright, David P.
  1985   "Purification from Corpse-Contamination in Numbers xxxi 19–24." *VT* 35:213–223.
  1987   *The Disposal of Impurity: Elimination Rites in the Bible and in Hittite and Mesopotamian Literature.* SBLDS 101. Atlanta: Scholars Press.
  1988   "Two Types of Impurity in the Priestly Writings of the Bible." *Koroth* 9:180–193.
  1991   "The Spectrum of Priestly Impurity." In *Priesthood and Cult in Ancient Israel*, ed. Gary A. Anderson and Saul M. Olyan, 150–181. JSOTSS 125. Sheffield: Sheffield Academic Press.
  1992   "Holiness, Old Testament." *ABD* 3:237–249.
  1994   "Review of *Graded Holiness: A Key to the Priestly Conception of the World*." *Hebrew Studies* 35:160–163.
  1999   "Holiness in Leviticus and Beyond: Differing Perspectives." *Interpretation* 53:351–364.
Wright, David P. and Richard N. Jones
  1992   "Leprosy." *ABD* 4:277–282.
Xella, Paolo
  1991   *Baal Hammon: Recherches sur l'identité et l'histoire d'un dieu phénico-punique.* Rome: Consiglio Nazionale delle Ricerche.
Youngblood, Ronald
  1978   "A New Look at Three Old Testament Roots for 'Sin'." In *Biblical and Near Eastern Studies: Essays in Honor of William Sanford LaSor*, ed. Gary A. Tuttle, 201–205. Grand Rapids: Eerdmans.
Zach, Wolfgang
  1986   *Poetic Justice: Theorie und Geschichte einer literarischen Doktrin: Begriff—Idee—Komödienkonzeption.* BAZeP 26. Tübingen: Niemeyer.
Zehnder, Markus P.
  1999   *Wegmetaphorik im Alten Testament: Eine semantische Untersuchung der alttestamentlichen und altorientalischen Weg-Lexeme mit besonderer Berücksichtigung ihrer metaphorischen Verwendung.* BZAW 268. Berlin: de Gruyter.
Zerafa, P.
  1973   "Retribution in the Old Testament." *Angelicum* 50:464–494.
Ziegler, Joseph
  1948   *Ezechiel.* EB 6. Würzburg: Echter Verlag.
Zimmerli, Walther
  1954   "Die Eigenart der prophetischen Rede des Ezechiel: Ein Beitrag zum Problem an Hand von Ez. 14,1–11." *ZAW* 66:1–26.
  1965   "The Special Form- and Traditio-Historical Character of Ezekiel's Prophecy." *VT* 15:515–527.
  1974   "Verkündigung und Sprache der Botschaft Jesajas." In *Studien zur alttestamentlichen Theologie und Prophetie: Gesammelte Aufsätze II*, 73–87. ThB 51. München: Kaiser.
  1979   *Ezekiel 1.* Hermeneia. Philadelphia: Fortress. [= ET of *Ezechiel.* BKAT XIII. Vol.1. Neukirchen-Vluyn: Neukirchener, 1969.]
  1983   *Ezekiel 2.* Hermeneia. Philadelphia: Fortress. [= ET of *Ezechiel.* BKAT XIII. Vol.2. Neukirchen-Vluyn: Neukirchener, 1969.]
Zink, J. K.
  1967   "Uncleanness and Sin: A Study of Job xiv 4 and Psalm li 7." *VT* 17:354–361.
Zobel, H.-J.
  1986   "מִשְׁפָּחָה." *TWAT* 5:86–93.

INDEX OF AUTHORS CITED

INDEX OF BIBLICAL TEXTS

Numbers	
3:31	97
4:18	164
5:2–4	136
5:7	233
5:13	147
5:15	221
6:13–20	125
9:13	164
10:33	192
11:1	171
12:10–15	127
13	192
15:30–31	164
16–17	166, 170
16:40	142
18:1–5	128
19	127, 174
19:2	174
19:13	128, 164, 175, 187
19:14–16	136
19:18	137, 174, 175
19:18–19	174
19:20	164, 175, 177, 187
20:20	69
20:23	210
22:36	210
23:1	97
23:4	97
23:14	97
23:21–22	70
23:29	97
25:12	107
31	174
31:21–24	173, 174, 177
31:22–23aα	174
31:23	176
31:23aβ	174
31:23b	174
33:44	209
35:33	146
35:33–34	128, 155
35:34	145
Deuteronomy	
1:33	192
2:4	209
3:24	69
4:28	67, 68
4:34	69
5:4	71
5:15	69
5:18	147
6:21	69
7:5	97
7:8	69
7:9	60
7:12	60
7:19	69
7:20	11
7:25–26	140
8:2	11
8:3	11
8:5	11
8:18	47
9:4–5	182
9:4–6	11
9:9	69
9:26	69
11:2	69
12:2	96, 97
12:3	97
13:16–17	56
19:21	227
21:1	98
21:13	44
21:23	136, 146
22:9–11	134
22:20–24	51
22:21	56
22:22	55
22:22–27	51
22:23–24	56
22:28–29	51
23:9	134
23:13–15	134
25:1	240
25:9	206
25:11	227
26:8	69
28	79
28:36	67, 68
28:53–57	92
28:64	67, 68
29:11	43, 46
29:13	46
29:16	67, 68, 141
29:20	46
32:23	94
32:23–24	94
34:10	71
34:12	69
Joshua	
7	165
8:29	136
10:26–27	136
11:16	96

SUPPLEMENTS TO VETUS TESTAMENTUM

2. POPE, M.H. *El in the Ugaritic texts*. 1955. ISBN 90 04 04000 5

3. *Wisdom in Israel and in the Ancient Near East*. Presented to Harold Henry Rowley by the Editorial Board of Vetus Testamentum in celebration of his 65th birthday, 24 March 1955. Edited by M. NOTH and D. WINTON THOMAS. 2nd reprint of the first (1955) ed. 1969. ISBN 90 04 02326 7

4. *Volume du Congrès* [International pour l'étude de l'Ancien Testament]. Strasbourg 1956. 1957. ISBN 90 04 02327 5

8. BERNHARDT, K.-H. *Das Problem der alt-orientalischen Königsideologie im Alten Testament*. Unter besonderer Berücksichtigung der Geschichte der Psalmenexegese dargestellt und kritisch gewürdigt. 1961. ISBN 90 04 02331 3

9. *Congress Volume*, Bonn 1962. 1963. ISBN 90 04 02332 1

11. DONNER, H. *Israel unter den Völkern*. Die Stellung der klassischen Propheten des 8. Jahrhunderts v. Chr. zur Aussenpolitik der Könige von Israel und Juda. 1964. ISBN 90 04 02334 8

12. REIDER, J. *An Index to Aquila*. Completed and revised by N. Turner. 1966. ISBN 90 04 02335 6

13. ROTH, W.M.W. *Numerical sayings in the Old Testament*. A form-critical study. 1965. ISBN 90 04 02336 4

14. ORLINSKY, H.M. *Studies on the second part of the Book of Isaiah*. — The so-called 'Servant of the Lord' and 'Suffering Servant' in Second Isaiah. — SNAITH, N.H. Isaiah 40-66. A study of the teaching of the Second Isaiah and its consequences. Repr. with additions and corrections. 1977. ISBN 90 04 05437 5

15. *Volume du Congrès* [International pour l'étude de l'Ancien Testament]. Genève 1965. 1966. ISBN 90 04 02337 2

17. *Congress Volume*, Rome 1968. 1969. ISBN 90 04 02339 9

19. THOMPSON, R.J. *Moses and the Law in a century of criticism since Graf*. 1970. ISBN 90 04 02341 0

20. REDFORD, D.B. *A study of the biblical story of Joseph*. 1970. ISBN 90 04 02342 9

21. AHLSTRÖM, G.W. *Joel and the temple cult of Jerusalem*. 1971. ISBN 90 04 02620 7

22. *Congress Volume*, Uppsala 1971. 1972. ISBN 90 04 03521 4

23. *Studies in the religion of ancient Israel*. 1972. ISBN 90 04 03525 7

24. SCHOORS, A. *I am God your Saviour*. A form-critical study of the main genres in Is. xl-lv. 1973. ISBN 90 04 03792 2

25. ALLEN, L.C. *The Greek Chronicles*. The relation of the Septuagint I and II Chronicles to the Massoretic text. Part 1. The translator's craft. 1974. ISBN 90 04 03913 9

26. *Studies on prophecy*. A collection of twelve papers. 1974. ISBN 90 04 03877 9

27. ALLEN, L.C. *The Greek Chronicles*. Part 2. Textual criticism. 1974. ISBN 90 04 03933 3

28. *Congress Volume*, Edinburgh 1974. 1975. ISBN 90 04 04321 7

29. *Congress Volume*, Göttingen 1977. 1978. ISBN 90 04 05835 4

30. EMERTON, J.A. (ed.). *Studies in the historical books of the Old Testament*. 1979. ISBN 90 04 06017 0

31. MEREDINO, R.P. *Der Erste und der Letzte*. Eine Untersuchung von Jes 40-48. 1981. ISBN 90 04 06199 1

32. EMERTON, J.A. (ed.). *Congress Vienna 1980*. 1981. ISBN 90 04 06514 8

33. KOENIG, J. *L'herméneutique analogique du Judaïsme antique d'après les témoins textuels d'Isaïe*. 1982. ISBN 90 04 06762 0

34. BARSTAD, H.M. *The religious polemics of Amos*. Studies in the preachings of Amos ii 7B-8, iv 1-13, v 1-27, vi 4-7, viii 14. 1984. ISBN 90 04 07017 6
35. KRAŠOVEC, J. *Antithetic structure in Biblical Hebrew poetry*. 1984. ISBN 90 04 07244 6
36. EMERTON, J.A. (ed.). *Congress Volume*, Salamanca 1983. 1985. ISBN 90 04 07281 0
37. LEMCHE, N.P. *Early Israel*. Anthropological and historical studies on the Israelite society before the monarchy. 1985. ISBN 90 04 07853 3
38. NIELSEN, K. *Incense in Ancient Israel*. 1986. ISBN 90 04 07702 2
39. PARDEE, D. *Ugaritic and Hebrew poetic parallelism*. A trial cut. 1988. ISBN 90 04 08368 5
40. EMERTON, J.A. (ed.). *Congress Volume*, Jerusalem 1986. 1988. ISBN 90 04 08499 1
41. EMERTON, J.A. (ed.). *Studies in the Pentateuch*. 1990. ISBN 90 04 09195 5
42. McKENZIE, S.L. *The trouble with Kings*. The composition of the Book of Kings in the Deuteronomistic History. 1991. ISBN 90 04 09402 4
43. EMERTON, J.A. (ed.). *Congress Volume*, Leuven 1989. 1991. ISBN 90 04 09398 2
44. HAAK, R.D. *Habakkuk*. 1992. ISBN 90 04 09506 3
45. BEYERLIN, W. *Im Licht der Traditionen*. Psalm LXVII und CXV. Ein Entwicklungszusammenhang. 1992. ISBN 90 04 09635 3
46. MEIER, S.A. *Speaking of Speaking*. Marking direct discourse in the Hebrew Bible. 1992. ISBN 90 04 09602 7
47. KESSLER, R. *Staat und Gesellschaft im vorexilischen Juda*. Vom 8. Jahrhundert bis zum Exil. 1992. ISBN 90 04 09646 9
48. AUFFRET, P. *Voyez de vos yeux*. Étude structurelle de vingt psaumes, dont le psaume 119. 1993. ISBN 90 04 09707 4
49. GARCÍA MARTÍNEZ, F., A. HILHORST and C.J. LABUSCHAGNE (eds.). *The Scriptures and the Scrolls*. Studies in honour of A.S. van der Woude on the occasion of his 65th birthday. 1992. ISBN 90 04 09746 5
50. LEMAIRE, A. and B. OTZEN (eds.). *History and Traditions of Early Israel*. Studies presented to Eduard Nielsen, May 8th, 1993. 1993. ISBN 90 04 09851 8
51. GORDON, R.P. *Studies in the Targum to the Twelve Prophets*. From Nahum to Malachi. 1994. ISBN 90 04 09987 5
52. HUGENBERGER, G.P. *Marriage as a Covenant*. A Study of Biblical Law and Ethics Governing Marriage Developed from the Perspective of Malachi. 1994. ISBN 90 04 09977 8
53. GARCÍA MARTÍNEZ, F., A. HILHORST, J.T.A.G.M. VAN RUITEN, A.S. VAN DER WOUDE. *Studies in Deuteronomy*. In Honour of C.J. Labuschagne on the Occasion of His 65th Birthday. 1994. ISBN 90 04 10052 0
54. FERNÁNDEZ MARCOS, N. *Septuagint and Old Latin in the Book of Kings*. 1994. ISBN 90 04 10043 1
55. SMITH, M.S. *The Ugaritic Baal Cycle. Volume 1*. Introduction with text, translation and commentary of KTU 1.1-1.2. 1994. ISBN 90 04 09995 6
56. DUGUID, I.M. *Ezekiel and the Leaders of Israel*. 1994. ISBN 90 04 10074 1
57. MARX, A. *Les offrandes végétales dans l'Ancien Testament*. Du tribut d'hommage au repas eschatologique. 1994. ISBN 90 04 10136 5
58. SCHÄFER-LICHTENBERGER, C. *Josua und Salomo*. Eine Studie zu Autorität und Legitimität des Nachfolgers im Alten Testament. 1995. ISBN 90 04 10064 4
59. LASSERRE, G. *Synopse des lois du Pentateuque*. 1994. ISBN 90 04 10202 7
60. DOGNIEZ, C. *Bibliography of the Septuagint – Bibliographie de la Septante (1970-1993)*. Avec une préface de PIERRE-MAURICE BOGAERT. 1995. ISBN 90 04 10192 6
61. EMERTON, J.A. (ed.). *Congress Volume*, Paris 1992. 1995. ISBN 90 04 10259 0

62. SMITH, P.A. *Rhetoric and Redaction in Trito-Isaiah*. The Structure, Growth and Authorship of Isaiah 56-66. 1995. ISBN 90 04 10306 6

63. O'CONNELL, R.H. *The Rhetoric of the Book of Judges*. 1996. ISBN 90 04 10104 7

64. HARLAND, P.J. *The Value of Human Life*. A Study of the Story of the Flood (Genesis 6-9). 1996. ISBN 90 04 10534 4

65. ROLAND PAGE JR., H. *The Myth of Cosmic Rebellion*. A Study of its Reflexes in Ugaritic and Biblical Literature. 1996. ISBN 90 04 10563 8

66. EMERTON, J.A. (ed.). *Congress Volume*. Cambridge 1995. 1997. ISBN 90 04 106871

67. JOOSTEN, J. *People and Land in the Holiness Code*. An Exegetical Study of the Ideational Framework of the Law in Leviticus 17–26. 1996. ISBN 90 04 10557 3

68. BEENTJES, P.C. *The Book of Ben Sira in Hebrew*. A Text Edition of all Extant Hebrew Manuscripts and a Synopsis of all Parallel Hebrew Ben Sira Texts. 1997. ISBN 90 04 10767 3

69. COOK, J. *The Septuagint of Proverbs – Jewish and/or Hellenistic Proverbs?* Concerning the Hellenistic Colouring of LXX Proverbs. 1997. ISBN 90 04 10879 3

70,1 BROYLES, G. and C. EVANS (eds.). *Writing and Reading the Scroll of Isaiah*. Studies of an Interpretive Tradition, I. 1997. ISBN 90 04 10936 6 (*Vol.* I); ISBN 90 04 11027 5 (*Set*)

70,2 BROYLES, G. and C. EVANS (eds.). *Writing and Reading the Scroll of Isaiah*. Studies of an Interpretive Tradition, II. 1997. ISBN 90 04 11026 7 (*Vol.* II); ISBN 90 04 11027 5 (*Set*)

71. KOOIJ, A. VAN DER. *The Oracle of Tyre*. The Septuagint of Isaiah 23 as Version and Vision. 1998. ISBN 90 04 11152 2

72. TOV, E. *The Greek and Hebrew Bible*. Collected Essays on the Septuagint. 1999. ISBN 90 04 11309 6

73. GARCÍA MARTÍNEZ, F. and NOORT, E. (eds.). *Perspectives in the Study of the Old Testament and Early Judaism*. A Symposium in honour of Adam S. van der Woude on the occasion of his 70th birthday. 1998. ISBN 90 04 11322 3

74. KASSIS, R.A. *The Book of Proverbs and Arabic Proverbial Works*. 1999. ISBN 90 04 11305 3

75. RÖSEL, H.N. *Von Josua bis Jojachin*. Untersuchungen zu den deuteronomistischen Geschichtsbüchern des Alten Testaments. 1999. ISBN 90 04 11355 5

76. RENZ, Th. *The Rhetorical Function of the Book of Ezekiel*. 1999. ISBN 90 04 11362 2

77. HARLAND, P.J. and HAYWARD, C.T.R. (eds.). *New Heaven and New Earth Prophecy and the Millenium*. Essays in Honour of Anthony Gelston. 1999. ISBN 90 04 10841 6

78. KRAŠOVEC, J. *Reward, Punishment, and Forgiveness*. The Thinking and Beliefs of Ancient Israel in the Light of Greek and Modern Views. 1999. ISBN 90 04 11443 2.

79. KOSSMANN, R. *Die Esthernovelle – Vom Erzählten zur Erzählung*. Studien zur Traditions- und Redaktionsgeschichte des Estherbuches. 2000. ISBN 90 04 11556 0.

80. LEMAIRE, A. and M. SÆBØ (eds.). *Congress Volume*. Oslo 1998. 2000. ISBN 90 04 11598 6.

81. GALIL, G. and M. WEINFELD (eds.). *Studies in Historical Geography and Biblical Historiography*. Presented to Zecharia Kallai. 2000. ISBN 90 04 11608 7

82. COLLINS, N.L. *The library in Alexandria and the Bible in Greek*. 2001. ISBN 90 04 11866 7

83,1 COLLINS, J.J. and P.W. FLINT (eds.). *The Book of Daniel*. Composition and Reception, I. 2001. ISBN 90 04 11675 3 (*Vol.* I);
ISBN 90 04 12202 8 (*Set*)

83,2 COLLINS, J.J. and P.W. FLINT (eds.). *The Book of Daniel*. Composition and Reception, II. 2001. ISBN 90 04 12200 1 (*Vol.* II); ISBN 90 04 12202 8 (*Set*).

84. COHEN, C.H.R. *Contextual Priority in Biblical Hebrew Philology*. An Application of the Held Method for Comparative Semitic Philology. 2001. ISBN 90 04 11670 2 (In preparation).

85. WAGENAAR, J.A. *Judgement and Salvation*. The Composition and Redaction of Micah 2-5. 2001. ISBN 90 04 11936 1

86. MCLAUGHLIN, J.L. *The* Marzēaḥ *in the Prophetic Literature*. References and Allusions in Light of the Extra-Biblical Evidence. 2001. ISBN 90 04 12006 8

87. Wong, K.L. *The Idea of Retribution in the Book of Ezekiel* 2001. ISBN 90 04 12256 7